To David

With many many thanks for all your interest and encouragement, and for your very tangible help in the realization of the project.

Joe

AMERICA'S SOCIAL CLASSES IN THE WRITINGS OF EDITH WHARTON

An Analysis of Her Short Stories

AMERICA'S SOCIAL CLASSES
IN THE WRITINGS OF EDITH WHARTON
An Analysis of Her Short Stories

Joseph Griffin

With a Preface by
Barbara A. White

The Edwin Mellen Press
Lewiston•Queenston•Lampeter

Library of Congress Cataloging-in-Publication Data

Griffin, Joseph, 1931-
  America's social classes in the writings of Edith Wharton : an analysis of her short stories / Joseph Griffin ; with a preface by Barbara A. White.
      p. cm.
  Includes bibliographical references and index.
  ISBN-13: 978-0-7734-4682-3
  ISBN-10: 0-7734-4682-6
  1. Wharton, Edith, 1862-1937--Criticism and interpretation. 2. Social classes in literature. I. Title.
  PS3545.H16Z658 2009
  813'.52--dc22
                              2009026169

hors série.

A CIP catalog record for this book is available from the British Library.

Front cover: Photo of Edith Wharton, courtesy of The Mount Archives, Lenox, Massachusetts

The Edwin Mellen Press   The Edwin Mellen Press
      Box 450   Box 67
  Lewiston, New York   Queenston, Ontario
  USA 14092-0450   CANADA L0S 1L0

            The Edwin Mellen Press, Ltd.
            Lampeter, Ceredigion, Wales
            UNITED KINGDOM SA48 8LT

        Printed in the United States of America

This is for

Joseph X Brennan

Table of Contents

Preface by Barbara A. White   i

Acknowledgements   iv

A Note on References   vi

Introduction   1

Chapter 1: The Short Stories: A History   7

Chapter 2: Ghosts   47

Chapter 3: The Upper Class   103

Chapter 4: The Upper Classes   155

Chapter 5: The Middle Classes   221

Chapter 6: The World of the Arts   239

Chapter 7: Town and Gown   313

Chapter 8: The Past   345

Chapter 9: And the Rest...   377

Afterword   429

Bibliography   433

Index   437

Preface

In his new book on Edith Wharton's short stories, Joseph Griffin notes approvingly that the stories can no longer be called "neglected," as Alfred Bendixen called them twenty years ago. The first book on the subject, my *Edith Wharton: A Study of the Short Stories* (1991), has been followed by numerous articles in *Edith Wharton Review* and other journals. Recent books on Wharton's work have paid close attention to the stories, which have also been increasingly featured in writings done abroad. The appearance in 2001 of the Library of America's two-volume *Collected Stories* has again brought Wharton's short fiction to the fore. This would seem to be a good thing, providing us with increased access to the stories. But as Griffin points out, twenty-three stories are not included in the Library of America volumes (four novellas replace them), and now that R.W.B. Lewis's *The Collected Short Stories of Edith Wharton* (1968) is out of print, "readers are left with a much-depleted oeuvre." Although the twenty-three missing stories do not include Wharton's best, Griffin gives a good explanation in his "Afterword" of what is lost in their absence.

Griffin's critical approach to the stories is to examine each in the Lewis *Collected Short Stories* "as a distinct entity," to "see each tale as a work in which the characters and situations are those of the context of the story itself." I must say I have trouble conceiving of a distinct story entity without the "by Edith Wharton" attached, and I think I was right to convince Professor Griffin that in his discussion of Wharton's ghost story "Mr. Jones" the reader deserves to be given some biographical information: the ghostly Mr. Jones bears Wharton's father's name. But whatever the merits (or lack of merit) of the biographical approach, I completely agree with Griffin that Wharton's short stories are rich enough to demand "a more comprehensive going-over" than may be gained with one mind-set or one critical eye.

A major strength of Griffin's book is his careful attention to Wharton's narrators and reflectors. Wharton herself alerted readers to the importance of point of view in her "Telling a Short Story," which is a chapter in *The Writing of Fiction* (1925). She insists that the storyteller's "first care" should be to choose the "reflecting mind deliberately, as one would choose a building site, or decide upon the orientation of one's house, and when this is done, to live inside the mind chosen, trying to feel, see and react exactly as the latter would.... " Ignoring the "reflecting mind," as early critics often did, tends to produce superficial readings or downright misinterpretations of Wharton stories. Griffin always pays careful attention to the "building site" and often convinces us that the story is more about the narrator or reflector's inner blindness than his or her external actions. Some slight tales, such as "The Dilettante" (1903), gain added interest thereby. ("The Dilettante" is one of the stories missing from the new Library of America collection.)

As Griffin notes, readers will inevitably question his categorization of the stories; there are always new and different groupings to be thought up and stories that overstep the bounds of their category and could in fact fit into several. "The Recovery" (1901), for instance, a story of a painter who learns he has been overrated, is an artist tale and has to do with class; it is also set in the town of Hillbridge, a setting Griffin includes in his category "Town and Gown." By and large, however, the categories are not too troublesome and are sometimes revealing. Griffin devotes two chapters to Wharton's portraits of class, what he calls her "realistic stories of upper-class life." Into one category, "The Upper Class," he places those tales in which the characters are members of a high social class relating to people of their own set. The other category, "The Upper Class," consists of stories of "the interaction of persons of elevated status among whom there is some important distinction of social class." These are tales of conflict based on the relative positioning of the classes. The interesting result of this placement is that the first category abounds with mediocre stories and the second contains several of Wharton's very best, including "Souls Belated" (1899), "The Other Two" (1904),

"Autre Temps...."(1911), and "Roman Fever" (1934). Is it the conflict, especially the element of social climbing, that spurs Wharton to her greatest achievement? On the other hand, why is it that the stories of art and artists, one of Wharton's favorite subjects, are so uniformly weak?

Griffin's work leaves students of Wharton much to think about for the future. Take, for instance, the stories he classifies as historical tales set in the distant past. His attention to narrative method in the history stories leads to a rich and subtle interpretation of the underrated "The Hermit and the Wild Woman" (1906) and to the suggestive conclusion that "the quality of the [history] story is in direct proportion to the successful integration of the framing story and its interior tale." This insight might be applied to a wide variety of other stories, as might the suggestion that Wharton's ghost tales and historical tales are more closely connected than has previously been thought. Many of the "connections" Griffin notices throughout his book are well worth pursuing.

Barbara A. White

Professor Emerita of Women's Studies

University of New Hampshire

Acknowledgements

Permission to cite materials in the Archives of Charles Scribner's Sons, Manuscript Division, Department of Rare Books and Collections, Princeton University Library has been graciously granted by the Princeton University Library. Permission to reprint portions of letters and papers from the Edith Wharton Collection at the Beinecke Rare Book and Manuscript Library of Yale University has been graciously given by permission of the estate of Edith Wharton, and the Watkins/Loomis Agency. Portions of Wharton's short stories are reprinted with the permission of Scribner, an imprint of Simon and Shuster Adult Publishing Group, from THE COLLECTED SHORT STORIES OF EDITH WHARTON by Edith Wharton. Introduction by R.W.B. Lewis. Copyright © 1968 by Williams R. Tyler. All right reserved. The front-cover photo appears by courtesy of The Mount Archives, Lenox, Massachusetts.

My thanks go to the University of Ottawa, who aided this project at every turn, initially with travel grants and research assistants. More recently the project benifitted from the help of Robert Major, Vice-Rector (Academic), and Lorrie Burns, Associate Dean (Research), Faculty of Arts, who encouraged and supported my request for funding in the final stages of the manuscript's preparation. Since my retirement I have been provided with office space at the Department of English: my thanks to successive chairs Keith Wilson, David Rampton, and Franz de Bruyn. My special thanks go also to my friends and associates Henry Imbleau, David Rampton and Peter Stich, who helped the project come to a completion in the most tangible ways. I have been ably assisted by Veronica Tremblay and Stephanie Desnoyers, who lent their word-processing skills, and especially to the latter, who formatted the manuscript. Most importantly my wife Paulette and children Julie and Martin were constant providers of interest and encouragement.

A Note on References

All citations from Edith Wharton's short stories are to *The Collected Short Stories of Edith Wharton*, edited by R. W. B. Lewis. Volume and page numbers appear in parentheses after citations.

The following abbreviations are used for citations to the following works:

EW: R.W.B. Lewis, Edith Wharton: A Biography

ICSS: R.W.B. Lewis, Introduction, in *The Collected Short Stories of Edith Wharton*

LEW: The Letters of Edith Wharton, edited by R.W.B. Lewis and Nancy Lewis

(Scribner Archives) refers to the Archives of Charles Scribner's Sons, Manuscript Division, Department of Rare Books and Collections, Princeton University Library. (EW Collection) refers to the Edith Wharton Collection at the Beinecke Rare Book and Manuscript Library of Yale University.

Introduction

The time has passed when one has to explain or justify an interest in the short stories of Edith Wharton. And no longer is it the case that her short stories are "the single most neglected aspect of her literary achievement," as Alfred Bendixen wrote in 1988 (8). Five and a half years later Bendixen was satisfied that "scholars are now also actively exploring...the later novels, the short stories, and her lifelong fascination with the gothic" (20). Beginning in the 1990's a large number of articles has been devoted to the short fiction. Foremost among journals that have featured such pieces is the *Edith Wharton Review*. The Spring 1993 issue of the *Review*, that issue devoted to "the art of the short story," ran essays on "The Other Two," "The Looking Glass" and "Permanent Wave," "Kerfol," and "Afterward," and articles on both the lesser- and the better-known Wharton stories turn up in the *Review* frequently. Other American journals have carried essays about the short fiction as well: *Studies in Short Fiction, American Transcendentalist Review, CLA Journal, Studies in American Fiction, American Literary Realism*, to name some. Also, recent book-length studies of Wharton's work by such scholars as Kathy Fedorko, Hildegarde Hoeller, and Carol Singley make frequent allusion to the short fiction by either brief critiques or cursory references—as earlier books did also, in fact. There has also been a recent upsurge in interest in the short fiction abroad, in England, France, Italy, Japan and Taiwan for instance, where books, periodicals, and conferences have featured studies of the stories.

The most notable manifestation of the growing interest in Wharton's short fiction was the appearance in 1991 of the first book on the subject, *Edith Wharton: A Study of the Short Fiction*, by Barbara A. White. White's book

2

appeared as part of the Twayne's Studies in Short Fiction Series, whose General Editor was Gordon Weaver, and it followed a format already established in previous books of the series. That format allowed for a White commentary of some one hundred pages on the stories. The rest of the book was devoted to verbatim passages of Wharton essays and letters related to her short fiction, and to two brief segments of critical commentary by R.W.B. Lewis and Sandra M. Gilbert. The task of commenting on eighty-five stories in a hundred pages (even considering that little need be said about several less-than-satisfactory pieces) was doubtless a daunting one for White, and one can be sure that such a large body of thematically varied and stylistically diverse work as Wharton's presented serious problems of coverage.[1] I will allude to much of White's commentary within and simply remark at this point that among the many merits of her critique are her tracing through of the suggestions and sub-currents of sexual abuse that are to be found in the short fiction, and her insistence on the importance of attending to the role of narrators and reflector characters.

The publication in 2001 of the two-volume *Collected Stories* by the Library of America brought Wharton's short fiction to public attention again. The new *Collected's* appearance occasioned much commentary in both the scholarly and popular press and drew the attention of well-known literary figures to Wharton's stories. *The New Yorker* published a review by Claudia Roth Pierpont, a fellow at the New York Public Library and the acclaimed author of *Passionate Minds* (2000), a study of women writers; *The Atlantic Monthly's* commentary was by Margaret Drabble, one of the finest living British novelists and biographers. Because these two reviewers took notably different perspectives on the subject of Wharton's short stories, their review essays can serve as points of departure for my own study.

Pierpont's approach is signalled by the caption under the full-page cartoon image of Wharton on the second page of the review: "Wharton's stories served as an emotional release that was unavailable to her in any other way" (67), and in the review Pierpont writes:

Far more than her novels, Wharton's stories are rooted in the fluctuations of her life; the longer, richer works, though unquestionably her great accomplishment, stand at a magisterial remove. In the wake of "Beatrice Palmato," recent studies have scoured the stories for tell-tale signs of her father-daughter incest, but readers of these volumes are apt to be struck with the exposure of far more everyday varieties of horror: moral cowardice, being unloved or unloving, making rational compromises in order to live and discovering that one has reasoned one's life away, unendurable loneliness that must be endured—and that seems to have been endured by Wharton from 1871 to 1937. (66)

Such a biographical stance, as Pierpont herself notes, has been a frequent one among Wharton critics and of course it constitutes a legitimate way of approaching the stories. Indeed, Wharton herself drew sharp attention to the phenomenon of self-exposure in some of her earlier tales. But the habit of fitting everything into a biographical mould has its dangers. Besides the temptation of reading too much life into the tales there is also the problem of what to do with those stories that only in a very general way suit the paradigm. Here is Pierpont addressing first the later stories in general and in particular "All Souls'," and then the best-known of the late tales, "Roman Fever." "Here," she writes, "the terror of absolute loneliness [is] made all the more chilling for so perfectly closing the circle of her work." Then: "But the great majority of these later efforts, read in sequence, resemble a series of elaborately stage-managed and stiffly posed *tableaux vivants*. Even in 'Roman Fever,' written in 1934 and possibly her most popular story, the steady grinding of authorial machinery overwhelms the characters' voices and the warm Roman breeze" (74). Warm Roman breeze indeed! And a sad commentary on what happens when one is not willing to look closely at a story and when one allows a preconceived notion to dominate.

Pierpont's damning with faint praise (or none at all) stands in radical contrast to Margaret Drabble's unequivocal celebration of Wharton the short-story writer. Drabble writes in *Atlantic Monthly*:

Edith Wharton was one of the great exponents of the genre (one would in her age have unhesitatingly referred to her as a master of it) and these two

> generous volumes, collected and edited by the novelist Maureen Howard, have a fine cumulative effect. Here are riches. Wharton attempted, and succeeded in, a dazzling variety of styles, from the fantastic to the realistic, from the satiric to the sentimental. Here are antiquarian themes—ghosts, fables, historical fantasies, and tales of crazed connoisseurs in love with the past. But here are also a number of incisive dissections of contemporary American and European customs. Wharton brought new acuity to the debate between manners and morals. And she knew how to shape a story. (166)

As well, Drabble's brief critiques of individual stories emphasize the substance of the stories themselves removed from considerations of their reflectiveness of Wharton's life. In a different, but related context, the art critic Lance Esplund, reviewing Hilary Spurling's recent biographies of Henri Matisse, writes: "A common weakness of artist biographies is their authors' attempts to psychologize the art; rather than engage with the art on its own terms, these writers insist on illustrating, interpreting, and explaining the work through the life and, in turn, the life through the work. Of course, a biography is bound to have an element of this, but these writers often end up reducing the art to little more than a biographical mirror" (93). In the face of the fact that much of the criticism of Wharton's short fiction has been of a biographical nature, Esplund's words alert us to the necessity of reading texts for their content, and Drabble's review (which is far too brief) serves as an example of such critical practice.

In the present study each of Wharton's published stories, i.e., each of the stories in the Lewis *Collected*, is examined as a distinct entity. Without dismissing the autobiographical elements of the stories out of hand, the present examination seeks to see each tale as a work in which the characters and situations are those of the context of the story itself. Of course, this has been done with many of the stories already: Wharton's better tales have received the most of this kind of critical attention, but these tales are so good that they cannot usually be circumscribed by one or two or three readings.[2] And then there are other pieces that have not been very carefully examined—or examined at all—as isolated fictions.

But the present work makes no pretentions to being the last word on Wharton's stories. As Drabble has mentioned, the richness and variety of Wharton's short-story oeuvre are remarkable: it promises, it deserves, it demands a more comprehensive going-over than one mind or one critical approach can bring to it. And there are aspects of the stories to which attention need be paid: the question of textual comparison, for instance, and of what can be gleaned about Wharton's habits of writing and progression of ideas. Maureen Howard writes in her Notes on the Text for the Library of America volumes: "[Wharton] tended to revise, sometimes lightly and sometimes substantially, between periodical and book publication..." (920).

Some readers will doubtless wonder about and/or disagree with the categories into which I have placed the stories, or about my placement of certain stories within certain categories. I am not always happy myself about my positioning of the tales. Inevitably, some stories might be relocated depending on one's perspective: in a word, there had to be a certain arbitrariness about the placement of some stories especially.

One more point should be made. Although I have written about each of Wharton's eighty-six published short stories as a distinct entity, I make no claims to having written a definitive analysis of any of the stories. Nor do I pretend to have incorporated into my discussion all of the relevant criticism of the stories. What I *have* attempted is to discuss each story in light of the context of the category in which I have placed it, and I have appended to each chapter a summary statement that attempts to identify the particular flavor and emphasis Wharton has given to a homogeneous group of fictions: to ghost stories, to stories about social class, to stories about persons in the arts, to stories about persons in and around the academy, to stories set in the historical past. Although I would not like to think that my commentaries on individual stories serve only a supportive function, there is a sense in which the more important units in this book are its chapter conclusions, to each of which, for purposes of their importance, I have given a title. I hope that readers will see a complementary relationship between examinations of single stories and chapter conclusions.

Notes

[1] White notes: "R.W.B. Lewis includes 86 stories in the *Collected Short Stories*..., but one of these, "Her Son" (1932), should be considered a novella, as Lewis later acknowledged" (XV).

[2] An excellent example of bringing a fresh perspective to a Wharton story is Alice Herritage Kinman's article about "Mrs Manstey's View," "Edith Wharton and the Future of Fiction." Kinman examines Wharton's story in light of critical views about fiction that were circulating at the time and as a fictional embodiment of ideas put forth by Jacob Riis, the New York journalist/photographer, excerpts of whose book *How the Other Half Lives*, had been published in *Scribner's Magazine* in December 1889, eighteen months before "Mrs Manstley's View" appeared in the magazine.

Chapter One

The Short Stories: A History

" ... the excesses of youth"

On May 26, 1890, Edward L. Burlingame accepted Edith Wharton's short story "Mrs. Manstey's View" for publication in *Scribner's Magazine*. As editor, he had already published a number of Wharton's poems, and although in his acceptance letter he referred to her fiction submission as "a slight sketch" (*EW* 61), he evidently had seen enough of the young woman's work to suspect a budding talent. A story of respectable quality, "Mrs. Manstey's View" gave little hint of either the major subjects and themes that would preoccupy Wharton or of the excellence that was to come. Nevertheless, it launched the career of a woman who would become a major figure in American letters. Published in *Scribner's* in July 1891,[3] this story of a lonely widow who is deprived of her only pleasure, the view into her backyard, by the building of an extension on a neighbouring house, helped to secure Wharton's fruitful association with the Scribner organization.

Buoyed by the acceptance of "Mrs. Manstey's View," Wharton submitted a second story to *Scribner's*, "The Fullness of Life," a fantasy that treated in thinly disguised manner her problematical relationship with her husband, Teddy. Burlingame found it "a capital conception" but returned it for changes. When Wharton found herself unable to make the revisions, Burlingame offered to do them himself, a proposal Wharton did not respond to. When "The Fullness of Life" appeared in the December 1893 *Scribner's*,[4] it was without the revisions the editor had requested: Burlingame had learned something about his "mutely mulish" apprentice (*EW* 65).

By the end of November 1893, Wharton had sent two more stories to Burlingame, both of which he accepted. "That Good May Come" elicited high

8

praise from the editor: he would accept "everything else of the same quality you are willing to give me" (*EW* 70). *Scribner's* carried this tale, of an aspiring poet who in order to raise money to buy a confirmation dress for his sister, writes a piece for a gossip publication, in May 1894.[5] The other story, "The Lamp of Psyche," also impressed Burlingame, and he wrote Wharton on November 24, 1894: "[making] the proposal officially and formally ... . How should you think of letting the firm publish a volume of [your] collected stories and sketches ... ?" (*EW* 70). "I need hardly say how much I am flattered by Messrs. Scribner's proposition," replied Wharton the next day (*LEW* 31). Her first collection was assured, but when it appeared in 1899 its contents were not precisely what Scribner's had envisaged. Meanwhile, "The Lamp of Psyche," probably Wharton's best story to date, featuring a woman who discovers that her husband's past has been less than exemplary, appeared in *Scribner's* in October 1895.[6]

Only one published piece of Wharton short fiction eluded the *Scribner's* imprint prior to that publisher's 1899 collection of her stories. This was "The Valley of Childish Things, and Other Emblems," a "waif" Wharton called it in a letter to Burlingame on December 14, 1895 (*LEW* 35), "a collection of fables" in another communication to him, on July 13, 1898 (Scribner Archives). Burlingame had rejected the story, admitting frankly that it was beyond his understanding (Wolff 84). Comprising ten short fables, some of which disguised only slightly the kind of dissatisfaction Wharton had expressed in her earlier stories, "The Valley of Childish Things, and Other Emblems" appeared in *Century* in July 1896.[7]

The Greater Inclination

When Scribner's had proposed a collection of Wharton's short stories in 1894, it had wished to include the work it had already published in its monthly magazine. But Wharton was not in agreement, and she wrote Burlingame on July 10, 1898: "As to the old stories of which you speak so kindly, I regard them as the excesses of youth. They were all written at the top of my voice [and] The Fulness of Life is one long shriek ... . I fear that the voice of those early tales will drown all the others: it is for that reason that I prefer not to publish them" (*LEW* 36). When the collection appeared, five years after it was suggested, it carried eight new works; "poor little stories," Wharton wrote a friend shortly after the collection came out, "[they] have been reclaimed ... inch by inch, from almost continuous ill-health and mental lassitude" (*LEW* 28).

Of the eight stories that made up this first collection, only two had prior magazine publication. "The Pelican" and "The Muse's Tragedy" appeared in *Scribner's* in November 1898 and January 1899, respectively.[8] "The Pelican" was a satiric study of "the familiar lady lecturer whose shallow effusions represented culture before lecture audiences throughout nineteenth-century America," to borrow Millicent Bell's description (236), and one of a number of tales Wharton set in the fictional college town of Hillbridge. "The Muse's Tragedy," also in a cultural vein but more serious in perspective than "The Pelican," blended themes of love and literature within a milieu that reminded Wharton's contemporaries of Henry James's work.

The Greater Inclination saw print in March 1899.[9] Its title, Wharton's choice after she had discarded four others, "referred to a loftier as against a meaner moral propensity," according to Lewis (*EW* 87), and suggests that there is some thematic design behind the eight stories. The six new stories touch upon a variety of themes and subjects. "The Journey" is a macabre piece about a middle-class woman who accompanies her husband's corpse on a long train trip, "an imaginative device," suggests Lewis, "for dispatching poor Teddy" (*EW* 85). "Souls Belated" is the first of a long list of stories of manners, a genre in which Wharton did her most attractive work. "A Coward" reiterates the frequent Wharton subject of the flawed male, but with comic overtones. The same subject recurs in "The Twilight of the God," but here Wharton uses a play-script technique with speakers introduced as in a drama and stage directions given within parentheses. It is in the last two stories of the collection that one sees most clearly "the greater inclination." "A Cup of Cold Water" features a young man who sacrifices his name and comes to the aid of a woman about to take her own life. In "A Portrait," a painter places his instinct to protect the sensibility of a young woman concerning her father's public reputation above his own artistic integrity.

The coming into being of *The Greater Inclination* was a painful experience for Wharton. She was initially set back by the fact that though Burlingame was keen to collect her stories, he had subsequently rejected, or requested considerable revision of, her new submissions. As well, she was awed by the realization that her consent to the collection committed her to a profession of writing (*EW* 75). The actual writing and revising proved a daunting task for her too, for it coincided with a period of ill health. And when she had practically completed her part of the work, she was distressed by the delay in the book's publication. Writing to Scribner's on August 25, 1898 she voiced her impatience: "It has taken me so ridiculously long to get together eight or nine stories that seemed to me fairly satisfactory. And now that they are all sitting in a row waiting to appear they seem to have arrived so long before it is time for the performance to begin. Well—!" (Scribner Archives).

The Greater Inclination proved to be an almost instantaneous success despite Wharton's fears that it would not "catch the general attention readily" (EW to William Crary Brownell, 3 April 1899, Scribner Archives). An in-house Scribner's communication on July 12 stated: "Of the newer books, the most successful is The Greater Inclination. The reviews have recognized it as an exceptional book, the first edition is gone" (Bell 246). Indeed the collection was reprinted, sold 3,000 copies in the United States, and within two weeks of its appearance drew the attention of the London publisher John Murray, who issued it in England. Somewhat surprised, and pleased at the popular success of her book, Wharton was, nonetheless, disappointed with Scribner's handling of post-publication matters. She complained about its poor advertising of her collection, threatening in an April 25 letter to Brownell, who was handling Wharton's volume at Scribner's: "Mr. Scribner's methods do not tempt one to offer him one's wares a second time" (*LEW* 30). She subsequently softened her tone, on September 26 thanking Brownell "for your kind note" and expressing her pleasure about the sales of *The Greater Inclination* (*LEW* 40). But two days later she gave more notice that she would not be a pushover, telling Brownell: "Since writing to you the other day I have received a letter from a leading publisher—who had already written me twice on the subject—offering me 15% on any volume I will give him" (EW to Brownell, 28 September 1899, Scribner Archives). Wharton's contract with Scribner's gave her only a ten percent royalty (Garrison 15).

" ... so young, and with it so clever"

During 1900 Wharton saw three stories published she had placed with the magazines. The subject matter and tone of two of these, "April Showers" and "Friends," is suggested by the fact that they were both taken by *Youth's Companion*, the Boston weekly intended to be "an amusing and instructive children's periodical unconnected with Sunday Schools," in the words of James D. Hart (958). The third story, "The Line of Least Resistance," was a particular favorite of Wharton's, and she was intent on its appearing in the next Scribner's collection, but her enthusiasm was dampened by an unexpected circumstance.

"April Showers" appeared in the January 18, 1900 issue of *Youth's Companion*.[10] The tale had been rejected by Burlingame seven years earlier, and one suspects that the reasons for its rejection were the very ones for which *Youth's Companion* favored it. Overtly didactic, the story deals with a young woman who, given to believe that her story has been accepted by a magazine, is dismayed to find that there has been an error and that in fact she is not to see her work published. The story is patently autobiographical, and Lewis points to an additional dimension of its personal element: "Edith Wharton gently spoofed her [own] adolescent novella [*Fast and Loose*] by quoting its last lines as the conclusion of what is presented as an insipid short story by a rather silly young girl" (*EW* 30).

Wharton's other contribution to *Youth's Companion*, "Friends," published consecutively in the August 23 and 30 issues,[11] had also been rejected by Burlingame under the title "Something Exquisite" in 1894 when Wharton and

Scribner's were assembling stories for *The Greater Inclination*. Wharton accepted Burlingame's criticism that the tale was maudlin and offered to revise it (*LEW* 32). It is easy to understand why Wharton saw "Friends" as a logical entry for her collection: the protagonist here also follows the greater inclination, giving over a teaching job that is rightfully hers to another teacher, whose financial need appears to her to be greater than her own. At the time she wrote Burlingame, Wharton had submitted the story to *Lippincott's*, and one assumes the response there was the same as at *Scribner's*.

Lippincott's did accept a Wharton story at this time: "The Line of Least Resistance" came out in its October number.[12] Wharton wrote Brownell on August 1, 1900: "I think [it] the best story I have ever written," and she was adamant it should appear in the next Scribner's collection scheduled for 1901 and that the volume should bear the title "The Line of Least Resistance." But after the story appeared in *Lippincott's* she sent a copy to Henry James. James praised some elements of her writing, but Wharton was stung by the general import of his remarks and perhaps by his patronizing tone: the story had "admirable sharpness and neatness, and infinite point and wit," wrote James. "Only it is a little *hard*, a little purely derisive. But that's because you're so young, and with it so clever" (*EW* 125). When the 1901 collection appeared it was without "The Line of Least Resistance" and bore the title *Crucial Instances*, a title, Wharton thought, that "keeps a sort of connection with 'The Greater Inclination'" (*LEW* 43).

Crucial Instances

All of the stories brought together in *Crucial Instances* were written in 1900 and 1901, and six of the seven appeared in the magazines during the same period: three were placed in the familiar *Scribner's* and three in *Harper's* and *Cosmopolitan*, well-known periodicals that were carrying Wharton fiction for the first time. "Copy" came out in the June 1900 issue of *Scribner's*.[13] Sub-titled "A Dialogue," it copied the playscript format of the earlier "The Twilight of the God" and had a similar plot featuring a married person meeting up with a lover out of the past. In August, *Scribner's* also published "The Duchess at Prayer,"

Wharton's supernatural, historical tale set in Italy, with illustrations by Maxfield Parrish.[14] August also saw the publication of "The Rembrandt" in *Cosmopolitan*, a story centering around a fraudulent painting and a conscientous curator.[15] "The Angel at the Grave" appeared in the February 1901 *Scribner's*.[16] An evocation of Transcendentalist Concord, its major character was the granddaughter of one Orestes Anson. *Harper's* published the next two Wharton stories, "The Recovery" and "The Moving Finger," in its February and March numbers respectively.[17] "The Recovery," another Jamesian story (its resemblances to James are noted by both Millicent Bell [332] and E.K. Brown [10]) centers on an American painter's recognition of the superiority of the European masters. "The Moving Finger," mentioned favorably by James himself (Bell 247), also features painting as its subject.

 Crucial Instances appeared on April 7, 1901[18] with one previously unpublished story, "The Confessional," added to the aforementioned six. The tale is atypical of the other stories in the volume: "the thing is done on such a large scale, with so much broader strokes than most of my stories," Wharton wrote Brownell on February 6 (Scribner Archives). "The Confessional" is the most complex and in some ways the most intriguing tale in the book with its meshing of time frames and its seal-of-the-confessional subject, and it perhaps gives *Crucial Instances* a distinctiveness it would not otherwise have. Generally the contemporary reviews of this second collection were favorable, although the consensus was that there was a falling off from the standard set in *The Greater Inclination*. Later assessments were pointedly critical. Blake Nevius wrote in 1953, for example: "In their wholesale deference to the popular tone of magazine fiction, the stories in *Crucial Instances* ... stand alone among Edith Wharton's earlier [short stories]. There is a marked reversion in these stories of contemporary life to the false sentiment and the conventionally 'inspirational' endings of the stories she published in *Scribner's Magazine* in the early nineties" (25-26). If Wharton sacrificed some of her former quality in this later volume, it was perhaps because she was being lured by the possibilities of the novel, and in fact she admits in her correspondence of this period that the writing of the stories was often a kind of respite she provided herself as she was working on her first piece of longer fiction, *The Valley of Decision.*

The Descent of Man, and Other Stories

Early in 1903, Scribner's was asking Wharton for another collection of short stories: the coming spring would be "a psychological moment" for its appearance. But Wharton was reluctant to produce a new volume so soon after *Crucial Instances*: she feared she was getting the reputation of "writing too much [and] publishing too hurriedly," and while she could not help her tendency to write a great deal, "it seemed ... distinctly better to 'espacer' the volumes a little more" (EW to Brownell, 22 February 1903, Scribner Archives). By mid-autumn, plans were well under way for a spring 1904 publication of a new collection. "I have ten stories for the April volume," Wharton wrote Brownell on October 17, noting that "it was agreed that one or two of the stories would be 'inédits'.... Now of the ten on hand at present," she went on, "all have been taken by magazines, but as two are going respectively to the Cosmopolitan and Collier's, I fancy that to my usual readers they will seem, in the volume, as good as new" (Scribner Archives).

All of the contents of the 1904 collection appeared in the magazines in 1902, 1903 and 1904, and most of them were taken by the upper-class *Scribner's* and *Harper's.* Wharton was very pleased with the stories as a group, telling Brownell at least twice that they were the best she had ever written (17 October 1903; 22 February 1904, Scribner Archives). "The Quicksand" and "The Reckoning" were published by *Harper's* in June and August 1902, respectively.[19] Both were stories of marriage in the upper classes, a subject that was always popular with Wharton. In November, *Scribner's* carried Wharton's first ghost story, "The Lady's Maid's Bell," with illustrations by Walter Appleton Clark that played up the spectral aspects of the story.[20] The following month *Harper's* brought out "The Mission of Jane," another story of upper-class marriage, this one of a satiric turn.[21] "The Dilettante," "A Venetian Night's Entertainment," and

"Expiation" all appeared in December 1903, in *Harper's*, *Scribner's*, and *Hearst's International-Cosmopolitan* respectively, and the decision of editors of upper-class and slick magazines alike to feature these stories in their Christmas numbers attested to Wharton's growing appeal.[22] "The Dilettante" centered on a male character type that surfaced often in Wharton's fiction: in Louis Auchincloss's words, "the cold cultivated aristocratic egoist who feeds on the life and enthusiasm of simpler souls" (*EW* 11). *Scribner's* used "A Venetian Night's Entertainment" as its lead piece and hired Maxfield Parrish to illustrate the story, and Parrish's full-color plate added a festive touch to this slight romantic tale set in eighteenth-century Venice. "Expiation," another satire, is about a writer, the success of whose books derives from the fact that her uncle, an Episcopalian bishop, condemns them from the pulpit. The remaining two entries in the collection appeared immediately prior to the volume's publication in April. "The Other Two" was published by *Collier's* on February 13; "The Descent of Man" in *Scribner's* the following month.[23] "The Other Two," widely acclaimed as one of the very best of Wharton's short stories, testifies to the high standard she maintained when she wrote for the slick magazines. "The Descent of Man," another of the stories of academe set in Hillbridge, reminds us again of Wharton's penchant for satiric writing.

The collected version of these nine works bore the title *The Descent of Man, and Other Stories* and a dedication: "To Edward L. Burlingame my first and kindest critic."[24] (Wharton had arranged with Brownell that the dedication would be kept secret until the book came out.) When Brownell sent Wharton reviews of the collection, she was dismayed that once again her stories were being compared to James's. "The continued cry that I am an echo of Mr. James (whose books of the last ten years I can't read, much as I delight in the man) [and] the assumption that the people I write about are not real because they are not navvies [and] char-women, makes me feel rather hopeless," she answered Brownell (*LEW* 91). Brownell's response was to comment on the paucity of real American critics and to agree that "it is unpleasant not to have one's uniquity recognized," but, he went on to say, "sometimes you seem to come out of the mix better than he does." As much as this support must have pleased Wharton, one wonders if Brownell's citing of a review that referred to her as "a masculine H.J." did much to quell her disappointment (*EW* 132).

In fact, a number of the commentaries on *The Descent of Man, and Other Stories* were very laudatory whether they mentioned James or not, and it is worth suggesting that perhaps Wharton made too much of the James allusions. Critics drew attention to her gift for irony and her "artistic perfection" (C.H. 226), and stories such as "The Lady's Maid's Bell" and "The Other Two" were singled out as being particularly meritorious. For later generations of critics who had the advantage of reading the whole of Wharton's *oeuvre*, the collection was considered superior, and it is fair to use Lewis's assessment, "probably the best of her collections of short stories ... . With it she reached full maturity as a satirist of American manners" (*EW* 133), as a representative one.

A quartette of "stray chicks"

When Wharton wrote Brownell on May 10, 1904 acknowledging receipt of six copies of her new collection, she wondered at the absence of a story called "The Letter" (Scribner Archives). Brownell replied that he had never heard of the story: "You have never referred to it. Your brood is so numerous you don't keep track of stray chicks" (*EW* 132). One of four stories published in the magazines between 1904 and 1908 that remained absent from Wharton's American collections, "The Letter" did appear in the English edition of *The Descent of Man, and Other Stories*, published by Macmillan. A romance set in the same period and milieu as the earlier tale "The Confessional," "The Letter" appeared in April 1904 in *Harper's*.[25]

The other uncollected stories of this period saw print in magazines in which Wharton's short fiction had not previously appeared. "The House of the Dead Hand" was published in *Atlantic Monthly* in August 1904; "The Introducers" in *Ainslee's* in December 1905 and January 1906.[26] Written earlier, in the spring of 1898, (Wolff 85) "The House of the Dead Hand" is a gothic tale set in Sienna. It has been virtually ignored in the earlier commentary on Wharton's work, and indeed Wharton herself did not include it in her later collection of ghost stories, a work in which it might have found a place. "The Introducers," yet another story of marriage and manners, has gone largely unnoticed as well, perhaps deservedly so.

The last of this group, "Les Metteurs en Scène" (translated as "The Stage Managers") is unique in the short story oeuvre, for it is the only story Wharton wrote in French and published initially in France. Weary of writing translations for French magazines, she decided to try her hand at an original story in her adopted language. The result was "Les Metteurs en Scène," published in *Revue des Deux Mondes* in October 1908,[27] the tale of an American matchmaker plying her trade in Paris. Though initially proud of her effort to write in her second language (EW to Scribner, October 1908, Scribner Archives), Wharton was not pleased with the outcome, telling Burlingame she would never look him or Henry James in the face again. When she met James soon after the story's publication, he patronized her mercilessly, saying, "I do congratulate you, my dear, on the way in which you've picked up every old worn out literary phrase that's been lying about the streets of Paris for the last twenty years, and managed to pack them all into these few pages" (*EW* 234). It makes an interesting comment on the artistic failure of "Les Metteurs en Scène" that in "The Verdict," a story published a few years before and probably written around the same time, Wharton has the character Jack Gisburn say to a friend: "Don't you know how, in talking a foreign language, even fluently, one says half the time, not what one wants to, but what one can?" (I, 663).

The Hermit and the Wild Woman

In the months immediately before the appearance of *The Descent of Man, and Other Stories* in April 1904, Wharton worked on two pieces she saw as potential contributions to this collection, "The Last Asset" and "The Potboiler." She feared, as she wrote Brownell on March 31, that her "New England conscience" had set her to "worrying all winter ... because I thought I was not giving you [and] the public your money's worth for the new volume" (Scribner Archives). But Brownell was able to assuage her anxieties, and the two stories were kept for a later collection. That collection eventually appeared in 1908 and at Wharton's initiative. Her burgeoning career as a novelist and her decision to publish *The Reef* with Appleton's had perhaps distracted Scribner's attention away from the fact that their prize find was still writing short stories and publishing them in their own magazine. When Charles Scribner wrote Wharton on September 3, 1908, he expressed his regret that *Scribner's* was losing *The Reef* for serialization but was "quite consoled by your offer of a new series of stories" (Scribner Archives).

Wharton's offer had come in a letter to Burlingame on June 7: "I seem to have afloat in magazines," she wrote, "enough 'Nouvelles' for another volume—si le coeur vous en dit for I made out this list" (Scribner Archives). Of the list of seven titles she submitted, "The Last Asset," "In Trust," "The Potboiler," "The Hermit and the Wild Woman," "The Verdict," "The Pretext," "The Choice," all but the last had been published in the magazines by August, and the first six along with "The Best Man" (substituted for "The Choice") became the contents of the promised collection. Both "The Last Asset" and "The Potboiler" appeared in *Scribner's*, in August and December 1904, respectively.[28] "The Last Asset," a brilliant story of manners, is, surprisingly, not much venerated in the canon. (It is impossible to understand E.K. Brown's dismissal of it as having "aucune valeur") (20). "The Potboiler," about three creative artists, broaches questions of artistic talent, commercial success, and ethical behaviour. "The Best Man," Wharton's only attempt at a story about politics, was published by *Collier's* in its September 2, 1905 number:[29] Wharton had submitted it at that time for the Collier Prize. *Scribner's* published one of Wharton's favorites, "The Hermit and the Wild Woman," in February 1906:[30] a medieval tale of passion and penitence, it had caused her much trouble in the writing. "In Trust" was issued in *Appleton's Booklover's* two months later.[31] A story of failed philantropy, it features Wharton's ever-popular theme of the moral dilemma. That theme recurs in "The

Verdict," and "The Pretext," both published by *Scribner's* with illustrations by Alanzo Kimball, the summer prior to the new collection's appearance, in its June and August issues respectively.[32] They were, Wharton wrote her friend Sarah Norton on April 12, "The only things I've done this idle winter" (*LEW*, 140).

Scribner's had the collected version of these stories out in September 1908, its title that of the lead piece, "The Hermit and the Wild Woman."[33] As early as March 11, 1904, Brownell had suggested this to Wharton as an appropriate title for an eventual collection (Scribner Archives), and she later concurred. "I think the volume had better be called 'The Hermit and the Wild Woman'," she told Brownell in a letter on June 20, "as that story made rather a hit.—I can't think of a collective name for such a wide-ranging lot of *donnée*" (Scribner Archives). *The Hermit and the Wild Woman and Other Stories* (the elongated title appeared on the book's title page but not on the cover) had sold about 4,300 copies by the end of the year, a modest sale that did not even earn back the thousand-dollar advance paid to Wharton. Once again Wharton was disappointed with the publisher's meagre publicity. "It had struck me that for these shreiking days," she wrote on October 2 in answer to Scribner's promise of a stepped-up advertising campaign, "that the book was being faintly advertised" (Scribner Archives).

The Hermit and the Wild Woman and Other Stories received a generally approbative reading by reviewers. Agnes Repplier's notice in *Outlook* reflected the pervasive praise of Wharton's craftsmanship with its reference to "sentences ... cut like gems" (693). Critics also commented not infrequently that the stories tended to be depressing, to lack any "touch of cheerfulness," as the anonymous critic in the *Nation* review put it (525). Some later commentators continued to catch glimpses, or larger views, of James: for Auchincloss the tales were "slender contrived James stories of artists and dilettantes..." (*EW* 18). The consensus, both contemporaneous and more recent, is that Wharton maintained her standard here but revealed little thematic newness or stylistic change.

Tales of Men and Ghosts

Evidence that the Wharton-Scribner affiliation was still strong two decades after its inception was readily available in the two years leading up to the publication of Wharton's next collection of short fiction in the fall of 1910. Of the ten stories that were to compose that volume, eight were carried in *Scribner's Magazine*, nearly all of the eight appearing under the caption "Tales of Men," which anticipated in part their title in collected form. The first of these, "The Bolted Door," appeared in March 1909.[34] A new kind of tale for Wharton—Lewis has called it "Poe-esque" (*EW* 253)—it concerns a man who is unable to convince anyone that he has murdered a cousin and who has become trapped in his own consciousness. June, July, and August saw three Wharton stories in *Scribner's*. "His Father's Son" deals with a man who has compensated for a dull life by inventing a fictive life for his wife via a series of letters he writes, and with the effects of this on his son.[35] "The Daunt Diana" features an art collector and centers on the question of the value of art.[36] "The Debt," a story Wharton considered one of her most successful (EW to Burlingame, 10 May 1909, Scribner Archives) takes up the subject of scientific and academic authenticity.[37] The October *Scribner's* carried "Full Circle," a story in which the theme of the double figures prominently.[38] *Century* published "Afterward" in January 1910, interrupting briefly the *Scribner's* monopoly on Wharton's stories:[39] one of the most successfully wrought of Wharton's ghost tales, it has not been given its critical due. In March and June, *Scribner's* resumed "Tales of Men" with "The Legend" and "The Eyes."[40] In "The Legend," Wharton, as she told Morton Fullerton in a letter of March 19, 1910, chose to represent Henry James in the guise of a character named Pellerin (*LEW* 202). "The Eyes," called by Lewis "a small masterpiece," is generally recognized as one of Wharton's best ghost stories. (*EW* 296). Wharton returned to *Century* with a long story, "The Letters," serialized in the August, September, and October issues, with illustrations by Sigismond De Ivanowski.[41] Here she drew upon her experience with and knowledge of Fullerton to fashion a rambling tale of male opportunism and female fidelity and commitment. The last of the "Tales of Men," "The Blond Beast," appeared in the September *Scribner's*.[42] Again, the central character is an opportunistic male but in this case one who acquires a moral sense.

The stories saw print in volume form on October 22, 1910. After considering "Men, Women and Others" and "Tales of Men and Others" (EW to Brownell, 10 August 1910, Scribner Archives) Wharton settled on the title *Tales of Men and Ghosts*, a title Scribner's favored as well (Brownell to Wharton, 16 August 1910, Scribner Archives).[43] It is difficult to form a consensus on the book's overall quality based on the reviewers' comments. When there was praise it was tepid, and the old reservations were expressed again: Wharton was still under the spell of James; the stories were undistinguished by any departure from the magazine style. Some praised the ghost stories; others regretted that Wharton had not given all of her time to writing studies of human nature. The sales of *Tales of Men and Ghosts*, a barely respectable 4,000, perhaps reflected the indifferent critical response. Nonetheless, Wharton was maintaining a small but steady readership.

More recent comment on the collection *Tales of Men and Ghosts* is as difficult to assess as was the initial critical response. Bell calls the stories "neater , 'snappier' .... They are studies in situation rather than character which have moved decidedly out of the penumbra of James into a lighter element" (360). Wolff notes "the recurrent preoccupation with the theme of the double—the alter ego, the shadow self" (202). Lewis, ever the biographer, and other recent critics tend to view the stories as reflecting aspects of Wharton's relationship with Fullerton, which coincided with the time of the writing of some of these tales. If there is a recurrent opinion worth noting, it is the enthusiasm with which "The Eyes" has been received.

Xingu and Other Stories

Four years after the publication of *Tales of Men and Ghosts* Wharton wrote Scribner: "I suppose I might collect another vol. of short stories next year" (6 January 1914, Scribner Archives). Scribner found the suggestion "most welcome" (19 January 1914, Scribner Archives), and plans were afoot for Wharton's sixth collection of short fiction. Wharton anticipated that her proposed collection would include some new and previously unpublished material: on February 20, for example, she wrote Burlingame that a story called "The Temperate Zone" was "nearly finished" (Scribner Archives). However, this story did not make its appearance until eight years after the proposed collection came out in 1916. In fact, all of the seven stories comprising the 1916 collection had previous magazine publication, and all but one, "Coming Home," had been written before the Great War (*EW* 394). Writing to Scribner on October 20, 1915, Wharton listed "Xingu," "Autres Temps ... ," "Kerfol," "The Long Run," and "Coming Home" as stories "I could put in a volume for the early spring" (Scribner Archives). Wharton had forgotten, "The Triumph of Night," a tale she had sent to *Scribner's* earlier, and an old story, "The Choice," published in *Century* in 1908, was added to flesh out the volume. Wharton's vast personal involvement in the war effort had not only limited her output but had also prevented her from providing the kind of material she would have liked to see in her new collection: during the period leading up to the 1916 publication, her correspondence makes more than one allusion to her desire to translate her wartime experiences into short stories.

The contents of the 1916 collection appeared in the magazines over a span of eight years in Wharton's familiar outlets, the upper-class magazines. The "oldest" of these stories was "The Choice," done during a trans-Atlantic crossing in May 1908 and published by *Century* the following November (*LEW* 146)[44] Written in "a burst of savagery and despair" (*EW* 128), "The Choice" belongs to that group of stories in which Wharton attempted to deal with her affair with Fullerton and her unhappy marriage. *Century* also carried Wharton's next story, "Other Times, Other Manners": it appeared in the July and August 1911 issues of the magazine.[45] One of her very finest—"probably her best short story," says Blake Nevius (175)—"Other Times, Other Manners" studies the effects of divorce in successive generations. In December of the same year, *Scribner's* brought out "Xingu," a throwback to Wharton's earlier satiric tales.[46] Set in her mythical college town of Hillbridge, the story holds sham culture up to ridicule and is perhaps Wharton's most effectively achieved satiric piece. Early the following year *Atlantic Monthly* published "The Long Run," the story helping to sell out the number in two days. (*EW* 318).[47] Here Wharton went back to a favorite subject, love in and outside of marriage, in a piece that suggested again the agony of her own marital predicament. *Scribner's* carried the last three of this group: "The Triumph of Night" in August 1914, "Coming Home" in December 1915, and "Kerfol" in March, 1916.[48] "The Triumph of Night" and "Kerfol" were ghost stories, both with Hawthornesque echoes, E.K. Brown has noted (27). "Coming Home" represents the closest Wharton came to publishing a war story. In June 1915, she had expressed to Scribner a desire to write "four or five short stories, not precisely war stories, but on subjects suggested by the war. So many extraordinary and dramatic situations are springing out of the huge conflict that the temptation to use a few of them is irresistible" (*LEW* 357). "Coming Home" was one of the few actualizations of this desire.

Scribner's produced the new collection in October 1916, using Wharton's choice for the title, *Xingu and Other Stories*, and supplementing the seven stories with her 1892 novella *Bunner Sisters*.[49] Wharton was pleased that "everyone seems to think [the collection] shows growth," as she wrote Gaillard Lapsley in December (*LEW* 185). In fact, *Xingu and Other Stories* sold better than had Wharton's more recent collections. Scribner told Wharton early in December that "the orders...show a good deal of life and we have ordered it printed a second time, for our first edition (6250) was small and we did not wish to run any chance of being out of print... The second edition is 2000 copies" (7 December 1916, Scribner Archives). By February the editors were able to tell Wharton: "For a collection of stories and in these times, we think "Xingu" did very well" (4 February 1916, Scribner Archives).

Xingu and Other Stories is remarkable for its high quality in a number of different genres of the short story. "Xingu" is surely Wharton's best satire (The anonymous *Nation* reviewer referred to its "delightful exuberant humor" [Lauer and Murray 329]). "Coming Home," its war story, was generally highly praised at the time. "Autres Temps..." (the title changed from "Other Times, Other Manners") ranks among Wharton's most successful stories of manners. Its two ghost stories, "Kerfol" and "The Triumph of Night" show different facets of the genre. One is hard pressed to find much commentary among non-contemporary critics on the collection as a whole, but the criticism of its individual stories suggests that it was close to being the best work in the genre Wharton produced to date.

"Writing a War Story"

Xingu and Other Stories marked the end of an era. It would be ten years before another collection of Wharton's short stories appeared. And when that collection did come out it bore the imprint of Appleton and Company; the long-standing affiliation with the house of Scribner had all but come to an end. Scribner's refusal, early in 1916, of Wharton's offer of her novel *Summer* for serialization in its magazine seems to have been the immediate cause of the Wharton/Scribner break-up. As a result, and in the aftermath of that rejection, misunderstandings between the two parties multiplied, and before long, much to Scribner's disappointment, Wharton was sending her novels to Appleton, who would place them for serialization with magazines—Appleton no longer had a magazine of its own— and then publish them in volume form. Wharton's move to Appleton was also motivated by financial considerations. Scribner was finding it difficult to compete in a market dominated more and more by large-circulation, low-priced popular magazines (*EW* 395), and Appleton "offered much bigger advances, better magazine deals, and more active advertising" (Aronson 7).

The falling-out with Scribner's led, of course, to a much-diminished relationship between Wharton and *Scribner's Magazine*. And the financial considerations that in part motivated Wharton's move drew her away from the other lower-paying upper-class magazines such as *Harper's* and *Atlantic Monthly* that had been her outlets in the past. Now, dealing with Appleton, she would have a go-between who would place her stories with the more popular magazines and seek out the best prices.

A case in point is "Writing a War Story," the only uncollected short story Wharton published between 1916 and 1926. "Writing a War Story" saw print in the popular *Woman's Home Companion* in September 1919, with illustrations by Charles E. Chambers.[50] Called "a flimsy tale" by Lewis (*EW* 422), its theme is the disappointment experienced by a poet when a war story she has written has been poorly received. Appleton had difficulty placing the story, offering it unsuccessfully to *McClure's*, *Saturday Evening Post*, *Metropolitan*, *Everybody's* and other magazines. "Each and all [said]," wrote J.H. Sears of Appleton to Wharton "that they wanted stories by you very much, that they regretted not taking this story, but it was not in their opinion suited to magazine publication." Finally *Woman's Home Companion* took the story, offering 350 dollars, but paying 500 at Sears' insistence (13 December 1918, EW Collection).

Here and Beyond

The idea for a first collection of short stories with Appleton and Company surfaced in January 1919, Wharton proposing it for that spring (EW to Appleton, 25 January 1919, EW Collection). The plan emerged again in 1923. In August of that year, Rutger Jewett, Wharton's editor at Appleton, wrote her that " the format of the [collection] would be that of the regular novel, only not so thick. Our idea is to produce attractive, distinguished looking books, selling the different stories separately, also combining them four in a box to be sold in a set" (30 August 1923, EW Collection). But in November Jewett changed his tune, asking Wharton to choose a title for a new collection and to list the stories to be included, and stipulating that the book would be put out "the first season where we are not issuing any other volume by you" (15 November 1923, EW Collection). Wharton responded with the title "Here and Beyond" and a list of six stories: "The Seed of the Faith," "Velvet Ear Pads," "The Temperate Zone," "Bewitched," "Miss Mary Pask," and "The Young Gentlemen" (3 December 1923, EW Collection). Jewett was pleased with Wharton's title and selections, specifying that Appleton would plan the book when all the stories had appeared in the magazines (21 December, 1923, EW Collection). When *Here and Beyond* was published two and a half years later, its contents were exactly as Wharton had anticipated.

The first of this group of stories to be published was "The Seed of the Faith," one of the last appearances in *Scribner's* of a Wharton story. When Wharton sent it to the magazine, Charles Scribner replied: "We should be delighted to publish this and any other stories which may follow," but explained that the house could no longer pay her the thousand dollars they usually did. "500 dollars would seem enough at this time," he went on, but he specified that because the story was long he could add an extra hundred (6 May 1918, Scribner Archives). Wharton accepted the price, for the sake of "my old affection for Scribner," but insisted that she could get better prices elsewhere and could not afford to pass them up "owing to a great reduction of my income, to the heavy taxes we are all suffering from, and to the unprecedented demands for help on all sides" (23 May 1918, Scribner Archives). "The Seed of the Faith," a story about missionaries in Africa, no doubt inspired by her trip to Morocco in 1917, appeared in *Scribner's* in January 1919.[51]

"Temperate Zone," another story initially slated to appear in *Scribner's*— Wharton mentioned it in letters to Burlingame as early as 1917 (10 May 1917, EW Collection)—ended up in *Pictorial Review*, a periodical that was to be a frequent outlet for Wharton's short stories over the next few years. This popular magazine was on a list Jewett prepared for Wharton in 1922: the list comprised magazines "outside the yellow group of Hearst periodicals" that paid high prices to contributors (1 June 1922, EW Collection). *Pictorial Review* published "Temperate Zone," one of Wharton's many stories about people in the arts, in its February 1924 issue, paying the handsome sum of 2,500 dollars (Jewett to EW, 17 April 1923, EW Collection).[52]

Pictorial Review published Wharton's next two stories as well: "Bewitched" and "Miss Mary Pask," both ghost tales, appeared respectively in the March and April 1925 issues of the magazine.[53] Jewett boasted to Wharton that he was able to get the high price of 2,750 dollars for "Bewitched," writing her that he had told *Pictorial's* editor, Arthur T. Vance, that "quality as well as quantity demanded consideration. He is always a good sport and came up to my figure" (30 January 1924, EW Collection). "Miss Mary Pask" was not the financial succcess of its predecessor, earning only sixteen hundred dollars (Jewett to EW, 21 June 1923, EW Collection). Perhaps Wharton herself tipped the scales in *Pictorial's* favor when she wrote Jewett: "I am sending you a ghost story that I wrote the other day while I was getting over the grippe. You will judge from it what a bad attack I had" (1 May 1923, EW Collection).

One of the other magazines Jewett had included on his list of likely markets for Wharton's stories was *Red Book*. When *Pictorial Review* turned down "Velvet Ear Pads," Jewett sent it to *Red Book* which bought it for 3,000 dollars (Jewett to EW, 13 March 1925, EW Collection). "Velvet Ear Pads" was a rarity for Wharton: a comic story. When she sent it to Jewett she told him: "I have tried it on a party of friends here who laughed so much that I hope it will have a success with a larger public" (29 January 1925, EW Collection). *Red Book* ran the story, about an absent-minded American professor, in its issue of August 1925, changing the title to "Velvet Ear-Muffs," much to Wharton's disapproval.[54] She asked Jewett to "transmit her protest to the editor," noting that "It is a sheer discourtesy to rearrange an author's language in accordance to some personal notion of the meaning of words" (19 August 1925, EW Collection). She received an apology from *Red Book* and an explanation that ear pads were used on patients after surgery (Karl Edwin Harriman to Jewett, 25 September 1925, EW Collection)—an explanation that did not satisfy her (EW to Jewett, 1 October 1925, EW Collection).

The last of the contents of the first Appleton collection in the magazines was "The Young Gentlemen," a bizarre tale about a widower who has secretly kept in his mansion for a lifetime, two sons, dwarves both physically and mentally. The story was turned down by the *Delineator*, another of the high-paying popular magazines: alluding probably to its reputation for avoiding controversial fiction, Wharton referred to it after the rejection as "that female journal" (EW to Jewett, 1 October 1923, EW Collection). Jewett was very high on the story, telling Wharton: "... the suspense sustained perfectly. The closing pages gave me an unaccustomed thrill." He no doubt communicated his enthusiasm to Arthur Vance, the *Pictorial Review* editor, who bought it for 2,500 dollars and published it in February 1926 (23 September 1923, EW Collection).[55]

Here and Beyond—the second term in its title referring to the three of its stories that are psychic in character—appeared in early May of 1926.[56] By mid-June it had sold some 8,000 copies in the United States and Canada (Jewett to EW, 18 June 1926, EW Collection), and four months after its appearance it had earned Wharton 3,200 dollars in royalties (Appleton and Company to EW, July 2, August 26, 1926, EW Collection). Its critical reception was at best tepid and in one case especially harsh. Though the most sympathetic of the reviewers singled out one or another story for particular praise—"Bewitched" and "The Seed of the Faith" came in for compliments by different critics—or commented on Wharton's well known verbal or structural grace, none praised the volume unequivocally. From the *North American Review* came unaccustomed condemnation: "Of all the silly, inconsequential, irrelevant bits of flub-dubbery," wrote J.T. Rogers, "these 'six exquisite gems,' as they are called, stagger criticism. There is, as far as we can see, not one page from the opening line of 'Here and Beyond,' the first gem, to the final word of release in 'Velvet Earpads' which deserves five seconds consideration" (225). It must have surprised and amused Wharton, if she ever saw the review, to realize that the reviewer had not noticed that the name of the book was not also the name of its lead story.

More recent evaluations have done little to redeem the early reputation of *Here and Beyond*. For Lewis, it "was perhaps the only volume of tales that has virtually nothing in it to commend" (*EW* 522); Wolff finds in it "not one genuinely remarkable story" (395). In the face of such a wave of disapproval it may sound presumptuous to say so, but there is at least one "exquisite gem" in the volume, "Miss Mary Pask," the point of which seems to have been missed even by those commentators who appear to have read the story.

Certain People

The unflattering critical reception of *Here and Beyond* had no apparent ill effect on Wharton's desire to write short stories, and a year later she was making overtures to Appleton about another collection (EW to Jewett, 17 November 1927, EW Collection). The substance of that collection was set when she wrote Jewett on April 30, 1929 listing "Mr. Jones," "A Bottle of Perrier," "After Holbein," "Dieu d'Amour," and "Atrophy" as the proposed contents. When the volume appeared in the fall of 1930, it contained these five stories, all published in the magazines in the later 1920's, and an earlier tale, "The Refugees," "the existence of which Wharton had entirely forgotten," her secretary wrote Jewett in January 1928 (27 January 1928, EW Collection). All of the six stories were placed with two periodicals, *Saturday Evening Post* and *Ladies' Home Journal*, new outlets for Wharton stories and among the most successful of the popular magazines.

The first of the group to be published was "The Refugees," an older story and the only one that derived from Wharton's charitable work during the Great War. The *Saturday Evening Post* paid 1,500 dollars for this "amusing" tale (*EW* 422) and published it in its issue of January 18, 1919.[57] "The Refugees" had been turned down by *McClure's* and *Metropolitan* "on the grounds that they could not pay so high a figure" as Wharton demanded (Jewett to Mary Cadwalader Jones, 22 November 1918, EW Collection).

The *Saturday Evening Post* also took "A Bottle of Perrier," Wharton's murder mystery set in the Sahara, publishing it in the March 27, 1926 issue under the title "A Bottle of Evian."[58] The *Post* rejected Wharton's title because of advertising considerations: Jewett had to explain to her that "the use of the word 'Perrier' might cost the *Post* many thousands of dollars because rival firms might cancel advertising contracts on the ground that they were exploiting Perrier at the expense of other brands." Because the price was so good (2,000 dollars) she should accept the minor change, Jewett went on, especially since other magazines were not enthralled with the story's subject (26 January 1926; 1 March 1926, EW Collection). Wharton suggested "A Bottle of Fizzy Water" as a substitute title, but apparently the *Post* went ahead with its choice without her prior approval (EW to Jewett, 10 February 1926, EW Collection). In the matter of the *Post's* acceptance of "A Bottle of Perrier," and of "The Refugees" as well, it can be noted that the magazine put aside its usual preference for stories of American life.

Wharton's next two stories made their appearance in *Ladies' Home Journal*, "Atrophy" in November 1927 and "Mr. Jones" in April 1928.[59] "Atrophy," a tale of marital infidelity, was first turned down by the *Delineator*, which preferred to introduce Wharton to its readers by either a serial or a longer story, and then bought by the *Ladies' Home Journal* for 2,000 dollars, "a good price for one of your shorter stories," Jewett told Wharton (31 May 1927, EW Collection). "Mr. Jones," another fine ghost story, also earned Wharton 2,000 dollars, the price and acceptance pleasing her considerably, for she "feared the tale might be too English for the American market" (EW to Jewett, 26 December 1927, EW Collection).

The *Saturday Evening Post* carried "After Holbein," Wharton's macabre story of old New York—one of the main characters was modelled on Mrs Astor—in its May 5, 1928 number.[60] Wharton had written it in March and it was sold at once for 2,500 dollars (EW, Notes and Subjects, 1928; Appleton to EW, 31 March 1928, EW Collection). The *Ladies' Home Journal* topped its own and the *Post's* prices when it took "Dieu d'Amour" for 3,000 dollars. This historical romance was published in October 1928.[61]

The collected version of these stories, *Certain People*, saw print in October 1930,[62] and by November 15 it had earned Wharton over 2,500 dollars. (Appleton's record of receipts, EW Collection). Jewett sang a familiar refrain a month later when he told Wharton: "*Certain People* is selling exceedingly well for a collection of short stories. Of course such a volume never sells as well as the longer novel. Evidently," he went on "the American woman prefers to spend the same amount of money for an armful of magazines which contain not only fiction but pictures of famous actors and film stars, also home decoration and household hints" (5 December 1930, EW Collection). The critical reception of *Certain People* reflected the book's commercial success: the *New York Times* wrote, for example, that "four [of the six stories] are above average in importance and one ['After Holbein"] is a triumph of short story writing" (9). Later criticism of the volume echoed this positive response, Lewis including *Certain People* in his general approbation of Wharton's last three collections (*EW* 522), and Wolff remarking that it "exhibits distinct signs of improvement [over *Here and Beyond*]"(395).

Human Nature

A little over a year after the arrival of *Certain People* on the scene Wharton was planning yet another collection with Appleton (EW to Jewett, 4 December 1931, EW Collection). Jewett encouraged the project, explaining though that the new collection would have to wait until after Appleton's publication of her novel *The Gods Arrive* so that it would not compete with the latter (16 December 1931, EW Collection). By summer and fall of 1932 the book's preparation was well under way, Jewett frantically badgering Wharton for proofs. Because Wharton was nervous about the difficulty of getting the stories placed in the magazines and the delays in their publication, Jewett decided on the order of the volume's contents ("Her Son," "The Day of the Funeral," "A Glimpse," "Joy in the House," and "Diagnosis") (Jewett to EW, 27 December 1932, EW Collection). Wharton chose the title, "Human Nature," although she also considered "Her Son and Other Stories," because her long tale "Her Son" had attracted so much attention when *Scribner's* published it (EW to Jewett, 27 October 1932, EW Collection).

All of the *Human Nature* stories appeared in the magazines in the space of a little over two years. "Diagnosis," a tragic tale of love and infidelity, was the first to see print, and Wharton had initially hoped it could be included in her previous collection, *Certain People*. But Jewett, eager to see stories pay off twice, discouraged, as he always did, the inclusion in a collection of a story that had not made a periodical appearance. He congratulated Wharton on "Diagnosis," calling it "one of your very best," and sent it to *Ladies' Home Journal*, "which has been eager to receive something from your desk" (11 July 1930, EW Collection). The *Journal* accepted "Diagnosis" immediately, paid 3,000 dollars for it—"a top-notch price" boasted Jewett—(18 July 1930, EW Collection) and to Wharton's disappointment published it only in November, too late for inclusion in *Certain People*.[63]

The publication of "Her Son," in *Scribner's* in February 1932 marked Wharton's final fiction appearance in that magazine.[64] When she sent this "long-short" story to Jewett, she feared it would be difficult to place because of its extreme length (30 June 1931, EW Collection). Jewett found the piece "stunning," but the undisclosed magazine editor to whom he sent it turned it down on two accounts: it would require two installments, and it was "unpleasant." "I've had it read by a considerable number of our people," Jewett cited the editor, "and all of them object to its sordid interpretation of a mother-love story" (7 October 1931, EW Collection). *Scribner's* took "Her Son" for 750 dollars and issued Wharton an invitation to enter the story in a contest they were holding (Alfred Sheppard Dashiell to Jewett, 9 November 1931, EW Collection).

With *Scribner's* diminished price, Wharton was beginning to feel the pinch of the Depression. Jewett described the lamentable state of magazine fiction in a letter written to her in May 1932:

All magazines are suffering from the drastic reduction in advertising placed in their pages. Business is at the lowest ebb that we have had since I have been in the business. Corporations which in the past have spent fortunes advertising food products, cosmetics, automobiles, etc, have cut their advertising appropriations to the bone. This means that the magazines have reduced their pages. As a result they are buying fewer stories and articles. The abominable method of cutting up fiction into small sections in order to place it next to advertisements is the reason for this curtailment. The editors are not allowed to print a long story consecutively in a manner agreeable to the reader. It must be used as 'fillers' on the advertising pages so that they can make good their promise that each advertisement appears next to reading matter. It is a detestable system for the reader. Small bits of short stories and novels are tossed to us like scraps of meat to a dog. (5 May 1932, EW Collection)

After *Ladies' Home Journal* turned down Wharton's "short sketch" "A Glimpse," Jewett was pleased to report that *Saturday Evening Post* had offered 2,000 dollars for it, "a good figure for these parlous times" (5 May 1931; 16 August 1931, EW Collection). The *Post* ran "A Glimpse," about the impact of two performing artists on an admiring observer, in its issue of November 12, 1932, chopping it up badly in the manner Jewett had described.[65]

The "parlous times" were again brought home to Wharton when her story "Joy in the House" began making the rounds. And her unhappy experience now with the magazines that had sought out her work and paid handsomely for it not long past led to her decision to abandon her long-standing reluctance to place her fiction with periodicals controlled by the Hearst organization. It did not help matters that Wharton was especially fond of "Joy in the House": she had written it "inside of a week. I had not had such an adventure for years," she told Jewett (5 March 1932, EW Collection). When *Pictorial Review* offered a "meagre" 750 dollars for "Joy in the House," Jewett turned it down (Jewett to EW, 26 April 1932, EW Collection). *McCall's, Saturday Evening Post, Delineator,* and *Ladies' Home Journal* all refused the story, most editors stating that they were looking for material that was lighter and more humorous (Jewett to EW, 21 June 1932, EW Collection).

The virtual rejection of "Joy in the House" spurred Wharton to an unexpected turnabout. She told Jewett:

... I am growing very much discouraged by the inane criticism that was made of late on my work by the editors of these magazines. As far as I can make out, the literary standards are, alas, much higher in the so-called "Hearst group". ... I shall have to pocket my scruples as so many others have done and offer my work to some of the magazines controlled by Hearst. I shall naturally prefer not to be associated with the particular papers which represent his political views. I remember you have often told me that in the case of the magazines he is the principal owner of many whose literary policy he does not interfere with. If this is the case I shall have to haul down my colours, and join with the great majority of my fellow authors in selling my goods to him. I have so many people dependent on me that I cannot have political scruples to interfere any longer and I gather from the price which Nash's magazine offered me for the English rights of "The Day of the Funeral" that my work is still in demand in that quarter. (24 June 1932, EW Collection)

Wharton drifted somewhat from this pro-Hearst position in the days immediately ahead, but when Jewett "confess[ed] defeat" in placing "Joy in the House" in the United States, she told him while on a trip to England that she would try "here," and sold the story to *Nash's Pall Mall Magazine*, a Hearst publication, for fifty pounds (Jewett to EW, 15 July 1932; EW to Jewett, 20 July 1932, EW Collection). *Nash's* published "Joy in the House" in its December 1932 number.[66] It is the story of a woman who, upon returning to her husband after a six-month affair with an artist, discovers that her lover has committed suicide.

With "The Day of the Funeral," another tale of marital infidelity, Wharton again ran into the editorial reluctance to offend popular sensibilities. The story was turned down by *Pictorial Review* and *Ladies' Home Journal*, the latter's editor writing that "In spite of its power, its artistry, it is a little too strong for a popular magazine audience" (Jewett to EW, 12 September 1931, EW Collection). After these rejections Wharton decided, reluctantly, to accept the suggestion of Gertrude Lane, editor of *Woman's Home Companion*, that she tone down the "immoral relationship between [the married man] Trenham and the girl" (Lane to EW, 11 September, 1931, EW Collection). "If American audiences prefer to be shown the awful consequences of misconduct, without having the dreaded word mentioned," she wrote acidly to Jewett, "it is usually easy for the novelist to comply" (23 September 1931, EW Collection). *Woman's Home Companion* paid 3,000 dollars for "The Day of the Funeral," holding on to it for nearly a year and a half before serializing it in its issues of January and February 1933 (Jewett to EW, 1 October 1931, EW Collection). The segments were illustrated by Roy F. Spreter and bore a title less likely to offend, "In a Day."[67]

Human Nature, the collected version of these stories appeared in March 1933, "Her Son" taking up half the book.[68] The reaction to the volume was positive, sustaining the favourable response that *Certain People* had garnered. Reviewers praised Wharton's clarity and precision of vision, but one senses in at least some of the critiques a certain fatigue with, as Theodore Purdy, Jr. put it in his *Saturday Review of Literature* piece, "this latest in the long canon...short stories of a limited and familiar Whartonian gallery of character studies" (549). In later years Cynthia Griffin Wolff saw in *Human Nature* "an even more remarkable recovery" than *Certain People* had shown: "...certain pieces ... are easily as good as her earlier short stories," she wrote (395).

The World Over

The stage was set for Wharton's last volume of previously uncollected short fiction in October 1934 when she included a list of its proposed contents to John L.B. Williams, who was replacing Jewett as her contact at Appleton. The list comprised six stories: "Pomegranate Seed," "Charm Incorporated," "Roman Fever," "Duration," "Permanent Wave," and an unnamed "long short story," very likely "The Looking Glass," (9 October 1934, EW Collection). When the collection came out in April 1936 it contained these stories and a seventh, "Confession." Six of the stories—"Duration" was the exception—were published in the magazines during the first half of the 1930's, all in the mass-circulation periodicals and three in *Hearst's International-Cosmopolitan*.

Saturday Evening Post carried "Pomegranate Seed" in its issue of April 25, 1931, paying 3,000 dollars for it[69] (Jewett to EW, 18 March 1931, EW Collection). This outstanding ghost story was first sent to *Ladies' Home Journal*, which had not so many years before paid a high price for another Wharton ghost tale "Mr. Jones." Now, however, Loring A. Schuler, the editor, although he called "Pomegranate Seed" "one of the most gorgeous pieces of writing he had ever seen ... a splendid story," feared that "the great mass of *Journal* readers would be lost and indignant because there is no explanation of the situation that has been so interestingly developed." Schuler went on to single out areas in which the incertitudes in the story might be clarified by Wharton in a revised ending (Schuler to Jewett, 16 January 1931, EW Collection). Surprisingly, Wharton revised the story, but evidently not to Schuler's satisfaction. It was also at Schuler's request that Wharton added a short note explaining the story's "classical" title.

With "Charm Incorporated," a "light fingered" (Lewis's term, *EW* 507) satire about marrying into the aristocracy, that circulated under the title "Kouradjine Limited" after its major female character, Wharton again suspended her disinclination to submit her work to the Hearst publications. After the story had been turned down by *American Magazine* and *Saturday Evening Post* (Albert Benjamin to Jewett, 28 September 1933, EW Collection), Wharton had it sent to *Hearst's International-Cosmopolitan*. In a letter to Jewett on October 26, 1933, she explained her position:

> I have just had a letter from Miss Giles who asks to see me on behalf of the new editor of *Cosmopolitan*. As you know I have held out firmly till now against the wiles of Mr. Hearst, but I have been the only one to do so. Many of my friends, for instance Aldous Huxley and Louis Bromfield appear to have succumbed at once, and I think you told me some time ago that in the case of the *Cosmopolitan* Hearst did not intervene personally. I have therefore decided to see Miss Giles and to ask point-blank what the situation is, and if I can reconcile it to my conscience I shall have to give them one of the stories you have in hand. (*LEW* 572)

Four days later Jewett was congratulating Wharton for selling "Kouradjine Limited" to *Cosmopolitan* and for making a Hearst appearance (30 October 1933, EW Collection). *Cosmopolitan* paid "a good figure" for the story (*LEW* 573) and published it in its February 1934 number under the title "Bread Upon the Waters," the new title supplied by Wharton at the editor's request[70] (Jewett to EW, 16 November 1933; EW to Jewett, 30 November 1933, EW Collection).

The publication of "Roman Fever," Wharton's brilliant tale of jealousy and passion in two American matrons, also had its connection to the Hearst affair. Early in 1934 William Lengel, a former Hearst minion and now editor of *Liberty*, a new popular weekly, wrote Wharton that she had promised to send him her stories if he ever worked for a magazine connected with Hearst (17 January 1934, EW Collection). When Lengel received "Roman Fever" the next summer, he wrote Wharton: "I am sure you must know how happy I am to have 'Roman Fever' for *Liberty*. And what a beautiful story it is" (17 August 1934, EW Collection). *Liberty* published the piece in its issue of November 10, 1934, paying 2,500 dollars for it[71] (Appleton-Century to EW, 8 August 1934, EW Collection). Lengel was anxious to have another short story from Wharton "soon" (24 September 1934, EW Collection).

Williams, now working as Wharton's agent at Appleton-Century, soon accepted Lengel's invitation, sending "Permanent Wave" a month later. This time Lengel turned down Wharton's story, however, reporting to Williams that he liked it "but was unable to convince his magazine"(Williams to EW, 26 October 1934, EW Collection). Before being accepted by *Red Book*, "Permanent Wave" was also rejected by *Saturday Evening Post* and *Ladies' Home Journal*. When *Red Book* offered 1,000 dollars for it, Wharton held out for 1,200 and got it (Appleton-Century to EW, 24 November 1934; Williams to EW, 6 December 1934, EW Collection). *Red Book* published this trifling story set in American academe in April 1935, and unknown to Wharton, changed its title to "Poor Old Vincent."[72] Wharton thought the new title gave "an entirely false direction to the story" and, moreover, objected to this unwarranted violation of a writer's rights, demanding an explanation from *Red Book* (EW to Curtis Brown Ltd., 7 August 1935; EW to Williams, 14 August 1935, EW Collection). The explanation, that *Red Book* was permitted by contract to make such changes and that they in fact had requested permission for the change, did not satisfy Wharton (Williams to EW, 29 August 1935, EW Collection).

Wharton's final two short-story magazine appearances were matters of some trepidation for her as well. The ghost tale "The Looking Glass" encountered many difficulties. Williams told Wharton in March 1934 that "One or two editors have said that they find ghost stories difficult in these days but I am certain a place will be found for your excellent story" (15 March 1935, EW Collection). But less than a month later Eric Pinker, Bleeker's permanent replacement as Wharton's agent, reported to Wharton that "Mr. Williams has covered a good deal of ground with no success having offered ["The Looking Glass"] to the Saturday Evening Post, the Ladies' Home Journal, Liberty, Collier's, McCall's, and the American Magazine. Assuming that the fiction editor of Collier's, as is his wont, covered the story for the Woman's Home Companion as well, only the Delineator and Red Book are left of the first class magazines which pay top prices. ... I presume," Pinker added, "you would not want the story offered to Pictorial Review that magazine now being owned by Hearst" (5 April 1935, EW Collection). Thus arose again the tempting prospect of sending the story to *Hearst's International-Cosmopolitan*, whose editor, Burton, was avid to publish more Wharton stories. Wharton's initial response to Pinker's opening was adamant. In an undated memorandum of this period she wrote: "I think it would be better for Mr. Pinker to avoid the Hearst group altogether." There was trouble, she explained, collecting the 5,000 dollars Burton owed her for "Bread upon the Waters" and trouble as well about the novella and novel Burton wanted for his magazine (EW Collection).

By the time Pinker got word of Wharton's renewed reluctance about a Hearst appearance, he had received her story "Confession" and was having trouble placing it. "Cosmopolitan Magazine is about the only one with a policy of publishing stories of this length," he wrote her. Then, after defusing the problem of Burton's reluctance about paying Wharton for "Bread upon the Waters" by telling her that Burton had sent his check to Jewett in good time, he went on: "My intention in all this is to lead up to the suggestion that you might reconsider your ban on the Hearst Magazine because from the commercial point of view the elimination of Cosmopolitan, Good Housekeeping, Pictorial Review and Harper's Bazaar as possible markets leaves the field considerably restricted" (28 May 1935, EW Collection). Wharton sent her go-ahead to "get a good price from Cosmo for "Confession," and the upshot was that Pinker sold "The Looking

Glass" and "Confession" to *Cosmopolitan* for 2,500 and 4,500 dollars respectively (EW to Pinker, 11 June 1935; Pinker to EW, 24 September 1935, EW Collection). "The Looking Glass" appeared in *Cosmopolitan's* issue of December 1935 under the title "The Mirrors," and "Confession," based on the Lizzie Borden case, in the issue of May 1936.[73]

The World Over appeared in April 1936 under the imprint of Appleton-Century (Appleton had merged with the Century organization in March 1933).[74] The collection bore the elegant dedication: "For my dear sister Mary Cadwalader Jones who for so many years has faithfully revised me in proof and indulgently read me in print." Its only new piece was "Duration," a humorous tale of old Boston. This story had been taken by *Woman's Home Companion* for a good price after Wharton had agreed to revise the ending, and then turned it down, causing Wharton no end of frustration. "When I think of my position as a writer, I'm really staggered by the insolence," she wrote to Jewett. "I am afraid that I cannot write down to the present standards of the picture magazines." (*EW* 507). She must have been relieved to see "Duration" and *The World Over* in print, for their final realization had not been easy.

The World Over was rewarded with generally flattering reviews on both sides of the Atlantic, although amidst the approbation one is surprised to find questioning of Wharton's depth. A youthful Graham Greene wrote that "the suave, well-bred tales are technically expert, though in the essential triviality of her anecdotes it's hard to recognize the author of...that superb horror story 'A Bottle of Perrier'" (950). *Saturday Review of Literature* called the contents "not deep...but dramatic...occasionally melodramatic...[and] entertaining" (19). As difficult to understand as such comments are, later ones by Louis Auchincloss about "Roman Fever," that it is "nothing but technique ... where the interest and excitement is concentrated in the last line that gives the whole meaning of what has gone before," are even harder to understand (*EW* 19). Happily better judgement prevailed, and the later commentators on *The World Over*—and on "Roman

Fever"—provide more thoughtful assessments: though they may question the scope of Wharton's vision, they do not challenge her profoundity.

Ghosts

Wharton's ghost stories, at least until the 1930's, when magazine editors hesitated to handle them because of their perception that readers wanted more cheerful material during hard times, had always been popular and in demand. The Wharton correspondence contains many requests from editors for new ghost stories and for permission to reprint published ones. In 1937, when Eric Pinker was having trouble placing Wharton's last ghost story, "All Souls'," and told her so, Wharton replied through her secretary that "all her ghost stories published in American magazines have aroused much more interest and curiosity than any other stories, judging from the number of letters she always received after publishing a tale of this kind" (6 March 1937, EW Collection). The idea for a collection of her ghost stories appears to have been initiated by Wharton herself when she broached the subject to Jewett in 1931. Jewett found the proposition "an excellent one," but thought such a collection might be premature: since some of her ghost stories had just appeared, readers might feel short-changed when faced again with material they had just read (22 May 1931, EW Collection).

The plan began to round into shape the following summer and fall. Wharton submitted a list of nine stories, proposed to write an introduction to the collection, and gave the book the title "*Shadowland*" (EW to Jewett, 5 August 1931; 3 October 1931, EW Collection). Jewett reported to Wharton that *Scribner's* would not stand in the way of such a volume—they held the copyright for five of Wharton's ghost stories that had appeared earlier in their magazine and collections (26 October 1931, EW Collection).

In the meantime, Scribner's was working up a plan of its own: they wanted to produce an omnibus volume of Wharton's short fiction including material that they as well as Appleton had published. Wharton responded to the Scribner's plan on December 16, 1931: "Would it be possible to make a mutual arrangement, whereby Messrs Appleton might include in their volume the ghost stories published under your name, and you might use other stories published under their names" (EW Collection). Subsequent letters of the two publishers expressed a mutual satisfaction with this arrangement (15 January; 28 January 1923, EW Collection), but the early enthusiasm did not translate immediately into the products envisaged, probably because of the same difficulties Wharton had experienced with the publication of her last group of stories in the magazines—a falling off in interest in ghost stories, and in short stories generally. The ghost-story volume appeared only after Wharton's death in 1937; the omnibus collection was never produced as initially conceived, although of course the *Scribner's* publication of the two-volume collection of the complete short story oeuvre in 1968 was effectively the utimate realization of that plan.[73]

Ghosts, the Appleton-Century collection, appeared some three months after Wharton's death, on August 11, 1937, bearing the author's dedication: "I entrust my spectral strap-hangers in gratitude and admiration to Walter de la Mare."[76] It contained the nine stories Wharton had listed in her letter to Jewett on August 5, 1931: "The Lady's Maid's Bell," "The Eyes," "Afterward," "Kerfol," "The Triumph of Night," "Miss Mary Pask," "Bewitched," "Mr. Jones," and "Pomegranate Seed." It also contained the preface she had promised to write and two additional stories: "A Bottle of Perrier," published in 1928, and "All Souls'," not previously published.[77]

The circumstances surrounding the circulation of "All Souls'," called "Week-end" before its publication, give some impression of the frustration that dogged the last days of Wharton the short- story writer. When she sent the tale to Pinker early in 1937, he responded with an already-familiar cautionary note: "While I personally like Week-end very much, I fear that it may be a little difficult to sell to the first-line magazines as there is among them a deep-seated editorial prejudice against anything to do with the supernatural. However, I hope that the merits of the story and the appeal of your name will be sufficient to overcome this prejudice" (26 February 1937, EW Collection). Pinker's hope was not realized, and less than five months later he wrote again, listing the magazines that had rejected "Week-End": *American, Collier's, Hearst's International-Cosmopolitan, Woman's Home Companion, Ladies' Home Journal, Good Housekeeping, This Week, McCall's* (13 July 1937, EW Collection). One refusal bore "the editorial criticism that the reader is left unsatisfied at the end because there is no explanation of the mystery—either natural or supernatural," Pinker later explained to Wharton, asking at the same time if she would "consider adding something to the end of the story ... to satisfy the average magazine reader's desire for something at least approaching a conclusive ending" (11 March 1937, EW Collection). Wharton apparently complied with the request, although her response may supply the key as to why the revised ending was in one way or another unsatisfactory to the editor in question. "I enclose herewith," she told Pinker, "a new ending for "Weak-End" for the use of magazine morons" (23 March 1937, EW Collection)—and we may assume that her misspelling of the title was intentional.

Notes

[3] "Mrs. Manstey's View." *Scribner's* 10 (July 1891): 117-122.

[4] "The Fullness of Life." *Scribner's* 14 (December 1893): 699-704.

[5] "That Good May Come." *Scribner's* 15 (May 1894): 629-642.

[6] "The Lamp of Psyche." *Scribner's* 18 (October 1895): 418-428.

[7] "The Valley of Childish Things, and Other Emblems." *Century* 52 (July 1896): 467-469.

[8] "The Pelican," *Scribner's* 24 (November 1898): 620-629; "The Muse's Tragedy," *Scribner's* 25 (January 1899): 77-84.

[9] *The Greater Inclination.* New York: Scribner's, 1899.

[10] "April Showers." *Youth's Companion* 74 (18 January 1900): 25-28.

[11] "Friends." *Youth's Companion* 74 (23 August 1900): 405-406; 74 (30 August 1900): 417-418.

[12] "The Line of Least Resistance." *Lippincott's* 66 (October 1900): 559-570.

[13] "Copy: A Dialogue." *Scribner's* 27 (June 1900): 657-663.

43

"The Duchess at Prayer." *Scribner's* 28 (August 1900): 153-160.

[15] "The Rembrandt." *Cosmopolitan* 29 (August 1900): 429-437.

[16] "The Angel at the Grave." *Scribner's* 29 (February 1901): 158-166.

[17] "The Recovery." *Harper's* 102 (February 1901): 468-477; "The Moving Finger." *Harper's* 102 (March 1901): 627-632.

[18] *Crucial Instances.* New York: Scribner's, 1901.

[19] "The Quicksand." *Harper's* 105 (June 1902): 13-21; "The Reckoning." *Harper's* 105 (August 1902): 342-355.

[20] "The Lady's Maid's Bell." *Scribner's* 32 (November 1902): 549-560.

[21] "The Mission of Jane." *Harper's* 106 (December 1902): 63-74.

[22] "The Dilettante." *Harper's* 108 (December 1903): 139-143; "A Venetian Night's Entertainment." *Scribner's* 34 (December 1903): 640-651; "Expiation." *Cosmopolitan* 36 (December 1903): 209-222.

[23] "The Other Two." *Collier's* 32 (13 February 1904): 15-17, 20; "The Descent of Man." *Scribner's* 35 (March 1904): 313-322.

[24] *The Descent of Man, and Other Stories.* New York: Scribner's, 1904.

[25] "The Letter." *Harper's* 108 (April 1904): 781-789.

[26] "The House of the Dead Hand." *Atlantic Monthly* 94 (August 1904): 145-160; "The Introducers." *Ainslee's* 16 (December 1905): 139-148; 16 (January 1906): 61-67.

[27] "Les Metteurs en Scène." *Revue des Deux Mondes* 67 (October 1908): 692-708.

[28] "The Last Asset." *Scribner's* 36 (August 1904): 150-168; "The Potboiler." *Scribner's* 36 (December 1904): 696-712.

[29] "The Best Man." *Collier's* 35 (2 September 1905): 14-17, 21-22.

[30] "The Hermit and the Wild Woman." *Scribner's* 39 (February 1906): 145-156.

[31] "In Trust." *Appleton's Booklover's* 7 (April 1906): 432-440.

[32] "The Verdict." *Scribner's* 43 (June 1908): 689-693; "The Pretext." *Scribner's* 44 (August 1908): 173-187.

[33] *The Hermit and the Wild Woman and Other Stories.* New York: Scribner's, 1908.

[34] "The Bolted Door." *Scribner's* 45 (March 1909): 288-308.

[35] "His Father's Son." *Scribner's* 45 (June 1909): 657-665.

[36] "The Daunt Diana." *Scribner's* 46 (July 1909): 35-41.

[37] "The Debt." *Scribner's* 46 (August 1909): 165-172.

[38] "Full Circle." *Scribner's* 46 (October 1909): 408-419.

[39] "Afterward." *Century* 79 (January 1910): 321-339.

[40] "The Legend." *Scribner's* 47 (March 1910): 278-291; "The Eyes." *Scribner's* 47 (June 1910): 671-680.

[41] "The Letters." *Century* 80 (August 1910): 485-492; 80 (September 1910): 641-650; 80 (October 1910): 812-819.

[42] "The Blond Beast." *Scribner's* 48 (September 1910): 291-304.

[43] *Tales of Men and Ghosts*. New York: Scribner's, 1910.

[44] "The Choice." *Century* 77 (November 1908): 32-40.

[45] "Other Times, Other Manners." *Century* 82 (July 1911): 344-352; 82 (August 1911): 587-594.

[46] "Xingu." *Scribner's* 50 (December 1911): 684-696.

[47] "The Long Run." *Atlantic Monthly* 109 (February 1912): 145-163.

[48] "The Triumph of Night." *Scribner's* 56 (August 1914): 149-162; "Coming Home." *Scribner's* 58 (December 1915): 702-718; "Kerfol." *Scribner's* 59 (March 1916): 329-341.

[49] *Xingu and Other Stories*. New York: Scribner's, 1916.

[50] "Writing a War Story." *Woman's Home Companion* 46 (September 1919): 17-19.

[51] "The Seed of the Faith." *Scribner's* 65 (January 1919): 17-33.

[52] "Temperate Zone." *Pictorial Review* 25 (February 1924): 5-7, 61-62, 64, 66. The title was changed to "The Temperate Zone" in *Here and Beyond*.

[53] "Bewitched." *Pictorial Review* 26 (March 1925): 14-16, 60-64, 69; "Miss Mary Pask." *Pictorial Review* 26 (April 1925): 8-9, 75-76.

[54] "Velvet Ear-Muffs." *Red Book* 45 (August 1925): 39-45, 140-148.

[55] "The Young Gentlemen." *Pictorial Review* 27 (February 1926): 29-30, 84-91.

[56] *Here and Beyond*. New York: Appleton and Company, 1926.

[57] "The Refugees." *Saturday Evening Post* 191 (18 January 1919): 3-5, 53, 57, 61.

[58] "A Bottle of Evian." *Saturday Evening Post* 198 (27 March 1926): 8-10, 116, 121-122.

[59] "Atrophy." *Ladies' Home Journal* 44 (November 1927): 8-9, 220-222; "Mr. Jones." *Ladies' Home Journal* 45 (April 1928): 3-5, 108, 111-112, 114, 116.

[60] "After Holbein." *Saturday Evening Post* 200 (5 May 1928): 6-7, 179, 181-182, 185-186, 189.

[61] "Dieu d'Amour." *Ladies' Home Journal* 45 (October 1928): 6-7, 216, 219-220, 223-224.

[62] *Certain People.* New York: Appleton and Company, 1930.

[63] "Diagnosis." *Ladies' Home Journal* 47 (November 1930): 8-9, 156, 159-160, 162.

[64] "Her Son." *Scribner's* 91 (February 1932): 65-72, 113-128.

[65] "A Glimpse." *Saturday Evening Post* 205 (12 November 1932): 16-17, 64-65, 67, 70, 72.

[66] "Joy in the House." *Nash's Pall Mall Magazine* 90 (December 1932): 6-9, 72-75.

[67] "In a Day." *Woman's Home Companion* 60 (January 1933): 7-8, 46; 60 (February 1933): 15-16, 104, 106, 118.

[68] *Human Nature.* New York: Appleton and Company, 1933.

[69] "Pomegranate Seed." *Saturday Evening Post* 203 (25 April 1931): 6-7, 109, 112, 116, 119, 121, 123.

[70] "Bread upon the Waters." *Hearst's International-Cosmopolitan* 96 (February 1934): 28-31, 90, 92, 94, 96, 98.

[71] "Roman Fever." *Liberty* 11 (10 November 1934): 10-14.

[72] "Poor Old Vincent." *Red Book* 64 (April 1935): 20-23, 116-119.

[73] "The Mirrors." *Hearst's International-Cosmopolitan* 99 (December 1935): 32-35, 157-159; "Confession." *Hearst's International-Cosmopolitan* 100 (May 1936): 34-37, 84, 86, 88, 90, 92, 94. "Confession" had already appeared in the British periodical *Story-Teller*, 58 (March 1936): 64-85, under the title "Unconfessed Crime." It was Wharton's habit at this period in her career to publish her short stories in English magazines after they were published in the United States. The usual order of publication was reversed in the case of "Confession."

[74] *The World Over.* New York: Appleton-Century, 1936.

46

[75] *The Collected Short Stories of Edith Wharton.* Ed. by R.W.B. Lewis, 2 vols. New York: Scribner's, 1968.

[76] *Ghosts.* New York: Appleton-Century, 1937.

[77] When Scribner's published *The Ghost Stories of Edith Wharton,* its version of *Ghosts,* in 1971, they included ten of the eleven stories from the Appleton-Century volume, replacing "A Bottle of Perrier," with "The Looking Glass," no doubt deeming the latter more of a ghost tale than the former. The Scribner's collection also included Wharton's Preface from *Ghosts,* and a segment entitled "An Autobiographical Postscript," a previously unpublished portion of Wharton's memoir, *A Backward Glance.*

Chapter Two

Ghosts

That Edith Wharton had a particular liking for ghost stories is evident: in the chapter "Telling a Short Story" in her 1925 book *The Writing of Fiction* the commentary on ghost stories heads up her entire discussion; she also drew special attention to the genre in the preface to her posthumous collection of stories, *Ghosts*. That they were a significant means of expression for her is equally evident, for they were literally the work of a lifetime of writing, the first, "The Lady's Maid's Bell," appearing in *Scribner's* in 1902 early in her career, the last, "All Souls'," her final completed work of fiction, sent to her agent in February 1937 not long before her death. During the first four decades of the century nine other Wharton ghost stories came out in the magazines and reappeared in her frequent short-story collections. There were only two collections of Wharton stories published after 1899 that did not contain at least one or two ghost stories. While they were never a main concern, never came near to displacing those realistic stories of upper-class life that were her stock in trade, they nevertheless satisfied some continuing urge in her to engage the supernatural sphere, in which it was possible to address significant aspects of the human condition that more familiar contexts seemed to have less capacity to do.

The exploration of human life generally became the *raison d'être* of the ghost stories, although in her theoretical remarks about the genre Wharton was wont to deemphasize the "moral" issue in favour of what she called the "thermometrical quality," "the cold shiver down one's spine" (Preface to *Ghosts* 878). But of course in seeming to diminish the "moral issue" she was merely bowing to the demands of the genre as genre: what makes a ghost story effective as a ghost story is the "cold shiver." But Wharton's practice gainsays any possibility that she meant her readers to be merely entertained by her stories of the supernatural, or that she wished to give the impression that these tales were to be taken more lightly than her realistic stories. Indeed the critical commentary on Wharton's ghost stories—and these stories are to date the most frequently discussed of all her short fiction—pays little attention to their "thermometrical quality." Critics such as R.W.B Lewis, Margaret B. McDowell, Allan Gardner Smith, Annette Zilversmit, Barbara A. White, Carol Singley, and Richard A. Kaye emphasize the manner in which Wharton exploited the ghost story genre by making it a forum for the dramatization of universally relevant psychological and moral questions. Kaye writes, for example, "It was through the ghost tales ... that [Wharton] most thoroughly dealt with the subject of homoerotic carnality" (11), and Singley points out that "The Eyes" and "The Triumph of Night" equate homosexuality with "selfishness, with decadence, and with a vampirish tendency in the older men to prey on the younger" (278) in their exploitation of those stories' homoerotic subtextual meaning.

"The Lady's Maid's Bell"

E.K. Brown has called "The Lady's Maid's Bell" one of Wharton's best ghost stories (14), other critics have given it some cursory attention, and recently Ellen Powers Stengel has placed it under the Freudian/Lacanian microscope. Stengel's analysis, as useful as it is, ignores major elements of the story and carps on its supposed faults ("Its title *riddled* with apostrophes, its discourse *hampered* by Wharton's *awkward* attempt to reproduce the rhetoric of the servant class") (3; italics mine). One senses that "The Lady's Maid's Bell" has not been given its due.

"With the ghostly tales of Wharton," writes R.W.B. Lewis, "one is inevitably interested not only in what happens in the plot, but in what happens in the telling of it" (*ICSS* XVI). This attention to narrative voice, to the ghost story as an exercise in telling rather than as a series of events described for a readership, characterizes "The Lady's Maid's Bell," Wharton's first attempt at the genre, published in November 1902 in *Scribner's*. In this, of course, Wharton reflects

Henry James, whose *The Turn of the Screw* she much admired, and as we hear Alice Hartley spinning out her yarn to an attentive listener or listeners (there is a sense that she is telling her tale to an addressee or addressees other than the reader) we are reminded of the group gathered around the Christmas fire, "sufficiently breathless," the enchanted listeners to the tale that is *The Turn of the Screw*.[78]

Readers have no way of knowing if Hartley's immediate audience is "sufficiently breathless," but she herself is assuredly not. It is a particular quality of "The Lady's Maid's Bell" that its teller is no longer terrified by the events she recounts, that she has had time, if not to assimilate them, at least to be resigned to the state of suspension in which they have left her. This ability to come to terms with the series of experiences she describes is perfectly in keeping with her personality as it emerges in both the facts given in her tale and in her manner of telling it. Mrs Railton, the woman who recommends her hiring as Mrs Brympton's lady's maid offers her this flattering assessment: "[Y]ou're the very woman I want for my niece: quiet, well-mannered, and educated above your station" (I, 458), and Hartley's conduct during the ordeal at Brympton and her verbal recapitulation of it bears out the validity of her patron's evaluation.

Mrs Railton's evaluation suggests the insightful, good-humoured, level-headed person Hartley proves to be. The reference to her being educated "above [her] station" has a particular appropriateness, for she demonstrates not only an intelligence superior to that of the other servants but also considerable perception about the lives of her employers and social superiors. She declines to question the groom who drives her to her new workplace, "for I was never one to get my notion of my new masters from their other servants" (I, 458). She remarks about Ranford that "The servants all liked him, and perhaps that's more of a compliment than the masters suspect." Having observed the apparent good relations between Brympton and Ranford, she says, "But then I knew how the real quality can keep their feelings to themselves" (I, 462).

As well, Hartley expresses herself with considerable wit. This is true particularly of her comments about Wace, the butler, "a serious slow-spoken man [who] went about his duties as if he'd been getting ready for a funeral.... He was a great Bible reader...and had a beautiful assortment of texts at his command." But on the day of Brympton's return to the house "[Wace] used such dreadful language, that I was about to leave the table, when he assured me it was all out of Isaiah; and I noticed that whenever the master came Mr. Wace took to the prophets" (I, 461). Here, Hartley's statement evolves into a consciously sardonic one. Her initial assessment of Brympton has the same tone: "He swung about when I came in, and looked me over in a trice. I knew what the look meant, from having experienced it once or twice in my former places. Then he turned his back to me, and went on talking to his wife; and I knew what *that* meant too (Wharton's italics). I was not the kind of morsel he was after. The typhoid had served me well enough in one way; it kept that kind of gentleman at arm's length" (I, 461). For the most part Hartley's wry commentary is restricted to the early parts of the story; as she recalls her ghostly companion across the hall she is less wont to indulge in light remarks, although even her account of the latter part of her stay at Brympton is occasionally leavened with references to Wace's Bible-quoting habit.

Hartley's wryness and good humor removes some of the edge from the frightening tale she is telling, of course. It also serves another important purpose: Hartley's listeners are being reminded that she is a person with her wits about her, a person not susceptible to delusion even though she has been forewarned about the gloominess of her new workplace and acknowledges its oppressive impact on her. At times when it appears she might be succumbing to the gloom, the rainy winter, her anxiety about the locked room, she maintains control: "Once or twice, in the long rainy nights," she recalls, "I fancied I heard noises there; but that was nonsense, of course, and the daylight drove such notions out of my head" (I, 463). And terrified as she is when summoned by the bell the night of Mrs Brympton's death, she has the presence of mind to interfere with Mr Brympton's attempt to accost his rival. The ghost Hartley sees and hears during her stay at Brympton is not the product of a lively and easily provoked imagination. It is a real presence, so real that initially she does not even question its ghostliness, so ghostly that when it walks in the snow it leaves no footprints.

It is more difficult to comment on the nature of the awareness of the other inhabitants of Brympton vis-à-vis the ghost. Among the servants an aura of mystery and fear surrounds the room which Emma Saxon, the former lady's maid of long standing, has occupied during her twenty-year tenure, but whether or not they see the ghost is not much of an issue. As for the four lady's maids who have occupied the post between Emma's death and Hartley's arrival, the suggestion is that the brevity of their stays has been a result of the kind of appearances Hartley has experienced, for the latter is intrigued by the fact that it is only lady's maids who quit Brympton. Mrs Brympton is certainly aware of the presence of the ghost, although not apparently in the substantial form in which Hartley sees her. Mr Brympton is the only other person described as seeing the ghost, and this occurs on the two occasions when both Hartley and the ghost are summoned by the bell, both occasions when Brympton is a threat to his wife's safety. The ghost may be seen as reminding Brympton of his own sexual voraciousness, especially as it is directed towards his wife. Hartwell's perception that the master sees the ghost in the same sense that she does, however, cannot be taken as absolutely valid, for she has no way of measuring the nature of his vision. For Brympton the ghost may very well be the product of a vivid imagination, summoned up by guilt and fear.

A good deal of the commentary "The Lady's Maid's Bell" has elicited emphasizes precisely this role of the ghost: its implication in the Brymptons' unhappy marriage. For Margaret McDowell, "the situation developed" is "that of a sickly sensitive wife persecuted by her husband and protected by the ghost of her former maid." ("Edith Wharton's Ghost Stories" 144). For R.W.B. Lewis, "the action turns on the brutish physical demands made by one Brympton upon his fastidious wife" (*ICSS* XVII). Annette Zilversmit writes of the ghost emerging to avenge a "sexually demanding husband" ("Edith Wharton's Last Ghosts" 297). Of course, these comments are on the mark, but none of them addresses Hartley's function within the drama played out among the Brymptons, their friend Ranford, and the ghost of the former lady's maid.

The key to Hartley's role in "The Lady's Maid's Bell" is the fact that her sympathy for and commitment to her new mistress establish her as the first worthy successor of Emma Saxon. Her first contact with Mrs Brympton sets up a strong bond between mistress and servant: "[W]hen she smiled [at me]," Hartley recalls, "I felt there was nothing I wouldn't do for her" (I, 459). Hartley's suitability to the job and her usefulness to Mrs Brympton are generally acknowledged in the house. After her return from some shopping on a particularly difficult day at Brympton, Mrs Blinder greets her by taking her hand and saying, "Oh, my dear. I'm so glad and thankful you've come back to us!" (I, 464). More and more frightened by the atmosphere of the house, Hartley fights off the temptation to leave: "Whether it was compassion for my mistress, who had grown more and more dependent on me, or willingness to try a new place, or some other feeling that I couldn't put a name on, I lingered on as if spellbound, though every night was dreadful to me, and the days but little better" (I, 469). In her commitment and perseverance, Hartley is the reflection of Emma Saxon, of whom Mrs Blinder has said, "No better walked the earth. My mistress loved her like a sister" (I, 461).

If there is a marked character likeness between Hartley and Emma, there is considerable physical resemblance between Hartley and Emma's ghost as well. As lady's maids both wear the same uniform, a dark gown and apron. To match the paleness and thinness of the ghost, Hartley has taken the job not long after suffering a serious bout with typhoid fever and often makes allusion to her paleness. (There is also in this regard, the fact that Hartley's arrival at Brympton after being "close to the grave" resembles Emma's own ghostly return.) Here again, the resemblance between the two is noted by other Brympton dwellers. Early during her stay, Mrs Blinder responds to Hartley's question "[W]hat did

[Emma] look like?" with "a kind of angry stare." Unable to deal with the significance of their physical resemblance, Mrs Blinder replies, "I'm no great hand at describing, and I believe my pastry's rising" (I, 461). When Mr Brympton confronts Hartley on the night of her first response to the lady's maid's bell, he exclaims "in a queer voice, '*You? How many of you are there in God's name?*'" (Wharton's italics). He has no doubt he has just been visited by the ghost, which Hartley had heard preceding her down the hallway. And a few minutes later as Hartley is ministering to Mrs Brympton, the latter "groped out with her hand" and spoke softly "*Emma*" (I, 466; Wharton's italics).

In one way or another it becomes clear at Brympton that Hartley is the double of Emma Saxon. What purpose does this serve? Effectively Hartley assumes the role Emma cannot entirely fill because of her ghostliness. Hartley becomes the speaking voice of her who can be seen but cannot talk, the hand of her who moves but cannot touch. This is true in her general care of Mrs Brympton. Most particularly it is actualized in the final moments of the mistress's life when both Hartley's words, "Sir, sir, for pity's sake look to your wife!" and her physical action of catching Brympton "by the sleeve" (I, 473) ensure the escape of Ranford. As Brympton tears open the door he is faced not with the presence of his rival, who has had time to get away, but with the vision of Emma. If Hartley and Emma cannot save their mistress, as they have on an earlier night, they succeed in saving her cherished friend. Hartley is the other self, the self who compensates for what Emma cannot do as a ghost, who becomes her active living self.

In acting out her part as the living presence of Emma Saxon, Hartley senses that she is being moved by a force beyond herself. Hartley recalls that upon her arrival at Brympton, Emma "gave me a look" (I, 459)—as if you were being sized up, the reader is tempted to add. Having passed this initial scrutiny Hartley subsequently has a sense of being led, and compelled to action. This is most explicitly so the day Emma leads her to Ranford's house in the village. As lady's maid and ghost set out together, Hartley tells how "She looked at me long and hard, and her face was just one dumb prayer to me" (I, 470). When Hartley tries to go back, "she turned and looked at me, and it was as if she had dragged me with ropes. After that I followed her like a dog." When they reach Ranford's, Hartley sees that "it was my turn to act.... I knew well enough that she hadn't led me there for nothing" (I, 471).

It is not only in the presence of Emma that Hartley feels the pressure of the ghost's will. Once "chosen" she notices an element of control being exerted. Her first words to her mistress, a spontaneous exclamation to the effect that she knows she will not feel lonely with her, "surprised me when I'd spoken them, for I'm not an impulsive person" (I, 459). As she becomes more terrified in later months and is tempted to leave, she has the sense of "something [holding] me back.... I lingered as if spellbound, though every night was dreadful to me and the days but little better" (I, 469). The figure across the hall is frightening and mysterious not only because of her ghostliness as such, but also because she makes demands from which Hartley cannot easily extricate herself but of whose nature she cannot be certain.

The mystery that remains veiled at the story's end for Hartley and her audience alike is the nature of the relationship between Mrs Brympton and Ranford; the question that she is perhaps unwilling to face is: what kind of liaison existed between the wronged wife and her sensitive friend. Impelled to take the side of her mistress caught in a marriage with a boorish and demanding husband, is she not giving sanction to an illicit relationship? Thus, the moral dilemma, in which Wharton characters frequently find themselves, wherein the more desirable of two or more solutions is less than an ideal one, haunts Hartley, though she seems unwilling or unable to admit it openly. At the time she is led to Ranford's house by Saxon, the relationship she has always assumed to be an innocent one, takes on the possibility of being something else. "I had never thought harm of my mistress and Mr. Ranford," she recalls, "but I was sure now that, from one cause or another, some dreadful thing hung over them" (I, 471). Indeed, Hartley's recounting of the story's love triangle suggests that she is more concerned with moral considerations than with the interplay of human character. What she observes about the defensiveness of Mrs Brympton's behaviour and about circumstances on the night of her death does nothing to resolve her dilemma, and in the final portion of her account concerning the funeral of her mistress her memory centers less on the rite itself than on the conduct of Brympton and Ranford.

Seen retrospectively by Hartley, the triangular relationship among the Brymptons and Ranford takes on something of the quality of a morality play with the principals portrayed as stereotypes. The innocent wife, victim of an insensitive husband, finds solace in the company of a warmer man with tastes akin to her own. Little is said of the motivation and background of Mrs Brympton and Ranford: they are both genteel souls fond of reading and walking and considerate of the servants. The former has struck Hartley as "perhaps a trifle cold" (I, 463), but she sees this more as a response to her husband than to other factors. Brympton is something of an ogre: "a big, fair, bull-necked man, with a red face and little bad-tempered blue eyes: the kind of man a young simpleton might have thought handsome, and would have been like to pay dear for thinking it" (I, 461), and "coarse, loud and pleasure-loving" (I, 462). Subsequent descriptions hint of a demonic Brympton. Hartley declares that "in the light of my candle, his face looked red and savage" (I, 466), and she twice makes allusion to "a red spot [coming] out on his forehead" (I, 467, 473) when he is under tension. Brympton is drawn with much stronger (and harsher) strokes than the other two, for whom Hartley feels considerable sympathy. Considering the moral problem the Ranford-Mrs Brympton relationship raises for her, it seems entirely possible to read Hartley's demonic portrayal of Brympton as a way of rationalizing her implicit acceptance of an unacceptable extra-marital affair.

It is not altogether surprising that the triangular relationship Hartley describes should have resolved itself into a stereotypical situation, for the salient elements of her experience at Brympton are the ghost of Emma Saxon and her own response to it. "The Lady's Maid's Bell" is primarily a ghost story, and

Wharton has laden it with the conventional apparatus of the genre. Events take place in the fall and winter, often as the rain threatens and the snow falls. The house is "big and gloomy...a vault" (I, 457), according to Mrs Railton. Hartley, coming upon the house after a period of absence, feels her "heart [dropping] down like a stone in a well" (I, 463). Most of all, Hartley describes her terror vividly and at length as she becomes more and more enmeshed with Emma Saxon. But for all of that, the thermometric reading of the reader is not likely to be very low. Assuredly Hartley was deeply frightened as she lived through the events she recounts, but her recapitulation of them has the effect of diminishing the terror for herself and her audience. Her tale is sprinkled with humor and wryness; as well, it is told in a colloquial voice and a low key, and is devoid of histrionics. The "zero at the bone" to borrow a Dickinsonian term, is largely absent here, and certainly by design.

It might be said that in this, the first of her ghost stories, Wharton was easing her way into the genre. Later forays into the supernatural world would reveal a truer "thermometric quality." "The Lady's Maid's Bell" is, nevertheless, a remarkable short story in a number of ways: in its use of the ghost and double figures in a significant manner; in its rendering of a credible character and voice for the recounting of the tale (it is worth noting that this is one of Wharton's very few entries into the world of servants on their own ground); in its method of articulating Hartley's guilt about sanctioning a possibly illicit liaison. Happily, the recent upsurge of interest in Wharton's ghost stories has helped to restore it to a deservedly prominent position in the author's short-story oeuvre.

"Afterward"

Wharton's next ghost story, "Afterward," published in *Century's* January 1910 number, has attracted little critical attention, and much of that unflattering. E.K. Brown calls it "assez banale" (22); for R.W.B. Lewis "it begins promisingly but wilts into melodrama" (*EW* 296). Allan Gardner Smith expresses a more positive attitude to the story, however, demonstrating that its deployment of metaphor and symbol in melding supernatural and psychological/moral elements deserves to be looked at closely (154-157). Published some eight years after "The Lady's Maid's Bell," "Afterward," in its use of a "real" ghost rather than one born of a character's imagination and in its choice of a female character as its center of consciousness, imitates its predecessor. But though the earlier story may have given Wharton a model to work from, "Afterward" makes its own particular use of its ghost and of its female consciousness and is finally characterized more by its uniqueness than its indebtedness.

"Afterward's" point-of-view character is Mary Boyne, a New Yorker, who with her wealthy husband, Ned, has taken up residence at Lyng, an ancient country house in Dorsetshire, the purchase of which has been made possible by Boyne's recent success in a mining coup in the American midwest. The fact that "the prodigious windfall of the Blue Star Mine" (II, 154) has come Boyne's way as a result of his unconscionable business practices unleashes the story's ghost. Yet "Afterward" is only in a secondary way concerned with Boyne's guilt and its ghostly manifestation; its major focus is the impact on Mary of the events generated by her husband's misdeeds.

The Boynes' choice of an English home has been dictated by their desire for a new life; "they could not get far enough from the world, or plunge deep enough into the past" (II, 154). If Boyne is motivated in his move to England by the need to escape the immediate and potential effects of misdemeanours, Mary, who at the time of their emigration is unaware of her husband's misdeeds, is merely gratifying her romantic bent. For her the house has "almost all the finer marks of commerce with a protracted past...the charm of having been for centuries a deep dim reservoir of life" (II, 154). Part of Lyng's charm is its reputation for harboring a ghost, one that in Mary's perception is merely an appendage to the house, that might be conjured up "if one could only get into close enough communion with the house," that might produce "the fun of the shudder" (II, 156). It is Mary's romantic preoccupation with ghosts as appendages to the past and specifically to her ancient home (her yearning for "the fun of the shudder") that blinds her to the significance of the present ghost, which

58

she sees but whose reality and meaning she immediately and for some time fails to recognize.

Mary's blindness to the ghost and its significance is a factor also of another romantic predisposition: her utter attachment to and confidence in her husband.[79] As she sits next to Boyne with the letter that tells her of Elwell's bringing suit against her husband, she breaks "the seal with the languid gesture of the reader whose interests are all enclosed in the circle of one cherished presence" (II, 160). She thinks in terms of "this new life" at Lyng having drawn "its magic circle about them" (II, 161). Even as she questions Boyne about the implications of the letter, her fears are quelled in his encircling arms:

> "It's all right—it's all right?" she questioned through the flood of her dissolving doubts; and "I give you my word it was never righter!" he laughed back at her, holding her close. (II, 162)

At no time does Mary's romantic inclination stand more squarely in the way of her recognition of the revenant Robert Elwell than on the morning of the latter's second and final visit to Lyng, the day after her fearful questioning of Boyne. She is suffused with the aura of antiquity and beauty that Lyng projects: "the spiced scents and waxy pinks and reds of old-fashioned exotics...[the] grass terrace, looking across the fish pond and yew hedges to the long house front with its twisted chimney stacks and blue roof angles, all drenched in the pale gold moisture of the air." The house itself "sent her, from open windows and hospitably smoking chimneys, the look of some warm human presence, of a mind slowly ripened on a sunny wall of experience. She had never before had such a sense of her intimacy with it, such a conviction that its secrets were all beneficent, kept, as they said to children, 'for one's good,' such a trust in its power to gather up her life and Ned's into the harmonious pattern of the long long story it sat there weaving in the sun" (II, 163).

Is it any wonder that this second visit of the same mysterious figure to Lyng in a matter of months does not alert Mary—even in the face of the fact that on its first visit it had vanished suddenly and even though Mary's own description of the figure's physical appearance equates to that of the first unexpected visitor? On both of the occasions of Elwell's visits (as well as elsewhere in the story) narratorial references are made to Mary's short-sightedness. These refer literally to her weak eyesight, of course, but one cannot ignore their broader significance in relation to Mary's lack of observation and perception. Mary cannot see the present ghost for the old ghost that lurks romantically in the shadows of Lyng, the ghost that would evoke nothing more than "the fun of the shudder" if it ever did appear.

The drastic consequence of the ghost's second visit—the permanent disappearance of Boyne—forces the truth on Mary and deromanticizes her life radically: Lyng, devoid of the material Boyne—who in any case has lost his original aura—is no Lyng at all. The enchanted circle has been broken beyond repair. It is important to note, however, that Mary's coming to awareness has not been entirely abrupt. In the letter-opening scene cited above, she has begun to realize her absolute ignorance of and complete removal from Boyne's business dealings. She had not recognized Elwell's name, although her husband claimed he had told her "all about him at the time." "I must have forgotten," she replies, as "vainly, she strained back among her memories." But now "for the first time, it startled her a little to find how little she knew of the material foundation on which her happiness was built" (II, 161). Such an insight is the beginning of knowledge, but in Mary's case the completion of her awareness is a long time coming. Allan Gardner Smith has commented astutely: "The ghost itself dramatizes, in its indeterminateness, the difficulty [Mary] experiences in bringing this material to a consciousness and recognition or becoming aware of the foundations of her domestic milieu" (154-155). The corollary to Smith's comment, of course, is that the disappearance of Mary's husband with the ghost coincides with her discovery of the foundations of her former happiness.

The complete knowledge of past events and of their significance does not come to Mary until very late in the story. It is Parvis, the Waukesha lawyer who visits Mary with an appeal that she assist Elwell's financially distressed widow, who serves as the proximate cause of Mary's enlightenment. Seemingly "surprised at her continued ignorance of the subject," he tells the whole story of Boyne's unethical practices, which "threw, even to her confused perceptions, and imperfectly initiated vision, a lurid glare on the whole hazy episode of the Blue Star Mine" (II, 172). When Parvis subsequently shows Mary a copy of the *Waukesha Sentinel* with the "glaring headlines, 'Widow of Boyne's Victim Forced to Appeal for Aid'" and containing side-by-side photos of Boyne and Elwell, she "[closes] her lids with the sharpness of the pain" of recognition of her favourite shot of her husband, then "[opens] her eyes with an effort" (II, 174) to the recognition of the identity of the ghost. The juxtaposed photos represent the major realities of Mary's life: Boyne, the center of her enchanted circle; Elwell, at once victim of her husband and author of his demise and of her own disenchantment.

If some aspects of the closing portions of the story tend to justify R.W.B. Lewis's comment that "it wilts into melodrama," there are a number of compensating elements about "Afterward's" concluding segments as well. The closing line alerts the reader to the implications of the title. As Mary lies virtually unconscious, she hears "Through the tumult...but one clear note," the voice of her friend Alida Stair responding to her early questions about how Lyng's ghost will be recognized: "You won't know till afterward. You won't know till long, long afterward" (II, 176). Variations on this statement are spoken in jest during Mary's first references to Lyng, but of course they always make allusion to the "romantic" ghost associated with the house. The final use of the statement echoes Mary's awareness that her real ghost has produced not "the fun of the shudder" but the pain of loss, solitude and disenchantment. The story's final word emphasizes Mary's new life. Just as the phrase in question has shifted in significance by the end of the story, so Mary is left bereft of her magic circle and prey to the outside world she has sought to escape by going to Lyng.[80]

It is interesting that the ghost in "Afterward," like its counterpart in "The Lady's Maid's Bell," is seen less in the light of the impact it has on the person whose conduct evoked it than of its influence on other characters. Assuredly, in both stories some attention is paid to the guilt that both Boyne and Brympton suffer as a result of their misbehaviour. But evidently Wharton found much more compelling the investigation of the reflected impact of the ghosts on innocent people caught in entanglements of which they are not the cause.

"The Eyes"

Wharton's next ghost story, "The Eyes," published only six months later in *Scribner's* in June 1910, enjoys a high place in its author's oeuvre. It is universally praised as a superior story and ghost story both, and it is probably the Wharton ghost story most amply commented upon in print. For R.W.B. Lewis, it is a "small masterpiece" (*EW* 296), for Blake Nevius, "one of the most remarkable" of her ghost stories (94). And Allan Gardner Smith (157), Cynthia Griffin Wolff (156), E.K. Brown (22), and Margaret B. McDowell ("Edith Wharton's Ghost Stories" 136) all echo these plaudits.

"The Eyes" breaks the pattern Wharton established in her first two ghost stories: here, the ghost is not a revenant, not a real presence visible and apparently human to persons among whom it moves, but a being seen only by the story's central character, Andrew Culwin, manifesting itself as a pair of disembodied eyes. Most of the critics mentioned above have commented on the success of the story in terms of the effectual employment of the ghostly eyes as a sign of Culwin's essentially corrupt nature, a condition rendered more horrendous by the fact of his own blindness to it, and it seems pointless to repeat here what so many commentators have already said on this point.

Commentary on the effect of Culwin's tale on his audience of two is less ample, and an investigation of this aspect of "The Eyes" suggests something of the subtlety and complexity of Wharton's story. Culwin's young protegée Phil Frenham and the unnamed narrator have totally different responses to their patron's story: the former's intelligent reaction to it and the latter's lack of insight draw our attention away from Culwin's ghost story as such, whose impact, in any case, has been diluted by its retrospective narration, and towards the horror of the present reality.

For Frenham the unfolding of Culwin's tale results in the realization that he is in the process of being manipulated in the ways both of Culwin's former victims have been. By the end of Culwin's account he has recognized the identification between his friend's eyes and the ghostly eyes of Culwin's past. His silence, and unresponsiveness to Culwin's attention are evidence to that. It is Culwin himself who has drawn the parallel between his second victim, Gilbert Noyes, and Frenham by his passing allusion to Gilbert's "head thrown back in the lamplight, just as Phil's is now" (II, 125). In the light of the endless patronization of Noyes and Alice Nowell cluttering Culwin's tale and particularly of the images and metaphors betraying his attitudes of superiority to and depersonalization of others, Frenham becomes sensitive to the fact of his own objectification at the hands of his patron. If Culwin has had Noyes "under the microscope," so had he had Frenham; if Culwin could say of Noyes that "telling him the truth would have been about as pleasant as slitting the throat of some gentle animal" (II, 124), he could say it of him.

Ellen Kimbel has commented on the dramatic function of the primary narrator of "The Eyes," writing: "While Culwin unknowingly reveals the hideousness of his nature, recognizing only at the end that the grotesque eyes are, in fact, his own, the narrator just as disingenuously reveals his own terrible obtuseness" (44). From beginning to end the narrator's recapitulation evidences this obtuseness. When introducing Culwin to the reader, he says: "He had always been possessed of a leisure which he had nursed and protected, instead of squandering it in vain activities" and "none of the disturbances common to human experience seemed to have crossed his sky." He fails to grasp the validity of Murchand's "ogreish metaphor" to the effect that Culwin "liked 'em juicy" (II, 116) even as he sees and responds to Frenham's reaction to the tale. Nor does he seem to realize the implications of Culwin's final self-recognition, rendering it as he does without interpretation or feeling.

If "The Eyes" can be read as a story of the double—in important ways it is reminiscent of Poe's "William Wilson"—with the ghostly eyes of Culwin's haunted nights representing the side of his personality that he will not acknowledge, certain interesting conclusions follow an examination of the radically different responses of Culwin's two listeners. If Culwin, in recognizing finally his other self, may be seen to have rid himself of his double, his former split self is maintained in the dual personages of Frenham and the narrator, the former embodying the side of Culwin that sees, the latter the side that does not. Allan Gardner Smith has written, "in [Wharton's] ghost stories, the horror of what is, of the suppressed 'natural', is greater than the horror of what is not, of the conventionally 'supernatural'" (158). What Frenham and Culwin finally see and what the narrator does not see (along with the *fact* that he does not see) horrify more than the haunting eyes of Culwin's past. Once again the word of Wharton's title has applications far beyond its most obvious referent.

"The Triumph of Night"

"The Triumph of Night" appeared in *Scribner's* in August 1914, four years after "The Eyes," but although it imitates its predecessor's use of the ghostly double, its manipulation of that phenomenon is decidedly different. Here the double is not a subjective projection of a persona by the persona in question: whereas the eyes Culwin sees are his own, the vision of George Faxon, the presiding consciousness in "The Triumph of Night," is of one other than himself, the double of a man with whose reputation he is familiar but whom he has never previously seen. The story has not garnered nearly as much critical attention as "The Eyes," although McDowell has praised it highly ("Edith Wharton's Ghost Stories" 141-143) and Smith has given it some fleeting recognition.

Smith's comment dealing with the nature of the story's ghost furnishes an interesting overture to a discussion of "The Triumph of Night":

> The issue of whether Faxon...encounters a phantom vision of Mr. Lavington, or merely hallucinates one, like the debate over the governess in *The Turn of the Screw*, means almost nothing. If he sees the phantom, it appears *to him*, as a person susceptible to its meaning; if he hallucinates it,

that does not mean he was incorrect. In either case, the issue is *why* rather than *whether*. Locally, that is, within the terms of the story, the phantom is clearly an illustration of the actual malignity of Lavington, beneath his mask of ingratiation and benevolence, as he cheats his nephew out of an inheritance. (154)

It does seem, however, that Wharton is weighting the story towards the second of Smith's hypotheses, that is, that Lavington's double is a figment of Faxon's imagination. As a young man whose "temperament hung on lightly quivering nerves" (II, 326) and who has been told by his doctor five months after the major events of the story, "You must have been bottling up for a bad breakdown before you started for New Hampshire last December" (II, 343), Faxon might very well be susceptible to hallucinatory visions. It is a point worth making that the binary nature of Lavington is a feature of Faxon's thoughts considerably before he sees his host's alter ego. Shortly after he meets Lavington's nephew Rainer, as the two young men sit shivering at the station awaiting the arrival of a train, Faxon is already questioning his new friend's assessment of his uncle as "a regular brick" (II, 328). The following portion of their dialogue establishes this clearly:

> "All the same you ought to be careful, you know." The sense of elder-brotherly concern that forced the words from Faxon made him, as he spoke, slip his arm through Frank Rainer's.
> The latter met the movement with a responsive pressure. "Oh, I *am*; awfully. And then my uncle has such an eye on me!"
> "But if your uncle has such an eye on you, what does he say to your swallowing knives out here in this Siberian wild?" (II, 328)

Faxon carries with him his initial disquietude about the ambivalence of Lavington as he enters his host's house. Here he receives "a violent impression of warmth and light, of hothouse plants, hurrying servants, a vast spectacular oak hall like a stage setting," but the house "for all its ingenuities of comfort, was oddly cold and unwelcoming" (II, 329). His view of the place as unreal and theatrical sustains his image of its presiding figure as one who puts forth a false front, who has a hidden persona.

Certain other details, which may initially seem merely to symbolize the binary nature of Faxon's vision of his host, may also be seen to predispose his already susceptible mind to seeing the ghost. The narrator's description of Lavington's house as it is approached from the outside suggests such a view: "At the end of the avenue the long house loomed up, its principal bulk dark, but one wing sending out a ray of welcome" (II, 329). The story's narrative method, its use of a third-person narrator who views events from Faxon's perspective throughout, ensures that such a detail is part of the point-of-view character's perception. In this case, Faxon may very well see reflected in the house its owner's double nature as it has emerged in his earlier conversation with Rainer at the railroad station.

Other details of a similar kind reveal in Faxon a consciousness acutely aware of the double nature of setting and object, particularly as these latter are identified with their owner Lavington. One example is the reference to the stairways in Overdale. As Faxon goes downstairs, supposedly to dinner, he finds that "two staircases, of apparently equal importance, invited him." However, the stair he chooses leads not to the dining room, and he realizes that he has "blundered into what seemed to be his host's study" (II, 330). The study, the site of the ghost's first appearance, is, of course, the place in which Lavington's scheme to secure his nephew's wealth is sealed. Rainer later tells Faxon that it is the other stair that leads to the dining room. It is in this room, where the ghost makes its second appearance, that the munificence of Lavington is demonstrated. Thus Faxon is aware of two stairways leading to two rooms, that equate to the two Lavingtons. An even more striking instance of the same sort occurs at the time of the ghost's second appearance. As he looks away from the two Lavingtons (the ghost "[gathering] into its look all the fierce weariness of old satisfied hate," Lavington with a "pinched smile...screwed to his bland face") Faxon catches "the soliciting twinkle of the champagne glass; but the sight of the wine turned him sick" (II, 337). There is no question that the stairs and champagne glass carry symbolic value. What is possible also is that they have psychological importance. Faxon's sensitivity to the relevance of these phenomena, indeed his manipulation of them, reinforces the possibility of seeing him as one for whom the envisaging of a Lavington double is quite feasible.

It is from his second sight of Lavington's ghost that Faxon flees into the frigid New Hampshire night, drawing Rainer after him, and to his death. As in other Wharton ghost stories, "the horror of what is, of the suppressed 'natural', as Smith says, "is greater than the horror of what is not, of the conventionally 'supernatural'" (158). What is appalling to Faxon, and ultimately to the reader, is that he has not paid heed to the warning proffered him, has not come to his new friend's assistance. As McDowell puts it, "The chilling effect of the tale...derives from Faxon's gradual recognition of the fact that he might have saved Rainer" ("Edith Wharton's Ghost Stories" 143). Faxon's most acute awareness of his failure and guilt comes in the closing paragraphs of the story, which detail his learning of Lavington's use of Rainer's fortune to solve his own business problems: as he reiterates his failure, Faxon recalls Rainer's death five months before: "the dreadful moment in the lodge when, raising himself up from Rainer's side, he had looked at his hands and seen that they were red..." (II, 344).

However, the story's depiction of Faxon does not permit us to see him as simply the guilt-ridden subject of a failure in human courage and love, for his dilemma is more complex than that, at least at a conscious level. The truth is that Faxon, in failing Rainer, has also failed himself; in failing to act on behalf of his friend, he has perpetuated a life pattern that he himself has characterized as desultory, uncommitted, and unsatisfying. The story is laced from the very beginning with references to Faxon's dissatisfaction with his own life. His years have been "mainly a succession of resigned adaptations" (II, 327) and his coming to Overdale to take on the job of secretary to Mrs Culme is merely the latest manifestation of his habit of taking up inconsequential positions. Inside Overdale he senses that he is "unutterably sick of all strange houses, and of the prospect of perpetually treading other people's stairs" (II, 330).

Faxon's sense of dissatisfaction with himself continues to be expressed after the ghost's second appearance when he realizes he is the only one who sees it. The realization of his being the sole repository of the ghost's warning triggers in him a self-consciousness that translates into a reiterated questioning of the reasons for his being "singled out as the victim of this dreadful initiation" (II, 339). It is in this context that his expressions of a failed life continue. The following passage, recording his thoughts as he flees Overdale, illustrates in a striking manner how elements of fear, failure, regret, and victimization fuse in his consciousness:

> Why else, in the name of any imaginable logic, human or devilish, should he, a stranger, be singled out for this experience? What could it mean to him, how was he related to it, what bearing had it on his case?... Unless, indeed, it was just because he was a stranger—a stranger everywhere— because he had no personal life, no warm screen of private egotisms to shield him from exposure, that he had developed this abnormal sensitiveness to the vicissitudes of others. The thought pulled him up with a shudder. No! Such a fate was too abominable; all that was strong and sound in him rejected it. A thousand times better regard himself as ill, disorganized, deluded, than as the predestined victim of such warnings! (II, 339-440)

The thoughts Faxon manifests in this passage and elsewhere reveal a young man so taken up with his own problems (his nervous agitation, his unsuccessful past, "perpetually treading other people's stairs") that he is unable to see, let alone seize, the possibilities of the moment. It never occurs to him that the chance of performing the significant act that has so long eluded him is within reach. It never strikes him that the opportunity of a "personal life," of a rich friendship with one for whom he has instinctively felt a strong affinity and in whom the feeling has been fully reciprocated is at his fingertips. What bearing had it on his case, indeed! His being singled out had all the bearing imaginable on his case. And so, Faxon can be seen as yet another of those Wharton characters who fail to see. The night that triumphs here is not merely the darkness that swallows up the innocent Rainer; it is the darkness that holds Faxon blind to his own possibilities even as they lie within his grasp. Once again Wharton takes a story to an additional psychological level that enhances its stature as a delineation of "the horror of what is, of the suppressed 'natural'."

"Kerfol"

Some eighteen months after "The Triumph of Night," "Kerfol" appeared in the March 1916 issue of *Scribner's*. A story that has not generated much critical comment, it marks Wharton's first experiment with a pure ghost story, i.e., one that is primarily concerned with a supernatural occurrence, and that does not see that occurrence in terms of its impact on the story's present-time characters and least of all on its narrator. In previous Wharton ghost stories narrators and characters contemporary to them are directly related by either cause or effect to the ghosts at hand, or significance is brought to bear on the fact that they are not so related.[81]

The fact that the events constituting the tale of the marriage of the lord and lady of the domain of Kerfol have taken place some three centuries previous and are available to the narrator only by way of a manuscript, has much to do with the purely ghostly nature of "Kerfol." Although distanced in time from the events he recapitulates, the narrator is interested in these events because of the human horrors that have provoked the ghostly retaliation that is at the heart of the tale. In fact "Kerfol" does begin in such a way as to indicate that the impact of the story's three-century-old events continues into the present. The ghostly dogs make an annual appearance at Kerfol on the anniversary of their act of vengeance: this is well known among the inhabitants of the area. But as "Kerfol" develops, the yearly return of the dogs is dropped completely as a point of interest, and effectively is limited to serving as a mechanism to get the "real" story under way.

One has the sense that with "Kerfol" Wharton wanted, for once, to steer clear of psychological matters and to tell a story merely for "the fun of the shudder," merely to exploit the possibilities of a ghost story as ghost story. It is useful to compare "Kerfol" to its predecessor "Afterward." In both stories friends of the central characters introduce them to attractive country estates which can be bought at bargain prices. Both central characters as well are attracted by the prospect of being associated with ancient houses with their stored-up history and romance. But after these superficial likenesses, the stories diverge radically, and it is in this divergence that one sees the particular quality of "Kerfol." "Afterward's" protagonist, Mary Boyne, is disappointed in her search for the ghost she conceives to be part of the very fabric of the house she inhabits. Blinded by this romantic penchant, she fails to see the ghost at hand and its implications. Kerfol renders up for the narrator of the other story its very real ghosts, but they remain interesting for themselves and the story they inhabit. Perhaps Wharton's chosen title, "Kerfol," a place name, dead-ended, without the potential for the thematic and imaginative expansiveness of such titles as "The Eyes," "Afterward," or "The Triumph of Night," is the best clue as to its author's limited intentions.

"Bewitched"

After a long interval of nine years, Wharton returned to the ghost story in 1925 with the successive publication of "Bewitched" and "Miss Mary Pask" in the March and April issues of *Pictorial Review*.

"Bewitched," set, like "The Triumph of Night," in a wintry New England countryside but amidst a lower social class, tells the story of a deceased woman, Ora Brand, who for a year has allegedly come back from the dead for meetings with Saul Rutledge the man who had been prevented from marrying her by her father, Sylvester. As the story opens, the "bewitched" man's wife, Prudence, has called a meeting to deal with the situation: present with her and her husband are Deacon Hibbins, Orrin Bosworth and Sylvester Brand. Saul admits to his complicity with the ghostly woman, and Prudence claims to have seen the two together. The three visitors agree that they will confront the ghost the next day at sunset, but Hibbins and Bosworth, travelling together, and Brand, all jump the gun and proceed to the trysting place on their way home. They are drawn to the dilapidated shack to which bare footprints lead, and in a confusing scene Brand shoots at the "white and wraithlike...something that [surges] out of the darkest corner of the hut" (II, 418). The next day the community hears that Venny, Ora's younger sister, has died suddenly of pneumonia.

Two critics who have had substantial comments to make on "Bewitched," Margaret McDowell and Allan Gardner Smith—R.W.B. Lewis swiftly dismisses it as "an artificial yarn which strives for effect by converting the figurative into the natural" (*ICSS* XVII)—agree essentially on the subtlety of the story. Smith's assessment is as follows:

> In a complicated misconception, the dead girl's father shoots what he takes to be [Ora's] spirit, and the narrative covers over a probable, ugly sequence of events under the screen of a limited point of view, showing only the outline of a corpse: the dead girl's sister has suddenly been carried away by "pneumonia". This leads the attribution of witchcraft to fall on its inceptor, Mrs. Rutledge, whose Saul, it seems, had married the witch, not met her. Mrs. Rutledge now reminds the narrator of a stone figure, with marble eyeballs and bony hands, a reference that picks up his early reminiscence of "soft bony hands" belonging to mad aunt Cressida, who strangled the canary he brought her as a boy. (152)

In other words, "Bewitched" is clearly open to the interpretation that there is no ghost at all; that Rutledge is being drawn not to a spectre, but to the wild and beautiful Venny; that Sylvester Brand's shooting of "the white and wraithlike something" is not a symbolic driving of a stake through the heart of Ora but the killing of Venny, whose pneumonia is but a cover for the real cause of her death; and that Prudence Rutledge is, by what she is and what she does, at the source of these troubles. McDowell's is a lengthier and more detailed discussion ("Edith Wharton's Ghost Stories" 145-151) than Smith's, fleshing out what Smith suggests and detailing the ill effects wielded on the other major characters by the witchly Prudence in her embodiment of both the harsh Puritan tradition and the loneliness and isolation of New England life.

The point that McDowell and Smith both make—the latter less tentatively than the former—is that regardless of whether or not Ora's perambulations are real, the story's true source of disruption in the community is Prudence. In this context, it is important to note that in "Bewitched" Wharton is exceptionally attentive to the physical appearance of her characters. One can read Wharton fiction in long stretches without coming across the number and detail of descriptions of the human face, figure, and dress that one finds in this story. Here, for example, is the reader's introduction to Prudence:

> It was doubtful, indeed, if anything unwonted could be made to show in Prudence Rutledge's face, so limited was its scope, so fixed were its features. She was dressed for the occasion in black calico with white spots, a collar of crochet lace fastened by a gold brooch, and a gray woollen shawl, crossed under her arms and tied at the back. In her small narrow head the only marked prominence was that of the brow projecting roundly over pale spectacled eyes. Her dark hair, parted above this prominence, passed tight and flat over the tip of her ears into a small braided coil at the nape; and her contracted head looked still narrower from being perched on a long hollow neck with cord-like throat muscles. Her eyes were of a pale cold gray, her complexion was an even white. Her age might have been anywhere from thirty-five to sixty. (II, 404)

Subsequent briefer descriptions of Prudence support and amplify this picture of a cold, rigid, impassive woman, who suppresses life, love, and vitality in her Puritanical commitment to labor and in her assimilation into the harsh New England setting: "her long thin hands" are "[w]ithered and wrinkled by hard work and cold" and "of the same leaden white as her face" (II, 406).

It is through the eyes of Orin Bosworth that we frequently see Prudence. Bosworth notices that "the inner fold of her lids was of the same uniform white as the rest of her skin, so that when she dropped them her rather prominent eyes looked like the sightless orbs of a marble statue" (II, 405). As she "glided" past him at Venny's funeral, it "looks [to Bosworth] as if the stonemason had carved her to put atop of Venny's grave.... When she bent over her hymn book her lowered lids reminded him again of marble eyeballs: the bony hands clasping the book were bloodless. Bosworth had never seen such hands since he had seen old Aunt Cressidora Cheney strangle the canary bird because it fluttered" (II, 419). Like Cressidora, Prudence stifles life: she cannot abide vitality and freedom.

Just how much Bosworth, the story's center of consciousness, perceives of the truth of events in the story is uncertain. For him, the remembrance of his aunt's cruel gesture and the news he hears from Prudence about her husband's affair with the ghost provoke thoughts of the supernatural and the reality of its intrusion in human affairs. While he does question the supernatural nature of various events he is naturally attuned to the supernatural: if a witch had been burned at North Ashmore, he does not consider the possibility that, like many witches burned at the stake, this one was the victim of human perversity and not a demonic presence. Finally, while he is more sophisticated than his fellow Ardmorites, "had had more contact with the modern world; down in Starkfield, in the bar of the Fielding House, he could hear himself laughing with the rest of the men at such old wives' tales," he realizes he is heir to the same tradition as his country friends: "the roots of the old life were still in him" (II, 412).

That the "roots of the old life" penetrated through many generations is what may be seen to account for the mystery of the present, for the "great many other things below the surface of [Bosworth's] thoughts" (II, 413). In the final analysis, whatever its supernatural possibilities, "Bewitched" portrays a society in which lurks the old Calvinistic denial of life. "The chill down [Bosworth's] spine" is brought on as much by the human evil perpetrated by persons as by any supernatural occurrence. The "witch" in Prudence is not a demonic visitor but the result of her withdrawal from human relatedness and warmth. In one way or another, whether as victims or as perpetrators, characters in "Bewitched" dwell under the shadow of the Old Testament texts Prudence lives by: the one that adorns the wall of her house, "The Soul That Sinneth It Shall Die," and the one she reads from Exodus: "Thou shalt not suffer a witch to live" (II, 405, 412). As McDowell has suggested, the principals in the story's trysts are victims of a lack of warmth and love. Rutledge himself, husband in a childless marriage, living in the wake of his wife's harshness, flies to the ghostly Ora or the living Venny. In the Brand household "father and daughter lead separate lives and Venny runs wild on the slopes of Lonetop Mountain" ("Edith Wharton's Ghost Stories" 149).

In short, the effects of a tradition and a lifestyle that squelches life, warmth, and love are pervasive in "Bewitched." And their pervasiveness is visible: hence the plethora of physical descriptions in the story. "[T]here was something animal and primitive about [Brand], Bosworth thought, as he hung thus, lowering and dumb, a little foam beading the corner of that heavy purplish underlip" (II, 408). Even Deacon Hibben is not immune from the telltale signs of life in an inhibiting society: "[his] mildewed countenance...[b]etween the blotches...had become as white as Mrs. Rutledge's, and the Deacon's eyes burned in the whiteness like live embers among ashes" (II, 406). In a word, Bosworth's apprehension, as he watches the snow fall relentlessly outside the window, "that a winding sheet [was] descending from the sky to envelop them all in a common grave" (II, 410), is less a fear about the future than an unconscious assessment of the present. In this most Hawthornesque of all of Wharton's short stories it is the natural, the everyday, the residual past that terrifies most.

"Miss Mary Pask"

"Miss Mary Pask" strikes upon the same general theme as its predecessor "Bewitched," albeit the setting and scope of the two stories are quite different: both are about the failure of love and the effects of this failure on persons, but "Miss Mary Pask" deals with private failures rather than ones indigenous to a certain society.

"Miss Mary Pask" is told in the first person and from a retrospective point of view by a dilettantish American who after becoming ill on a visit to Egypt is recuperating in Brittany. While there he decides to visit Mary Pask, an old acquaintance who has lived alone since the marriage of her sister Grace Bridgeworth. Just as he sees Mary coming down the stairs to greet him, the narrator remembers that she has been dead for a year: the figure approaching him is the ghost of Mary Pask. Partly because of this experience he suffers a nervous collapse, and it is several months before he can bring himself to tell Grace Bridgeworth of his vision, but during his painful attempt to inform her, she gives him the news that Mary has not died, that what had been considered her death was but a "cataleptic trance." The ghost the narrator has concluded to be such is no ghost at all but the living Mary Pask.

"Miss Mary Pask" is not a ghost story in the strict sense, of course. In Wharton's earlier stories of the genre there was always the possibility that ghostly appearances occurred, even in the face of some evidence to the contrary, and even if the ghosts, in some cases, were but subjective imaginings of certain characters. In this story the reader is given no choice but to conclude that there is no ghost. Wharton's decision to include the story in her last collection, *Ghosts*, though, has gone unquestioned, and understandably so, for the narrator effectively experiences Mary as a ghost on the basis of his ignorance about her false death. As well, the various conditions at the time of his visit to Mary's cottage aid and abet his subjective vision of her: the fog-enshrouded night, the dark and gloomy cottage, the suspicion that he is not entirely cured of his recent sickness. Under the circumstances it is entirely plausible that he should flee in horror from her wraith-like presence. In the few minutes he sees Mary he is only able to pronounce four words, "You live here alone?" (II, 379); all his other attempts at coherent speech die within him so terrified is he by the seeming spectre. Nor is the narrator's predicament assuaged by the several ironic references Mary makes to her "death": "I've had so few visitors since my death, you see"; "The dead naturally get used to it [i.e., loneliness]; "When [my sister] got the news of my death—were you with her? Was she terribly upset?" (II, 379) "People don't like me much since I've been dead" (II, 380).

Given the above circumstances, which establish conclusively that the narrator believes himself to be in the presence of a ghost, it is difficult to accept the contention of Margaret McDowell that his escape into the night constitutes merely a cowardly retreat from one who wishes to relieve her terrible aloneness. Writes McDowell: "He recoils from her as if she is indeed a vampire; and he resists her appeal to him to stay longer and to assuage her unendurable loneliness. Instead he yields to his fear and becomes obsessed with the need to flee from her" ("Edith Wharton's Ghost Stories" 138). In her attempt to establish the insensitivity of the narrator, McDowell seems overly zealous. In fact, there is sufficient evidence to illustrate her subject's moral failures, his serious disregard of persons, elsewhere in the story. It is an important dimension of "Miss Mary Pask" as well that the narrator is not conscious of his own ineffectuality as a person and that in commenting patronizingly and negatively on others he is unwittingly defining himself. As Allan Gardner Smith puts it: "[the story] brings to light an aspect of male attitudes which is not 'secret'...within the terms of the story, but is unexpressed by the narrator because it is invisible to him" (152).

One need not read very far into the story before seeing the shallowness and blindness of the narrator. His early put-downs of the Pask sisters establish him as one who sees himself in a superior light: "Mary Pask was like hundreds of other dowdy old maids, cheerful derelicts content with their innumerable little substitutes for living"; Grace was "a handsome, capable and rather dull woman, absorbed in her husband and children and without an ounce of imagination" (II, 374). But each assessment has its own comment to make on the unmarried and unattached dilettante, pampering himself with some desultory landscape painting on the Brittany coast after contracting a "touch of fever" in Egypt, and about to be "rest-cured and built up again [presumably because of his experience at Mary Pask's] at one of those wonderful Swiss sanatoria where they clean the cobwebs out of you" (II, 373).

If "Miss Mary Pask" documents grave failures of love, it is, again, in his superficial evaluations of Grace's attitudes to her sister that the narrator's true self is revealed. Grace herself can be blamed for seriously neglecting her sister. The most flagrant example of this is the fact that she has not visited, indeed does not appear to have even communicated with Mary during the year that has elapsed since her cataleptic trance. Given this tangible sign of indifference, all Grace's ritual protestations of love ring hollow. "You know my darling Mary has a little place near Morgat," she tells the narrator. "[I]f you ever go to Brittany, do go to see her. She lives such a lonely life—it makes me so unhappy" (II, 373). "You know it's years since Mary and I have been together—not since little Molly was born," she says on another occasion. "If only she's come to America! Just think...Molly is six and has never seen her darling auntie.... If you go to Britanny promise me you'll look up my Mary" (II, 374). When the narrator visits Grace months after having seen Mary, "the ready tears overbrimmed her eyes. 'I do reproach myself more and more about darling Mary.' [she adds] tremulously" (II, 383). What should be seen here is that the narrator takes Grace's words and gestures at face value, without questioning their genuineness. "Grace and [Mary] were greatly attached to each other, I knew," and their parting at the time of her marriage to Bridgeworth "had been Grace's chief sorrow" (II, 373), he says early in his narration. And it is without the least bit of conscious irony that he can refer to Grace somewhat later as "one of the sweet conscientious women who go on using the language of devotion about people whom they live happily without seeing" [sic] (II, 374).

The narrator's response to Mary Pask is remarkably similar to Grace's. He too is moved by the memory of Mary. He too "meant to come back when I was patched up again," and as he rests in his Swiss retreat "more and more tenderly, but more intermittently, [his] thoughts went back from [his] snow mountain to that wailing autumn night above the *Baie des Trépassés* and the revelation of the dead Mary Pask who was so much more real to me than ever the living one had been" (II, 382). These tender sentiments are set aside at the news of Mary's being alive. The closing words of the narrative are decisive: "I felt I should never again be interested in Mary Pask, or in anything concerning her" (II, 384). Like Grace's, the narrator's love is contingent on removal and remoteness, sentimental and uncommitted—in fact, no real love at all.

Not the least of the merits of "Miss Mary Pask" is its vivid imaging of an intensely lonely woman. Effectively, Mary's apparent death, her cataleptic trance, have left her enduring a kind of death-in-life, as her poignant remarks to the narrator, cited above in another context, amply demonstrate. Because of traditional suspicions surrounding apparent death, the peasants in the area avoid her—even the woman who works for her leaves her house without speaking. The people from whom she might rightfully expect love and concern, especially Grace and her family, and the narrator, have abandoned her. The narrator's dismissal of Mary indicates a withdrawal from life and love, and his act is not a surprising one given the attitudes and opinions he reveals during his narration. One wonders if the critical assessment of Annette Zilversmit that the narrator is "exploitive" ("Edith Wharton's Last Ghosts" 297), and of McDowell, that he is "hedonistic" ("Edith Wharton's Ghost Stories" 138) do not err by understatement. Fear, self-absorption, passivity, and blindness finally damn the narrator more than do the active vices. He is very nearly a non-entity, a shell of a man, perhaps the closest thing there is to a real ghost in "Miss Mary Pask."

"Mr. Jones"

Wharton followed up "Miss Mary Pask" and "Bewitched" with "Mr. Jones," published in the April 1928 issue of *Ladies' Home Journal.* This story bears notable resemblance to "Afterward" and "Kerfol" from earlier in her career. In "Mr. Jones" the center-of-consciousness character is Lady Jane Lynke, who comes into ownership of Bells, a country estate in Sussex. From her first visit on she is obstructed by a mysterious Mr Jones[5], who exercises a domineering influence at the house and who remains invisible and inaccessible to her, transmitting his wishes by way of his elderly niece, Mrs Clemm, the housekeeper. With the support of a friend, Stramer, Jane, ignoring the orders of Mr Jones, discovers in examining old family papers that a former lord of the manor, the fifteenth viscount of Bells, had confined to the house during his long-standing absences his deaf-and-mute wife, Juliana, and that during these periods, and especially during the last three years of her life after her husband's death, she had been under the immediate control of a Mr Jones. It becomes clear that the historical Mr Jones has continued to exert his influence in ghostly form, and in the closing portion of the story Jane and Stramer discover that Mrs Clemm has been choked to death by the spectral Mr Jones. [82]

The story's immediate resemblances to "Afterward" and "Kerfol" are easily seen. Like her fictional predecessors Mary Boyne and "Kerfol's" narrator, Jane comes upon a country estate of striking antique beauty and is moved by the aura of its history and romance. Like Mary Boyne especially, Jane is surprised by the spectral presence that intrudes on her secure and comfortable life. "Mr.

Jones," however, departs in important ways from each of its "models," and it is useful to examine the story in the light of the other two.

"Mr. Jones" and "Kerfol" have resemblances particular to themselves. Both tell tales of horror set in the distant past, tales that have the same subject: the incredibly harsh and sadistic treatment of wives at the hands of their husbands. The essential difference between the two stories is the fact that "Mr. Jones" does not limit itself to the past in the way "Kerfol" does. The latter's interest is mainly in the lives of the Cornault-Barrigan-Lanrivain triangle, with the exception that the ghostly revenants make their appearance to the present-time narrator on the day of his visit to Kerfol: but for the fact that he is horrified by the cruelty of the husband and by the revenge of the dogs, the events of the past do not reach into the narrator's life. In "Mr. Jones," however, the past intrudes into the lives of Jane, her novelist friend Stramer, and the household servants in the most immediate and palpable ways, and one is left at the open end of the story with a sense of impending menace, of threat to the central character herself.

At the heart of the difference between "Mr. Jones" and "Kerfol" is the distinctive role of the ghosts in the stories. The dogs of Kerfol are avengers: their work has been done and their annual appearance serves a commemorative purpose for the people of the area. Mr Jones the revenant sustains his role as accessory to his master and as the presiding power at Bells. His passive harassment of Jane constitutes his attempt to maintain his power over women, and women of a higher social class; his suffocating of Mrs Clemm perpetuates his cruelty and malevolence, his inheritance from the Viscount, and serves as a warning to his present mistress. Clearly Mr Jones remains a lethal force, imparting more than merely a chill of fright.

A comparison of "Mr. Jones" and "Afterward" reveals the entirely different treatment of the stories' central characters. Mary Boyne, the chatelaine of Lyng, has lived her life in the shadow of her husband, entirely reliant on him and unquestioning of his business dealings, the source of her ease and content. It is only after Ned's permanent disappearance that Mary is forced into a life of her own, and her awakening after her husband's passing gives the story an interesting psychological dimension.   Lady Jane Lynke, though more appealing as a character *per se*, remains essentially a static personality. Unmarried at thirty-five, and contentedly so, she leads a productive and fulfilling life of travel, study, and writing. Her independence, resourcefulness, and *sang froid* are evident in her enjoyment of living alone at Bells and her coping with the mysteries of a new home with a minimum of discomfort and agitation.   And even though she eventually has the company of Stramer to buttress her courage in the face of the obstructive Mr Jones, nevertheless it is she who removes the manuscripts from the blue parlor's citron wood desk, violating Bells' major taboo.

When Georgiana the servant girl arrives shortly thereafter with news of Mrs Clemm's collapse and Jane proceeds upstairs with Stramer to find the housekeeper dead, one senses that Wharton's interest is not in engaging the kind of deeper theme that makes "Afterward" a more engrossing and probably better short story.   As she stands looking at the strangled Mrs Clemm, Jane can only summon up the bland reaction: "Oh, poor thing! But how—?" And as "with a shiver of fear [she draws] down the housekeeper's lids" (II, 615) and listens silently to Stramer's badgering of Georgiana and the latter's terrified reply, none of the frightening elements of her own predicament registers on her: her own potential danger at the hands of Mr Jones, or the fact that it is her action that has indirectly brought about Mrs Clemm's death.   Evidently it is not Wharton's purpose to pursue more profound moral and psychological matters, though they are there for the pursuing.

The gradual revelation of the life at Bells of distant generations in the past gives "Mr. Jones" the quality of a mystery story whose solution is arrived at by Jane and Stramer. The add-on inscription "in small cramped characters, 'Also His Wife'" (II, 595), that follows the elaborate description of the titles and offices of the fifteenth Viscount of Thudeney adorning his sarcophagus intrigues Jane on her first visit to Bells. "Mr. Jones" is among other things the unravelling of the mystery surrounding the pathetic reference to Juliana. With the help of Stramer the novelist, one by occupation interested in and adept at the concoction of plots, Jane comes to an understanding of the dreadful significance of the words "Also His Wife," words that epitomize the meaning of the story and that might have been used, Allan Gardner Smith remarks, as the story's title (156).

One other comment about "Mr. Jones" is appropriate in connection with the imaging of its ghostly title character. Like previous Wharton revenants Mr Jones is a real presence. But he does not have the substantiality of such earlier ghosts as Bob Elwell of "Afterward" or Emma Saxon of "The Lady's Maid's Bell." Here is the narrator's rendering of Jane's first view of Mr Jones: "Some one was in the room already; she felt rather than saw another presence.... What she saw, or thought she saw, was simply an old man with bent shoulders turning away from the citron wood desk. Almost before she had received the impression there was no one there, only the slightest stir of the needlework curtain over the farther door. She heard no step or other sound" (II, 603-604). And of her second glimpse: "[She] saw in the long dazzle of autumn light, as if translucent, edged with the glitter, an old man at the desk," and detected on the needlework "the same faint tremor as before" (II, 611). However, the uncertainty suggested in these descriptions is resolved by other details provided, to which both Jane and Stramer are privy: "the trace of dusty footprints—the prints of broad-soled heelless shoes" (II, 610) in the muniment room and the blue parlor, and "a circle of red marks [on Mrs. Clemm's throat]—the marks of recent bruises" (II, 615). The ghostly Mr Jones is clearly there, if not in very solid form, resembling one of Poe's supernatural presences more than a conventional Wharton ghost.

"Pomegranate Seed"

One of three ghost stories produced during the closing years of Wharton's life, "Pomegranate Seed," published in the April 25, 1931 issue of the *Saturday Evening Post*, takes its place among a group of short stories whose titles and contents draw on classical myth. In this case the myth is of Persephone's enforced confinement in the underworld during the winter months, punishment for having broken her promise of abstinence by eating pomegranate seeds.

Wharton's attraction to this particular myth surfaces in at least two of her other texts: a poem entitled "Pomegranate Seed," and a war novel of the same title, written by the fictional writer Margaret Aubyn in Wharton's novel *The Touchstone*. It is not surprising that at the time of and prior to its publication, Wharton received requests for elucidation of this story's title, as Barbara White reports (25), from publishers and readers alike, for the story's relationship to the myth is not transparent. One recent attempt to establish firm connections between "Pomegranate Seed" and the myth of Persephone's confinement in the underworld can be found in Candace Waid's *Edith Wharton's Letters from the Underworld*. Writes Waid:

> As Wharton rewrites the story of Demeter and Persephone in "Pomegranate Seed," the Persephone figure is at first the husband Ned Ashby, over whose fate the deceased wife, Elsie Corder Ashby, and the living wife, Charlotte Gorse Ashby, struggle. Elsie Corder Ashby, the writer of the letters, is the author of the ties that bind. The middle name of the living wife, Gorse, is the name of a prickly plant sacred to the goddess Demeter, suggesting her association with the maternal figure in the myth. However, Wharton's rewriting of the myth is also a reading of the story of Demeter and Persephone. In "Pomegranate Seed," the seed is singular; it points to Charlotte Gorse Ashby's illicit reading of a single letter—an act that seals the fate of all the characters at the close of the story. Charlotte Gorse Ashby becomes the Persephone figure at the close of the story as she, instead of her husband, eats the forbidden fruit.... [She] is transported to the erotic underworld.... [She] opens the letter from the underworld: the letter from her husband's deceased wife. She also reads a letter which calls her to "come" to the underworld. In this sense Demeter shares with Persephone the experience of the underworld—only her hell is the barren winter of the soul experienced by the abandoned woman on earth. "Pomegranate Seed" links the experience of mother and daughter as it explores a deeper story in the cyclical myth of female replacement. (195-196)

Such an explanation announces the attention being placed on the supernatural in recent criticism of "Pomegranate Seed" and other ghost stories. Waid's reading, with its emphasis on the underworld, on the ghostly features of the story, echoes other recent commentaries, such as Sandra M. Gilbert's. For Gilbert, "Pomegranate Seed" depends on the portrayal of a woman who speaks "from beyond the grave.... If not in life, Wharton here implies, then in death, beyond the boundaries of logic and the logic of boundaries, a kind of female victory becomes possible, albeit a cryptic and problematical one" (168).

However, Margaret McDowell, writing in an earlier time, has made the point that "Pomegranate Seed" is "finally imposing for its moral and psychological significance, not simply for its convincing supernatural aspect" ("Edith Wharton's Ghost Stories" 139). Focusing her attention more directly on the living wife than on the ghost, McDowell suggests that among the main causes of the victory of "death and negation" in the story are "Charlotte's distrust, possessiveness and cowardice" (140). Because "Pomegranate Seed" is written with Charlotte, the living wife, as the point-of-view character, it seems reasonable to assume that Wharton was at least as interested in delineating the anatomy of failure as she was in depicting a victory of the supernatural.

"Pomegranate Seed" depicts Charlotte at the outset returning on a March afternoon to her home from the great boisterous city. "She turned her back on [New York], standing for a moment in the old-fashioned, marble-flagged vestibule.... The sash curtains drawn across the panes of the inner door softened the light within to a warm blue through which no details showed.... The contrast between the soulless roar of New York, its devouring blaze of lights, the oppression of its congested traffic, congested houses, lives, minds, and this veiled sanctuary she called home, always stirred her profoundly. In the very heart of the hurricane she had found her tiny islet—or thought she had" (II, 763). One recognizes here Charlotte's likeness to the earlier Mary Boyne of "Afterward," who "cannot get far enough away from the world" (II, 154) and whose happy life depends upon a combination of tradition, security, and romantic love, in a word, on elements that reside outside her own person. Like Mary, Charlotte fears, however, that so soon in her marriage potential danger has beset her "tiny islet."

There is in the initial stages of Charlotte's period of apprehension the flash of an insight as to the nature of the threat to her content. Again juxtaposing her own fortress of security with the outside world, she thinks: "Outside there, skyscrapers, advertizements, telephones, wireless, airplanes, movies, motors, and all the rest of the twentieth century; and on the other side of the door something I can't explain, can't relate to them. Something as old as the world, as mysterious as life...." But the insight is short-lived—indeed, she herself dismisses it with her "Nonsense: What am I worrying about?" (II, 767). Entirely consistent with her habit of escape from the modern world, she refuses to confront the issue that has raised itself in her consciousness. In fact, it is only after her husband disappears that she realizes the supernatural nature of her rival.

As the events of the story's first day wear on, the day of the arrival of the by-now-familiar gray letter, Charlotte's conception of the threat substantializes into images of "an old entanglement" and "a mistress," and this in the face of her strong sense of Kenneth's utter devotedness to her. It becomes increasingly evident that in her complete misreading as to the source of the mysterious letters, Charlotte is directed by "the secret she hardly acknowledged to her heart—her passionate need to feel herself the sovereign even of [Kenneth's] past" (II, 767). It is this desire to maintain control of her husband's entire existence that gets in the way of her pursuing the insight about "something as old as the world—as mysterious as life," and it is the same desire that continually thwarts her from following through her frequent resolutions to actualize intentions that emanate from her better self. The following is but one example of this kind of occurrence. When Kenneth returns to his bedroom after having endured Charlotte's cross-examination, we are provided with a description of the latter's ambivalence: "Her first movement was one of compunction; she seemed to herself to have been hard, unhuman, unimaginative. 'Think of telling him that I didn't care if my insistence cost me his love! The lying rubbish!' She started up to follow him and unsay the meaningless words. But she was checked by a reflection. He had had his way, after all; he had eluded all attacks on his secret, and now he was shut up alone in his room, reading that other woman's letter" (II, 774). And so when Kenneth emerges for dinner her onslaught continues, culminating in his capitulation to her request that they go away on a holiday together.

In the description of the aftermath of Charlotte's illusory victory over her husband during the late evening before and the earlier part of the day of his disappearance, one sees that Wharton has laden the text heavily, though not obtrusively, with a military imagery that is highly suggestive of the attitude of her central character. "[Charlotte] had fought through the weary fight and victory was hers"; "she would have to renew her struggle day after day till they started on their journey" (II, 778). As Charlotte gazes at her reflection in a mirror, "It made her feel young again to have scored such a victory. The other woman vanished to a speck on the horizon, as this one, who ruled the foreground, smiled back at the reflection of her lips and eyes.... As she brushed back her light abundant hair it waved electrically above her hand like the palms of victory" (II, 779). Even as the unexpected absence of Kenneth begins to dampen her spirit she is buoyed by the image of her conquest: "Of course he had gone to see that woman—no doubt to get her permission to leave," Charlotte speculates. "He was as completely in bondage as that; and [she] had been fatuous enough to see the palms of victory on her forehead. She burst into a laugh and, walking across the room, sat down again before the mirror. What a different face she saw! The smile on her pale lips seemed to mock the rosy vision of the other Charlotte. But gradually her color crept back. After all, she had a right to claim the victory..." (II, 780). Charlotte emerges from these scenes as one preening over her conquest, as one more taken with the victory over her husband than with the husband himself. Wharton seems to propose here a kind of female Hercules/Narcissus figure in whom resides the seeds of her own destruction.

To be sure, factors other than Charlotte's failure play a part in Kenneth's disappearance and the dissolution of the Ashby marriage, and McDowell singles out the nature of the blame the two other principals must share: "Kenneth's inertia, nostalgia and resentment...and Elsie's craving for continued power over one whom she has supposedly cherished in the past for his own sake" ("Edith Wharton's Ghost Stories" 140). But the given emphasis of the story suggests that it is Charlotte's failure that most intrigues Wharton. In her jealousy, possessiveness, self-centredness, insecurity, and belligerence Charlotte proves herself unworthy of Kenneth's love. Her inability to grant Kenneth a life of his own, her being rendered insecure at the thought that there might be parts of his life unknown or unknowable to her point to her essential smallness of character. She is no match for her rival from the other world. Athough Elsie shared with Charlotte the need to dominate her husband's life (and Kenneth is aware of the possessiveness of both his wives) nevertheless Elsie possesses the advantage of being envisioned, the remembered one, and measured against this the present-time realness of the petty Charlotte cannot stand up.

As in many of Wharton's ghost stories, "Pomegranate Seed" might be seen to relegate its ghost to a secondary place. While the ghost's presence here satisfies the needs of the genre and fulfills the dramatic need of a foil in the story, one can, again, make a legitimate case for the primacy of the human element.

"The Looking Glass"

The companion "ghost" story to "Pomegranate Seed" in Wharton's 1936 collection *The World Over* has occasioned little critical comment. First published in *Cosmopolitan* in December 1935, "The Looking Glass" is certainly the least ghostly of all Wharton's stories in the genre. The ghost in this story is that of the young man Harry, with whom Mrs Clingsland alleges to have been smitten, who "went down on the Titanic" (II, 851) and who now communicates to her, she supposes, "from the other world...from the Over There" (II, 854) via an intermediary: unlike other Wharton ghosts whose existence is but a subjective one, Harry never reveals himself directly to his earthly "connection." This circumstance of the ghost's removal from the action, along with the fact that Cora Attlee tells her story to her granddaughter a considerable time after it occurred mitigates considerably the spectral element of "The Looking Glass," to the point where it is the narrator, Cora, who becomes the center of interest. In this attention to the narrator as character, "The Looking Glass" has much in common with Wharton's first ghost story, "The Lady's Maid's Bell," for in recalling her life with her former patroness, Cora inevitably reveals much of herself. Like Hartley,

Mrs Brympton's lady's maid, Cora revels in the role of *raconteuse*, and in her concentration on the events and personages of the past lets down her guard and inadvertently sketches a self-portrait: the tale told to her granddaughter becomes a looking glass in which her fictive and readerly addresses may see Cora's real self reflected.

Of considerable interest regarding "The Looking Glass," as well, is the fact that it is one of the few short stories in which a major character draws particular and frequent attention to her Roman Catholicism. Wharton's knowledge of and interest in matters Roman Catholic are well known. She numbered among her friends the Abbé Arthur Mugnier, a Parisian parish priest, who was a habitué of her salons, and during her winter stays at her Riviera home, Sainte-Claire le Chateau Hyères, she was associated with the Catholic community there. In "The Looking Glass," one of her last short stories, written at a time when she was undoubtedly thinking about Catholicism, she created a character whose self-portrait is drawn in lines deriving from that character's adherence to the Roman Catholic faith.

Cora Attlee's telling of her story (the story within the story) is triggered by a remark she makes to her granddaughter Moyra as the latter takes her turn sitting with the elderly woman. Bored and listless, preoccupied with an upcoming date (Cora thinks), Moyra is startled by her grandmother's confession of "the wrong I did to Mrs. Clingsland" (II, 844). Surprised that such an apparently virtuous old woman harbors skeletons in her closet, Moyra repeatedly requests the details, until finally her grumbled remonstration, "It's not much fun sitting here all this time, if you can't even keep awake long enough to tell me what you mean about Mrs. Clingsland" (II, 848), launches the old woman into her tale. Thus Cora is given the opening she wants, that she probably, consciously or unconsciously, instigated in the first place, for it is clear even to Moyra "that [the wrongs] being unconfessed lurked disquietingly in the back of her mind" (II, 846).

Cora's tale takes up the larger part of "The Looking Glass," and it is told non-stop and without interruption to Moyra. It is introduced with a brief preamble in which Cora alleges to have had clairvoyant powers and to have used them to assuage the emotional torment of women stricken with worry over their husbands and sons overseas during the Great War. Singling out one such occurrence, Cora recalls:

> I got more and more sorry for those poor wretches that the soothsaying swindlers were dragging the money out of for a pack of lies; and one day I couldn't stand it any longer, and though I knew the Church was against it, when I saw one lady nearly crazy, because for months she'd had no news of her boy at the front, I said to her: "If you'll come over to my place tomorrow, I might have a word for you." And the wonder of it is that I *had*! For that night I dreamt a message came saying there was good news for her, and the next day, sure enough, she had a cable, telling her her son had escaped from a German camp....
> For I *did* see things, and hear things at that time.... And of course the ladies were supposed to come just for the face treatment...and was I to blame if I kept hearing those messages for them, poor souls, or seeing things they wanted me to see? (II, 848)

Cora's preoccupation with the guilt she experiences over her alleged clairvoyance ("I made it all straight with Father Divott years ago" [II, 848-849], she says) is germane to the ensuing story about her deception of Mrs Clingsland. The passage cited above sows in the reader's mind the suspicion that Cora tends to deceive herself, a suspicion that has become a certainty by the end of the story. The clairvoyance can be put into question by the conscious emphasis in Cora's tone at certain points. It is not Wharton's habit to italicize words to indicate rhetorical stress; usually the statement itself is left to carry any desired emphasis. The italicizing of "had" and "did" in Cora's apologia above suggests that the lady protests too much. More tellingly perhaps Cora gives away her hand when she asks if she should be blamed for "seeing things they wanted me to see." (Did her "voices" tell her only what she wanted to hear? Was she never warned of impending disaster?) Perhaps what Cora "made straight with Father Divott years ago" was her breaching of the truth as well as her participation in a forbidden activity.

"The wrong I did to Mrs. Clingsland" is the concern of Cora for the major part of the story. The wrong itself, the duping of Mrs Clingsland into believing that her young lover speaks to her from the other world, his words transmitted to her by Cora, is but one aspect of the story-teller's revelation. Cora's recapitulation of events, though genial and humorous, is a complex of many serious elements: a rationalization of her actions, an explanation and attempted justification of her material success, an attempt to explain away Mrs Clingsland's self-centredness and vainglory, an attempt to implicate Divine Providence in events as a way of self-justification. The portrait of the lower middle-class Irish-Catholic masseuse and beautician that emerges from the story-teller's own narration is possibly the best representation of a middle-class woman in the whole Wharton short-story oeuvre.

Cora's depiction of Mrs Clingsland must be seen in the light of her attitude toward those "people prowling about in the background that I didn't like the look of: people, you understand, that live on weak women that can't grow old" (II, 850). She speaks of a woman who had "sucked people dry selling them the news they wanted, like she was selling them a forbidden drug" (II, 851-852). Effectively, Cora may be said to take her place among the very people she condemns, for the false information she provides to her mistress had resulted in material advantage to herself and her family. For years the Attlee family has known—"(though they did not know why) that it was through [Mrs. Clingsland's] help that Grandmother Attlee had been able, years ago, to buy the little house at Montclair, with a patch of garden behind it, where, all through the depression, she had held out, thanks to fortunate investments made on the advice of Mrs. Clingsland's great friend, the banker" (II, 845). By the end of her grandmother's story Moyra knows why, of course, but she also learns something of the rationalization and opportunism the old woman has used in the securing of her material advantage. Cora makes little attempt to conceal her taking advantage of Mrs Clingsland. Recalling her interceding with her mistress on behalf of the impoverished and sickly young man whose assistance she has coopted in her grand deception, she remarks: "So I used to keep the poor young fellow well looked after, and cheered up with dainties. And you'll never make me believe there was anything wrong in that—or in letting Mrs. Clingsland help me with the new roof on this house, either" (II, 854). Again, recalling seeking Mrs Clingsland's help at the time of the young man's death, she says, "I had hard work making her believe there was no end to the masses you could say for a hundred dollars; but somehow it's comforted me ever since that I took no more from her that day. I saw to it that Father Divott said the masses and got a good bit of the money" (II, 858). Statements such as these bring a somewhat harsher light to bear on Cora's earlier explanation of her decision to deceive Mrs Clingsland; "What I was after was to make her believe in herself again, so that she'd be in a kindlier mind toward others" (II, 852). Assuredly she has been a major beneficiary of the kindlier mood induced in her patroness by her deception.

A large part of Cora's preoccupation in the story of her duping of Mrs Clingsland is with the attempt to salvage some good, some "kindness," for a woman she clearly believes to be without much redeeming quality. Mrs Clingsland neglects her husband, ignores her daughter, and manipulates her son shamelessly, and Cora is clearly aware of this, rendering the details of her employer's unconcern within her own family and sometimes managing the details so that Mrs Clingsland will not appear in too bad a light. Mrs Clingsland's treatment of her children is a case in point. She has coddled her son as a toddler, "[b]ut when his long legs grew out of the pants, and they sent him to school, she said he wasn't her own little cuddly baby any more" (II, 849). Then, when he has become a young man she has had him escort her to lunch and cabarets, fawning on the deflected attention she imagines his attractiveness brings her, until he realizes he is being used. Cora's assessment of the relationship of Mrs Clingsland and her daughter points to her tendency to rationalize away the mother's faults: the daughter was of "a plain face and plain words,... With her mother she was cold and scared; so her mother was cold and scared with her" (II, 849).

As she is, in her own way, open in admitting that she has benefitted from Mrs Clingsland's largesse, so is Cora honest about her motivation for whitewashing the outrageous conduct of her patroness. It is to Cora's advantage to believe that Mrs Clingsland is an essentially loving woman, that her near-absolute self-absorption and vanity masks the real person underneath, for it justifies her taking extraordinary measures, *i.e.*, simulating supernatural intervention, "to make [Mrs. Clingsland] believe in herself again" (II, 852). Yet Cora's insistence on the older woman's goodness is shot through with doubt, just as is her attempt to justify duping her and using her to her own advantage. Thus, her story of "the wrong I did to Mrs. Clingsland" is characterized by ambivalence.

The kind of self-questioning and guilt that underlies much of Cora's story is a factor of her adherence to the Roman Catholic faith. In the first place, Cora's speech is spiked with Catholic references: Catholicism flows as naturally from her as does her occupation of masseuse and beautician. The sight of Mrs Clingsland lying disconsolately in bed, in tears at the thought that her advancing years have shorn her of her beauty, moves Cora to the sentiment that she looks like "a martyred saint on an altar" (II, 846) and to the question: "But what are you saying to me about beauty, with that seraph's face looking up at me this minute?" (II, 847). The familiarity with Catholicism evidenced here surfaces most visibly in Cora's knowledge of the Church's theology of sin, guilt, and reconciliation. As a younger woman, she claims, she has continued exercising her clairvoyant gifts "though I knew the Church was against it" (II, 848), but she has since confessed her sin to Father Divott and discontinued its practice. (Whether or not she possessed and made use of clairvoyance is not so much the point here as her recognition of the Church's attitude to that activity and her acceptance of the doctrine of confession and forgiveness.)

Cora's preoccupation with her offenses to Mrs Clingsland is brought into relief by and directly related to her repentant attitude about her forbidden practice of clairvoyance. Her phrasing of this preoccupation, put as a direct question to Moyra, is the pivotal element of "The Looking Glass," for it demonstrates the ambivalence about the speaker that helps to make her the amusing person she is: "And I hope I'm a good Catholic, as I said to Father Divott the other day, and at peace with heaven, if ever I was took suddenly—but no matter what happens I've got to risk my punishment for the wrong I did to Mrs. Clingsland, because as long as I've never repented it there's no use telling Father Divott about it. Is there?" (II, 844). Again Cora demonstrates her knowledge of moral theology: because she has benefitted from and continues to benefit from the material advantage her deception of Mrs Clingsland has brought her, she cannot repent, and she cannot be given absolution in the confessional for the wrong done to Mrs Clingsland. Thus her quandary, and her attempt to relieve herself of her guilt by making her non-sacramental confession to Moyra.

But it is difficult to take Cora's moral dilemma very seriously—and questionable that she is very distraught about it herself, for details of the story conspire to delineate Cora as more a figure of amusement than of moral concern. If Mrs Clingsland is a person who is more to be pitied than censured, Cora beguiles and bemuses more than she shocks. She is reminiscent of those Shakespearean comic characters (Falstaff of *Henry IV*, Part I, for example) who in their attempts to extricate themselves from predicaments of their own making, devise the most outlandish rationalizations and become ludicrous in the process. Cora implicates God and Father Divott both in her deceptions. Seeing at one point how circumstances seem to play so readily into her hands, she remarks: "But it's wonderful, as Father Divott says, how Providence sometimes seems to be listening behind the door" (II, 853). She prays for Divine help in the working out of her deceptive plan, taking care "to say a Novena against Father Divott finding me out" (II, 854). Noting that she has given Father Divott a portion of Mrs Clingsland's donation for masses for the repose of the soul of her accomplice she ripostes to Father Divott's refusal (as she anticipates) to give her absolution by saying, "so he was a sort of accomplice too, though he never knew it" (II, 858).

How reconcile Cora's evident need to unload her conscience with the cavalier manner of her confession? Perhaps Wharton accomplishes this through an early statement of her primary omniscient narrator: "Like many humble persons of her kind and creed, she had a vague idea that a sin unrevealed was, as far as the consequences went, a sin uncommitted; and this conviction had often helped her in the difficult task of reconciling doctrine and practice" (II, 845). In any case, "The Looking Glass" brings this narratorial observation and its practitioner to life most vividly. The story may also reflect, as radically different as its central character is from its author, something of the dilemma Catholicism posed for Wharton towards the end of her life.

"All Souls'"

"All Souls'," Wharton's last completed short story, was published posthumously in *Ghosts*, the only story in that collection that had not seen print previously. It has won much praise and been the subject of many interpretations. Leon Edel saw in "the acute and eerie sense of absence, separation, desertion [and] panic" Wharton's foresight of her own death (White 106). For Allan Gardner Smith the story suggests "several lines of thought." He reads it as "a parable of frustration...in which Mrs. Claymore [sic] fantasizes a situation which expresses [her] sexual desires in suitably censored and transformed version"—all of this amplified by the suggestion of the text that her servants have "gone to join an orgiastic coven" (150). Smith sees "All Souls'" as well as a dramatization "of the psychic deformations entailed by Mrs. Claymore's [sic] inheritance of an authoritarian male position in relation to the house and servants" (151), and as a documentation of Wharton's "interest in the haunting *by absence* (Smith's italics) in everyday life rather than by presence in an extraordinary one" (151). In a more recent comment on "All Souls'" Barbara White makes an interesting case for reading the story as yet another fictionalization of "the incest secret" that haunted Wharton for much of her life.

Undoubtedly "All Souls'" has the capacity to support a variety of readings, to concretize different subtexts. Yet its pure spectral quality dominates, and in this light its narrative perspective is of particular interest. Sara Clayburn has spoken of her experiences of some years before to a cousin, probably female, who has then decided to transcribe them in the interests of clarifying her cousin's story in order to counter versions of it "that have become so exaggerated, and often so ridiculously inaccurate" (II, 879). There is about both Sara's transmission of events and the narrator's recapitulation of them much that is tentative and uncertain. "I'll efface myself, and tell the tale," the narrator says, " not in my cousin's words, for they were too confused and fragmentary, but as I built it up gradually out of her half-avowals and nervous reticences. If the thing happened at all—and I must leave you to judge of that—I think it must have happened in this way..." (II, 881). It is the perceived and created story of the narrator that is the substance of "All Souls'," not some experienced event. This is possibly what the narrator has in mind when she says early in her account, "[T]his isn't exactly a ghost story" (II, 880): Sara's ghost and experience may have a reality only in her mind and in the verbal rendering of the narrator. Enigmatically then, this most ghostly of Wharton's tales, the one that elicits most convincingly the experience of fright, the one in which the narrator's account captures the fear that characterized Sara's alleged experience and does not allow extraneous matters to diffuse its effects, the one inscribed so long after the supposed occurrences took place, is but a subjective construction. Whereas Wharton in her other ghost stories most often attempts to convince us of the reality of her ghosts, here the very authenticity and reality of Sara's experience is put into question. And yet the story delivers on the promise of the title of the volume for which it was specifically written.

The presence that sets in motion the two periods of Sara's terror is, in the narrator's opinion, "either a 'fetch' [the apparition of a living person] or else...a living woman inhabited by a witch" (II, 896). In either case the woman Sara meets on consecutive All Souls' eves[83] betrays herself as spectral, particularly in her second appearance, by the repetition of the circumstances of Sara's first meeting with her, and by her sudden disappearance when Sara pursues her behind the clump of hemlocks. She functions, effectively, as a ghost, and although her presence in the story is minimal, she is seen as the *sine qua non* of Sara's terror.

That terror is brought on and gradually increased by the silence in which Sara soon feels herself to be totally immersed. In severe pain, in need of assistance because of a serious injury to her ankle, she is made anxious by the reality of her isolation, but the silence of her house comes to outweigh even practical considerations of her state of health and becomes a force of its own, taking on a palpable, sinister, virtually embodied presence: an "inexorable and hostile silence,...an impenetrable substance made out of the world-wide cessation of all life and all movement" (II, 887). Sara senses that the silence "accompanied her...moving watchfully at her side, as though she were its prisoner and it might throw itself upon her if she attempted to escape" (II, 888-889).

As her sense of anxiety increases, Sara begins to image the silence in terms of the snow falling outside. Initially on the day of her ordeal "the snowy morning seemed almost reassuring," but as she becomes aware of her isolation, the silence "seemed to be piling itself up like the snow on the roof and in the gutters" (II, 885). Now, "in this snowy winter light [the house] seemed immense, and full of ominous corners around which one dared not look" (II, 887), and "the quality of the silence which enveloped her" had "no break, no thinnest crack in it anywhere. It had the cold continuity of the snow which was still falling steadily outside" (II, 888).

But Wharton does not stop at the graphic description of the atmosphere of Sara's growing anguish: she interiorizes it as well, recording the physical manifestations of fear and terror within her protagonist. As Sara becomes conscious that something is amiss in her house, "[s]he began to feel a nervous apprehension" (II, 884). Picking up the telephone receiver, "she noticed that her hand trembled," and when she realizes there is no telephone communication with the outside, "[h]er heart began to hammer" (II, 885). Later, aware of her total isolation, "her latent fear...was like an icy liquid running through every vein, and lying in a pool about her heart." And as she approaches the kitchen and hears a man's voice—the first sound that has broken the relentless silence—she is "cold with fear" (II, 889).

When on All Souls' eve of the following year Sara makes her escape from Whitegates, her flight to New York triggered by the afternoon reappearance of the strange woman she meets walking near her home, we are given more evidence of the horror of her first All Souls' experience: both her extreme state of agitation, as described by her cousin the narrator, who received her in her flat, and the fact of Sara's escape itself, suggesting her anticipated horror at the thought of a repetition of the previous All Souls' experience, vouch for the efficacity of the story as ghost story.

*   *   *   *   *

Revenants, Doubles, and Other Specters

Ghosts is the only one of Wharton's collections of short stories published with a preface, and that preface deals, not surprisingly, with ghosts and ghost stories.[84] The preface was written around the same time as "All Souls" (indeed, certain references occur in both pieces, including one to Osbert Sitwell to the effect that ghost stories have in a modern mechanized age lost much of their force). It seems germane to note that of the stories in *Ghosts*, all but one published in previous Wharton collections, "All Souls'," the new story, is the one that most conforms to the theory developed in the preface. "For the ghost should never be allowed to forget that his only chance for survival," writes Wharton prefatorially, "is in the tales of those who have encouraged him, whether actually or imaginatively—*and perhaps preferably the latter* (Italics mine). It is luckier for a ghost to be vividly imagined than dully 'experienced'" (II, 877). The narrator's and Wharton's building of a tale from the sketchily retold experience of Sara Clayburn is a direct application of Wharton's dictum to narrative practice. The same can be said for "All Souls'" as the practical application of Wharton's view of the element of fright in ghost stories: "...the 'moral issue' question must not be allowed to enter into the estimating of a ghost story. It must depend for its effect solely on what one might call its thermometrical quality; if it sends a cold shiver down one's spine, it has done its job and done it well. But there is no fixed rule as to the means of producing this shiver, and many a tale that makes others turn cold leaves me at my normal temperature" (II, 878). Unlike other Wharton ghost stories where the moral question is decidedly dominant, where the cold shiver is more the product of the reader's recognition of some underlying immorality or enormity than of her feelings of terror and fright, "All Souls'" places the emphasis on the ghostly intrusion that itself inaugurates the emotional and physical impact on the victimized character. In a word, "All Souls'" appears to be a kind of programmed response to the preface of *Ghosts*, the latter essay more applicable to it than to the other stories that have just been discussed.

In the other ten tales that constitute the collection *Ghosts*, the various spectral presences, as real and vital as they may be, are subordinated to those elements that their presence is used to expose or delineate. This subordination of the spectral does not occur in "All Souls'," and sets it apart clearly from its companion pieces. One way to establish this is to note that its central character, Sara Clayburn, is totally overwhelmed by her ghost and ghostly experience. When her cousin, the narrator, introduces her, she likens her to Whitegates, her house—she is solid, stable, "calm, matter-of-fact"—and remarks about "how unlikely it would have seemed that what happened at Whitegates should have happened...to her" (II, 880). Observing Sara moving through her house on a broken ankle, daring to open the pantry slide-door, courageously going from room to room, we are impressed with her physical toughness, her mental and emotional hardiness. But when we see her a year later arriving unannounced at her cousin's apartment in New York, sure now of the supernatural nature of the strange woman she has met again this All Souls' eve, we realize that the indefatigable woman of a year ago is now completely undone by her experience. The ghost has vanquished Sara: her cousin's recapitulation of events emphasizes the domination unequivocally, Wharton's story "All Souls'" is a story of spectral dominance. Nowhere else in *Ghosts* are the stories limited to the kind of absolute ghostly victory that characterizes "All Souls'."

Of the stories examined in this chapter, only one, "The Looking Glass," does not merit the title ghost story. Assuredly it has a ghost of sorts, Mrs

Clingsland's sailor Harry, "who went down on the Titanic" (II, 851) and who is resurrected by Mrs Clingsland and Cora, each for her own purposes. But the story is essentially a humorous one, whose early interest in Harry's ghost soon gets swallowed up in the more down-to-earth elements of Cora Atlee's tale to her granddaughter Moyra. Two of the stories do not have ghosts *per se* but may be said to be ghostly. The ghost in "Miss Mary Pask" is a living woman imagined to be ghostly because the protagonist/narrator who sees her mistakenly believes her to be deceased. The ghost alleged to exist by Mrs Rutledge of "Bewitched" is surely the living woman Venny Brand and not her revenant sister Ora. In two other stories, "The Eyes" and "The Triumph of Night," the mysterious appearances that break in upon characters' consciousness are doubles: in the first, the eyes of which Culwin and the narrator speak are versions of Culwin's eyes; in the second, the spectral person seen only by the point-of-view character, Faxon, is the double of Lavington, the real self that resides behind the hypocritical exterior. The remaining half-dozen tales feature revenants, real presences, some of whom also function as doubles. "The Lady's Maid's Bell's" ghost, Emma Saxon, is clearly Alice Hartley's double and a certain presence in the story. "Afterward's" ghost, the revenant Elwell, is seen not only by his guilt-ridden manipulator, Boyne, but also by Mary Boyne, who is guiltless in his exploitation, and by the servants who have spoken with him on his second visit to Lyng. The dogs of "Kerfol" are absolutely real—if mysterious-looking—to the prospective buyer of the Brittany estate Kerfol. And the ghostly Mr Jones is real enough to the down-to-earth chatelaine of Bells—and surely to his human emissary Mrs Clemm, who is choked to death by him. Finally, in "Pomegranate Seed" and "All Souls'" Wharton presents uncharacteristic spectral manifestations. In the former, the first Mrs Ashby manifests her presence not through a personal appearance but by sending letters from the grave, their grayness and their near-illegibility suggesting their source. In the latter story there is considerable uncertainty in the mind of the narrator about the ghost, shown in her tentativeness about identifying it. "I take it," she says, "that the strange woman who twice came up the drive at Whitegates on All Souls' eve was either a 'fetch,' or else, more probably, and more alarmingly, a living woman inhabited by a witch" (II, 896). In short, Wharton has exploited in these stories a sampling of supernatural possibilities, at the same time varying her narrative methods, using both female and male perspectives, and placing her ghosts in a range of social milieux and physical terrain.

In all the *Ghosts* stories save for "All Souls'," which is totally and unequivocally committed to its spectral effects, and "The Looking Glass," whose spectral element is negligible, ghosts and ghostly manifestations are used in support of themes that relate to human goings-on. In the best of these tales there is an admirable wedding of the supernatural with the natural, in which our understanding of characters' psychology is enhanced by the use of preternatural considerations and effects. In "Afterward," for example, there is a most effective playing off of Mary Boyne's imagined romantic ghost, which she identifies with the newly purchased Lyng, and the very unromantic and actual ghost of Bob Elwell: her recognition, finally, of the truth of her husband's disappearance spells her coming into a more realistic and mature attitude about human beings and ghosts both. In "Bewitched," the ghost conjured up in Prudence Rutledge's imagination, the figure she has envisaged consorting with her husband, is made to be an entirely credible subjective manifestation, given her coldness, her strictness, her representativeness of the long-standing Calvinist tradition. In "The Eyes," we realize that the substantive of the title is not merely a reference to the tortured eyes that stare back at the totally corrupt Andrew Culwin. They in fact allude as well to the unseeing inner eyes of the unnamed narrator. His recapitulation of events, and especially of Culwin's tale, takes place at some time removed from the night in question: "We had been put in the mood for ghosts that evening," his story begins (II, 115). Thus readers are able to ascertain that in the very rendering of his narrative he remains blind to its evil implications.

Indeed, the theme of inner sightlessness, of imaginative unawareness, runs through a considerable number of these ghost stories. First-person involved narrators or third-person narrators in their commentary and dramatic suggestiveness about their reflector characters often reveal themselves or their focus characters to be ignorant of important elements of their make-up. In some cases the lack of awareness is of little consequence to the outcome or larger significance of a story, as in "The Lady's Maid's Bell," for example. Here Alice Hartley's unconscious revelation of her imagistic demonization of Mr Brympton is a means enabling her to come to terms with the questionable relationship of two people she likes: it has little to say about the story's overall purposes but much to say about her character —in what is essentially a first-person tale of character revelation. In another first-person narrative, "Miss Mary Pask," the story-teller's unwitting revelations about himself, as those of the primary narrator in "The Eyes," are of far more dramatic consequence. This dilettantish self-absorbed painter, in his observations about Mary Pask and her sister, shows himself to be removed in grave ways from human commitment and association. In "Pomegranate Seed," the third-person narrator presents us with an equally self-absorbed Charlotte Ashby, whose interior narrative about her relationship to her husband, dominated by "her passionate need to feel herself the sovereign even of [her husband's] past" (II, 767), shows little if any sign of awareness of the liabilities to her marriage of her aggressive and dominant attitudes. "Afterward" and "The Triumph of Night," both third-person-narration stories, are even more explicit in their exploitation of themes of inner blindness. "Afterward's" central character, Mary Boyne, is frequently described, prior to her coming to awareness of the significance of her husband's mysterious visitor, in terms of literal myopia. There are references to "her weak sight" (I, 158), to "her short-sighted gaze" (I, 164), to "her short-sighted eyes" (I, 167). Then, in what might be called the story's climax, the narrator says:

> She opened her eyes with an effort, and they fell on the other portrait. It was of a youngish man, slightly built, with features somewhat blurred by the shadow of a projecting hat brim. Where had she seen that outline before? She stared at it confusedly, her heart hammering in her ears. Then she gave a cry.
> "This is the man—the man who came for my husband!" (I, 174)

In "The Triumph of Night," the theme of Faxon's blindness is emblemized in imagery of night and darkness. Realizing too late that he has failed to save Rainer and himself, Faxon reflects: "And if he had not fled from it, dashed wildly away from it into the night, he might have broken the spell of iniquity, the powers of darkness might not have prevailed" (II, 344). It might be noted here that these themes of the liabilities of inner blindness are pervasive in Wharton's short-story oeuvre: she has successfully used the ghost-story genre to engage one of her favored fictive interests.

An examination of two other ghost stories draws attention to yet another Wharton habit that is visible elsewhere in the canon. "Kerfol" and "Mr. Jones," published twelve years apart, highlight Wharton's penchant for revisiting a story that she seems to have considered unsatisfying or incomplete or in some way improvable. "Kerfol" and "Mr. Jones" are based on similar domestic situations that have occurred at a time considerably removed from the stories' present. In the former, whose past-time segment is set in Brittany in the early seventeenth century, the chatelaine of Kerfol, Anne de Cornault, has been cruelly and sadistically treated by her husband, who suspects that during his frequent absences from home she has engaged in a relationship with another man. The latter story's past-time reference is to early nineteenth-century Sussex. Here the fifteenth Viscount Thudeney of Bells has married the daughter of a wealthy East India merchant, a woman who can neither hear nor speak, and has confined her to Bells from her marriage on, his orders to be carried out by the house's major domo, a Mr Jones. "Kerfol" devotes most of its length to the story of the estranged couple, the story reconstructed by the prospective buyer of the estate from ancient court documents. Its only significant present-time allusion is to the strange-acting dogs the narrator sees on his visit, the revenants of the pet dogs de Cornault has killed to spite his wife. In "Mr. Jones," Wharton redistributes the elements of past and present, bringing the latter to the fore and fashioning a story in which the new owner of Bells, Lady Jane Lynke, confronts the revenant of Mr Jones and learns of his role in the history of her house. "Kerfol" remains a historical romance with ghosts. "Mr. Jones" brings the story's ghost into the present time blending the intrigue of the ghost story with the interest generated by the solving of the mystery of the enigmatic look on the face of the painting of Lady Thudeney in the Blue Room at Bells.

The continuity between Wharton's ghost stories and short fiction as a whole that is illustrated by such thematic and methodological similarities is evident in other areas as well, nowhere more than in the social settings chosen for the stories. Wharton's primary interest in upper-class life is axiomatic, and though the ghost tales do not so much concern themselves with the upper classes as upper classes, they are usually placed in terrain that is identifiable as upper-class. There are exceptions, of course, but the exceptions remind us that in her larger fictional oeuvre Wharton moved from time to time away from her usual milieu. Thus, "Bewitched" occupies the same rural and cultural space as *Ethan Frome*; "The Looking Glass," set in lower-middle-class Bayonne, New Jersey, lines up with such tales as "Mrs. Manstey's View"; in "Miss Mary Pask" we glimpse the artist's world as well as a Brittany seaside house, the abode of the titular character, a home several cuts below the country domains and affluent urban spaces that are the living places of the inhabitants of most of the ghost stories. Brympton, Overdale and Whitegates in the American northeast; Bells and Lyng, in the English countryside; and Kerfol in Brittany, with their bevies of servants and gardeners, their extensive size, their ample grounds, their storied pasts, speak to the social status of their owners and potential buyers. So do the Ashby brownstone in New York and Culwin's well-appointed rooms. All of these settings denote the social status of their owners, and they very often function as well to undercut the pretensions and perceived status of their occupants. In Wharton's stories about upper-class life *per se* such elements take on added significance.

Notes

[78] Jacqueline S. Wilson-Jordan's article, "Telling the Story That Can't be Told: Hartley's Role as Dis-eased Narrator in 'The Lady's Maid's Bell,'" addresses the question of Alice

102

Hartley's first-person narration in this, one of only two Wharton stories that uses a first-person female narrator. In the larger fictive construct that constitutes "The Lady's Maid's Bell," Hartley is indeed *telling* the story that can't be told, as the article's title indicates, and not *writing* it, as Wilson-Jordan insists in her critique.

[79] Janet Ruth Heller argues that the Boynes are secretly alienated from one another and that when Mary confronts Boyne with having conducted unfair business "their underlying alienation has come out into the open" (18). I do not find Heller's argument convincing. The story details quite unequivocally Mary's early attachment to her husband. See Heller. "Ghosts and Marital Estrangements: An Analysis of 'Afterward.'" *Edith Wharton Review*, 10 (Spring 1993): 18-19.

[80] Wharton had at one point entitled the story "The Call" on a typescript, then crossed it off and substituted "Afterward." The typescript in question is in the Edith Wharton Collection at the Beinecke Library, Yale University.

[81] An interesting exception to the lack of critical attention to "Kerfol" is Helen Killoran. "Pascal, Brontë, and 'Kerfol': The Horrors of a Foolish Quartet." *Edith Wharton Review* 10 (Spring 1991): 12-17. Killoran makes an elaborate case for reading the story as a historical murder mystery set during seventeenth- and eighteenth-century Jesuit-Jansenist conflict, and uses certain parallels between Brontë's *Wuthering Heights* and "Kerfol" to suggest that the latter's narrator is unreliable. While the first part of the article is compelling and helps to make sense of the enigmatic reference to Pascal at the end of the story, Killoran's insistence that the narrator is not trustworthy is not convincing. Her argument that he has become lost and has not even found Kerfol is a tenuous one, and her use of his hostess's words, "There isn't one dog at Kerfol" to suggest, again, that he has gone to the wrong place is scarcely germane given the context of the story. (One recalls that the same words are part of the testimony of Anne de Cornault at the trial, and that they are meant there to indicate the supernatural appearance of the dogs on the night of her husband's death.) In any case, whether or not the narrator is deluded, he still has an experience that is consistent with what he learns in the manuscript.

[82] One recalls that Wharton was a Jones, and the story's Mr Jones evokes something of the negative impact of Wharton's father on his daughter's early life.

[83] How explain in the story the error in the dating All Souls' eve? Sara Clayburn encounters her ghost on the final day of October in consecutive years. In the Christian liturgical calendar, October 31 is the eve of All Saints' or All Hallows' day (hence the term Halloween). The eve of All Saints' day is properly November 1, the day before All Souls' day, November 2.

[84] Wharton's preface to *Ghosts* is reproduced in *The Collected Short Stories of Edith Wharton*, Vol. II, pp. 875-878. Page references are to this volume.

Chapter Three

The Upper Class

In calling the present chapter "The Upper Class" and the following one "The Upper Classes," I am making this distinction: the present chapter has as its subject those Wharton stories in which the characters are members of a higher social class who are, generally speaking, relating to people within their own set; the following chapter focuses on stories of people of a higher social class as they relate to people of higher social classes other than their own.

We can assume that most of the stories discussed in this chapter have as their subject the New York upper-class group, however that may be defined in a given story—and it is not defined or identified in anything but a general way in the stories themselves. The setting is most often explicitly New York City or places where upper-crust New Yorkers spend their holidays or leisure time; where New York is not mentioned we can assume that the place is New York or environs. The exceptions to this are two tales set among the Boston elite, the first- and last-published in this group, "The Lamp of Psyche" and "Duration" respectively.

In both Boston stories Wharton makes a point of suggesting the superiority of upper-class Bostonians over New Yorkers, and it is interesting that the New York stories are framed at beginning and end by the Boston pieces. Although it is a truism that the old New York aristocracy had begun its decline before the period when these stories were written and that Wharton included this as an element in her longer fiction, this decline is not an explicit and pervasive theme in this group of short stories, though it is salient in the 1928 tale "After Holbein." What *is* common to virtually all New York stories here is the fixing of attention on members of the upper class as they relate to one another in the married union or in other heterosexual associations.

"The Lamp of Psyche"

"The Lamp of Psyche," published in *Scribner's* in October 1895, has the distinction of being the first story Wharton produced about people of the upper class, the subjects that would occupy her attention in most of her longer fiction and in a substantial proportion of her shorter tales. Although the story has not attracted a great deal of critical attention, it deserves a close look because, as Cynthia Griffin Wolff notes, it stands at "a significantly more distinct remove from [her] first three tales; within a limited context, [Wharton] was beginning to exercise real control over the fictive process"(81). Cued by the title to its use of classical myth (and aided by R.W.B. Lewis's footnote in the *Collected Short Stories* briefly recapitulating the story of Psyche and Cupid) the reader is alerted to Wharton's conscious attempt to ground her story in another fiction so as to avoid the temptation of story-telling that is too overtly autobiographical.

While certainly faithful to the story from which it draws its inspiration, "The Lamp of Psyche" goes far beyond that legend and concocts a rich and realistic fiction of manners around it. In this, the first story in which she puts under scrutiny the social elite into which she was born, Wharton places the coming into the light of her Psyche character, Delia Corbett, against the background of the conflicts and tensions brought on by distinctions between Boston's and New York's upper classes, by differing attitudes in these classes about the disposal of time and money, and to the American Civil War. These conflicts and tensions are artfully blended into a composite of forces which have in various ways formed and which presently affect the story's major characters: Delia; her husband, Laurence; and her Aunt Mary Mason Hayne.

The Corbett marriage has brought together members of Boston and New York society. Delia has been raised in her aunt's Boston home. Laurence "was a New Yorker, and entirely unknown, save by name, to [Delia's] little circle of friends and relations in Boston; but she reflected, with tranquil satisfaction, that, if he were cosmopolitan enough for Fifth Avenue he was also cultured enough for Beacon Street" (I, 47). Laurence had passed the early acid test administered by Aunt Mary, and that, and his obvious knowledge of art and his sophistication and taste in conversation, surely qualified him for admission to Beacon Street society. But if his means and savvy, his travel, his ability to bring himself off satisfactorily in Paris salons qualify him as a cosmopolite by the standards of Fifth Avenue, he is found wanting in the human qualities. In branding his absence from the Civil War as cowardice, Aunt Mary undercuts Laurence's pretentions to any real aristocratic status. And when Delia, alarmed at her aunt's accusation, assesses her husband as "a man who never did anything. His elaborate intellectual processes bore no flower of result; he simply *was*" (I, 53), she has been awakened to the emptiness of even his cultural pursuits. Thus Delia's early judgement about her husband's embodiment of the quintissential virtues of upper-class Boston and New York is put in serious question by the time the couple returns to France.

The inaction that has governed Laurence's life, and the ultimate inaction would be withdrawal from what was considered a just war by Northerners, is in radical contrast to Aunt Mary's activism and altruism. She is, Delia tells her husband, a woman of "kindergartens, and associated charities, and symphony concerts and debating clubs." Though Laurence early on refers to Aunt Mary as "a bundle of pedantries" (I, 46), after meeting her he alters his judgement when he confides to his wife that her relative is "a bundle of extraordinary vitalities" (I, 50). While there is no reason to question the sincerity of his reevaluation, his commendation of Aunt Mary never translates to imitation, nor is there any evidence that he has even seen the possibility that he might devote a small portion of his time and resources to the public good. To Delia's reflection that "In [light of Aunt Mary's life] her own life seemed vacuous, her husband's aims trivial as the subtleties of Chinese ivory carving, and she wondered if [Laurence] walked in the same revealing flash" (I, 51), we must conclude that her enlightenment has not reached him. Not only is his commitment to humanity a token one—Delia admires his "[giving] a coin to a crossing sweeper or [lifting] his hat

106

ceremoniously to one of Mrs. Hayne's maidservants (he was always considerate to poor people and servants)" (I, 54)—but also he fails to conclude that if Aunt Mary is somewhat off the standard in home decoration and personal dress, it is because she invests her enthusiasms, her time, and her money elsewhere. If Aunt Mary's "smoky expanses of canvas 'after' Raphael and Murillo which lurched heavily from the walls" (I, 49) do not match up to Laurence's "fruity bloom of Renaissance bronzes, and the imprisoned sunlight of two or three old pictures" (I, 46), and if her gown might have been "an unaltered one of her mother's," it is because "she never had time to think of her house or her dress" (I, 49).

It is not surprising that as one who is committed to humanitarian causes Aunt Mary would seize on Corbett's defection from the Civil War as a significant flaw in his background. She is evidently of New England Abolitionist stock, and Delia, having been raised in her home, shares her aunt's attitude about emancipation. The spontaniety with which the latter "[descends] from the train into [the African-American chore man Cyrus's] dusky embrace" upon the couple's arrival in Boston says much about her upbringing, and her guilty wish "that [Cyrus] could have been omitted from the function of their arrival" —for "she could not help wondering what her husband's valet might think of him" (I, 48) —suggests her fear about some prejudice being unveiled. A point to be made as well, is that if the lifting of eyebrows that Delia expects Cyrus's presence to bring on does not put in question Corbett's own claims to cosmopolitanism, it at least does bring on a doubt about the broadness of New York society's understanding of that term. And the same comment applies to Corbett's remark about the miniature portrait of the Union soldier he gives Delia: "All the pieties of one's youth seemed to protest against leaving it in the clutches of a Jew pawnbroker in the Rue Bonaparte" (I, 56).

The coming to light in Delia occurs as a result of the dynamic, latent and overt, set up between her husband and her aunt. Left widowed by her first husband, Benson, whom she had married at nineteen "because he had beautiful blue eyes and always wore a gardenia in his coat" (I, 44), she has scarcely settled into her second marriage. Little wonder that her first two months as Mrs Corbett have left her with an idyllic picture of her new state and new husband: Benson had been something of a wastrel, and her first days with Corbett have been spent travelling around Europe and then accomodating herself to lavish lodgings at the Hotel Drouet in Paris. It is hardly surprising that "Love had set his golden crown upon her forehead and the awe of the office allotted her subdued her doubting heart. To her had been given the one portion denied to all other women on earth, the immense, the unapproachable privilege of becoming Laurence Corbett's wife" (I, 42). But in light of Delia's recognition, at firsthand sight, of her aunt's all-out altruistic effort and then of the discovery of Corbett's non-participation in the Civil War (a discovery prompted by Aunt Mary's questioning her on the subject) the most admirable man she has ever met loses much of his stature in his wife's eyes.

If Delia's early idolization of her husband seems far-fetched, it is well to remember, besides the aforementioned circumstances of the new and untried state of the present marriage and the unsatisfactory nature of her first union, that Corbett is in point of fact a man of some quality and that she is still able to think of him, even after she has put his courage in question, as "admirable in every relation of life, kind, generous, upright; a loyal friend, an accomplished gentleman" (I, 54). Aunt Mary's endorsement of Corbett— "He's delightful" (I, 51), she tells her niece—suggests that the latter's admiration of her husband is not altogether misplaced. To be noted is a certain openness on the part of Delia of the rightness of her vision of Corbett, and in repeatedly questioning herself "if to a dispassionate eye he would appear as completely, as supremely well-equipped as she held him, or if she walked in a cloud of delusion, dense as the god-concealing mist of Homer" (I, 45), she reveals that she is not merely an innocent and blind neophyte wife.

Delia's coming to the knowledge of the truth about Corbett, of his not measuring up to the ideal man he has the potential to be, is of two parts. Her initial realization, that compared to Aunt Mary he is a mere dilettante, dissipates under the heat of the possibility of his cowardice. On the couple's return to France, questions of Corbett's life of inaction have disappeared as Delia is calmed by "the recollection of her husband's delightful house in Paris, so framed for a noble leisure" (I, 53). It says much about Delia that her vicarious guilt at the sight of Aunt Mary's feverish commitment and action so easily disappears in the face of the ease and excitement of the times she sees opening up before her: she is as taken by that as her husband is. But she remains plagued by the possibility that Corbett is a coward, to the point of asking him about his military service and branding him with her aunt's epithet.

It is Corbett's acknowledgement of his civic negligence that provides the lamp whereby Delia sees the whole truth about her husband, and she is perceptive enough to realize that his flaw is not merely of the past. "[K]nowing what he had once done," she reflects, "it seemed quite simple to forecast his future conduct. For that long-past action was still a part of his actual being; he had not outlived or disowned it; he had not even seen that it needed defending." Delia's awakening constitutes not merely a disillusion but a fear as well, casting a harsher light than might be expected on the story's close: "for the passionate worship which she had paid her husband she substituted a tolerant affection which possessed precisely the same advantages" (I, 57).

Wolff's statement that "The Lamp of Psyche" shows Wharton "beginning to gain control over the fictive process" (81) is no doubt meant to suggest that the latter was learning how to rid her fiction of an overt autobiographical tone. However, if the tale is an admirable one, "one of her better short stories" (81) Wolff insists, it shows still something of the heavy hand of the apprentice. This is noticeable, for example, in Wharton's over-playing of the symbology of "the crudely executed miniature of an unknown young man in the uniform of a United States cavalry officer" (I, 55). Rather than allow the significance of the breaking of the picture's crystal cover to stand for itself, Wharton explains the symbol in the opening sentence of the story's final paragraph: "Her ideal of him was shivered like the crystal above the miniature of the warrior of Chancellorville" (I,

57). But at the same time one sees the hint of the subtlety and density that would become a hallmark of Wharton's fiction. How aptly and adeptly Wharton characterizes the preeminence in Corbett of art over life in these his comments to Delia about the miniature: "It's awfully bad isn't it? —but some poor soul might be glad to think that it had passed again into the possession of fellow countrymen" and "What a daub! I wonder who he was? Do you suppose that by taking a little trouble one might find out and restore it to his people?" (I, 56).

"The Twilight of the God"

"The Twilight of the God," the first of a pair of stories Wharton wrote in the style of a brief playlet, appeared in her 1899 collection of short fiction, *The Greater Inclination*. As in a drama script, characters' names appear prior to their spoken words, and from time to time what might be called stage directions appear in parentheses. As well, each of the two parts of "The Twilight of the God" is preceded by a brief italicized passage addressing such matters as setting, costumes and "staging." Blake Nevius has commented that here, as in Wharton's early stories and novels generally, "dialogue is frequently Jamesian in its hesitations, seeming *non sequiturs*, and unfinished statements" (35). It might be added that because of the story's drama structure the reader is left without the usual aids towards gaining an understanding of the dialogue: since there is no exposition of the characters' underlying motives or emotional baggage, or of their non-verbal reaction to what is said to them, one arrives with more difficulty than usual at a sense of speakers' verbal intent.

Verbal intent is at the heart of the significance of "The Twilight of the God." The story is made up of two pieces of dialogue, each essentially uninterrupted, spoken on the afternoon of a summer weekend in the Newport, Rhode Island home of a fashionable woman who has been called away to care for a sickly aunt. In the first segment, two guests and close friends of the hostess, Mariana Raynor, the married couple Isabel and Lucius Warland, engage in an exchange that reveals the former as an aggressively witty woman who takes pleasure in out-duelling her husband, a seemingly devoted spouse but one who, having failed in his investments, is seeking a post with the public service in Washington. It is clear from the exchange that the Warland relationship has reached a very tenuous stage, which is not relieved by the imminent arrival of another weekend guest, the former beau of Mrs Warland, a man named Oberville.

Section II features the promised meeting of the reunited lovers and climaxes when Oberville confesses that he has earlier broken off his relationship with Isabel "because I couldn't face a scene!" Oberville's admission that he had been "a damned coward" (I, 147) brings an end to Isabel's dream of a better life: although her former suitor is more her equal in wit and intelligence than is Warland, she opts for the latter's devotedness and plans to use the former's influence in the effort to help her husband obtain the job he wants in Washington.

Thus Wharton repeats the theme she had deployed just a short time before in "The Lamp of Psyche": the disillusion experienced by a woman whose man of choice fails to satisfy her high expectations of him. But compared to the earlier story, "The Twilight of the God" is a frothy handling of the subject. Its form denies it the possibility of being as serious a treatment. While not without its superficial charms, "The Twilight of the God" is somewhat flawed even within the limitations of its chosen form. For one thing, one is tempted to apply Oberville's retort to Isabel, "You speak in enigmas" (I, 149), to a goodly number of the latter's comments especially. As well, the high seriousness suggested by the title is somewhat diminished by the flimsy substance of the story itself. Wharton was aware that her story was not up to the early standard she had set, and she had submitted to her editor Burlingame's request that it be reworked (Wolff 84). It is surely significant that the only time she used the playlet form again, in "Copy," a story published five years later, she returned to the subject of old lovers meeting again, and rid that story of the obtuseness and frivolousness of its predecessor.

"The Mission of Jane"

If "The Mission of Jane," published in the December 1902 issue of *Harper's*, continues Wharton's exploration of the subject of marriage in the upper classes, its perspective and outcome vary considerably from those of her two earlier studies of the same subject, "The Lamp of Psyche" and "The Twilight of the God." Whereas the latter two stories approach the institution of marriage from the perspective of women, this story does so from a male viewpoint. Also, the relationship examined in "The Mission of Jane" develops from a weak and problematical to a more successful one, in contrast to the relationships in the earlier tales, in which the marital relationships are seen to be in a state of decline.

Although "The Mission of Jane" enters into its examination of the marriage of Julian and Alice Lethbury at an unspecified point in its age, it is clear that the couple is still young enough to have children. It is clear as well that the relationship is in a state of stasis: the spouses seem to be conditioned to accepting the fact that each, for his or her own reasons, is set in a rather unrewarding and bland association: Lethbury is disappointed with what he perceives to be the intellectual dullness and naiveté of his wife; Alice is embarrassed by and resentful of the show of superiority that characterizes his comments and attitudes to her. Having clearly established this habitual condition of the Lethbury union, "The Mission of Jane" proceeds to tell the story of the rejuvenation of the marriage, wrought by the arrival of the adopted baby Jane.

The anticipation and arrival of the infant in the Lethbury household sets off profound changes in the attitudes of the new parents towards their marriage and towards one another, and in this the story maintains its serious perspective. The transformation for the better effected in Lethbury is especially striking, for it places him in sharp contrast to a goodly number of Wharton male protagonists in the other stories. Many of these latter show themselves to be irretrievably arrogant, self-satisfied, and condescending in their human associations. Although as we see him early in the story Lethbury seems struck from that mold, he soon reveals his capacity for acquiring self-knowledge, and his ability to acknowledge his errors and insensitivity. When Alice opens her heart to him about their past together, he is startled and moved by the loneliness of her life; he "groaned" at the emptiness of her days when she tells him, "Sometimes I've felt that when dinner was ordered I had nothing to do till the next day" (I, 366). And "in his rapid reconstruction of the past he found himself cutting a shabbier figure than he cared to admit. He had always been intolerant of stupid people, and it was his punishment to be convicted of stupidity" (I, 367). Lethbury's awareness of his wife's suffering and of his own part in it deters him from anything but complete cooperation in Alice's plan for adoption, although his insistence on retaining the baby's name, Jane, rather than re-christening her a more lady-like Muriel or Gladys betrays the social reservations he has about the adoption procedure. As for Alice herself, the child transforms her: "The girlish bubbling of merriment that had seemed one of her chief graces in the early days" (I, 367) has returned.

But if Jane's adoptive parents are initially buoyed by the infant's arrival, the child's development from childhood to young adulthood brings on a series of problems for the parents and for the couple as an entity that ultimately sends them to their knees in the face of Jane's overwhelming presence within the family, and they long for their daughter's departure to a family of her own. This stage in Jane's growth and the effect she has on family and household triggers Wharton's whimsical sense, and the story takes on a decidedly humorous and satiric tone. Speaking of the inevitable concerns about the growing child's health, the narrator writes: "But her unknown progenitors had given her a robust constitution, and she passed unperturbed through measles, chicken pox and whooping cough. If there was any suffering it was endured vicariously by Mrs. Lethbury, whose temperature rose and fell with the patient's, and who could not hear Jane sneeze without visions of a marble angel weeping over a broken column" (I, 371). Here Wharton makes use of hyperbole and anti-climax for comic effect. In other places the narrative of Jane's development is given a mock-parable turn, as when Alice tells Julian "after one of Jane's historical flights," i.e., her pseudo-dissertations on historical events: "She is getting too clever for me, but I am so glad that she will be a companion to you" (I, 372). The story's strongest satire comes in its portrayal of Winstanley Budd, Jane's suitor and eventual husband. Writes the narrator: "Politeness gushed from [Budd] in the driest seasons. He was always performing feats of drawing-room chivalry, and the approach of the most unobtrusive female threw him into attitudes which endangered the furniture.... [T]he velocity of Mr. Budd's gyrations increased with the ardor of courtship, his politeness became incandescent, and Jane found herself the center of a pyrotechnical display culminating in the 'set piece' of an offer of marriage" (I, 375).

In the end, after the comic suspense caused by Jane's deferring of her decision to accept Budd's offer, the Lethburys are relieved and assuaged by the daughter's departure. It is a sign of Wharton's (or her editors') lack of confidence in the story's ability to make its own point that it ends with the explicit "Jane had fulfilled her mission after all; she had drawn them together at last" (I, 379). But at the same time, the tale, the first in which Wharton looked at her own set with a wry eye, unquestionably establishes her comic and satiric gifts. The appearance of "The Mission of Jane" predated the 1905 publication of *The House of Mirth* by only three years. And though the satire in that novel is put to a more serious purpose the two works have important common traits, not the least of which is that wonderful wedding of word and phrase, of sense and tone, that would become a Wharton hallmark.

"The Dilettante"

Published in *Harper's* in December 1903, "The Dilettante" resembles two slightly earlier Wharton stories, "The Twilight of the God" and "Copy," that appeared in 1899 and 1900 respectively. The two earlier tales are constructed as brief dramas with characters' names preceding their spoken words and with stage directions written in parentheses and fitted into the text.[85] In "The Dilettante" Wharton uses the conventional short story format, yet the latter two thirds of the story comprises a dialogue between the major characters which has the immediacy and urgency of a dramatic script. Wharton had no doubt learned something about the structuring of dialogue from her experience writing the two earlier playlets. She had probably come to realize as well that her experiments in dramatic form had not provided her with the depth and detail available in the less restricted narrative format of the short story.

One sees the advantage provided to the story-teller by the narrated form in "The Dilettante" when one realizes what Wharton is about: the laying bare of the character of the heartless young dilettante Thursdale. In order to see clearly the significance of the unmasking that occurs during Thursdale's conversation with his friend Mrs Vervain, we must be made aware of the Thursdale whose seven-year relationship with Mrs Vervain has been marked by a fear of and a withdrawal from love, involvement, and commitment. Wharton effects this in the opening third of the story, in which her third-person narrator, who assumes the point of view of Thursdale, exposes the reflections of his protagonist as the latter decides to pay a late-afternoon visit to Mrs Vervain, after seeing his lately acquired fiancée, Ruth Gaynor, off at the train station. The critic Barbara White makes the point that Wharton's choice of Thursdale as the point-of-view character is fortuitous: "Thursdale's cruelty to Vervain, which is based clearly on his sense of male entitlement ... is effectively presented through his own thoughts. The feelings, perceptions, and reactions of the 'reflecting mind,'as Wharton calls it in 'Telling a Short Story,' characterize it more tellingly than an outside view" (59).

The narrator's description of Thursdale's impulse to visit his friend—"he had felt the dilettante's irresistible craving to take a last look at a work of art that was passing out of his possession" (I, 411)—aptly encapsulates major elements of the story. It characterizes Thursdale as one who has, after an unhappy brush with the emotional life early in his career, dealt with women in a desultory and superficial manner and used them to pass the time. It points to the fact that Thursdale has formed Mrs Vervain to his own design, and in a very real sense has controlled and monopolized her, possessed her, for seven years. It suggests that because of the recent appearance of Ruth Gaynor on the scene, Mrs Vervain is now disposable. At the heart of Thursdale's forming of Mrs. Vervain and at the heart of the story's significance is the suppression of outward emotional display. Thursdale "had taught a good many women not to betray their feelings, but he had never before had such fine material to work with [as Mrs Vervain]... she had acquired under the discipline of his reticences and evasions, a skill almost equal to his own..."(I, 412). His tutoring of Mrs Vervain in "the science of evasion" (I, 411) has allowed him to rationalize away her profound attachment to him, a fact that becomes evident during the course of their conversation, while he retains the benefit of her time, attention, and material means. It is an eloquent testimony to Thursdale's overweening selfishness and egoism that his finding Mrs Vervain at home "struck [him] as another proof of his friend's good taste that she had been in no undue haste to change her habits. The whole house appeared to count on his coming..." (I, 413).

It is also a sign of Thursdale's twisted sense of the order of things that he has reversed the usual moral positions of spontaneity and dissimulation, placing the second above the first as a desirable human trait. Mrs Vervain's agitated response to Thursdale's surprise visit and his reaction to it illustrate this penchant in him:

> "You?" she exclaimed, and the book she held slipped from her hand.
> It was crude, certainly, unless it were a touch of the finest art. The difficulty of classifying it disturbed Thursdale's balance. (I, 413)

Thursdale's use of the word 'crude,' and on one occasion, of the word 'crass,' to designate spontaneous, words, actions, and gestures recurs a number of times in the story and underlines his long-standing commitment to the attitude it betrays. Of a younger Mrs Vervain he says, "She had been surprisingly crude when he first knew her, capable of making the most awkward inferences, of plunging through thin ice, of recklessly undressing her emotions" (I, 412). Now the story of the undressing of the refinements that had always marked the Thursdale-Vervain relation is signalled in the successive use of the terms 'crude' and 'crass'. In the first case Mrs Vervain is telling her friend that Gaynor had visited her privately "to know if anything had happened."

"Had happened?" he gazed at her slowly. "Between you and me?" he said with a rush of light.

The words were so much cruder than any that had ever passed between them, that the color rose to her face; but she held his startled gaze. (I, 435)

Then Mrs Vervain's exposition of the details of his fiancée's visit to her strikes Thursdale even closer to the bone:

At last [Mrs Vervain] said slowly: "She came to find out if you were really free."

Thursdale colored again. "Free?" he stammered, with a sense of physical disgust at contact with such crassness. (I, 516)

Finally, it is Thursdale himself who actively involves himself in the "crudeness" that he has hitherto merely "heard" and commented on. Here, Mrs Vervain is explaining Ruth Gaynor's decision to withdraw from the proposed marriage because there has been no sexual liaison between Thursdale and Mrs. Vervain:

"That's just it," [says Mrs Vervain]. "The unpardonable offense has been in our not offending."

He flung himself down despairingly: "I give up! What did you tell her?" he burst out with sudden crudeness. (I, 417)

But of course what Thursdale perceives as crudeness is ultimately saving, and probably for the first time since its inception, the dialogue between them is carried on at a natural and spontaneous level. They both blush freely because they say things, hitherto left unsaid, which cause them embarrassment. In the end "It was extraordinary how a few words had swept them from an atmosphere of the most complex dissimulations to this contact of naked souls" (I, 418). For the first time Thursdale allows himself to see the complete love Mrs Vervain bears him, as she admits that his affections have irrevocably gone to a rival.

The reader never gets to meet that rival, but on the basis of the words of the two principal characters she stands as testimony to the power of simplicity and directness. Mrs Vervain, reporting to Thursdale on her recent interview with the young woman, admits she is no match for the latter. "...I have never known a girl like her; she had the truth out of me with a spring" (I, 417, Mrs Vervain tells Thursdale, the specific truth she is alluding to being the fact that she has never been Thursdale's mistress. And on her ensuing recapitulation of Ruth Gaynor's response to this information, Mrs Vervain points out that the young woman is one whose style is driven by substance and not form when she remarks of her that "she mixed her metaphors a little" (I, 417).

As for Thursdale, the breaking away from his long-developed accent on form over substance during his interview with his old friend equates to his burgeoning recognition of the truth, and the narration of the conversation between the two is as permeated with references to light coming to their minds as it is to the aforementioned examples of the vocabulary of crudeness.   When Mrs Vervain exclaims, "How you must care!—for I never saw you so dull" (I, 418), she is acknowledging the fact that Thursdale is abandoning his own instruction. And although it may be seen to be in Thursdale's favor that he chooses not to seize the option his friend offers him and thus "save" the two women of the moment, it must be remembered that it is totally in character for him to remain uninvolved and uncommitted.   The irony of Thursdale's position in the end, that now that the enlightened man might very well be a worthy partner for Ruth Gaynor she has already rejected him, should not be overemphasized: his carefully cultivated habits of a lifetime can surely not be expected to disappear in an instant, and his sense of loss may very well be accompanied by considerable relief.

By the time Thursdale is ready to leave Mrs Vervain's, he has realized the entire truth about the utter devotion of his hostess.   As it becomes apparent that Mrs Vervain will doubly jeapordize her own reputation by allowing herself to be perceived by Ruth Gaynor as both mistress and liar, "something in [Thursdale] cracked...and the rift let in new light" (I, 418).   The story's final moment is given to Mrs Vervain: "The door closed on [Thursdale], and she hid her eyes from the dreadful emptiness of the room" (I, 419).   It would be inaccurate to read this close as melodramatic, for the description of the woman that it embodies sustains the projection of her that informs the entire story. Her blindness vis-à-vis the evil in Thursdale is at its most pronounced when she speaks to him of the letter of rejection Ruth Gaynor has sent him: "There will be no letter," she tells him. "I mean that she's been with you since I saw her—she's seen you and heard your voice. If there is a letter she has recalled it—from the first station, by telegraph" (I, 419). If Mrs Vervain's conversation had the effect of bringing enlightenment to Thursdale, she herself has remained blind—to the strength of Ruth Gaynor's resolve, to the pathological attachment she retains for Thursdale. The "new light" that Thursdale receives is surely an awareness of the extent to which he has been responsible for the present condition of his longtime friend.

"The Dilettante" is one of those Wharton stories that has received little attention by critics. The early commentator E.K. Brown was right in praising it highly, and it belongs on the list of neglected Wharton tales that should be brought to public attention. It is probably the Wharton story that is the most Jamesian: in the subtleties of the depicted mental processes, in the refinement of the dialogues and of the language generally, in the psychological sophistication of the theme. It is a small gem, a model of brilliance, economy, and precision.

"In Trust"

From time to time in the Wharton short fiction *oeuvre* one comes across a pair of stories that have close thematic or formal similarity, the second of which shows a marked artistic improvement over an earlier one that has pre-dated it by only a short time. Such is the case with, "The Portrait" (1899) and "The Potboiler" (1901), as well as with "The Twilight of the God" (1899) and "The Dilettante" of the present chapter. "In Trust" and the later "The Verdict" can also be seen to have the same kind of interrelationship. "In Trust," published in April 1906 in *Appleton's Booklover's* magazine, has as a major theme the stultifying effect produced on a man who is committed to a philanthropic project by his entry into a moneyed marriage. The theme is revisited in "The Verdict," published two years later.

"In Trust" begins with little hint given of its eventual concerns. Its unnamed narrator, speaking in the first person, introduces himself and two fellow Harvard graduates, Paul Ambrose and Ned Halidon, "in the good days, just after we left college" (I, 616). By the time the story ends Ambrose and Halidon have undertaken successive marriages to a woman, Daisy, and the great architectural undertaking dreamed of by Ambrose and strongly supported by his two friends, the building of an Academy of Arts, remains unaccomplished. Because the story covers such an extended period of time and such a span of the life circumstances of the narrator's two friends, it lacks the immediacy of many Wharton stories and stands in radical distinction to "The Verdict," the tale to which it may be seen to bear some thematic and substantial resemblance. The fact that it is told by a first-person narrator who is at some distance from his friends and from Daisy, and the fact that he rarely introduces Daisy to us directly—he is only once himself in her company, and then briefly—have much to do with the story's attenuation: because Daisy is at the heart of the failure of Ambrose's grand plan to be realized and because both her husbands seem powerless to counter her effective (but not malicious) sabotaging of the plan, the story's narrative rather than dramatic approach to the dynamic of the marriages stands in the way of its ultimate artistic success.

In its early stages "In Trust" is centered on Ambrose's inaction in the face of his proposed enterprise. Ambrose admits that "Big sums frighten me" (I, 619) and that the project needs a Halidon to see it through successfully. Thus the stage is set for the latter's ultimate failure to effect what Ambrose himself could not. The foundation of the story's conclusion is laid in the ironic closing paragraph of its first section, in words spoken by Halidon: "Heaven knows what will become of the scheme, if Paul doesn't live to carry it out. There are a lot of hungry Ambrose cousins who will make one gulp of his money, and never give a dollar to the work. Jove, it *would* be a fine thing to have a carrying out of such a plan—but he'll do it yet, you'll see he'll do it yet!" (I, 620).

The dimming and eventual quenching of Halidon's aspirations by the wet blanket of Daisy's and her family's material needs is observed by the narrator from the outside. Indeed, the latter sees the erosion of Ambrose's design even within the latter's own marriage. He sees the manifestations of this erosion in the improvement of the quality of his friend's cigars, the growing stylishness of his wife's attire, and the frequency and extension of the young family's travels. When he visits the new Daisy Halidon, the narrator is convinced that: "*She's* not living for anything but her own happiness," but cannot understand why the husband has reneged on his commitment. As time goes by he notices that Halidon "had thickened—thickened all through. He was heavier, physically, with the ruddiness of good living rather than of hard training (I, 624); that "he was duller" (I, 626); that he is caught between embarrassment about the misplacement of Ambrose's money and rationalization of his and Daisy's use of it. In the end the narrator understands that Halidon has capitulated to Daisy's imperatives, and by leaving the marriage he has the relief of ceasing to be "[Ambrose's] pensioner—seeing his dreams turned into horses and carpets and clothes—" (I, 630).

Halidon does retain his dream, if in a quixotic way. His last words to the narrator are of "Paul's work." "It won't come in *my* day, of course—" he says. "I've got to accept that, but my boy's a splendid chap, and I tell you what it is old man. I believe when he grows up *he'll put it through*" (I, 631). Halidon's three-year-old son, Daisy's son, is hardly a realistic repository of his father's hopes that Paul's work will be revived, and in the detail of Halidon's escape to the Mananas somewhere in "the East" we see reiterated, in the use of the place-name, the empty aspiration suggested in his paean to Daisy's son.

"In Trust" ends with a brief scene set in the narrator's club, where he hears other men speaking of Halidon's death and feels compelled to correct casual acquaintances about the false impression they have of his friend. "I never knew a man who had better reason for wanting to live!" (I, 631) he retorts to one who had noticed Halidon's despair. The narrator's remark reveals once more his own sense of the betrayal of Ambrose's objective and of the frustration and shame Halidon experienced in his failure. It also reminds us that the narrator has been from the beginning a prod to Halidon's conscience. In thus making himself the center of consciousness the narrator draws attention away from the loci of tension in the story, its two marriages. This is, as much as anything else, the reason why "In Trust" attracts our attention in only a casual way. The absence of critical commentary is testimony to the weakness of "In Trust."

"The Choice"

"The Choice," first published in *Century* in November 1908, harks back to earlier Wharton stories in which she aired, in transparent disguise, her problematical relationship to her husband, Teddy. Like her first batch of tales in the 1890's, some of which she regarded as "the excesses of youth...and written at the top of [her] voice" (*LEW* 360), and which she withheld from volume collection, "The Choice" was initially of some embarrassment to her. Written on May 8, 1908 at one sitting during an Atlantic crossing (Wolff 151) the piece was not collected until 1916. R.W.B. Lewis writes, with reference to Wharton's withholding it from her 1908 collection, *The Hermit and the Wild Woman*, that "Edith had perhaps recoiled a little from its naked virulence, though after revising it somewhat (and after another period of life with Teddy) she liked it well enough to give it to the *Century* for an autumn issue" (*EW* 233).

Lewis also reminds us of the nature of the story's evocation of Wharton's marital predicament: "'The Choice' is about a married woman who wishes above all things that her husband would die. Cobham Stilling, like Teddy Wharton, is a trustee of his wife's estate, and as the story opens...has speculated or gambled away a good portion of it. But it is not impending financial ruin, it is the man himself who has driven Isabel Stilling to the verge of frenzy and into the arms of a lover. Stilling is addicted only to good cigars and water sports..." (*EW* 228). Lewis's biographical commentary is echoed by other critics as well, notably Cynthia Wolff (151-152) and Shari Benstock (186), and in fact most of the criticism of "The Choice" is limited to its reflectiveness of Wharton's unhappy marriage and to her admission of Fullerton to her intimate life. But although "The Choice" is not by any means a superior tale—E.K. Brown calls it mediocre and says it should have been let die in *Century* (27)—it deserves to be looked at in its own right as a story of upper-class life, and abstracted from its autobiographical considerations. It is certainly interesting in its depiction of a parasitical husband and a wife/mother caught up in an untenable plight of conflicting loyalties.

"The Choice" is set in Highfield, a summer resort where the wealthy New Yorker Cobden Stilling presides over his mansion The Red House and his property of "many horses...many green-houses...many servants...and three motors and a motorboat for the lake" (II, 345), gloating among the locals over a prestige he doesn't enjoy with his peers in New York. His pride in and flaunting of his impressive toys, especially his new motorboat, signal the primacy of the pleasure principle in Stilling and mark him as a boy/man, one whose affluence is put on flamboyant display and to the service of his own enjoyment. One is given a strong sense of the child in Stilling when, without the courage to inform his wife about a recent financial loss and about his intention to have her "sign a note for it" (II, 349), he begs his lawyer, Austin Wrayford, to perform these services for him. Stilling's juvenile handling of this situation is evident in his response to Wrayford's embarrassment and hesitancy about acceding to his client's wish: "And she'll take it better from you; she'll *have* to take it from you. She's proud. You can take her out for a row tomorrow morning—look here, take her out in the motor launch if you like. I mean to have a spin in it myself, but if you'll tell her—"(II, 349). His childish proffer of a reward to Wrayford and particularly his complete obliviousness to his own immature conduct brand him as a case of arrested development. Stilling's most pathetic moment occurs at story's end with its closing words, spoken by him: "Poor Austin! Poor Wrayford...terrible loss to me...mysterious dispensation. Yes, I do feel gratitude—miraculous escape..." (II, 356). In both his absolute blindness as to the cause of his rescue and in his narcissistic concentration on himself, Stilling strikes the nadir of his immature attitude and behaviour.

Faced with the prospect of a continuing marriage to such a man—a man "who thinks only of himself" (II, 354), she tells her lover Wrayford—Isabel Stilling yearns for release, yet is hesitant in the final analysis to dispatch her husband and disband the union.   Despite her unquestionable attachment to Wrayford, she has second thoughts about disrupting a relationship that will deprive her son of his father and that will "put his mother out of doors" (II, 353). It is true that at the time of Stilling's imminent arrival at the boathouse, she watches as Wrayford "[drops] to his knees and [lays] his hands upon the boards of the sliding floor," and that she does nothing to disrupt her lover's murderous intent when she sees that the floor "[yields] at once, as if with a kind of evil alacrity; and at their feet they [see] under the motionless solid night another darker night that moved and shimmered" (II, 355).   Yet as she looks into the water where husband and lover struggle for their lives, "she [cries] out the names of each of the two men in turn."   Indeed, it is subsequently Stilling who seems foremost in her concern as she thrusts an oar down into the water "crying out her husband's name" and screaming "Cobham! Cobham!" (I, 356).

The story ends on a high moral note: Isabel and Wrayford rise above their baser instincts to a higher ideal of human conduct.   The latter, in his act of opening up the floorboards to Stilling's blind footfall, the former, in her passive complicity with her lover's act, are taken by the impulse of the moment.   But the ensuing actions of both reflect their regret: Wrayford in his courageous leap into the water to save his rival, Isabel in her evident effort to save both men.   The actions of both contrast radically with Stilling's self-centered "I wish old Austin could have known that I was saved!" (II, 356).

With its early attention to Stilling's insecurity in the presence of his New York social equals and its ongoing contrasting of Stilling with Isabel and Wrayford, "The Choice" does seem to make a point about upper-crust New Yorkers.   Of course it is difficult for readers knowledgable about Wharton's life not to read the story as its author's personal unburdening. In this context it is important to note that Wharton displays an uncharacteristically heavy hand in the story, especially in her recurring references to an encroaching storm that will coincide with the calamitous events of the conclusion. Wolff's comment seems a valid assessment: "'The Choice' is not one of Wharton's better efforts. Clearly her energies are still too divided, her experiences still too new in her mind for her to return to the writing of fiction with mastery" (152).

"The Long Run"

"The Long Run" reminds us of Wharton's habit of returning to a particular subject that she had covered in a minor or ineffectual manner in a short story written earlier. In "The Long Run," published in the February 1912 issue of *Atlantic Monthly*, Wharton revisits the territory of "The Choice," a tale of only marginal quality, published some four years before. Specifically, she revisits a triad of upper-class New Yorkers familiar from the previous story: the hearty but oafish husband, his unhappy wife, and the male of superior intelligence and style who is engaged in an intimate relationship with the wife, shifting, however, the focus away from the husband and on to his male rival. "The Long Run" is a story far superior to its predecessor, this contention borne out by the fact that it avoids, as "The Choice" does not, the appearance of airing its author's marital problems and her entertaining of new suitors.

Testimony to the popular success of "The Long Run" is that it helped to sell out the *Atlantic Monthly* issue in which it appeared in just two days (*EW* 318). The story received strong commendation from critics as well—Lewis called it "superb" (*ICSS* XII), and for E.K. Brown its dialogues possessed truth and astonishing vivacity (28)—but it has not been given the close critical attention it richly deserves. The rightness of its narrative approach and especially the finely calibrated depiction of its central character give it a quality that should rank it among the very best of Wharton's short stories.

"The Long Run" is introduced by an unnamed first-person narrator who, after acquainting us with his friend Halston Merrick's background, turns the story over to the latter and becomes the sole confidant of Merrick's life story of missed opportunity and unconscious self-indictment. The setting of the first meeting between the narrator and Merrick is "one of the Jim Cumnors' dinners" (II, 301) where "the people of the old vanished New York set" (II, 304) are being entertained. The fact that he and his friend have not met for twelve years allows the narrator to perceive the vast change that has taken place in Merrick: the man whom he has thought to be full of vitality and adventurousness, who has worked in diplomatic posts and government, who has published "a small volume of delicate verse" (II, 302), whom he remembers for "his quickness of perception...and sureness of response"(II, 302), has become conventional and dull to the point where the two old friends, tactfully left alone by their hostess after dinner, are hard pressed to carry on a conversation together.

Thus the introduction of a narrator other than Merrick, who will subsequently tell his own story, allows us to have an outside perspective on the transformation that has taken place within Merrick—necessary because we come to realize as the latter relates his past that he is not to be entirely trusted as an objective evaluator of himself especially. The primary narrator's telling the story's opening scene at the Cumnors' serves another and related purpose as well. It places the former Paulina Trant in the setting in which the narrator and the reader can see clearly what she has become, a rank-and-file member of the "old vanished New York set...mostly cut on the same convenient and unobstrusive pattern" (II, 304). Because he has known her before and remembers her uniqueness of person and personality, the narrator is able to confirm for Merrick and for us that the present Mrs Reardon, "her gray dress...handsome but ineffective...her pale and rather serious face [wearing] a small unvarying smile which might have been pinned on with her ornaments" (II, 303), bears little likeness to the old Paulina. The closing image in Section I, the scene at the Cumnors', establishes the conventionality of Paulina's life in Merrick's assessment of her husband as "the best fellow in the world" and in the narrator's description of him as "a large glossy man with strawcolored hair and red face, whose shirt and shoes and complexion seemed all to have received a coat of the same expensive varnish," whose "big booming voice" cries out "'What I say is: what's the good of disturbing things? Thank the Lord, I'm content with what I've got!'" (II, 305). Reardon surely puts Merrick in mind of Trant, who is a less hearty version of the same conventional type represented by her present husband. Merrick will later describe Trant as "that pompous stick," a "wooden consort"and "gray" (II, 309), and as one who translates "his arbitrary classification of whatever he didn't understand into 'the kind of thing I don't approve of,' 'the kind of thing that isn't done,' and 'the kind of thing I'd rather not discuss'" (II, 310).

It is the sight of the plain and conventional Paulina Reardon and the reminder of her first marriage to Philip Trant called up by the presence of Reardon that trigger Merrick's invitation to his friend to visit him the following weekend at his retreat at Riverdale. At this visit, the setting of the remainder of "The Long Run," Merrick unburdens himself to the narrator of the story of the failed relationship with Paulina which in his mind accounts for both the radical transformation he and the narrator have detected in her, and the loss of spirit perceptible in Merrick by both himself and his friend.

Merrick's recapitulation of events centers around the evening that Paulina is about to embark on a long European vacation with her husband. For some time Paulina and he had been involved with one another in a liaison of friendship and love that by mutual acknowledgement far transcended the relationships and marriages of convenience common among their social class. On the evening in question, Paulina comes to Merrick's Riverdale home and offers to leave her husband permanently and spend the rest of her life with him. Merrick meets Paulina's invitation with protestations, reservations, and rationalizations that suggest he is not up to Paulina's challenge. As Lev Raphael puts is: "Merrick stuttered, hesitated, argued, hoping to spare 'her the humiliation of scandal and the misery of self-reproach'. In reality he could not match her passion and vision, was ultimately 'pusillanimous'..."(198). Raphael's use of the word 'pusillanimous' repeats Merrick's own self-accusatory adjective, used by the latter as he relates to the narrator his sense of the utter nobility of Paulina's offer: "...she had recklessly and magnificently provided me with the decentest pretext a man could have for doing a pusillanimous thing" (II, 323). Of course the fact that Merrick recognizes his own pusillanimity does not make him any less so, and we should recognize that his conduct in the critical stages of his relationship with Paulina betrays his inability to match his beloved's grand vision and passion.

But Raphael's conclusion concerning Merrick's visit to Paulina after Trant's death with the avowed intention of proposing marriage may have missed the mark. He was, Raphael writes, "too ashamed of his failure of spirit to propose..." (II, 198). In fact, the alleged reason for the passing up of his resolution to ask for Paulina's hand is surely the biggest of Merrick's rationalizations. It is interesting to compare the descriptions he offers the narrator of the two occasion on which he refuses to commit himself to a permanent relationship with Paulina. In the first of these descriptions, of the visit of Paulina on the eve of her departure for Europe with her husband, Merrick's recapitulation is replete with detail after detail of Paulina's thrusts and his defensive parries: he has every reason to believe that his logic will be grasped by his understanding bachelor friend. Merrick's recounting of the second meeting is remarkable in its lack of detail. We are to assume that the passionately open and now-liberated Paulina has suddenly become speechless. Merrick collapses what must have been an at least interesting reunion into one paragraph describing his "bland retreat" (II, 323) from the fixed intention of his visit. He has talked himself out of asking the question and he leaves at the first opportunity without having done so.

The truth is that Paulina is Merrick's superior not only in passion and vision but in courage as well. It is she who assumes the initiative in both action and word in the matter of moving toward a resolution in her relationship with Merrick. Her courage is clear when one contrasts her gesture of inviting her lover to share his life with her in the face of the proscriptions of society with Merrick's inability to push through his desires even when there is no societal interdiction. Merrick may very well be correct to conclude, at the time he has planned to propose marriage to her, that she saw "the memory of the gesture I hadn't made" as "forever parodying the one I was attempting!" (II, 323). But there is no evidence that this would have been her reaction, and indeed she has at that occasion greeted him with kindness and compassion. Regardless of his fears and. reservations though, he should have been capable of taking his chances—and he is not.

In fine, Merrick is a reactor rather than an actor, and it is interesting that the story makes a point of suggesting that he takes his lead from Paulina in the ideational and verbal realms as well.   For one thing, his version of the two masters no man can serve, mentioned in his conversation with the narrator the evening of the Cumnors' dinner party, is an imagistic translation of something Paulina has said to him on the night of his rejection of her. For Merrick, the mutually exclusive masters are "theory and instinct. The gray tree and the green. You've got to choose which fruit you'll try; and you don't know till afterward which of the two has the dead core" (II, 306).   Paulina has told him so much years before—and without benefit of hindsight.   Responding to his fear that she is not seeing the long-term impact of her proposal clearly enough, she has said to him: "No; there's one other way, and that is *not* to do it!   To abstain and refrain; and then see what we become, or what we don't become, in the long run, and to draw our inferences.   That's the game that almost everybody about us is playing, I suppose; there's hardly one of the dull people one meets at dinner who hasn't had, just once, the chance of a berth on a ship that was off for the Happy Isles, and hasn't refused it for fear of sticking on a sand bank!" (II, 319).   As well, Merrick admits using Paulina's metaphor of the ship (one instance of which informs the aforementioned statement) which he adapts and extends with considerable sophistication in his account to the narrator.

Merrick's tale of failed love is laden with images and metaphors of ships, ship travel, and travel and discovery generally. Some are Paulina's, but many are the product of his own fertile imagination. When he complains to the narrator that when he has unhappily dispatched Paulina from his life, "Poetry, ideas—all the picture-making processes stopped" (II, 321), we realize, particularly in regard to the "picture-making processes," that his loss has not been permanent, for his story is a rich tapestry of visually realized concepts. Besides the already-mentioned ship and travel images, one might mention others that illustrate Merrick's natural gift for picture-making. He differentiates between "the great enduring loves" and "the little epidermal flurries;" he speaks of many a man searching for a great love as thinking "he was seeking a soul when all he wanted was a closer view of the tenement;" he refers to the way that Paulina "in the gray Trant atmosphere...flashed with prismatic fires" (II, 309).

But of course there is more to the artistic process than making word-pictures. What Merrick seems to establish during the course of delivering his oral tale is that he has retained something of the capacity to produce literary art. The proof that a more comprehensive creative capacity has failed Merrick is in the book of essays he shows the narrator during their Riverdale reunion: both reader and writer know that the new work does not match the earlier book of sonnets whose Muse has been Paulina. That Merrick has been unable to actualize his literary potential into another successful piece of art has to do more with attitude than with ability, and the key to his failure resides in his statement to the narrator at the close of Section II: "Out of that very door they went [i.e., Paulina and the Muse]—the two of 'em, on a rainy night like this: and one stopped and looked back, to see if I wasn't going to call her—and I didn't—and so they both went" (II, 307). In this despairing declaration, which reiterates its author's image-making ability, Merrick betrays himself to be blind to the possibility of transforming his disastrous experience into a lasting piece of written art: it can be justly said that his rationalizing his failure in love extends to his excusing away his artistic failure. He is able to tell an oral tale about his experience to a sympathetic, admiring, and uncritical friend whose concurrences encourage the teller's excuses and stratagems, but he lacks the character to transform his relationship with Paulina into a written work that will shed a unique light on their liaison. Indeed he has opted away from writing that experience and produced a book of mediocre essays whose subjects probably pale by comparison with the experience that has so deeply affected him.

If Merrick has failed to join the woman of his dreams in a permanent union and failed to equal the success of his early sonnets in another piece of literary art, he *has* become a successful entrepreneur. Although little is said by either the narrator or himself about his role as head of the Merrick Iron Foundry at Yonkers, we must assume that Halston Merrick runs a reasonably successful enterprise. And if we are always given the sense that the Works is something of a burden Merrick would like to be rid of—he has fallen heir to the family business at the time of his father's death—he has never removed himself from it, and in fact has taken a house nearby "to be near the Iron Works." Early in the story we are told by the narrator that "he had a chance to free himself; but when it came he did not choose to take it" (II, 302). Later we learn from Merrick himself that "It was about that time...that I definitely decided not to sell the Works, but to stick to my job and conform my life to it" (II, 321). Although Merrick's decision to "stick to my job" bespeaks a long-term commitment to an endeavour and thus is an exception to the way he has acted in other areas of his life, it must be seen that it also has much in common with his decisions not to take up Paulina's offer of a permanent liaison with her and not to propose marriage to her when that becomes possible: in each case he passes up the chance he has yearned to act on. He is consistently unable to seize the moments that will allow him to change his prosaic existence.

Something must be said as well about Merrick's early career, which is summarized at the outset of the story by the narrator, who presents this portion of his friend's life in an altogether favorable light. For him "Merrick had been a vivid and promising figure in young American life" (II, 301). But it may be appropriate to question the narrator's interpretation of Merrick's pre-Foundry days. Was the latter's "private secretaryship to our Ambassador in England" as much of an "adventure" as he suggests? (II, 301). Why did he fail to win election to the State Senate? Is his working subsequently in municipal affairs not something of a come-down after his involvement at a higher political level? There is for the objective observer at least as much to wonder about as to praise about Merrick's post-Harvard career, and without pressing the point too vehemently, one might argue that there is to be found some foreshadowing of Merrick's future in his past.

In the final analysis Merrick has passed up "the chance of a berth on a ship that was off for the Happy Isles" (II, 318), proferred by Paulina. He has traded off "the high seas" for a life centered in the Iron Works—aptly named to suggest the non-emotional penchant in him—and balmed by the easeful security of his bachelor life. He has preferred to remain—to use Paulina's image—"tied up to Lethe Wharf" (II, 316). He relates his tale to the narrator in his "little place at Riverdale" where he goes "when the world is too much for him" (II, 305). As she so often does in her fiction, Wharton has rendered interior space and background so as to lend material support to her theme. The Riverdale house is "a pleasant setting of books and prints and faded parental furniture" (II, 305). Here the friends "dined late and smoked and talked...in his book-walled study till the terrier on the hearthrug stood up and yawned for bed" (II, 305-306). Here, attended by servants, sipping drinks with his bachelor friend and patting his pet terrier, Merrick launches into his story of retreat and surrender. He is a kind of anti-Emersonian working man (as opposed to Man Working) ensconced in his ivory tower, indulging himself in a tale of romantic might-have-been in a place lined with books, the very symbol of second-hand experience. It is possibly not coincidental that books are mentioned twice in the narrator's brief description of Merrick's den, and that the terrier, the recipient of his friendly but unreciprocated pats, is also mentioned twice: the repetition seems to suggest his life of capitulation to vicarious experience and to a vaguely soothing relationship that requires little return from him.

132

Not a great deal has been written about "The Long Run," the prevailing wisdom in earlier and more recent criticism being that the story is one of the twinned tragedy of Merrick and Paulina. Lewis writes, for example, that "the lovers linger on, like Ethan and Mattie, psychically if not physically mutilated"(*EW* 318), and White notes that the story contains a dialogue between reason and intuition, and that although Merrick, the voice of reason, wins out, both characters are unhappy and realize their mistake (70-71). While these conclusions have validity, they seem not to respect entirely the given focus of the story. Raphael comes closest to recognizing the full import of "The Long Run" when he writes that Merrick "could not match [Paulina's] passion and vision" (198), but he stops short of observing that Merrick's "pusillanimity" extends to his failure to propose to Paulina when he has the opportunity and to his failure as a creative artist as well. Halston Merrick is one of the best-realized of a substantial group of Wharton males who, for all their privilege and gifts, fail to confront life courageously, and in its happy wedding of characterization, substance, setting, and narrative perspective "The Long Run" can stand with the best of Wharton's short stories.

"Atrophy"

Even though "Atrophy," published in the November 1927 issue of *Ladies' Home Journal*, appeared some fifteen years after "The Long Run," it bears an unmistakeable resemblance to the earlier story in the nature of its depiction of the extra-marital affair that is at its center. Although "Atrophy" examines its focal situation from a woman's point of view and although it examines the extra-marital affair in its current circumstances rather than retrospectively—thus offering an entirely different slant than does "The Long Run"—it is difficult to ignore the fact that Wharton insists on certain common details about the lifestyles of the stories' central male characters. When the protagonist, Nora Frenway, visits her lover's bachelor home at Westover, she is shown by the chambermaid "into the low paneled room that was so full of his presence, his books, his pipes, his terrier dozing on the shabby rug" (II, 504). Not only does this passage evoke the description of Merrick's quarters at Riverdale, but it also suggests something of the easeful, secure, catered world, the space that is removed from any intimate feminine presence, that one finds in the house in which Merrick tells his story of failed love—and failed courage—in "The Long Run."

"Atrophy" also signals its connectedness to "The Long Run" by the manner in which Nora Frenway's view of love imitates that of Paulina Reardon, albeit in very muted fashion. The expression of her desire for a visionary union with Christopher Aldis is a rerendering of Paulina's invitation to her lover to set off for the metaphorical open sea of adventure and mystery. As Nora rides on the train towards Aldis, she views through the window "miles and miles of alluring tarred roads slipping away into mystery" and is reminded of "How often she had dreamed of dashing off down an unknown road with Christopher!" (II, 502). These reverberations from the earlier story that inform "Atrophy" must be considered in one's conclusions about a tale that is markedly different from its predecessor.

"Atrophy" is structured for most of its length as a story of inner consciousness. Though told in the third person by a narrator who has entry into the mind of Nora Frenway, the story often gives the impression that the latter is reflecting in the first person. In the following passage, for example—and there are many others like it—it is as if she were engaged in a concentrated and passionate address to self: "Yet here she was on her way to Westover.... Oh, what did it matter now? That was the worst of it—it was too late for anything between her and Christopher to matter! She was sure he was dying" (II, 502). The revelation of the active mental consciousness is pervasive in Section I of the story, which covers her train trip from Grand Central Station in New York to Westover Junction. Early in Section II, set inside Aldis's house at Westover, the focus shifts to the dialogue between Nora and Aldis's spinster sister, Jane, but we are often brought back here as well into the subjective observations and reflections taking place in the protagonist's mind.

The appropriateness of casting "Atrophy" as a modified interior monologue is evident when one considers Nora's growing isolation and alienation as she proceeds towards her lover's sickbed and then realizes that she will not succeed in seeing him. On the train she is self-conscious about her illicit relationship and fearful of being recognized, even though "neither the porter nor her nearest neighbors...seemed in the least surprised or interested by the statement [to the porter] that she was traveling to Westover" (II, 501). She stays to herself and is lost in her thoughts until roused by the announcement "Westover *Junction*," when "She started up and pushed her way out of the train" (II, 504). Once inside Aldis's house, her hopes for an immediate meeting with Christopher are dashed by a parlormaid who ushers her into "a stiff lifeless drawing room" where she waits alone. Here her sense of alienation is strong and is expressed in her interior response to the immediate setting. "The drawing room [was] the kind that bachelors get an upholsterer to do for them, and then turn their backs on forever. The chairs and sofas looked at her with an undisguised hostility, and then resumed the moping expression common to furniture in unfrequented rooms." Here it is not simply the fact that she has been shunted aside into an inhospitable room that leaves her "with a sense of emptiness and apprehension" (II, 505). There is also evident in her reaction to the furniture an intimation, perhaps at an unconscious leval, that she has been rejected by Aldis: if her lover has turned his back on the room, then she, in feeling the looks of the chairs and sofas to be hostile, is surely registering a sense of fear that her lover is turning his back on her. This sense of rejection anticipates the subsequent stone-walling of Jane Aldis, who engages her in an inane dialogue; "twaddle," "conversational rubbish" and a "stifling web of platitudes" [II, 507-508], Nora internally labels it, as she sits seeing her chances for a meeting with Christopher dissipate with the imminent departure of the return train to New York. Nora is as effectively trapped in her isolation as the blue-bottle fly she hears "[banging] against the window" (II, 510).

Critics have given "Atrophy" scant attention. Shari Benstock calls it "a disturbing story about aging" (423), R.W.B. Lewis one that deals with "the emotional and psychological challenge of adultery" (*ICSS* X). An extended comment on the story comes from Barbara White, who reads it as a confrontation between Nora and Jane Aldis, the latter avenging herself on Nora—by refusing her access to her brother—because Nora "always ignored her" in the past (100). It is true that Jane is immediately responsible for preventing Nora from seeing Aldis, but one wonders if there are not larger implications to Jane's unwillingness to allow the meeting. It seems inconceivable that if the relationship between Nora and Christopher is as strong and reciprocal as the former suggests in the course of her interior monologue, the latter would not have made some arrangement whereby a meeting could be effected.

The details of "Atrophy" as a whole conspire to suggest that in fact Aldis does not wish to see Nora. He is certainly not so ill that he cannot receive her. He has been visited by his cousin Hal Brincker the day before, and the fact that Aldis has received the man whom he has always considered a "blighting bore" (II, 509) brings home to Nora the painful realization that she is not wanted at Westover and no longer desired by Aldis. Although she has come hoping against hope that a meeting is possible, it is clear that once inside his home she has the innate sense that she is not welcome—and this even before Jane greets her. The hostility she feels in the house is palpable. In her concentration on Aldis's bachelorhood in passages that emphasize the self-sufficiency and comfort of his life style, Nora betrays her recognition that she is no longer required as a mistress. It is worthy of note that in the long, desultory conversation with Jane she suffers through she never directly asks if she may see Aldis: she in unable to hear the truth Jane's answer will carry. Wharton has aptly called her story "Atrophy," for the relationship between Nora and Christopher has wasted away from lack of nourishment on the latter's part.

"Atrophy" springs from the same root as "The Long Run," a certain attitude held by Wharton about unhappily married but venturous women and their

136

liaisons with affluent bachelors. Her own experiences with bachelors, both real and virtual, no doubt served as models for the two stories in question. Despite its close resemblance to "The Long Run," "Atrophy," however, retains its individuality, especially in its dramatization of the inner pain of the deceived Nora Frenway.

"After Holbein"

"After Holbein" interrupted a succession of Wharton stories about the New York upper class that dwelt upon the predicament of married women caught up in extra-marital relationships with men uneager to relinquish their secure and easeful bachelor lives. It disrupts the continuity in theme found in such tales as "The Long Run," "Atrophy," and "Diagnosis" measuring a span of over thirty years work, by presenting not a realistic but a surrealistic tale of New York. Published in the May 5, 1928 issue of *Saturday Evening Post*, "After Holbein" dramatizes the meeting between two socialites in their declining years, both enacting a charade in which the illusion and emptiness of their lives is exposed.

A key to the significance of "After Holbein" is its title, which is neither used nor explained in the story proper. William T. Going writes that the title refers to "the elaborate series of woodcuts, the *Dance of Death*, by the sixteenth-century artist Hans Holbein the younger":

> The motifs of the woodcuts are everywhere apparent in the story. In almost every engraving Holbein has Death carrying the hourglass of life. Anson Warley's vertigo is "only the dizzy plunge of the sands in the hour-glass, the everlasting plunge that emptied one of heart and bowels, like the drop of an elevator from the top floor of a skyscraper...". For Anson Warley Death appears as the "petrifying apparition" of Evelina Jaspar in grotesque purple wig and diamond necklace. And for Mrs Jaspar Death appears in the guise of the fastidious elegance of Anson Warley's impeccable evening clothes with the "thin evening watch" in the proper pocket.... Like Holbein's figures who are guided by Death into grasping graves despite their fixed glassy stares, Mr Warley and Mrs Jaspar "advance with rigid smiles and eyes staring straight ahead" into their last mock-banquet of life, and later Anson steps out into the cold night "to where a moment before the pavement had been—and where now there was nothing." (1-2)

In casting her sights on two ancient and decrepit denizens of New York society, Wharton was moving away from her conventional interest in character and psychological conflict among members of the upper class and focussing on the class itself. Thus "After Holbein"concerns itself with the demise of the old society, with its attitude to its servants and employees, and with the latter's attitudes towards their employers. The story is the dance of death of two of society's representatives, but it is also suggesting that the ballroom has gone dark and that a new order of priorities prevails.

"After Holbein"is structured as a sequence of looks at its two major characters, its final section initially bringing together Anson Warley and Evelina Jaspar in the latter's Fifth Avenue mansion, then in its closing paragraph suggesting either a literal death or a farther deterioration in the person of Warley. "After Holbein" is Warley's story: he is a major presence in all but one of its six sections, and we are given access to his consciousness by a third-person privileged narrator. Although Evelina has elicited much interest because of the opinion that her portrait is modelled on Lloyd Morris's sketch of Lady Astor (Nevius 192-193), her dramatic impact is more a factor of Wharton's creativity than of the character's historical resonance. And as strong and vivid as her presence is in the story, she is unquestionably subordinated to Warley in importance: we see her exclusively from the outside and are never given entry to her inner self.

It is an important element of "After Holbein" that all the contacts of the two major characters that occur in the story—other than their meeting with each other in Evelina's dining room—are with servants and other employees. People of their own social set enter the story only by allusion. There are references to the social acquaintances of both principals, and one in particular, an oft-repeated list of Evelina's dinner guests—the Italian Ambassador, the Bishop, Mr and Mrs Torrington Bligh, Mr and Mrs Benjamin Bronx—is mindful of the lists of Jay Gatsby's guests in Fitzgerald's novel. There is also a pointed mention of Evelina's family members, which hints at the woman's obsolescence and at the

138

coming of a new social order. After introducing a description of the setting of
Evelina's dinner table, the narrator continues, "There were no longer real flowers;
the family had long since suppressed that expense; and no wonder, for Mrs. Jaspar
had always insisted on orchids. But Grace, the youngest daughter, who was the
kindest, had hit on the clever device of arranging three beautiful clusters of
artificial orchids and maidenhair, which had only to be lifted from their shelf in
the pantry and set in the dishes..." (II, 557-558). While these details show that
Evelina's kin humor her desire for extravagance, they also confirm her isolation
even within her own family and aid and abet her image as a last and lonely
retainer of an all but moribund tradition.

The sense of isolation that characterizes Evelina's existence extends to
Warley's life as well and is observable not only in the two's desolate encounter in
the dining room but also in the absence of significant relationships with people of
their set. If we exclude their encounter in Evelina's house, which is bizarre and
surreal, we find them relating only to their social inferiors. In these relations,
servants and employees function as props for their employers' anachronistic lives.
Only sixty-three years old and hardly a fit subject for senility, Warley is a pathetic
figure as he drifts in mind in and out of the real world, imagines himself the
object of beautiful young women's attention, and unloads his frustrations about
his dwindling physical health and fitness, and failing mental sharpness and
awareness on his valet, Filmore, a man most probably his senior by several years.
Barbara White's assessment of Warley's treatment of Filmore is astute and
accurate: "...Warley treats Filmore as an extension of himself, projecting onto him
his frustration with old age. Thus he accuses Filmore of being forgetful and deaf
and thinks of replacing him with a younger valet" (94).

Evelina is tended by a host of assistants, five of whom are mentioned by
name: Miss Dunn and Miss Cress, nurses, one of whom seems to be on duty at all
times; Lavinia, a lady's maid, who is her senior in years; Manson, an old butler,
absent from the story because he hasn't appeared for work; and the doltish
George, a footman, who fills in for Manson. These servants' attitudes towards

their mistress range from servile fidelity by the two males, to professional concern by Miss Dunn, to adulation on the par of Lavinia: they seem in awe of the memory if not of her present condition. Miss Cress represents a younger generation and is something of an outsider to the class's ways. She has her own life in the city, enjoys the movies, the new art form, and hopes she will soon be engaged. Though not above laughing at the doddering Evelina and the slavishly faithful Lavinia, Miss Cress is alert to see that the latter's thoughts are with the absent "poor old [Manson]" whose "memory was going...". "If the daughters send him off—and they will—" Miss Cress understands Lavinia to be thinking, "where's he going to, old and deaf as he is, and all his people dead. Oh, if only he can hold on till she dies, and get his pension..." (II, 546). Thus the devoted Lavinia carries more of *noblesse oblige* than the members of the class from whom it is presumed to emanate. It is surely Wharton's point here that for all the superficiality and busybodyness of Evelina's lifestyle, her servants are better off in her hands than in those of her callous daughters.

Miss Cress treats Evelina insensitively, even cruelly. She compliments the old woman on her necklace when the latter hasn't yet put it on. Of her, the narrator remarks: "It always amused Miss Cress to give [Evelina] these little jolts though she knew Miss Dunn and the doctor didn't approve of her doing so. She knew also that it was against her own interests and she did try to bear in mind Miss Dunn's oft-repeated admonition about not sending up the patient's blood pressure, but when she was in high spirits...it was irresistible to get a rise out of the old lady" (II, 541-542). Critics have noticed that the story shows no pity for its focus subjects (Auchincloss 38; Nevius 194; White 93) and Miss Cress contributes to this, but it is the narrative voice that is the major offender. Descriptions especially of Evelina's physical and mental deterioration abound, and the images provided at the mock banquet featuring her and Warley sustain the aura of personal enfeeblement and even dementia: it is difficult to accept Barbara White's contention that "distinction should be made...between the society Mrs.

Jaspar and Mr. Warley represent and the characters themselves, for Wharton does show sympathy for them as individuals" (93).

Margaret B. McDowell's assessement of "After Holbein" broaches the subject of Wharton's attitude, placing it in the larger context of the story: "Tragedy lies not in the death of the principals...but in the pointless lives they have led. Excessive sympathy for the characters would have weakened the inevitability of [the] final scene: Anson has lost 'the Alps and the cathedrals' he had once dreamed of, but he and Evelina have had the sterile satisfactions that they settled for. They have paid for their own souls. Both have made life itself a dance of death. 'After Holbein' is a parable that the wages of wasted talent are death and that complacency may indeed be the greatest of social sins" ("Edith Wharton's 'After Holbein'" 58). This well-known and widely anthologized story is surely one of Wharton's saddest and most tragic, documenting not only the demise of a society but dramatizing as well the passing of two of the most pitiful of its principals.

"Diagnosis"

With "Diagnosis," published in the November 1930 issue of *Ladies' Home Journal*, Wharton returned to the subject that interested her in such earlier upper-class stories as "The Long Run" and "Atrophy," the egocentric, selfish male seen in his relationship with women. A story little commented on by critics, "Diagnosis" had the questionable distinction of being rejected by fourteen British periodicals before Wharton discontinued trying to place it overseas (Benstock 435). Its refusal in England can probably be blamed on editors' perceptions that the story was too complex to appeal to their general readership rather than on any inherent weakness. Shari Benstock's contention that it is "the weakest story" in the 1933 collection, *Human Nature*, notwithstanding, "Diagnosis" is a tale of some force and complexity as suggested in E.K. Brown's early comment that Wharton "never developed an ironic situation with such power, and never established on a more solid base a conclusion that astonishes the reader and pleases him at the same time" (37).

"Diagnosis" follows directly in the vein of its two upper-class predecessors, "The Long Run" and "Atrophy," bringing its own uniqueness to the subject of the relation between the egotistical male and the put-upon woman. Though its male perspective makes it similar to "The Long Run," it differs from that story in adopting a dramatic rather than narrative approach to a long-term relationship: "Diagnosis," told by an outside narrator who is privy to Paul Dorrance's consciousness and who adopts a judgemental attitude towards him, follows the action as it ensues. "Atrophy" differs from "Diagnosis" in offering a female perspective on the relationship in question and in concentrating its focus over a period of a few hours. By adopting its own narrative perspective and voice, and its own time frame, each of the stories exploits variations on a theme that is an overriding one for Wharton and that makes its appearance in several other stories that reach beyond the confines of the present chapter.

Barbara White's critique of Paul Dorrance, the central and point-of-view character in "Diagnosis" is shrewd. Referring to the latter and to "The Dilettante," she writes: "Wharton very skillfully makes the reflecting minds reveal their own narcissism, and she connects Thursdale's and Paul Dorrance's selfish detachment to their certainty, which is supported by social institutions, that women exist to serve them—to provide aesthetic enjoyment; listen, even to the praise of their rivals; comfort as death approaches; and finally become angels mourning at the grave.... She gives Thursdale and Dorrance no redeeming qualities" (60). "Diagnosis's" Dorrance alternately remains emotionally detached from and attaches himself to Eleanor Welwood, his mistress of fifteen years, as his own needs require. He is almost a parody of egocentricity and selfishness as he boasts to himself of "his own shrewdness. He had kept his freedom, kept his old love's devotion—or as much of it as he wanted—and proved to himself that life was not half bad if you knew how to manage it" (II, 727).

But White's assessment of Eleanor is perhaps open to some extension. White writes, in summary, that "Paul does not discover until many years later, after Eleanor's death, that she had known all along about the mistaken diagnosis, had been informed by the doctor and never told him." She continues: "'Woman's revenge' might be a more accurate term than 'feminist revenge' in that it scarcely seems the height of feminism to trick a man into marriage" (60). Putting aside the questionability of the notion that a man who has monopolized a woman's life for fifteen years after having been the cause of her divorcing her husband in the first place can be said to be "tricked into marriage," it must be asserted that Eleanor has acted with duplicity in not ridding her new husband of his illusion. However, to leave it at that may be doing Eleanor some injustice, and it is appropriate to suggest that her hiding the truth from Dorrance may have been motivated by something other than revenge.

On the basis of details provided in the story, it does not appear to be consistent with Eleanor's character to call her vengeful. Dorrance's doctor, who has known her well, attests to her "kindness, her devotion, ...her goodness, her charity, the many instances he had come across among his poor patients of her discreet and untiring ministration.... She always gave too much of herself—that was the trouble" (II, 738). The truth is that Eleanor has seized upon the opportunity of Dorrance's "bad news" to secure for herself a period of time during which she can, because he has an intense need of her, offer him her heart secure in his total commitment to her.

The story of Eleanor's relationship to Dorrance is the story of the waxing and waning of the human heart. At the time of her divorce from her first husband, Eleanor has hoped that marriage with Dorrance will ensue; disappointed that it hasn't, "she has silenced her heart." But when Dorrance, terrified by the fear of death proposes marriage to her, she quickens to life. "The shadow of her terrible fear [of his imminent passing] seemed to fall from her, as the shadow of living falls from the newly dead. Her face looked young and transparent; he watched the blood rise to her lips and cheeks" (II, 727). Knowing that Dorrance's desire for her is contingent on his perception that he is doomed to die, she of course keeps the truth from him initially, and when in Europe she notes the distinct improvement in his health, "she forbore to emphasize it" (II, 729). When he announces to her that "the New York diagnosis was a mistake," he is "arrested, silenced, by something in his wife's face which seemed to oppose an invisible resistance to what he was in the act of saying" (II, 731). However, the fear expressed here that Eleanor's tenuously acquired state of bliss may be at an end is suspended by Dorrance's decision not to return to New York to resume his former life. "Oh, this fellow here may be all wrong," he says to her of the Viennese specialist who has "restored life to him." "Anyhow, he wants me to take a cure somewhere first.... But wouldn't you rather travel for a year or so? How about South Africa or India next winter?" (II, 732).

Dorrance's decision to return to America brings an end to Eleanor's charmed life. He reflects, that though she has been "a perfect companion while he was ill and lonely," she is "an unwitting encumbrance...now that...he was restored to the life from which his instinct of self-preservation had so long excluded her" (II, 734). Eleanor soon becomes ill, and her fatal disease is twice hinted to be an illness of the heart that is more emotional than physical. As her bodily health seems to improve, the story has it that "the doctors would have been perfectly satisfied if her heart had not shown signs of weakness" (II, 736). And the attending physician's own remark to Dorrance after Eleonar's death, "I only wish it had been in our power to prolong [her life]. But these cases of heart failure..." (II, 739), is especially ambiguous (and suggestive) concerning the nature of her ills. As Dorrance ponders the meaning of Eleanor's unfinished deathbed statement, "Well, it was worth it! I always knew—," readers will suspect (although Dorrance admits "that he would never know what she found worth it") (II, 737) that Eleanor intended to say that her short life with a husband who cherished her companionship while he was ill and lonely proved a satisfying interval for her.

Dorrance's utter inability to deduce the inference behind his wife's deathbed statement signals, of course, his hopeless self-absorption. It also points to the essential irony that informs "Diagnosis." His "increasing satisfaction with his own shrewdness" (II, 727); his conviction about Eleanor's "obtuseness" (II, 728); his labelling of her via the epithet "Sancta Simplicitas" (II, 729); his numerous patronizing references to her as "child," "poor child," "poor thing," "poor Eleanor," all draw attention to his flawed view of the relative intelligence and perceptiveness of himself and his wife. In a less overt way they also point to Eleanor's emotional maturity and acquired satisfaction in the affairs of the human heart.

In "Diagnosis" Wharton is playing another variation on the theme that preoccupied her in "The Long Run" and "Atrophy," two stories discussed in earlier pages of the present chapter. In both of these earlier stories Wharton used inner house space and home furnishings to delineate the male protagonists' habit of isolating and insulating themselves from and against what they considered to be demanding female intrusions on their lives. "Diagnosis" follows the same pattern. At the outset Dorrance lives alone but attended by servants in a "high-perched flat...the window [looking] south over the crowded towering New York below Wall Street which was the visible center and symbol of his life's works" (II, 723). Upon his return to New York after his European travels with Eleanor, it is precisely this kind of intrusion into his sacrosanct bachelor space that alerts Dorrance to the sense of suffocation he now feels in his marriage: "Eleanor Welwood did not ring his doorbell now," he reflects one day, "she had her own latchkey; she was no longer Eleanor Welwood but Eleanor Dorrance, and asleep at this moment in the bedroom which had been Dorrance's, and was now encumbered with feminine properties, while his own were uncomfortably wedged into the cramped guest room of the flat" (II, 733). "Diagnosis" imitates the high quality of its two aforementioned predecessors. Its one flaw, the premise whereby Dorrance attributes a diagnosis meant for another patient to be one assessing his own condition, does not in any major way detract from the considerable impact of the story.

"Duration"

It is difficult to discuss "Duration," a humorous story published towards the end of Wharton's life in her 1936 short fiction collection, *The World Over*, without making reference to "After Holbein," the highly serious and tragic tale she had written just a few years before. Each piece centers on a male and a female member of the American upper class and on the particular dynamic that determines the relationship of the two characters in each case. It is tempting to read "Duration" as Wharton's attempt to right the balance after the unrelieved darkness of "After Holbein," and in this context one notes that she has shifted the milieu away from New York to Boston, as if to suggest that the former place presents no tempering possibilities and that one must look elsewhere for a less self-destructive upper class.

However, such a positive view of Boston society is not entirely warranted based on Wharton's portrayal of it in "Duration." In an earlier story of the Boston upper class, "The Lamp of Psyche," published in 1895, Wharton had promoted the superiority of Boston over New York society in her contrasting of characters representative of each city. That story's male protagonist, the New York-born Laurence Corbett, is at first considered by his wife to be "cosmopolitan enough for Fifth Avenue...also cultivated enough for Beacon Street" (I, 47). But Mrs Corbett's Aunt Mary, knowledgeable in the arts like her niece's husband, leads a life given over as well to the service of the community, and ultimately Mrs Corbett recognizes that her husband is empty and insular. "Duration" in cursory fashion imitates the earlier story's celebration of Boston as a place where art and good taste are still considered important and where there is a higher value placed on them than their mere asking price. When the story's presiding voice, Henley Warbeck, returns home after years of absence, he sees that "The Copley portraits looked down familiarly from the walls, the old Pepperel Madiera circulated about the table," and reflects that "In New York, Copleys and Madieras, if there had been any, would have been sold long since" (II, 862-863). But in its sense of superiority and exclusiveness, directed even at members of its own class, and in its penchant for inbreeding, the Boston of "Duration" is more an object of ridicule than emulation.

Like the other elements of "Duration," the subject of inbreeding is directed to humorous ends. "The whole immense Warbeck connection, the innumerable Pepperels, Sturtesses, and Syngletons, the Graysons, Wrigglesworths and Perches...the remote and neglegible Littles, whose name gave so accurate a measure of their tribal standing" (II, 860), forms a society in itself, its people intermarrying freely, thus perpetuating its membership and its names. The branches of the family have reached beyond Beacon Street and Commonwealth Avenue to Frostingham, Massachusetts and even Rhode Island, where the name South Perch adorns the place of residence of Syngleton Perch, the cousin who threathens to upstage Martha Little at her hundredth-birthday celebration.

The action in "Duration" turns on a rehearsal for Martha Little's centennial celebration. Formerly the victim of the family's internal snobbery, she has risen in prestige by virtue of her durability, and the Warbecks are preparing to mark her centenary of life with pride and enthusiasm. The once "effaced, contourless, colorless" (II, 859) Martha is now confident, assertive, and in charge, and finds a victim for her rancor about the past in the person of Syngleton Perch, who resents the fact that he is being virtually left in her wake. In fact Martha is by far Perch's physical superior, and much of the humor in the latter two thirds of the story is directed at Perch's inferior motor control. Perch has, literally, to be propped up, and at one point during the rehearsal his legs are described as "jerking upwards as he attempted to raise himself on his elbows" (II, 870). The story ends with a bit of slapstick: as Perch is being guided towards Martha, the latter "made an unexpected movement. Its immediate result...was to shoot forward [Martha's] famous ebony stick which her abrupt gesture...drove directly into the path of Uncle Syngleton. In another instant...the stick entangled in the old man's wavering feet, [and he shot] wildly upward, and then [fell] over with a crash" (II, 871).

Barbara White's conclusion about "Duration," that "the comedy falls flat because Martha Little's revenge is just as unpleasant as her relatives' earlier treatment of her" (84), may not meet with general approval. The story is after all parodic and not realistic. In any case, it is well to note that the two ranking senior citizens of "Duration" have carried into their old age a certain healthy combativeness, *joie de vivre*, wit, and personal pride that contrasts them to the considerably younger but more pathetic Anson Warley and Evelina Jaspar of Wharton's more serious and more arresting study of old age, "After Holbein." Although "Duration" does not match the high quality of the earlier story, it does display a trait that one rarely finds in Wharton, a sense of comic mischief that has its own allure.

*   *   *   *   *

Marriages, Triangles, and Males in Retreat

If Wharton's ghost tales frequently use country settings—in eight of them the characters move against rural backgrounds—her stories of the upper class locate themselves in an urban milieu or in places close to the city that are the habitual haunts of an urban upper class. In most cases the city in question is New York, which is alluded to in the stories either by name or by some landmark: "In Trust," "The Long Run," "After Holbein," and "Diagnosis" are explicitly New York City stories. We may assume, as well, that other city tales are meant by Wharton to have this same setting, even though this is not made explicit within them, and this is true of "The Mission of Jane" and "The Dilettante." Of the remainder of the stories in this group, "The Twilight of the God," placed in Newport; "The Choice," set in "the Highland summer colony" (II, 345) to which the central character repairs to escape the social pressures he experiences in New York; and "Atrophy," focussed on a New York woman who has come to visit her lover at his home upstate from the city, there is clearly a casting of attention on persons belonging to one or another section of New York society. The only stories here that are not about New York are the Boston tales, the early "The Lamp of Psyche" and the late "Duration." In moving away from the country terrain of the ghost stories to upper-class New York City, Wharton is signalling the salience of social intercourse in the lives of well-to-do and status-oriented people: if ghosts and ghost tales may be said to flourish in places and seasons of isolation, the sophisticated metropolis is the suitable site for the commingling of persons and hence for dramas of the marriage game and of the intrusions upon the stability of the wedded state, dramas that are pervasive in these stories of the upper class.

An examination of Wharton's ghost tales as measured against her stories of the upper class also allows us to note the move away from the high seriousness of the former towards a tone that is noticeably less grave in the latter, although this is not invariably the case. That the ghost tales seldom depart from their serious tone is understandable: characters alarmed about either the threat or appearance of ghosts and narrators preoccupied with recounting the spectral are not likely to be light-hearted or undetached. Freed from the compulsions of inherent gravity that the ghost tales require, Wharton's stories of the upper class—as well as her stories on other subjects—are unloosened and give rein to the varieties of lightness and even levity dictated by their subject matter, their narrators' attitudes, their personages' characters and personalities.

A number of the pieces examined here indulge in one sort or other of comic or quasi-comic display: breeziness of tone, wit, satire, and in "Duration," slapstick. Even in an essentially serious tale such as "The Lamp of Psyche" one finds from time to time an airiness about the prose. Here is a description of Delia's experience as a child in her grandmother's home: "[She] after the death of her parents, had even spent two years under Mrs. Hayne's roof, in direct contrast with all her apostolic ardors, her inflamatory zeal for righteousness in everything from baking powder to municipal government" (I, 48). And here is Aunt Mary's first look at Delia's husband: "[Her] eyes, through the close fold of Delia's embrace, pierced instantly to Corbett, and never had that accomplished gentleman been more conscious of being called upon to present his Credentials" (I, 49). Such passages do not so much impinge on the gravity of the subject matter as impart a certain conviviality to the story-telling. "The Twilight of the God" is built on wit. Verbal wit and its absence define the two men with whom Isabel Warland engages in conversation in this playlet as well as the contrasting light in which she holds them: her husband, Lucius, is not up to matching her repartee; her ex–lover John Oberville is more adept at following her. Wharton uses Isabel's verbal cleverness to establish her intellectual sophistication and psychological advantage over both men. "The Mission of Jane," indulges in the same kind of narrative lightness that one finds less pervasive in "The Lamp of Psyche," and in gentle humorous satirical commentary, particularly about Jane and her bumblingly ardent suitor, Winstanley Budd. The satire in "After Holbein," where both elderly pitiable principals are held up to ridicule, is not so gentle and the humor here is mitigated by our sympathy for Warley and Evelina— this despite the narrator's obvious effort to undercut their standing.

Four of these upper-class tales are devoid of any humor at all. "The Dilettante," "The Long Run," "Atrophy," and "Diagnosis" present us with characters who are self-absorbed, seemingly without a sense of humor or the capacity to access their humorous impulses. In "The Dilettante" the clever exchanges between Thursdale and Mrs Vervaine, although they provoke superficial smiles, remain under the pall of the embargo against emotional display that characterizes their discourse. Such restraint begets stiffness and is the very enemy of humor. The central characters in "The Long Run" and "Diagnosis" provide the deadly serious tone to both stories, the first by the mixture of evasiveness and regret that marks his narrative of lost opportunity and lost love, the other by his preoccupation with his perceived illness and his utter selfishness and blind egotism. This absence of humor of course does not invalidate either story, although "The Long Run" is a more engrossing and complex study of its protagonist, Halston Merrick. "Atrophy" presents us with essentially the same situation as these two tales of male egotism and retreat from women, but its presentation of the predicament from the woman's point of view lends it a certain freshness. Nora Frenway too is a figure of self-absorption and alienation, and the story is most effective in its delineation of the isolation of an ardent woman left behind by an uninterested lover. There is a strong complementary relationship between "The Long Run" and "Atrophy" that speaks to the plight of women in Wharton's fictive society. When Paulina Trant tells Merrick, "A little trip along the coast won't answer. It's the high seas—or else being tied up to Lethe Wharf. And I'm for the high seas, my dear!" (II, 301), is she not pointing to the Nora Frenways of society, mistresses of men uncommitted to their lovers, short trippers along the coast, whose destiny is abandonment?

Of the eleven stories seen in this chapter, all are about family, eight have marriage as a preoccupation—"The Dilettante" is about a thwarted marriage—six focus on triangular relationships of greater or lesser intensity, and a significant number portray men in retreat from women and/or as immature, as boy-men. Family is only of passing interest in "After Holbein": Warley is a bachelor and Evelina's family is only cursorily mentioned. In "Duration" the subjects are the members of an extended Boston upper-class family seen at a time of reconciliation and celebration. Only one other of the eleven tales pictures a happy family, "The Mission of Jane." Shaky as the story opens, the Lethbury marriage is stabilized by the adoption of a daughter, then solidified by the daughter Jane's marriage and departure. The family has been saved from potential disaster by husband Julian's realization that he takes his wife too lightly. The likes of Julian Lethbury is not often encountered in Wharton's short fiction: he is a man of social standing and easy means who not only alters his ways but is also open to the insight that allows him to see the danger of his attitudes. Unlike Wharton characters, males especially, who do not see, he detects that "he had not seen before" and "felt as though he had touched a secret spring in Alice's mind" (I, 306) when he recognizes his early failure as a husband.

In most of the stories the marriages are problematical, although sometimes they carry on in spite of obstacles to their success. The Corbetts of "The Lamp of Psyche," though devoted to one another, may yet see their idle, if cultivated, lives jeopardized by a lack of commitment to causes that reach beyond themselves. It

is instructive to juxtapose certain passages from "After Holbein" with others from
"The Lamp of Psyche" that might be taken to suggest that the good innocent
cultured Corbetts may become the jaded innocuous and inept Anson Warleys a
few decades beyond. Here is a description of the Corbetts upon their return to
Paris: "He and his wife entertained their friends delightfully and frequented all the
'first nights' and 'private views' of the season, and Corbett continued to bring
back knowing 'bits' from the Hotel Drouet and rare books from the quays; never
had he appeared more cultivated, more decorative, more enviable, ... (I, 55). And
here is "After Hoblein's" narrator:

> It was in the interest of this lonely fidgety unemployed self that Warley, in
> his younger days, had frequented the gaudiest restaurants, and the most
> glittering Palace Hotels of two hemispheres, subscribed to the most
> advanced literary and artistic reviews, bought the pictures of the young
> painters who were being the most vehemently discussed, missed few of the
> showiest first nights in New York, London or Paris, sought the company of
> the men and women—especially the women—most conspicuous in fashion,
> scandal, or any other form of social notoriety.... (II, 532)

But for the detail of Warley's bachelorhood, the two passages are virtually
interchangeable. In "In Trust," the successive husbands of Daisy, Paul Ambrose
and Ted Halidon, see a substantial fortune meant for the construction of an
Academy of Arts dwindle away in marriages in which Daisy's penchant for
luxury and travel must be satisfied and which, the closing lines of the story
suggest, were less than happy.

Fear and weakness on the part of both husbands and suitors, more or less
serious than that experienced by Daisy's husbands, is a pervasive factor in the
stories seen in this chapter. Many of Wharton's male characters might be called
cases of arrested development, to use Harvey Stone's characterization of Robert
Cohn in Hemingway's *The Sun Also Rises*. Lucius Warland of "The Twilight of
the God" is unable to pay his bills and, more interested in his yachting races,
hands over to his wife the job of interceding with the influential Oberville on his
behalf for a secretaryship in Washington. "The Choice's" Cobham Stilling,

another lover of boats, has his lawyer inform Mrs Stilling that she must sign for a loan to cover his business failure. If men like Stilling and Oberville betray their cravenness by their fear of "[facing] a scene," as the latter puts it, others fail courage in more pervasive ways and in ways more hurtful to themselves and the women who have a right to expect more of them. Thursdale, the title character of "The Dilettante," restricts, indeed repels, all emotional expression in the relationship with the woman whose life he has manipulated and monopolized for some time, clearly establishing his fear of and retreat from women. The domineering males in "Atrophy" and "Diagnosis," Christopher Aldis and Paul Dorrance respectively, withdraw from intimate relationships with women when circumstances suit. Halton Merrick of "The Long Run" prefers to give up the chance of a permanent relationship with his married mistress, Paulina Trant: he prefers to maintain the status quo, to remain attached but unconnected to her in a permanent liaison.

Wharton, the author, with Ogden Codman, of *The Decoration of Houses*, and one given to the exploitation of interior place in her fiction, emblemizes the retreat from women of these last three male characters by the use she makes in the respective stories of inside house space, decoration, and furnishings. One is reminded in this regard of her ghost story "The Eyes" and its locale. "Seen through the haze of our cigars and by the drowsy gleam of a coal fire,"says the narrator, "[was] Culwin's library, with its oak walls and dark old bindings..." (II, 115). Here, as in "The Long Run," "Atrophy," and "Diagnosis," male spaces are private sanctums, beyond womanly intrusion (where even the servants are usually males), modishly masculine, secure.

The upper class identified in these eleven stories is a generic upper class, and the personages who people them are not a homogeneous social set. This has to do in part with the fact that the tales' composition ranges over a period of some forty years, at a time when New York society was undergoing radical change. Most of the characters here are well to do, some wealthy enough to not have to work. Some are entrepreneurs or lawyers, a number give evidence of

153

considerable intelligence by the sophistication of their thought and the refinement of their speech, some are Harvard men. For the most part, though, Wharton's critique of this heterogenous group is a negative one, and only two major characters stand up as positive models, one, in his reflectiveness of the better aspects of his humanity and social standing, the other in her utter repudiation of the standards of her class. Julian Lethbury of "The Mission of Jane" successfully passes muster, but the story in which he is found is one that presents his family as a rather isolated entity somewhat removed from the society at large, and it is difficult to determine his attitudes towards the larger social milieu. Paulina Trant of "The Long Run" is immersed in her society, has twice married men who embody its superficiality, but would have been willing to withdraw from it in favor of a more satisfying life had her lover had the courage to join her. But for the most part characters here are seen askance, and on a number of counts: superficiality, idleness, dilettantism, social climbing, cowardice, indecision, conformity, inner blindness, wastefulness, Philistinism. It is interesting that this block of stories is framed by two tales of upper Boston society, a society that is pictured to be not without its faults, but one that has retained some allegiance to older standards.

Wharton pursued her study of upper-class life in another group of stories in which she examined persons of one upper social class in their contacts and conflicts with persons of another upper social class or other upper social classes. If the tales in the present chapter deal exclusively with American people in America, the stories of contact and conflict among upper-class groups frequently move their locale to Europe, where distinctions in social class are often more pronounced. In all of this group of stories though, whether set in Europe or in America, distinctions of social class are at the heart of things: they are the very substance on which the tales are built.

Note

[85] The early Wharton critic E.K. Brown has commented on the resemblance between "The Dilettante" and "Copy" (17)

Chapter Four

The Upper Classes

In these dozen stories, published over a span of nearly four decades, Wharton treats of the interaction of persons of elevated status among whom there is some important distinction of social class. As in the stories discussed in the previous chapter Wharton is writing here from a New York perspective, although half of the tales place their action in various European settings: Paris, Rome, the Alps, the south of France. In some of these European stories, American characters, usually from New York or with New York connections, come up against a European aristocracy into which they desire access or against which they consciously or unconsciously measure themselves; in others they merely move against the European backdrop (realistically and/or symbolically relevant) in their conflicted circumstances whose source is to be found in their distinctions of class.

In the other half dozen stories that limit their action to New York or Newport, Wharton plays various themes on the subject of the problems arising among persons of different classes who are married, or contemplating marriage, or caught up in conflicting attitudes about the permanence of the married state. It is fair to say that in most of these stories the conflicting social classes which the characters represent are on the one hand an established New York elite and on the other hand the parvenu group that seeks entry into the established class—or has already achieved entry to it. Most of the European stories play out the same themes.

The dramatic impetus in these stories of conflict between the social classes is a factor of the *relative* positioning of the classes. The stories are less interested in identifying or defining the contending classes than in establishing that there are important differences between them that provoke conflictual situations. At the same time, Wharton does make clear, if sometimes oblique, references to the classes she is considering in some of these stories. I make no effort to define the classes as sociological entities: this would involve a study unlike the one I have undertaken and outside the domain of literary criticism. In this chapter I refer to upper classes in a most general way and include the new American professional/merchant group that had attained or was attaining wealth and social standing during the period in which these stories are set.

In the tales discussed here, as in her ghost stories, Wharton reached the zenith of her artistic performance. The frequent anthologizing of "Roman Fever," "The Other Two," and "Autres Temps..." testifies to the excellence of the stories of this *genre*. Other lesser-known stories in this group deserve more of a hearing as well: "The Last Asset," "Her Son," and "Confession," for example. In these stories in which she is on her own ground, so to speak, in a broad social sense if not in a particular personal way, Wharton attains a striking, and sometimes a stunning, level of performance.

"Souls Belated"

"Souls Belated," first published in Wharton's 1899 collection *The Greater Inclination*, was the first of a dozen or so stories about the upper classes in which the author directs focus on matters of divisiveness or animosity among people of different, sometimes only slightly different, social status. In this story the central characters, an American couple, find themselves in an exclusive Italian lake resort populated with highbrow English guests who aim to set the moral and social standards for the other clients. Among these clients are an unmarried couple who have signed in under the name Linton but who are in reality Lord Trevanna and Mrs Cope, a commoner. The central characters, the lovers Ralph Gannett and the just-divorced Lydia Tillotson, themselves represent two strata of society. If Gannett is a member of the New York elite, Lydia "[comes] from a small town and [has entered] New York through the portals of the Tillotson mansion" (I, 106). Although Wharton's main interest in "Souls Belated" is the relationship between Lydia and Gannett, and particularly the former's preoccupation with her own moral and social predicament within that relationship, the fact that she has "come in" to the New York upper set from the outside has a large part to play in defining the person Lydia is.

The question of social class has much to say as well about Lydia's two men, Tillotson and Gannett. Lydia's former husband has lived scrupulously by the standards of the class as dictated by his mother. He is literally his mother's boy and lives with Lydia after their marriage in his mother's mansion. Here they conform to the prescribed regimen and practise the virtues of prudence, common sense, convention, and punctuality that Tillotson has "reverently imbibed with his mother's milk" (I, 106). Gannett, himself a member of the same social set—he has been a regular dinner guest at the Tillotson mansion, where he has met Lydia—is less hidebound by the conventions than are his hosts, more evidently his own man, more engaging and adventurous a personality, hence his appeal to Lydia. Nonetheless, it is clear that he is also inured to the essential dictates of his society. His utter surprise at Lydia's reluctance to marry him and his spontaneous lapses in sensitivity about the precarious situation in which Lydia finds herself after she receives her divorce papers—as when he asks her, "Where would you go if you left me?" (I, 124)—attest to the extent to which he is in the grip of the conventions.

Because she comes to New York life from the outside and as a young woman, Lydia is not hardened in the ways of the class to the degree her consorts are. She is, therefore, less prone to follow the dictates of society and of a mind more apt to perceive the flaws inherent in them. Because she is a woman from the outside, it is easier for her to see, as well, that the persons most liable to suffer the ill consequences of a slavish adherence to convention are women. Beyond this she is far and away the most intelligent of the characters we confront in the story, and Gannett is mature enough to perceive and accept her high intelligence. It is surely Lydia's intelligence that is at the core of the story, and we see it at work in the early interior monologue in which she assesses the liabilities of the current relationship in which she is engaged, in her insight about the current uncomfortable nature of her association with Gannett, in her ability to communicate her situation to him, and in her projection about her future plight. One of the most intriguing features of "Souls Belated" is the airing of the whole question of Lydia's entrapment, fallen into unawares: the young woman, in her inner reflections and subsequent conversations with her lover, demonstrates a keen sense of the subtleties and complexities of her predicament.

But for all her protestations against the hypocrisy of the social conventions and for all her sentiments of high personal idealism, Lydia fails to turn ideas into practice. We are prepared for her return to Gannett and certain marriage by her earlier defection from ideals during her two-month stay at the Hotel Bellosguardo. The extremity of the shift between theory and practice that takes place in Lydia is evident when one considers that hours before registering as Gannett's wife at the hotel she has engaged her lover in an extended appeal for his understanding of her position on the conventions. "We neither of us believe in the abstract 'sacredness' of marriage;" she says, "we both know that no ceremony is needed to consecrate our lives for each other; what object can we have in marrying, except the secret fear of each that the other may escape, or the secret longing to work our way back gradually—oh, very gradually—into the esteem of the people whose conventional morality we have always ridiculed and hated?" (I, 110). "And if we don't believe in the conventions," she asks, "is it honest to take advantage of the protection they afford?" (I, 111).

The extent to which Lydia is distracted from her good intentions during her stay at the Hotel Bellosguardo is suggested during a conversation she has with Mrs Pinsent, the gossipy apologist for the snobbish Lady Susan Condit. If Lydia is made uncomfortable by Mrs Pinsent's exposition of Lady Susan's iron-handed methods of maintaining "a certain tone" (I, 113) at the hotel, she shows no sign of it. And Mrs Pinsent's patronizing of Lydia and Gannett and her blatant put-down of the former provoke no response from the young woman: "[Lady Susan] took at once to you and Mr Gannett," Miss Pinsent tells Lydia, "—it was quite remarkable really. Oh, I don't mean that either—of course not! It was perfectly natural. We *all* thought you so charming and interesting from the first day—we knew at once that Mr. Gannett was intellectual, by the magazines you took in..." (I, 114). It is clear that Lydia is more conscious of not being seen amiss than of the slights directed towards her by Mrs Pinsent. Having been told, and having seen herself, that the Lintons are to be ignored, Lydia reacts with "displeasure" at Mrs Linton's desire to speak to her: "She certainly did not want to speak to Mrs Linton" (I, 115).

Of course it is Lydia's conversation with Mrs Cope (Mrs Linton has revealed her true identity to her) and that flashy woman's reminder to Lydia that "you and I were both in the same box" (I, 118) that triggers her self-recognition. Lydia subsequently tells Gannett that he must "tell Lady Susan and the others" (I, 121) of their unmarried state; she expresses her personal guilt to Gannett: "I've behaved badly, abominably, since we came here: letting these people believe we were married—lying with every breath I drew—" (I, 121) and she resolves to leave the hotel and Gannett. If anything, she seems more adamant in denouncing the hypocrisy of her position at this point than she was in earlier conversations with Gannett about the evils of adhering to the conventions of the class, and one expects her to follow through on her promise to herself. There is evidence though that her prolonged residence at the Hotel Bellosguardo has hardened her somewhat in the ways of the society she alleges to reject. One would hardly expect her, for example, given the fervor of her renewal after the meeting with Mrs. Cope, to flinch from her resolve to reveal her unmarried state. Yet in requesting Gannett to "go and tell Lady Susan and the others" (I, 121) she is doing exactly that. Her reluctance here foreshadows her inability to depart on the boat the next morning even as she is in the very act of attempting it.

The question of Lydia's inability to turn her principles into action is a fundamental one in the story. Margaret McDowell writes: "In 'Souls Belated' [Wharton] implies that marriage may be an artificial formality and a mere extraneous convention when love invests a liaison outside of marriage, but that compromise with conventions may undergird love more satisfactorily than the troublesome seeking of freedom from conventions" (*Edith Wharton* 83). Clearly the resolution of the profound conflict within Lydia in favor of marriage is not to be seen as an entirely negative one. In wishing to continue her relationship with Gannett she is opting for the man and not the class. Although Gannett does not understand his lover's position and commits gaffes that are the result of that misunderstanding, he is certainly the moral and intellectual superior of Tillotson. When Lydia reflects that "It was the abundance of Gannett's intentions that consoled her...for what they lacked in quality. After all it would have been worse, incalculably worse, to have detected any overreadiness to understand her" (I, 111), she is acknowledging his ability to be his own man, hence his superiority, certainly to Tillotson, and probably to his peers.

Gannett's ability to be his own man places him in sharp contrast to Mrs Cope's lover, Lord Trevanna, and indeed the resemblances between the Cope-Trevanna and the Lydia-Gannett relationships suggest that the former is being used as a foil for the latter. Both couples include a woman who comes from a lower social level than her man. The women also, each in her own way, take the initiative in the relationship leaving the men to react to their leads. These similarities but serve to introduce us to the vast differences between the two pairs of lovers. Lord Trevanna has been taken in tow by Mrs Cope who takes advantage of his callow youth and his attraction to her striking beauty, but the efforts of his family to intrude on his idyll have come too late. Mrs Cope is loud, aggressive, somewhat gaudy, and anxious to marry Trevanna. Lydia and Gannett are sensitive to one another's needs, and unopportunistic. They are superior to their counterparts both as individuals and as a couple, and it is interesting that Wharton's contrast shows the American "aristocrat" in a better light than the English lord, and the American woman from outside the inner social sanctum as the superior human being.

Although the merits of "Souls Belated" have not been catalogued in much detail in the literature on the story, its excellence has been appreciated. For

Lewis it is "one of [Wharton's] three or four finest stories" (*EW* 81), for Wolff "one of her best short stories" (85), for Brown, "the conflict of passion is treated in an admirable way" (6). "Souls Belated" is an auspicious start to a series of stories that occupied Wharton intermittently throughout her career: tales of upper-class life treated specifically as upper-class life.

"The Line of Least Resistance"

After focussing, in "Souls Belated," on the dangers of entrapment for women in marriage within a society governed by appearances and conventions, Wharton turned her attention to the liabilities men risked in contracting society marriage. In "The Line of Least Resistance," published in *Lippincott's Magazine* in October 1900, a year and a half after "Souls Belated" appeared, she examines the plight of a wealthy New York husband and father who finds himself unable to leave a marriage in which he is openly cuckolded by his youthful wife. Set in Newport, one of the summer playgrounds of affluent New Yorkers, "The Line of Least Resistance" effectively details the extent to which its protagonist, Mindon, sees himself the provider for his wife, Millicent, of the ample and luxurious domestic trappings which she has married him to acquire and which she now uses to advantage in the exercise of her marital infidelity.

"The Line of Least Resistance" is told by a third-person narrator who records the action as Mindon experiences it. In stories told from this perspective, the reader is left to judge whether or not the narrator is projecting a realistic view of the situation in which the protagonist finds himself. Mindon responds to his being manipulated by his wife with a clear mind and with resentment, and his pained understanding of the injustice of which he is the victim shows itself in many ways and can be assumed to have been present for a considerable time before he makes the decision to abandon his marriage on the day the story is set. His sense of the injustice done him is, for a time at least, balanced by a certain tolerance to his unpleasant situation. As the narrator tells us early in the story: "Mr. Mindon was shrewd enough to see that he reaped the advantages of his wife's imperfect domesticity, and that if her faults were the making of her, she was the making of him. It was therefore unreasonable to be angry with Millicent, even if she were late for luncheon, and Mr. Mindon, who prided himself on being a reasonable man, usually found some other outlet for his wrath" (I, 216).

But his reasonableness notwithstanding, Mindon finds himself more and more shaken by the circumstances of his life and the events of the day as he moves towards the discovery that brings about his decision to leave Millicent. He is irritated that Millicent is late for lunch; indeed, he seems to experience a permanent irritation, which manifests itself in a chronic stomach problem, a source alleged by Millicent of her displeasure with him.   His emotional and physical discomfort is largely a factor of the huge demands that Millicent's lifestyle make on his pocket book, a circumstance the narrator frequently comments about.   Her extravagant requirements in dress, entertainment, and generally keeping up the appearances of social standing are such that "literally and figuratively, he had gone on making larger and larger allowances, till his whole income, as well as his whole point of view, was practically at Millicent's disposal" (I, 217-218).

In a word, Mindon has little if anything to say about the conduct of affairs within his own family and household, even though he is their chief support.   The most striking example of his mere nominality as head of the house is the indifference and even insolence with which his servants respond to him.   The latter react to Millicent's ill temper by treating him with disrespect.   At his order that his daughters' pet dog be removed from the room, "[t]he butler continued to gaze over his head, and the two footmen took their cue from the butler"(I, 217). The children's governess is only somewhat less discourteous to Mindon: she is all but indifferent to her charges' girlish recalcitrance: when he points out to her that the children are late for dinner, she replies that "Gladys was always unpunctual" and "perhaps her papa would speak to her" (I, 216).

Mindon is most put out by the indifference of his young daughters, whom he recognizes to be "costly replicas of their mother" (I, 216).   He especially resents that the family puppy has been a gift from by Frank Antrim, his wife's lover, and recognizes that he has been displaced in Gwendolyn's affections by Antrim. His act of kicking the puppy is born of resentment for its donor, and his insistence on buying Gwendolyn "a much handsomer and more expensive one...a prize dog" (I, 217) is a frustrated attempt to restore himself to his daughter's good graces. His alienation from his two daughters signals the hopelessness of his plight within his house. When he tries to "go and play with the little girls" later during the afternoon "he found them dressing for a party, with the rapt gaze and fevered cheeks with which Millicent would presently perform the same rite. They took no notice of him, and he crept downstairs again" (I, 218).

If Mindon's discovery of Antrims's gift-giving to his daughters makes him feel disqualified as a father, his subsequent finding of the incriminating note written by Antrim to Millicent renders him redundant as a husband and launches him for the first time into a retaliatory mode. Significantly the knowledge of his wife's infidelity prompts only secret suffering and solitary action. By retreating to a local hotel he has once again followed the line of least resistance, repeating the pattern that has characterized his life within his household. His retreat from confrontation is but yet another manifestation of earlier kindred actions. Displeased with Antrim, he kicks the dog; upset with Millicent, he resolves interiorly to avenge himself on the servants; disappointed with his servants' bad manners, he contemplates attacking the governess. Apparently the strongest stand he has ever taken is to ask Millicent "to be reasonable" (I, 219). His hurt is real but remains hidden: his desire to confront even the servants scarcely translates into fact. No one but the dog feels the brunt of his anger.

The inability to confront that lies behind Mindon's silent and secretive departure to the Newport hotel is shortly thereafter repeated during his meeting with the three men who have been dispatched to save the family name. Mindon is of course no match for this triumvirate who represent the institutions that dictate and control conduct and manners in society: Laurence Meysey, the experienced man of the world who sees that Mindon's offended sensibility must be put behind the protection of the family; Ezra Brownrigg, Mindon's uncle and the senior partner in his law firm, who insists that a divorce would negatively affect business; and the Reverend Doctor Bonifant, rector of Mindon's church, for whom the family is sacrosanct above all other considerations. In the face of their onslaught, Mindon's stammering insistence that he wants a divorce wilts away. As in all other showdowns he takes the line of least resistance. "It's for the children" (I, 226), he murmurs as the story ends, and he may very well mean it. But the lightness with which his grievances are handled, the fact that his wife's infidelity is tacitly accepted and not even addressed by his interlocuters is shocking, to say the least. "Under certain conditions, what is unknown may be said to be nonexistent" (I, 226), says Doctor Bonifant, and Mindon's dilemma, indeed Mindon himself, remains effectively nonexistent even to this man of the cloth.

Mindon is a finely drawn example of a male character that is a staple of Wharton's fiction of manners. He is replicated in such men as Gus Trenor and Lily Bart's father from *The House of Mirth*, to mention two, men who are driven by their wives' and their society's desire to provide a suitably affluent lifestyle for their families and whose familial lives become devoid of fulfillment as a result. Mindon is an important character—and "The Line of Least Resistance" an important story—because he is developed beyond the type to which he belongs. His salient quality is his passiveness, and he is best understood if this is kept in mind. His inability to confront even his employees suggests that he is without a strong sense of self, and the narrator's evocation of Mindon's vision of himself as "a tiny object - the quivering imperceptible ego" being swept back to shore (I, 219) at the time he finds Antrim's note makes this explicit. Because he is aware of his own ineffectuality, Mindon's realization that he can take a stand—albeit a non-confrontational one—fills him with inner exaltation. He "felt a sudden increase of stature.... There was a fierce enjoyment in his sense of lucidity" (I, 220). He has risen "to the rarified heights of the unexpected" (I, 221). However, his ecstasy is short-lived, and he soon realizes that his latest surrender to the line of least resistance has "set him once more adrift on a chartless sea of perplexities"

(I, 222). The one quality he alleges as positioning him above the abuse that circulates around him, his reasonableness, is itself a self-deception: the decision to marry an attractive younger woman, who is probably outside his social set, cries in the face of his pretended reasonableness.

Mindon's marriage to Millicent and the subsequent intrusion of Antrim into the family places "The Line of Least Resistance" within the context of a fiction of manners. Because Antrim has given gifts to the children and because he has allowed them to call him by his first name he has been guilty of "bad form" (I, 218), he has offended against the prescriptions of the class into which he has been granted access by Millicent. The suggestion here is that he is an outsider, unaware of the manners expected of him. More to the point, Mindon is alerted by Antrim's lapse to his wife's *faux pas* in allowing her lover to act in this manner and he takes a certain pleasure in the fact that "Millicent had been guilty of that kind of failure she would have least liked him to detect—a failure in taste..." (I, 218). It is not unreasonable to suggest that she herself has been an outsider to Mindon's class and has used her beauty, youth, and a certain style to insinuate herself into a higher set by taking advantage of the innocent and innocuous man who becomes her husband. In her ascendancy to wealth and status she resembles both Lydia Tillotson and Mrs Cope of "Souls Belated," but if she shares the latter's brazenness she is entirely without the former's intelligence and sensitivity.

It is something of a mystery why "The Line of Least Resistance" has not garnered more attention than it has. Wharton herself was happy with it, considering it her best story to date, and she had planned to collect it in a volume that would bear its name. (*EW* 125) Its absence from her 1901 collection may have accounted for its contemporary neglect. The reason why it has not been the subject of more recent commentary can possibly be explained by the fact that it finds itself in a group with other stories of manners of such high quality: "The Other Two," "Roman Fever," "Autres Temps...," and "Souls Belated," for example. "The Line of Least Resistance" is another of a considerable list of Wharton short stories that deserves closer attention.

"The Quicksand"

"The Quicksand" appeared in *Harper's* in June 1902, two years after *Lippincott's* publication of "The Line of Least Resistance." It repeats its predecessor's examination of two social classes and of how the differences between them help us to understand the underlying tension and resolution that are at the heart of the story's significance. "The Quicksand" is also reminiscent of such Wharton short stories as "The Twilight of the God" and "Copy," relatively short pieces written during the same period, which Wharton chose to structure as brief plays. "The Quicksand" is made of three pieces of dialogue, the first between the central character, Mrs Quentin, and her son Alan, the other two, between her and Hope Fenno, a young woman whom Alan seeks to marry. Expository prose is kept to a minimum and is at times used to describe physical background that might appear as stage directions or stage settings in a formal dramatic script.

The earlier portions of "The Quicksand" establish that the parties in this drama of courtship belong to different New York social classes. It is clear from the earlier dialogue between Alan and his widowed mother that Hope is of an older established elite. Indeed Alan's first reference to Hope in the conversation in which he informs his mother that the young woman has refused to marry him is a reference to her social group. "It's painful to see them think" (I, 399), he says, establishing her identity with her family and her people—"them," those who can be expected to deliberate so carefully about a marriage decision, those, unlike him and his kind, who might bring a different, an old-fashioned, scale of values to bear on such a decision.

As well, the settings of the conversational exchanges in the story serve to demark the social group to which each family belongs. The Quentin house, where Alan has come to inform his mother of Hope's decision, bears the hallmarks of an establishment of the *nouveau riche*: "One felt it to be the result of a series of eliminations: there was nothing fortuitous in its blending of line and color. The almost morbid finish of every material detail of her life suggested the possibility that a diversity of energies had, by some pressure of circumstance, been forced into a channel of narrow dilettantism. [Mrs. Quentin's] house...was never so distinguished as when it was empty" (I, 397). With its self-conscious emphasis on stylishness and novelty, it contrasts sharply to the Fenno home, described during Mrs Quentin's visit there to plead, at her son's request, for a change of heart in Hope.

> [The Fenno drawing room] was the kind of room in which no member of the family was likely to be found except after dinner and after death. The chairs and tables looked like poor relations who had repaid their keep by a long career of grudging usefulness; they seemed banded together against intruders in a sullen conspiracy of discomfort.... The room showed none of the modern attempts at palliation...and Mrs. Quentin, provisionally perched on a green reps Gothic sofa...concluded that, had Mrs. Fenno needed another seat of the same size, she would have set out placidly to match the one in which her visitor now languished. (I, 401)

The descriptions of the respective home furnishings and decorations, however, do not function merely as indicators of social strata. Embedded in the physical descriptions are signs of the ways in which each interior reflects the social and personal preoccupations of its owner. Thus Mrs Quentin's "fastidiousness" about home decoration is seen to be not only a measure of her *parvenu* status but also of her hunger for perfection. Similarly, Mrs Fenno's furnishings reflect not only her state of financial depletion, her "failure," but as well the conservatism identified with an established class. Indeed, the reasons alleged by Quentin for Hope's refusal of his offer of marriage are closely tied to his perception that because she belongs to an older New York social caste, she is inhibited by the standards of that class against accepting him. Quentin repeatedly seizes upon the absence of spontaneity, intuition, and feeling in the Fennos with his almost obsessive characterization of their "thinking" side. "It's painful to see them think," he tells his mother. "She's been thinking—hard.... The result of her cogitations is that she won't have me. She arrived at this by pure ratiocination— it's not a question of feeling, you understand" (I, 398).

With Quentin's disappearance from the foreground of the story after Section I, considerations of social distinctions are largely displaced by ones of personal and moral significance, one of the several ways by which Wharton signals the erosion of sharp distinctions between social classes. Quentin himself, in spite of his conscious demarcation of classes, suggests in his own rhetoric the blurring of the very distinctions he insists on. He addresses his mother as "a nice old-fashioned intuitive woman" (I, 398) and "You dear archaic woman" (I, 399). Of Hope's "prejudices" he remarks: "...those she has are brand-new; that's the trouble with them. She's tremendously up to date. She takes in all the moral fashion papers, and wears the newest thing in ethics" (I, 399). But in erasing distinctions he only draws attention to them, and in any case all his considerations about social class are put to the grand effort he is making to rationalize away the reason Hope has rejected him: his editorship of the grossly immoral scandal sheet *The Radiator*.

In the narration of Mrs Quentin's meeting with Hope in the Fenno home, the drama-like construction of the text is again evident in the two-character dialogue and the attention given to setting description. It is surely significant that in detailing Mrs Quentin's consciousness of her surroundings and her conversant's representativeness of them, Wharton is suggesting Mrs Quentin's inability to detach herself from her son and be true to her own sense of what is right. Her attitudes especially during the early part of the visit reflect those of Alan as he has revealed himself in his earlier conversation with his mother. "To Mrs. Quentin's fancy, Hope Fenno's opinions, presently imparted in a clear young voice from the opposite angle of the Gothic sofa, partook of the character of their surroundings. The girl's mind was like a large light empty place, scantily furnished with a few massive prejudices, not designed to add to anyone's comfort but too ponderous to be easily moved" (I, 401-402). Blinded by her love—"Alan is a perfect son," she tells Hope—she is less than herself. Hope here emerges as the superior of the two. Although the older woman carries the conversation, raising reason after reason why the latter's fears are unwarranted, Hope meets all her remonstrations with intelligence, wit, and clarity. By the end we sense that Hope has won her point. The principles the Quentins have tended to denigrate have stood her in good stead. She has been cowed neither by Mrs Quentin's experienced outlook, nor by her admiration for her, nor by her own love for Alan.

The second meeting between Mrs Quentin and Hope takes place six months later at the Metropolitan Museum, significantly, on neutral ground, away from the home of each. The tension between the two women is palpable given the circumstances of Hope's refusal of Alan and Mrs Quentin's unsuccessful effort to have her change her mind. When the latter, referring to their last meeting, announces early in the dialogue, "You were right—that day—and I was wrong" (I, 406), the tension is intensified. Mrs Quentin's surprising statement launches her into her counter-offensive upon Hope, who has declared moments earlier that she has changed her mind about marrying Alan. Once again Mrs Quentin dominates the exchange, this time even more strongly. The history of her relationships with the two men whose lives have been committed to the dissemination of scandalous news is told passionately, graphically, and unequivocally. She has felt "walled up alive" (I, 407), and at the time of her husband's decision to sell the *Radiator* she recalls, "I saw that we were in a vicious circle. The paper, to sell well, had to be made more and more detestable and disgraceful...the ground seemed to give under me: with every struggle I sank deeper" (I, 408). Hope responds to Mrs Quentin's story wordlessly, sitting "motionless, her eyes on the ground" (I, 410) as the latter walks away.

As sometimes occurs in Wharton's short fiction, the story told within the main story ends up shouldering the latter off-center. In "The Quicksand," it is this inner tale from which the title is derived. And the dramatic is superceded by the narrative as Mrs Quentin becomes more *raconteuse* than actor in the final pages. That notwithstanding, the earlier portions of the scene in the Metropolitan yield some interesting observations in terms of their dramatic caste. The fact that Hope pronounces her change of mind, her abandonment of principle in a place that is physically removed from her own home has symbolic significance: it suggests

170

that, removed from her environment, she is without the sustaining vision that guided her previously. And the fact that Mrs Quentin has told her story and delivered her message in the house of art and away from the two houses that have previously tended to blur her judgment has more than merely symbolic force. It can be said that as "The Quicksand" shifts into a monological mode it finds a new center, away from the houses of Quentin and Fenno and within the personal experience and moral integrity of its main character.

"The Quicksand" has not received a great deal of critical attention in the literature about Wharton's short fiction, perhaps because its earlier dramatic edge is not sustained. Nevertheless, its characterization of Mrs Quentin is remarkable, and Allen F. Stein has perhaps best expressed that character's most notable quality: "...by staying in a hideous marriage Mrs Quentin has gained more than she would had she sought to escape it. Brought by her marriage to an awareness of the intransigence of evil in human nature, including her own, Mrs. Quentin has been purged of illusions. She has won her way into the house of pain and from its vantage point can see her way clear to shielding another from a dark triumph like her own" (221).

"The Other Two"

"The Other Two," one of Wharton's most anthologized and also most commented upon stories, had its original appearance in the February 13, 1904 issue of *Collier's*. Lewis has favored it with the highest praise, calling it "very likely the best short story Mrs Wharton ever wrote," (*ICSS* XIV) and "the most nearly perfect short story Edith Wharton ever wrote and a model in the genre of the comedy of manners" (*EW* 134). Brown comments that "The Other Two" shows Wharton in such a light as to make the short fiction of Katherine Mansfield appear mediocre (14-16). Nevius reflects Lewis's evaluation when he writes, "There is no better capsule demonstration than in 'The Other Two' of the imaginative use to which Edith Wharton put her interest in manners" (72). As well, the story is the subject of other extended comment by Wolff, White, and Stein. The result of all this attention is that it has been given a very thorough critical going-over, to the point where it is difficult to find a facet of the story that has been left untouched. The question of Alice Waythorn's "elasticity" and "pliancy" and the role this plays in her rising through the ranks to the highest social level (Wolff, 108); the objectifying of Alice by Waythorn (White 17); the fact that Waythorn comes around to perceiving "the folly of his seeing himself above [the world]" (Stein 262): all of these important topics have been more than adequately covered.

Given this happy state of the coverage of "The Other Two," there seems little point in repeating what has been said often and well. Rather, the emphasis in the ensuing discussion will be on the ways in which the dynamic among different strata of society affects the life of the story. This element of "The Other Two" seems to have been less the subject of comment than other elements and deserves some mention.

Alice herself has belonged to "society," has had an "undoubted connection with a socially reigning family"—but away from New York City, in Utica—and has contracted a first marriage to Haskett, a man below her station,—"a runaway match at seventeen" (I, 381). Alice's second marriage, to the New Yorker Gus Varick has "rescued" her "from the outer darkness" (I, 382) and brought her into society. But Varick has not satisfied her material aspirations, for we are told that prior to the present time of the story "he had dabbled only in the shallow pools of speculation, with which Waythorn's office did not usually concern itself" (I, 384). Indeed Varick has admitted as much to Waythorn, saying, "The fact is I'm not used to having much money to look after.... It feels uncommonly queer to have enough cash to pay one's bills. I'd have sold my soul for it a few years ago!" (I, 387). Alice's present marriage to Waythorn, who is Varick's social equal, has been motivated by the former's more tangible financial success. It is interesting to note that Waythorn, forced into working with Varick in the seeing through of the latter's promising speculative plan out of a sense of solidarity with his business partner Sellers, is not keen to assist his wife's former husband. "He did not care a farthing for the success of Varick's venture," we are told (I, 387). It is obvious why. He had just witnessed his wife's action of preparing his coffee in precisely the same way as she had performed that service for Varick and realizes that Alice retains some remembrance of and feeling for Varick. The vision of a wealthier Varick, a Varick still attractive to Alice, constitutes some threat to Waythorn.

Because "The Other Two" is told by a narrator who has access to Waythorn's consciousness, it adopts his attitudes about class and wealth. Stein writes that "It is not long before [Waythorn] learns that neither Haskett nor Varick is a bad sort, and that his marriage, rather than isolating him from the world, not only brings him into close contact with it but teaches him, as well, the folly of seeing himself as above it" (262). But although he "had been finding out about Haskett, and all that he had learned was favorable" (I, 391), and although "he could not but respect [his] tenacity [i.e., about his concern for Lily's welfare]" (I, 392), he can never forget Haskett's lower social status. If he boasts that Haskett no longer reminds him of "a piano tuner" (I, 392), his attitude towards him remains patronizing, as evidenced by his reference to details such as his "commonness," his "boarding house" (I, 394), and his lack of breeding. Waythorn's most conspicuous betrayal of his inability to judge people on their own merits, and Wharton's finest touch in a story that is filled with fine touches, is his response to the way Haskett sits while in the Waythorn home: "In the library he found Haskett occupying a chair in his usual provisional way. Waythorn always felt grateful to him for not leaning back" (I, 394).

In fact, Haskett is a paragon of character: devoted, forthright, tenacious, humble, and self-aware, a model of fatherly concern and devotion, a very tiger in his insistence on the best upbringing for his daughter. We may be tempted to question his perspicacity when he complains to Waythorn about Lily's governess. "I don't like the woman," he says. "She ain't straight, Mr. Waythorn—she'll teach the child to be underhand. I've noticed a change in Lily—she's too anxious to please—and she don't always tell the truth. She used to be the straightest child Mr. Waythorn—" (I, 390). But his inability to see that his daughter's eroding truthfulness and encroaching manipulativeness are the product of her mother's influence may merely mask the fact that he wishes to see no ill in his former wife.

Waythorn's enigmatic laugh at the conclusion of "The Other Two" has occasioned a number of attempts by critics to explain it. Considering that Waythorn is not the kind of man who would be likely to shed many tears if he lost Alice, and considering that he recognizes her for what she is, is it not possible that he is revelling mildly at the self-created mental image of himself as the third of "another three," so perceived by some future Alice Waythorn conquest? The beauty of "The Other Two," among other of its qualities, is its capacity to allow just such a speculation.

"The Last Asset"

Another superb story of social climbing appeared six months after "The Other Two": *Scribner's* carried "The Last Asset" in its issue of August 1904. In this tale Wharton moved away from New York to a European setting, placing her American protagonist and characters in Paris, the site of their forays into continental life. "The Last Asset" might by seen as a "Daisy Miller" in which focus is shifted away from the daughter and on to the mother: both Wharton's story and James's deal with aspiring Americans' wishes to enhance their social positions through successful marriages for their daughters, but in place of the inept Mrs Miller of Schenectady, Wharton's story features the highly manipulative—and successful—Mrs Newell "from somewhere in western New York" (I, 604), and in place of the very spontaneous and ebullient Daisy, a withdrawn, though similarly genuine Hermione Newell. Within the Wharton short-story canon "The Last Asset" is reminiscent of the earlier story "Souls Belated." It too features American protagonists translated to a European milieu, and one of its minor characters, the flamboyant and beautiful English woman Mrs Cope, prefigures the doubtlessly attractive and clearly persuasive Mrs Newell.

A major strength of "The Last Asset" is the development of the character of Mrs Newell, of whom the point-of-view character Garnett reflects in summary during Hermione's wedding ceremony: "One and all [the other guests] were there to serve her ends and accomplish her purpose: Schenkelderff and the Hubbards to pay for the show, the bride and bridegroom to seal and symbolize her social rehabilitation, Garnett himself as the humble instrument adjusting the different parts of the complicated machinery, and her husband, finally, as the last stake in her game, the last asset on which she could draw to rebuild her fallen fortunes" (I, 615). Garnett's capsule assessment of Mrs Newell covers the years since her husband's financial failure. The present time of the story dramatizes the most precarious portion of that history, the moment when its central figure, having managed to marshall those resources that are necessary to her social survival and even permanent success and comfort, finds herself poised on the edge of a likely disaster should she not be able to enlist her estranged husband as the final implement in the realization of her purposes. Mrs Newell's efforts to secure a place in society have always been tenuous. In Garnett's view, she "really moved too fast;... She used up everything too quickly—friends, credit, influence, forbearance. It was so easy for her to acquire all these—what a pity she had never learned to keep them!... If she exhausted old supplies she always had new ones to replace them. When one set of people began to find her impossible, another was always beginning to find her indispensible" (I, 593). Now Garnett sees that she has almost used up her possibilities: "there were limits—there were only so many sets of people, at least in her classification, and when she came to an end of them, what then?" (I, 593-594). The window open to her is near to being shut: the du Trayas family is close to withdrawing its support for their son's marriage to Hermione, and Mrs Newell's alliances with money and aristocracy are largely contingent upon that union being effected. Hence the urgency of Garnett's mission to convince Sam Newell to make the mandatory appearance at his daughter's wedding.

Wharton's narrative method is to acquaint us with Mrs Newell's past (and to a lesser extent her husband's) through the ruminations of a removed narrator. The narrator speaks via the consciousness of the young society reporter Garnett, follows Garnett about Paris as he responds to his patron's initial summons, and then proceeds, out of sympathy with Hermione, to accept the mission of conscripting Sam Newell for the all-essential appearance at the church of Saint Philippe du Roule. Evidently Garnett serves a central role in "The Last Asset": he is present at all the action and he furnishes both facts (which we must accept as accurate) and opinions (the validity of which we are free to judge for ourselves) about past and present. Often in Wharton stories, narrators and reflectors are not to be taken at their word. As well, because of the persons and actions they are engaged with, narrators and reflectors tend to deflect attention away from themselves. In "The Last Asset" Mrs Newell and her manipulations are striking enough, and Sam Newell's abjectness startling enough, to lull us into ignoring the important change that is one of the story's most subtle features: the growth in awareness and sensitivity taking place in the *New York Searchlight's* London correspondent, Garnett.

When Garnett arrives at Ritz's to keep his appointment with Mrs Newell we find a very superficial young man who, by virtue of his job as a journalist reporting on society people and events, is primarily impressed with exterior show and excitement. He is immediately taken with Mrs Newell, whose "appearance was brilliantly fresh, with the inveterate freshness of the toilet table; her paint...impenetrable as armor. But her personality was a little tarnished: she was in want of social renovation." His habit of evaluating persons in terms of their usefulness in society is demonstrated on this occasion by his assessment of Hermione: "With the smartest woman in London as her guide and example," he reflects, "she had never developed a taste for dress, and with opportunities for enlightenment from which Garnett's fancy recoiled she remained simple, unsuspicious and tender, with an inclination to good works and afternoon church, a taste for the society of dull girls, and a clinging fidelity to old governesses and retired nursemaids" (I, 595). So blinded is Garnett by the social primacies of his *métier*—and these are brandished before him in the person of his glamorous hostess—that he fails utterly to appreciate the character and personal charm of Hermione. He receives Mrs Newell's information about her daughter's

176

impending marriage with "a long silent stare," then "a cry of wonder" and "somewhat unseemly astonishment." Confronted with the name and status of Hermione's intended, he responds with "deepening wonder," generated by the huge social implications of the match. "Hermione a bride!" he exclaims inwardly, "Hermione a future countess! Hermione on the brink of a marriage which would give her not only a great 'situation' in the Parisian world but a footing in some of the best houses in England!" (I, 597). When Mrs Newell responds to Garnett's surprise with "You've never appreciated her" and "You've no imagination" (I, 598), she is drawing attention, inadvertently perhaps, to the extent to which Garnett has failed to recognize in Hermione the human quality that transcends his own shallow standards, the very quality that has drawn the attention of Comte Louis du Trayas.

Garnett's initial reaction to Mrs Newell's request that he act for her in securing her husband's presence at Hermione's wedding is not favorable. His mind is changed by the sight of the genuine feeling he perceives between the young engaged couple during Mrs Woolsey Hubbard's dinner party. The catalyist, at least in part, for Garnett's shift in attitude is Mrs Newell's current companion, Baron Schenkelderff, for whom he conceives an immediate dislike: the latter's looks, and his past involvement in what appears to have been a questionable business affair upset him. If her association with Schenkelderff lowers Mrs Newell in Garnett's eyes and signals the beginnings of his disenchantment with her, the vision of Hermione's living out her life in the shadow of her mother's new friend absolutely seals his conviction that "Hermione's marriage must take place" (I, 603). It is the sense "that in this case, at least, the sins of the parents should not be visited on the children" (I, 607) that informs Garnett's refusal to take no for an answer from Sam Newell on the day he proposes that the latter must submit to his wife's wish.

Garnett leaves Newell after relaying to him Mrs Newell's request with the knowledge that the old man's consent is far from assured. It is the unplanned interview with Hermione, instigated by the latter, that provides him with the ammunition with which he can win the battle over Mr Newell's consent. During this brief interview Garnett is "astonished at the passion of [Hermione's] accent; astonished still more at the tone with which she went on" (I, 610) protesting at the unreasonableness of her mother's demand to her father. Garnett is "deeply struck" by the girl's selflessness, her sensitivity to the shame to which her father has been put and will be put if he accedes to Mrs Newell's plan: she is willing to forgo her own marriage in order to save what she feels will be her father's huge embarrassment. When towards the close of their conversation Garnett thinks, "'It might be the best thing'...but did not give utterance to the thought," he is visualizing his likely moment of success with Newell, who will not fail to be moved by Hermione's insistence that Garnett tell her father "what I've said to you!" (I, 610).

Garnett's admiration for Hermione in this scene is triggered not simply by her utter thoughtfulness and generosity. He is "astonished" and "deeply struck" by the change he perceives to have occurred in the young woman. His earlier response to her has been of a "vague personality...merely tributary to her parent's... [whose] youth and grace were, in some mysterious way, her mother's rather than her own," as one who "Burning at best with a mild light...became invisible in the glare of her mother's personality" (I, 595). Now he views her with "increasing wonder," and "he had never supposed her capable of such emotion as her voice and eyes revealed" (I, 609). Garnett's observations during the wedding service reveal that his attitudes to Mrs Newell and Hermione have moved to a diametrically opposed position. The woman whom he had but days before admired is now a puppeteer for whom family, friends, and acquaintances have "become mere marionettes pulled hither and thither by the hidden wires of her intention," and he feels a "deep disgust" for the scene she has engineered and for his own participation in her plan. The young bride who had a short time ago disappeared in her mother's shadow is now an "illuminated presence" (I, 615). What has happened, of course, is that Garnett now sees things as they have always been. The change has taken place not in the Newell women but in him: shorn of the superficiality become second nature to him over years of writing about the social life by the sight of genuinely experienced emotion and selfless generosity, he understands the real life that lies beneath facades.

The path of Garnett's redemption is hidden beneath the exceptionally compelling events and manipulations that are the outer substance of "The Last Asset," to the point where he, the only dynamic character in the piece, can be virtually forgotten. Indeed, in two of the most recent commentaries about the story, by Barbara White and Allen Stein, the question of Garnett's evolution is not mentioned. Certainly these two critics have much to say of value about "The Last Asset," and White comments astutely on the implications of the title by extending their possibilities beyond the story's explicit mention of it: "[Mrs. Newell's] husband...as the last stake in her game, the last asset on which she could draw to rebuild her fallen fortunes" (I, 615). White notes that Baron Schenkelderff "has been cast out of society for financial misdealings and has seized on Mrs Newell as his 'last asset'" (78). Would it be stretching matters too far to suggest, as well, that the title has implications in connection with Garnett? Now that the latter has seen the meretriciousness of his chosen profession and will be hard put to practise it with any conviction, cannot he too be said to be thrust back on the ultimate "last asset" of the human person, the truth-seeking mind?

"The Introducers"

In "The Introducers," published serially in the *Ainslee's* issues of December 1905 and January 1906, Wharton returned to the subject of the intercourse between the social sets, but not with as much success as she had in her previous two stories of the genre, "The Last Asset" and "The Other Two." The story is reminiscent of an 1899 tale "The Twilight of the God," also set in Newport, and structured along the lines of a playlet. One wonders if "The Introducers" had not been initially conceived by Wharton as a playlet as well, for it has a number of the characteristics of that art form without technically adopting the format of a drama. Its two major characters converse only with each other and they do so always in the same setting and at the same time of day. Early in the story the male character Frederick Tilney muses as he looks out over the ocean from "a shaded seat invitingly placed near the path which follows the shore: 'Sometimes I feel as if the sea, and the cliffs, and the skyline out there, were all a part of the stupid show—the expensive stage setting of a rottenly cheap play—to be folded up and packed away with the rest of the rubbish when the performance is over'..." (I, 531). Certainly Tilney conceives of his present role in life as that of a player in an insignificant drama, and it appears that Wharton has structured her story as a play to accentuate the artificial quality of the occupations its two protagonists hold within the social orbit they presently inhabit, itself a false and make-believe one.

Wharton's premise for "The Introducers" is a fresh and interesting one: its two principals, youthful members of a higher American class, are employed by two *nouveau riche* parties, Tilney by the bachelor Hutchins Magraw, and Belle Grantham by the Bixby family, as social secretaries. They have come into such employment because their hirers know they will be able to instruct them in the manners necessary to inhabit the higher class to which they aspire and more particularly because they will furnish them with the contacts that will facilitate their entry into the class. Thus the two are introducers, and it is understood that the most valuable introductions they will be able to make are those that match wealthy young men and women to the sons and daughters of an old established class: effectively, Tilney and Belle have been hired to be match-makers.

The "cheap play" their roles give them access to observe—as members of their own class they are aware of the efforts to keep the new-comers out; as the privileged employees of *nouveaux riches* they observe first-hand the efforts that are made to penetrate the sacrosanct domain of their own social group— displeases them immensely. Part of the drama they witness is particularly distasteful to them because they see themselves cheapened in the bargain: because their financial means are relatively meager, they find themselves playing with the temptation to marry "down" merely to insure for themselves lives of comfort and leisure. "The Introducers" resolves itself into the story of how Tilney and Belle pass up the lure and choose each other as life partners, more because they recognize their strong fellow feeling and reciprocal attraction and less because they are members of the same upper class—though there may be a complementary factor present in these elements.

Setting of place and time assumes a major function in "The Introducers." The aforementioned bench, with its undisturbed view of the landscape it offers in the early morning prior to the cluttering of the scene by the denizens of Newport, is a symbol central to the story's significance and so perceived by the protagonists. "[I]t's good," Tilney reflects (and Belle later tells him that she uses the bench for the same purpose) "to come out and find it here at this hour, all by itself, and not giving a hang for the ridiculous goings-on of which it happens to be made the temporary background" (I, 531). It is from the bench that he observes Cliffwood, the Bixby mansion, with its "fantastic chimneys and profusely carved gables which made the neighboring villa rise from the shrubberies like a *pièce montée* from a flower-decked dish" (I, 533). It is here that he and Belle discuss their respective efforts not to have their charges look ridiculous in high society. It is here that Belle quotes to Tilney Aline Leicester's statement to her, "Belle, I see the Bixbys in your eyes, but I don't see them in my ballroom," and tells him that Aline's "latest pose is to snub the new millionaires" (I, 536). It is here that Tilney and Belle arrange to have each other meet, respectively, Sadie Bixby and Hutchins Magraw at Aline Leicester's Louis XV dance. In short it is from the bench overlooking the pristine sea and cliffs in the pure early morning air that the two see clearly the distasteful drama of the classes—including their own roles in it—for what it is.

It is on the bench, or near the bench and in view of it, that the developing love relationship between Tilney and Belle is played out. We see them expressing reciprocal admiration and then betraying their anxiety that each will be lost to the other if the arranged liaisons with Sadie and Magraw draw them away, and finally pledging their allegiance to one another. Tilney's final words, the closing words of the story, suggest the broader implications of the bench as symbol of togetherness: "Don't you see that Magraw and Miss Bixby must be sitting there together, and that, in that case, nothing remains for you and me but to find a new seat for ourselves?" (I, 554). Not only have Tilney and Belle renounced their desire for material advancement and settled for each other, but also Sadie and Magraw appear to have put aside their designs for marriage into the higher set in favor of an attachment to one another.

If the bench functions in "The Introducers" as a symbol fixed in place, Wharton has fleshed out her story with another important symbol, this a dynamic one whose shifts and alterations signal the psychological state of the two youthful protagonists. On the first day of Tilney's appearance on the bench, "The morning was brilliant, with a blue horizon line pure of fog" (I, 530). That state of the atmosphere continues as Belle makes her appearance and the two learn of their identical responses to both the natural setting and the social milieu. On a later morning when Tilney is fearful of a possible entanglement between Belle and Magraw, "The morning was chilly and veiled in a slight haze, too translucent to be called a fog, but perceptible enough to cast a faint grayness over sea and sky" (I, 545). Later still, on a morning when Tilney mistakes Sadie's silhouette for Belle's, he muses, "It's odd—it's odd how the fog distorts a silhouette. I could have sworn I should have known her anywhere and yet this deceptive vapor—or my nerves, or the two together—make her look so much shorter—and I'll swear I never saw her swing her arms as she walked" (I, 548-549). But once assured that the figure is not Belle's and that Magraw is sitting with another woman on the bench, he easily recognizes "the indistinct gleam of a white dress halfway down the Cliffwood lawn" to be Belle's, "even though the fog had thickened" (I, 549). Similarly, when he finds himself "face to face with Miss Grantham," she, as well, "suddenly [discerns] him though the fog" (I, 550). Finally, realizing that their two charges now share the bench, Tilney and Belle are "charged with a gradual rush of inner enlightenment" (I, 554) that dispels their fears for good.

"The Introducers" has received virtually no critical attention and is surely not up to the standard of Wharton's better fiction of manners. It is probably longer than it needs to be, and once the social context of its personages has been set out and the protagonists' vision of life becomes clarified, there is not much to hold the readers' attention, and the ending is telegraphed long before it occurs. Yet "The Introducers" is noteworthy because of the manner in which Wharton introduces an effective symbology and sustains it to accent the story's social and interpersonal themes.

"Les Metteurs en scène"

The following footnote appears on the first page of "Les Metteurs en scène" in Volume I of *The Collected Short Stories of Edith Wharton*:

> Revue des Deux Mondes, LXVII, October 1908 (Translated by Becky Nolan, French Graduate Program, Yale University). The French title is retained as appropriate in the Parisian setting. It is a theater phrase meaning "The Stage Managers." (I, 555)

The note occasions two comments, the first in the form of a question. Why did Scribner's not hire a professional translator to render Wharton's French text into English? As solid, no doubt, as Becky Nolan's credentials were as a graduate student in the Yale French Department, would it not have been preferable that one with professional experience in the translation of literary texts from French into English be assigned this job? The question of the artistic accuracy of the translation of "Les Metteurs en scène" is particularly relevant in view of the fact that Wharton herself was preoccupied around the period of the story's appearance by the problem of communicating in a second language. In "The Verdict," published four months before "Les Metteurs en scène" and a story no doubt in her mind around the time she was engaged with her French tale, the character Jack Gisburn asks, "Don't you know how in talking a foreign language, even fluently, one says half the time, not what one wants to but what one can?" (I, 662). It would be useful to have a professional translation of "Les Metteurs en scène" if only to verify the validity of Ms Nolan's work.

The other comment, suggested by the second portion of the note in the Scribner's collection, is that Wharton's French story is close in spirit to "The

Introducers" in its view of the marriage-making process as an activity suitable for portrayal as theater. In "Les Metteurs en scène," as in the earlier story, the match-makers are both members of the upper class who are without the material resources to lead lives of financial independence and who are materially sustained by those *nouveaux riches*, mainly Americans, who seek introduction into the European aristocracy through marriage. Wharton sets the scene in Paris and creates as her stage-managing tandem a French aristocrat and a young American woman. Jean Le Fanois, the point-of-view character for a removed third-person narrator, is an "aristocratic Parisian" (I, 555) who "for almost ten years,...[has] led the tiresome and ambiguous life of a promoter of 'nouveaux riches' in Parisian society" (I, 557). His associate, Blanche Lambart, has come "from more refined stock than most Americans who try to storm Parisian society. Everything about her betrayed a careful education, an abundance of social graces, the habit of moving in elegant circles" (I, 558).

Like their counterparts in "The Introducers," Frederick Tilney and Belle Grantham, Le Fanois and Blanche are strongly tempted by the prospect of "breaking into" the *nouveau riche* set to ensure a life of comfort for themselves, but "Les Metteurs en scène" resolves its principals' dilemma on that score in a far different way. For the romantic conclusion of "The Introducers," in which Tilney and Belle find each other, "Les Metteurs en scène" substitutes a less idyllic solution. Le Fanois succumbs to the lure of wealth in his engagement to marry the American millionaire Mrs Smithers and so misses his chance for a union with Blanche, which would have provided him with the best of the two worlds he seeks. There is also about "Les Metteurs en scène" the view of the Parisian aristocratic set—including Le Fanois—as wasteful, superficial, and *ennuyé*. Blanche, although she has tired of being poor and actively seeks a successful marriage, does not compromise herself in the grossly venal way Le Fanois does. In her refinement she emerges superior to Le Fanois and his group of *aristocrates du faubourg*.

Wharton was unhappy with her experiment of writing fiction in French. Lewis reports her "[admitting] to Brownell [her editor at Scribner's] that she would never dare look him or Henry James in the face after this rash undertaking." And her fear of James's displeasure was confirmed by the former's saying to her, "I do congratulate you, my dear, on the way in which you've picked up every old worn-out literary phrase that's been lying about the streets of Paris for the last twenty years, and managed to pack them all into those few pages" (*EW* 234). Although Wharton holds her own in the earlier descriptive and narrative portions of the story, the potentially dramatic later dialogue of the two principals falls flat. One only has to compare it to the conversation in such a tale as "The Dilettante"to see how little at ease Wharton was with the dialogue in her French story. But if Wharton and some of her friends considered "Les Metteurs en scène" a failure, and if she never again undertook to publish fiction in French, it missed the mark because her standard was so high. It is interesting to note that E.K. Brown, himself a critic who wrote in French, hesitated to criticize her effort in the story, noting of the style that it was *"excellent, fermé, ramassé et concis"* (22).

"His Father's Son"

Because "His Father's Son" centers on the family of a successful businessman whose home and enterprise are in Wingfield, Connecticut, a family that cannot be said to be upper-class in any real sense of the term, the story's inclusion among this group of commentaries on tales about people of higher social standing may very well be put into question. However, "His Father's Son" is about, among other things, social standing and accession to the New York upper classes, hence its discussion here.

The story appeared in *Scribner's* in June 1909 and is one of the very few in the Wharton canon in which a date is used to fix its temporal context. Mason Grew the successful entrepreneur informs his lawyer son that the first letter written by the pianist Dolbrowski to Mrs Grew is dated January 10, 1872. If we assume that young Ronald Grew, who is practising corporate law with a New

York firm, is in his early thirties, we may conclude that the present time of the story coincides more or less with the period of its writing, in other words that Wharton was making a point of telling us that she was placing the story in her own time.

It is difficult to say if Wharton intended the story to have a special autobiographical resonance. At least two critics have seen that as a very strong possibility. R.W.B. Lewis writes, for example:

> [I]t may be that it was only at this time that Edith first heard the rumor about her own irregular paternity. If so the story implies that she rejected it decisively.
>
> There are, nevertheless, one or two interesting parallels. Edith Jones, born in January 1862, was, according to allegation, not the daughter of the soberly upper-middle-class George Frederic Jones, but of the cultivated foreign-born tutor of her brothers. In "His Father's Son" young Ronald Grew persuades himself that he is not the son of the solidly bourgeois buckle manufacturer Mason Grew, but of the distinguished European pianist Fortuné Dubrowski.... But it is all an innocent hoax and a misunderstanding; Mrs. Grew had never even met Dubrowski and the tender letters she was supposed to have written him were in fact composed, for a variety of reasons, by her husband. (*EW* 254) It was crude, certainly, unless it were a touch of the finest art. The difficulty of classifying it disturbed Thursdale's balance. (I, 413)

Gloria C. Erlich contends that Mason Grew's love of music and language places him in the same category of male characters with artistic traits—Newland Archer of *The Age of Innocence*, for example. Of these characters Erlich notes: "Whether their aesthetic interests are dominant or vestigial, in most cases these men are married to worldly women who value financial over intellectual assets. This recurring pattern seems to stem from Wharton's grief for her own father's wasted potential, a loss that she attributed to her mother" (139).

It is intriguing to speculate about whether Wharton's unusual use of a date in this short story signals some particular personal preoccupation she wishes to accent. Taken on its own "His Father's Son" is without much subtlety. The title, often in a Wharton story a key to the relative complexity or transparency of a piece, is here alluded to twice in specific terms by the senior Grew to his son as he both harps on the reason for the latter's success and explains away his suspicions about his paternity. The depiction of Mason Grew is straightforward and obvious also and reminds us that Wharton's most interesting male point-of-view characters are those whose real selves are hidden over by all manner of guises, defenses, and motivations.

One important aspect of the portrayal of Mason Grew has elicited little or no comment, and in the context of the present discussion of stories about the interplay of social classes should not be left unmentioned. At one level "His Father's Son" is about the accession of Ronald Grew to the higher regions of New York society, and it is a source of pride for the father that the son's Groton and Harvard education, his Columbia law school degree, and his employment with a New York corporate law firm have given him the wherewithal to contract a likely marriage into the city's elite class. These advantages have been made possible not only by the father's brains but also by the financial resources of his company, Secure Suspender Buckle of Wingfield, Connecticut.

But if young Ronald's social ascent has begun in Wingfield and ended in New York where he will shortly land in the bosom of the Waltham Bankshire family by way of their daughter Daisy, the elder Grew has made Brooklyn the end of his line. He is satisfied to live in the "sociological isolation of Brooklyn" (II, 36) where its geographical nearness to New York will allow him to bask in the sunshine of his son's success. Because his essential creativity and intelligence have always been kept under wraps, because these qualities have never been recognized, Mason Grew lives out his latter days in the reflected glory of Ronald's acceptance into metropolitan society, the tangible recognition for him of his son's quality and hence of his own: "He wanted to be near enough to New York to go there often, to feel under his feet the same pavement that Ronald trod, to sit now and then in the same theaters, to find on his breakfast table the journals which, with increasing frequency, inserted Ronald's name in the sacred bounds of the society column" (II, 36-37). Ronald's anticipated future, and even his present, possess both the trappings and the essence of what his own life might have been had he had the opportunity to capitalize on the cultural and social potential of his talents. "Where did you say you were dining?" Grew asks his son at one point. "With the Waltham Bankshires again? Why, that's the second time in three weeks, ain't it? Big blow-out, I suppose? Gold plate and orchids— opera singers in afterwards?" (II, 37). And the huge importance his reflected status has for him is betrayed in Grew's protests to Ronald when the latter insists on visiting him in Brooklyn.

> "And when you come bouncing in I never feel sure there's enough for dinner—or that I haven't sent Maria out for the evening. And I don't want the neighbors to see me opening my door to my son. That's the kind of cringing snob I am. Don't give me away, will you? I want'em to think I keep four or five powdered flunkeys in the hall night and day—same as the lobby of one of this Fifth Avenue hotels. And if you pop over when you're not expected, how am I going to keep up the bluff?" (II, 37-38)

For all their humor—if indeed Grew is attempting to be funny—Grew's words here belie his preoccupations about social standing.

"His Father's Son" is in the end a slight story and not likely to be the object of any major evaluation. It is without the subtlety or obliqueness of Wharton's best work. It is, also, close to being unique in her short-story *oeuvre* in its depiction of a male point-of-view character who is utterly transparent.

"Autres Temps..."

"Autres Temps...," one of Wharton's finest stories—"probably her best short story," says Blake Nevius (175)—appeared in two installments in *Century*, where it was titled "Other Times, Other Manners," in July and August 1911. Here the play is not between representatives of different social classes but between attitudes that prevail in higher New York society from one generation to the next. The central character, Mrs Lidcote, returning to the United States after a protracted period in Europe, finds that although standards and manners among her set have eroded considerably, she continues to be judged by the norms that rendered her *persona non grata* a generation or so before. "Autres Temps..." is set during the few days Mrs Lidcote spends in the United States (in New York and at the luxurious country home of her daughter at Lenox). It is about its protagonist's recognition that times and manners have changed, but that her own undesirable status in the community, the result of her divorce as a young woman, has not altered: her daughter considers her an impediment to her husband's future success, and the man who has sought her hand in marriage for years must finally concede that her social peers do not accept her. Thus "Autres Temps..." is both a study of social class and an examination of personal anguish: it is, as Barbara White remarks, "no more about changing social mores than how it feels to be a pariah" (8).

White also notes and illustrates the manner in which "spatial metaphors dominate the story. Wharton's descriptions make the past seem like a material presence in Mrs. Lidcote's consciousness" (74). Nowhere is this more evident than on the story's first page, a description of the woman's thoughts as the ocean liner she is aboard approaches New York harbor: "As the huge menacing mass of New York defined itself far off across the waters," Mrs Lidcote "shrank back into the corner of the deck." She feels of her past that "it would always be there, huge, obstructing, encumbering, bigger and more dominant than anything the future would ever conjure up" and that "[it] was a great concrete fact in her path" (II, 257). What is remarkable about these references is that she imagines her past in the same terms as she does the menacing and encroaching presence of New York.

For the moment the analogy she initially makes is an arbitrary one, but we soon realize that in fact New York *is* her past; the sense of oppression Mrs Lidcote experiences almost palpably as she nears the city has been effected by the city's social set. When Mrs Lidcote reflects on the reason for her return to the United States, to see her daughter through the throes of her own divorce and remarriage, "she could hear the whole of New York saying with one voice: 'Yes, Leila's done just what her mother did. With such an example what could you expect?' " (II, 257). As well, the city's role as oppressor extends beyond merely time past: "It was not only because she felt still so unprepared to face what New

York had in store for her.... The past was bad enough, but the present and future were worse, because they were less comprehensible, and because, as she grew older, surprises and inconsequences troubled her more than the worst certainties" (II, 258-259).

Mrs Lidcote's apprehension about her visit to New York turns out to be justified, although she errs about the sources of her future pain. When she perceives during her first few hours on shore that her daughter Leila suffers no ill at the hands of her peers because of her divorce and remarriage, she assumes, understandably, that her own fall from grace has been forgiven and forgotten. "It's extraordinary," she tells Franklin Ide. "Everything's changed. Even Susy [her cousin Susy Sufferin] has changed; and you know the extent to which Susy used to represent the old New York. There's no old New York left, it seems. She talked in the most amazing way. She snaps her fingers at the Purshes. She told me—*me*, that every woman had a right to happiness and that self-expression was the highest duty" (II, 263). But Mrs Lidcote's elation is short-lived. Although in the glow of her surprise at the extent to which the old New York has changed she is able to overlook her daughter's being too busy to welcome her off the boat, and although basking in "the deep sense of well-being that only Leila's hug could give" (II, 268), she is able to put aside the sense of "petrified politeness" she experiences before luncheon at the hands of "the assembled group of Leila's friends" (II, 269), it does not take Mrs Lidcote long to realize that the daughter considers the mother's past an immense liability to her husband's, hence her own, success.

The extent to which Leila considers herself endangered by her mother's presence in her house, and the extent of the embarrassment and hurt she is willing to subject her mother to with the connivance of cousin Susy and the knowledge of numerous house-guests of both generations, comments articulately on the young woman's preoccupations and priorities, and by extension, those of her class, or more accurately, the state to which the class has sunk. In obliging her mother to "stay quietly up here till Monday" (II, 272), Leila breaks rudimentary rules of decency that prevail in any social group with regard to a person treating a person, a hostess behaving towards a guest, a daughter acting towards a mother.   In literally shutting up her mother in her rooms for the weekend Leila demonstrates her sense of what is significant in her hierarchy of things, a sense that is articulated by Susy when she tells Mrs Lidcote about the level of affluence and status to which Leila has been raised by her new marriage: "You won't know Leila. She's had her pearls reset. Sargent's to paint her.... The house was built by Wilbour's father you know, and it's rather old-fashioned—only ten spare bedrooms.... Their idea is to keep the present house as a wing.... They're thinking of Egypt for next winter, unless, of course, Wilbour gets his appointment" (II, 266).   Of course Leila's attempt to lull her mother into acceptance with her show of material goods and comfort fails. As Mrs Lidcote stands in her rooms looking at the sofa "heaped up in cushions" and "a table laden with new books and papers," she cannot "recall ever having been more luxuriously housed, or having ever had so strange a sense of being out alone, under the night, in a wind-beaten plain" (II, 274-275).

"Autres Temps..." is about, among other things, the decline of a class and the erosion in morals and manners of persons within that class, including the older and younger generations. The one mild exception is "the little Wynn girl" (II, 271) who dares to speak warmly with Mrs Lidcote at lunch but who is without the resources to withstand her mother's whisking her away to Fishkill for the weekend to keep her away from Mrs Lidcote. In the face of Mrs Lidcote's humiliation the males have made themselves virtually invisible. And Susy Suffern, who according to Ide "snaps her fingers at the Purshes" (II, 263), the family of Leila's first husband—"the Purshes who are so strong! There are so many of them, and they all back each other up—" (II, 262) wilts in the face of Leila's insistence on her support to ensure that her mother be made to stay out of the way.

When Mrs Lidcote remarks, early in the story and before she comes in contact with her daughter, her cousin, and their friends, "There's no old New

York left it seems" (II, 263), she is referring to the possibility that the old grievance against her no longer applies. Her words turn out to be both wrong as they apply to her particular predicament and also prophetic in a far broader sense than she intends. Her shipboard neighbors whom she overhears saying "Oh, *Leila's* all right" (II, 259); Leila, who greets her mother with "It's all right, you old darling!" (II, 267); and Susy and Ide, who repeat variations of the same, are all wrong.   For Mrs Lidcote nothing is right.   Not only is her reputation unchanged but also the standards of the class to which she belongs have deteriorated beyond recognition, and the persons on whom the story focuses most sharply, Leila, Susy, Ide, and the ambassadress Mrs Boulger all demonstrate the falling away of the old manners.   Mrs Boulger's bad form is seen as she disembarks from the Utopia.   As Mrs Lidcote descends to the main deck "the throng swept her against Mrs. Lorin Boulger's shoulder, and she heard the ambassadress call out to someone, over the vexed sea of hats: 'So sorry! I should have been delighted, but I've promised to spend Sunday with some friends at Lenox'" (II, 263). Mrs. Boulger's shouting out of her social plans for everyone to hear is singularly maladroit—whether or not she is aware of the presence of her hostess's mother beside her.

The descriptions of Susy's, then Leila's, visits upstairs as they attempt to dissuade her, without telling her why, from going downstairs to be with the other guests are in the best tradition of the fiction of manners.   Both Susy and Leila are aware of the inappropriateness of what they are asking their guest to do, and unschooled and undisciplined in the traditional ways of covering up the embarrassment and stress they have put themselves under.   When Mrs Lidcote asks Susy, "Is it your idea that I should stay quietly up here till Monday?" the latter "set down her cup with a gesture so sudden that it endangered an adjacent plate of scones" (II, 272).   When her mother asks Leila, "Do your visitors know that I'm here?" the latter answers, "Do they—of course—why, naturally" and becomes "absorbed in trying to turn the stopper of a salts bottle."   Finally, pressed to a showdown by her mother's question "Will [your guests] think it odd that I *do* [appear downstairs for dinner]?" Leila breaks down completly: "...the color stole over her bare neck, swept up to her throat, and burst into flame in her cheeks. Thence it sent its devastating crimson up to her very temples, to the lobes of her ears, to the edges of her eyelids, beating all over her in fiery waves, as if fanned by some imperceptible wind" (II, 274).

Mrs Lidcote's conduct as she copes with Susy and Leila is exemplary. Although she knows that something is amiss she maintains her composure. She is not an obtuse person slow to recognize that she is being stone-walled: it simply never crosses her mind that the woman who has just convinced her that times have changed, and the daughter she has travelled half way around the world to see and who has greeted her so warmly would engage in such discourteous plotting against her. And when she does recognize clearly what is going on at the moment Leila betrays her blushing embarrassment, Mrs Lidcote is the soul of control: rather than disclose her own discomfort and disillusion she comforts her daughter in the latter's abashment. If "Autres Temps..." is a story about the falling off of standards, it provides a striking example of what characterized the best qualities of the class to which Mrs Lidcote belonged and of the person she is.

Only Franklin Ide seems for a portion of the story to share Mrs Lidcote's high character, but he too in the end reveals himself to be unworthy of the trust his friend places in him. For much of the story he appears convinced that Mrs Lidcote is just imagining that society continues to reject her. He is most adament about this during their last meeting when to Mrs Lidcote's question "Then you don't think Margaret Wynn meant to cut me?" he answers, "I think your ideas are absurd" (II, 277). Throughout the scene he presses his point, unable and/or unwilling to see that Mrs Lidcote's feelings of rejection are justified. In the end he is unable to back up his convictions and accept her invitation to go down with her to visit the Wynns, and we may very well conclude that he has learned something during his earlier meeting with the Wynns himself that, unwilling as he is to admit it, has established the validity of Mrs Lidcote's position. The consecutive reasons Ide provides her as to why they shouldn't visit the Wynns—

"They told me they'd had a tiring day at the dressmaker's. I dare say they have gone to bed" (II, 280) and "I believe—I remember now—Charlotte's young man was suggesting that they should all go out—to a music hall or something of the sort. I'm sure—positively sure that you won't find them" (II, 281)—establish him as being of a piece with Leila. Mrs Lidcote "saw the blood rise slowly though his sallow skin, redden his neck and ears, encroach upon the edges of his beard, and settle in dull patches under his kind troubled eyes. She had seen the same blush on another face..." (II, 281). She of course recognizes as well the remarkable similarity in the circumstances leading up to the blush of each of the two persons for whom she has the most regard. Neither proves worthy of her finally. Neither will share her life in the ways that she and they would like. Yet her compassion will never allow them to be removed from her love.

"Autres Temps..." is a remarkably effective story in its delineation of the erosion of standards of decency and decorum in a social class and in its concretely illustrated depiction of a lonely woman under duress. It also has the distinction of presenting one of the most noble women in the Wharton short-story *oeuvre*. Mrs Lidcote is a refreshing contrast to many of Wharton's older women, who control and manipulate the lives of people within their reach. She is assured yet compassionate, loving yet strong-willed, pained yet courageous, a woman for all seasons, and it may be said that her society is further lessened for having rejected her.

"Her Son"

Although Wharton's long short story "Her Son" appeared in *Scribner's* as late as 1932, its idea had been alive in its author's mind as early as June 1925, when "Wharton was told the following true story," according to Cynthia Wolff. "It was a good subject and it made up into a splendid tale" (395-396):

> Mansfield (the actor) and his wife lived together before they were married, and had a child. The secret was kept, the child (son) smuggled away, looked after, but never seen by either of them. They then married and had another son, whom they adored. Mansfield died. The widow was left alone with her boy. He died at 22 of fever, in an American training

194

camp, during the war. Utterly alone, she is now traveling in Europe, looking for a trace of the other, the repudiated son!—what a subject—(EW Collection)[86]

Wharton's splendid tale is narrated in the first person by Norcutt, an American diplomat who has known the central character, Katherine Glenn, prior to the time of the events that constitute the story he tells, and who assumes the role of friend, confidant, and adviser to her as she becomes more and more enmeshed in a situation she is ill-suited to control or transcend. Norcutt narrates his tale retrospectively and chronologically, maintaining the reader's interest with a series of surprising revelations that demand a chronologically organised account. But his presence in the story goes beyond merely narrating it: his friendship with Catherine's husband and knowledge of the Glenn family past; his native intelligence: his fraternal-like attachment to Catherine; and his willingness to familiarize himself with the complex evolving association among Boy and Chrissy Brown, young Steve and Catherine force him into the active role as participant, as both initiator of and reactor to significant events of his narration. Despite his strong bias in favor of Catherine and the disfavor in which he increasingly holds the Browns, and especially Chrissy, Norcutt remains the conventional objective narrator: we sense that his recording of what happened is a true one. Norcutt differs from several other of Wharton's involved narrators whose prejudices reveal themselves as their narrations ensue and whose recapitulations result in stories that are as much about themselves as they are about their subjects.

The class distinctions in "Her Son" are clear and painstakingly documented. Catherine Reamer, "a beautiful girl—from Kentucky or Alabama—" has been "left an orphan, and penniless, when she was still almost a child," and raised by her "fatuous, impecunious" (II, 621) uncle. But her natural gifts have been noticed and she has married Stephen Glenn, a New Yorker, "a man who was a permanent ornament to society, who looked precisely as he ought, spoke, behaved, received his friends, filled his place on the social stage exactly as his world expected him to" (II, 621-622). And although "the old ladies thought [Glenn] might have done better...Catherine Reamer...rose above these hints as she had above the perils of her theatrical venture. One had only to look at her to see that, in that smooth marble surface there was no crack in which detraction could take root" (II, 622).

As for the Browns, they are the most obnoxious of social climbers, their chances of advantaging themselves all but impossible for their quality is all surface. Chrissy Brown is "slim, active, and girlish...but the freshness of her face was largely due to artifice, and the golden glints of her chestnut hair were a thought too golden." She had "the alert cosmopolitan air of one who had acquired her elegance in places where the very best counterfeits are found" (II, 631). Boy Brown is "a small dry man dressed in too-smart flannels, and wearing a too-white Panama" (II, 631) whose "lordly conception of the life of pleasure [is] exemplified by intimacy with the headwaiters of gild-edged restaurants and the lavishing of large sums on racing and cards" (II, 632-633).

But Boy Brown remains a virtual non-entity in the story and, having established his essential plebianism in a few deft strokes, Wharton focusses squarely on Chrissy to enlighten the class dynamic that is played out in "Her Son." Norcutt is made most acutely aware of the social inferiority of Chrissy when he sees her together with Catherine. "The women were so different," he perceives, "so diametrically opposed to each other in appearance, dress, manner, and all the inherited standards, that if they had met as strangers it would have been hard for them to find a common ground of understanding..." (II, 631). As the story plays itself out and as Chrissy "improves" in her exterior by virtue of her stripping her adversary of her money, the differences between them remain as pronounced as ever—more pronounced perhaps. In the final scene we see a physically weakened and emotionally debilitated and aged Catherine vanquish Chrissy with the shot that strikes at the utter pretention, fakery, and cheapness of the latter. In her weakened position, her poverty, her debility Catherine is able to launch at Chrissy "that little shaft" that Norcutt sees "she must have been waiting for years to launch": "My dear—your hat's crooked" (II, 668). Both Catherine's closing remark and Norcutt's recognition of its impact highlight the fact of the story's strong underpinnings in social class.

Of course, it is not Chrissy Brown's lower social class that stigmatizes her but her attempts to effect a status she does not enjoy. This is the least of her moral lapses, which are manifold and serious and bespeak a woman for whom expediency and self-gratification are the highest goals. In her venality, her dishonesty, her insensitivity, her disregard of persons she rivals the lowest of all of Wharton's worst characters. Her cruelty to her benefactress Catherine is flagrant. And her interference in the life of the ill young man Stephen by her seduction of him in the first place and by her preventing him from pursuing a healthy relationship with Thora Darcy, a woman his own age, are self-serving in the most reprehensible ways—as is her manipulation of Stephen as an instrument whereby she effectively acquires all or most of Mrs Glenn's fortune. What appears to be her only saving grace for an extended portion of the story, her maternal feeling for Stephen, turns out to be simply another one of her false poses.

Her junior partner in the duping of Catherine, Stephen, comes off, finally, rather better than his accomplice. Wharton's description of the initial meeting between Norcutt and Stephen suggests that the former reads the young man's intrinsic decency accurately. "I felt that I was going to like him a good deal better than I had expected.... I was taken at once by the look of his dark-lashed eyes..." (II, 629). The text offers many examples of Stephen's uncomfortableness living with his lie. In the following, Norcutt has been recapitulating Stephen's story about his past:

> The war was over, he had worked for a time at Julian's, and then broken down; and after that it had been a hard row to hoe till mother Kit came along. By George, but he'd never forget what she'd done for him—never!
> "Well, it's a way mothers have with their sons," I remarked.
> He flushed under his bronze tanning, and said simply. "Yes—only you see I didn't know." (II, 634)

Another time, when he is discussing with Norcutt the real possibility of an early death, Stephen is obviously uneasy about his duplicity:

> "if I should drop out—you can never tell—there are Chrissy and Boy, poor helpless devils. I can't forget what they've been to me...done for me....though sometimes I daresay I seem ungrateful...."
>
> I listened to his embarrassed phrases with an embarrassment at least as great. "You may be sure your mother won't forget either," I said.
>
> "No; I suppose not. Of course not. Only sometimes—you can see for yourself that things are a little breezy.... They feel that perhaps she doesn't always remember for how many years...." He brought the words out as though he were reciting a lesson. "I can't forget it...of course," he added painfully. (II, 640)

Here Stephen's embarrassment derives from a source other than the one Norcutt surmises, and he has been primed by his tutors to say what they want him to say.

In the end, Stephen is conscience-stricken, resolving that "I won't take another dollar from Katherine—not me" (II, 654), telling Norcutt, who insists he go away with the Browns, "I'd rather be dead. I'd rather hang on here till I *am* dead" (II, 654), and leaving his promising paintings to Catherine as an atonement offering. Just before his death he has to be restrained by Norcutt from confessing his lie to Catherine, for Norcutt knows the devastating effect this would have on the now-feeble woman who is convinced Stephen is her son.

Katherine's error in accepting unquestioningly that she is Stephen's mother flies in the face of her repeated insistence early in the story that she is incapable of committing the error she so tragically does commit. "I couldn't be mistaken—" she assures Norcutt during one of their first encounters, "I should always recognize him. He was the very image of his father. And if there were any possibility of my being in doubt, I have the miniature, and photographs of his father as a young man." Norcutt immediately recognizes the rashness of her hope when she shows him a photograph of her first son. He thinks, "The vague presentment of a child a few months old—and by its help she expected to identify a man of nearly thirty!" (II, 627). Indeed Norcutt's early assessment of Catherine Glenn is clouded with reservations, and the woman is a rather striking exception to Wharton's women of means, most of whom are more intelligent, resourceful, self-assured, effectual and socially active than is Catherine. If she seems to grow in stature as the story progresses it is more because Norcutt comes to sympathize with her as he recognizes that in her long-standing fragility she is no match for the opportunistic Chrissy Brown. In fact there is little of psychological change in her. The beautiful, reserved, aloof woman whose life has been marked by tragic loss—she has been bereaved of one son in the Great War, lost track of another son, then lost her husband—finds herself in the end deprived of the one element that seemed to have allowed her to salvage some meaning and connection for herself. Catherine Glenn engages our sympathy more than our interest. She is one more acted upon than acting. Her terrible loneliness and naive hopefulness make her a sitting duck for the predatory Chrissy Brown.

Although Catherine's life prior to the present time of the story is not in itself a major concern of Wharton's in "Her Son," the information we are given about it is helpful in explaining the paradoxes of the woman's personality. She is a person who has always been taken in hand by others. After being orphaned "she had been passed about by one reluctant relation to another" until her uncle "had taken the girl into his house." It is interesting also that as a young woman she was an actor and "followed a strolling company across the continent" (II, 621). In choosing a wife and in electing to put up for adoption the child born prior to their marriage, Glenn has acted "exactly as his world had expected him to" (II, 622) as well. Catherine has been her husband's choice because she satisfies certain societal requirements, and although she rationalizes the giving up of the son on the basis of the shame it would bring her uncle, it is very likely her husband's professional standing that was seen to be an obstacle to keeping the child. In any case, giving up the baby has been death to her. "Ah, you've understood! Thank you. Yes, I died" (II, 625), she tells Norcutt. It is hardly surprising, given the series of circumstances of her prior life, that a woman we would expect by virtue of her obvious exterior quality to be confident, outgoing, resourceful and astute, is not.

The fact that Catherine is essentially a static personage, as are, indeed, the other players in this tragic piece, makes the story one more of plot than of character, and this is unusual in the Wharton short-story *oeuvre*. The longest of Wharton's tales—forty-nine pages in the *Collected Short Stories*—"Her Son" in a sense justifies its length with its series of surprising revelations from both Catherine's past and from the period of Norcutt's experience with the unconventional Brown-Catherine-Stephen triangle. These points of surprise keep the extended tale going and maintain our interest. At the same time "Her Son" is an astonishingly well-developed account of human loneliness on the one hand and of inhuman cruelty on the other.

"Roman Fever"

Less than three years after publishing the extended and leisurely "Her Son," Wharton placed "Roman Fever" in *Liberty's* November 11, 1934 issue. "Roman Fever" is a radical contrast to "Her Son," a story of manners that is both dense and brief. (It covered eleven pages in the *Collected Short Stories* and only five in *Liberty*.) Probably the best known of Wharton's stories—it is a frequent choice of anthologists—it is, as Lewis says, "a brilliant piece of short fiction" (*EW* 522), certainly one of her finest accomplishments. One marvels at Auchincloss's comment, "At times [Wharton] would try her hand, almost as one might try a puzzle, at a story that was nothing but technique, like 'Roman Fever,' where the interest and excitement is concentrated in the last line that gives the whole meaning of what has gone on before" (19).

One is hard-pressed to know where to begin a discussion of this superb piece, so rich in possibilities it is. "Roman Fever" is a story of the clash of social classes, a theme that is not necessarily always considered in the tale's numerous critiques.[87] Lewis notes that "The dialogue of the tale takes place in the mid-1920s on the Janiculum Hill above Rome. But the minds of the 'two American ladies of ripe but well-cared for middle age' drift back to the turn of the century to old New York..." (*EW* 522). If the conversation between Grace Ansley and Alida Slade on the afternoon of the story's present time appears initially to be one between social equals, the fact is that in the latter's mind at least, and very likely in the former's as well, there is a consciousness that an important distinction in blood line exists between them, one that certainly has a part to play in the animosity that marks Alida Slade's conduct that afternoon. An extended description of her lower social status, not openly admitted by Alida to be a real liability, is set up by the awareness that her own daughter, Jenny, comes off second best in comparison to her contemporary, Grace's daughter Barbara:

> Funny where [Barbara] got [her superiority], with those two nullities as parents. Yes Horace Ansley was—well, just the duplicate of his wife. Museum specimens of old New York. Good-looking, irreproachable, exemplary. Mrs. Slade and Mrs. Ansley had lived opposite each other—actually as well as figuratively—for years. When the drawing-room curtains in No. 20 East 73rd Street were renewed, No. 23 across the way was always aware of it. And of all the movings, buyings, travels, anniversaries, illnesses—the tame chronicle of an estimable pair. Little of it escaped Mrs. Slade. But she had grown bored with it by the time her husband made his big *coup* in Wall Street, and when they bought in upper Park Avenue had already begun to think: "I'd rather live opposite a speak-easy for a change; at least one might see it raided." (II, 835)

One can only assume that Alida's self-consciousness about her friend's old New York roots was an element during their association as young women during the fateful period of their previous visit to Rome. It is not difficult to imagine a youngish Alida being cowed by her "good-looking, irreproachable, exemplary" friend to the point of fearing the appeal the latter would have for her own fiancé.

If the Slades' move uptown, made possible by Delphin's financial "*coup*," enabled them to remove Alida from the constant reminder of her friend's superior status and provided her with the means of asserting a certain superficial superiority over her, Alida's thoughts and statements on the afternoon of the story's telling provide ample evidence that she has never come to terms with Grace's class. "Would she never cure herself of envying her?" Alida asks herself as she speculates about Grace's future in her new Roman home near her married daughter, where she would "never be in their way...she's much too tactful. But she'll have an excellent cook, and just the right people in for bridge and cocktails..."(II, 839).

One can understand Alida's envy, for the conversation between her and her friend reveals the latter to be a model of self-assurance, decorum and control, qualities in which Alida is excelled by Grace. Wharton has contrived to make of the two women symbolic and realistic examples of what one imagines the old New York class and the rising wealthy commercial class would be. Grace is smallish in stature, unobtrusive, passive, quiet, subtle, and inoffensive; Alida is larger in size, loud, assertive, "vivid," and aggressive. The fact that we are given more access to Alida's mind than to Grace's reflects this active/passive contrast: much of the former woman's thinking, as we observe it in the story, is directed towards her animosity for Grace. Alida's first sally is blatantly antagonistic and not at all lightened by its parenthetical "ever so respectfully, you understand": "And I was wondering...wondering how two such exemplary characters as you and Horace had managed to produce anything quite so dynamic [as Barbara]" (II, 838). And although Alida briefly pulls in her horns she is not long able to desist, and within minutes her attack is back out in the open for good and persists to the point where she in fact invites the closing verbal Ansley thrust that demolishes her.

Grace, it must be said, has foreseen the disaster her aggressor has been building towards and attempted to forestall it. Initially she does not allow herself to become embroiled in the preamble to the unfortunate outcome Alida is preparing. When she realizes that the situation is getting out of hand she makes attempts to cut off movement towards the revelation she senses will be inevitable. First she tries to dissuade Alida from talking about the note the latter had written inviting her to the Colosseum to meet secretly with Delphin Slade. Then, when the revelation comes that Grace has answered the note and Grace answers the other's shock with "It's odd you never thought of it, if you wrote the letter," she moves again to dispel the now-immanent danger. "Mrs. Ansley rose and drew her fur scarf about her. 'It is cold here. We'd better go...I'm sorry for you'" (II,

843). The reader feels reasonably sure that at this point Grace has no intention of making any farther revelation. But Alida must have what she senses will be assuredly her last word. Responding to the other's statement that Delphin Slade has showed up for the tryst, Alida says, "Yes, I was beaten there. But I oughtn't to begrudge it to you, I suppose. At the end of all these years. After all, I had everything. I had him for twenty-five years. And you had nothing but that one letter that he didn't write" (II, 843). Again, one senses that Grace tries to restrain herself. She is silent for a time, but finally cannot resist the temptation to counter Alida's last blow.

In saying what she does, that Delphin Slade has fathered her child Barbara, Grace is, among other things, consciously or unconsciously retaliating to Alida's opening thrust earlier on. The latter's "I was wondering...how two such exemplary characters as you and Horace had produced anything so dynamic" (II, 838) is the spoken and only slightly less offensive equivalent of an inner reflection she has indulged in earlier on: "Funny where [Barbara] got [her edge] with those two nullities as parents" (II, 835), and indeed of the mindset that has colored her entire afternoon. And if she does not recognize the entire implication of Grace's confession—she must be utterly shocked by the revelation it contains—she will sooner or later realize that her friend is telling her that amongst the principals who form the romantic triangle that is at the heart of the story, it is she who is the non-entity, "the nullity": Delphin and Grace are responsible for the superiority of Barbara, and only Alida can be "blamed" for the relative mediocrity and plainness of Jenny.

One of the ways of looking at "Roman Fever" is as the tale of two women who have harbored silent animosity towards each other for years and who are now confronting each other over what is essentially a matter of pedigree, of bloodline. At the same time Wharton is plainly undercutting the notion of the validity of the traditional view of superiority based only on class. For one thing, Delphin, a man of the rising class, has sired a young woman of intrinsic quality. And Grace, supposedly the representative of the old New York patrician values has in the gravest ways fallen from the standards expected of her ilk when as a young woman she seduces the fiancé of her close friend, and when in the present time of the story she loses control in the face of Alida's verbal and psychological onslaught and inflicts deep pain on her with her closing revelation. Grace values her own discipline, control, and decorum to the point of feeling superior to Alida, and Alida prizes her freedom, spontaneity and unharnessed ways above what she considers her friend's hidebound stolidness—neither woman is able to see the other in a way that transcends class. As Wharton puts it, "So these two ladies visualized each other, each through the wrong end of her little telescope" (II, 836).

That said, Grace does garner more of our sympathy. Initially at least the reader tends to side with her because of her reticence, her casualness, her apparent lack of guile. Alida is not a particularly appealing person in her aggressiveness, her smugness, her lack of sophistication. Her sureness about her own judgement and intelligence is gravely prejudiced when we realize that neither in the time after Grace's tryst with her fiancé, nor during the intervening years, nor on the afternoon of the story's present has she recognized the telltale signs of an arranged marriage and its aftermath. Alida herself reminds Grace of events that ensued: "...you were married to Horace Ansley two months afterward....As soon as you could get out of bed your mother rushed you off to Florence and married you. People were rather surprised—they wondered at its being done so quickly; but I thought I knew. I had an idea you did it out of *pique*—to be able to say you'd got ahead of Delphin and me. Girls have such silly reasons for doing the most serious things. And your marrying so soon convinced me that you'd never really cared" (II, 842). We tend therefore to consider that Alida has unintelligently and belligerently set herself up for a fall and has received her just desserts. Of course Grace's more favorable positioning in our eyes in no way attenuates the cruelty of her initial flirtation or the sally that brings the story to a close, although it must be said in her favor that she appears to make courageous efforts to avoid delivering the latter.

Although it might be said that for most of the way "Roman Fever" is Alida's tale inasmuch as she carries the conversation and becomes the aggressive force, Grace is, in her verbal passivity and in her actions and reactions to Alida's escalating obnoxiousness, a most interesting subject of study. Wharton suffuses her portrait of Grace with shades of red: hence her preoccupations push through despite her near silence. Because her daughter Barbara, the product of her illicit liaison, and Rome and the Colosseum, the site of it, are never far from the consciousness and conversation of the ladies during the afternoon, Grace is clearly embarrassed in the presence of the woman she has so flagrantly deceived: "she colored slightly" at Bab's, "'we haven't left our poor parents much else to do'" (II, 833) and "again colored slightly" when, in the speculation about when their daughters will come back that day, Alida comments, "Do you even know back from *where*? I don't!" (II, 834). Nor is Grace without conscious guile. When Alida celebrates "her [own] gaze upon the Palatine" as "the most beautiful view in the world," she remarks, (and Alida notices the "stress" in her voice) "It always will [be] to me"; when Alida reminds her, "When we were first here we were younger than our girls are now," she "[murmurs] 'Oh, yes, I remember'" (II, 834). Wharton's placement early in the story of the important stage property, "a twist of crimson silk run through by two fine knitting needles" (II, 833), serves at least two purposes: the piece is an objective imposed emblem, a symbol, of Grace's on-going sense of guilt; at a realistic level it provides Grace from time to time with a place of retreat when Alida's aggressiveness and her own self-consciousness become too oppressive. There is ample matter in the silk and the knitting and the needles for at least one essay on the function of these elements in "Roman Fever".[88]

It would be negligent to leave off a discussion of "Roman Fever" without commenting on the role of its Roman setting, and Barbara White writes incisively in this regard:

> The Roman setting is, of course, not only essential in providing a context for the disease [of the title] but also completely appropriate to a

story about the past.... In the beginning of the story the city seems a mere decorative backdrop. Only gradually, as the past wells up to overwhelm the two women, does the reader come to feel the presence of the Roman past and realize that Rome is an integral part of the story.... [Grace and Alida] literally as well as figuratively view the ruins of the past; "the dusky secret mass of the Colosseum" that seems to loom over them at the end of the story has long been an actor in their drama. (11)

White's mention of disease and insistence on the importance of the city in the story point to "Roman Fever's" affinities with Henry James's "Daisy Miller."

It would be hard to imagine that Wharton did not write "Roman Fever" without "Daisy Miller" in mind. The title of her story repeats the crucial event in James's novella, in which a young woman is struck down by the disease named for the city with which it is identified and apparently with good reason. There is explicit reference made in "Roman Fever" to an instance in the past in which a young woman dies of the disease, under similar circumstances to Daisy's death. Wharton also raises the question of the diminishing status of Roman fever as a threat to human life, allowing her to emphasize more the metaphorical implications of the story's title term in her own tale. In other important ways Wharton's story takes a position different from James's.

"Daisy Miller" presents its title character through the perceptions of the dilettantish and conventional Frederick Winterbourne. At the same time Winterbourne is a major element in his own story, courting Daisy but losing her, and finally mourning her loss and his own irresponsible loss of her. The story also features the Italian Giovanelli who contests gaining the affection of Daisy with Winterbourne. These two males play prominent roles in James's story: they are front and center in the action and are drawn in detail by the author, most especially the involved narrator Winterbourne, who may very well be meant to be the subject of the study James intended when he subtitled "Daisy Miller" "A Study." "Roman Fever" devotes its attention exclusively to the four women who are the focus of the story's present time: two widowed mothers and their more-or-less strikingly attractive daughters. Delphin Slade and Horace Ansley, the husbands and fathers, are relegated to their long-concluded roles as providers, sires, and consorts: they are not given any play, and their persons remain virtually unknown to us. For all the day-dreaming Grace indulges in during the early parts of "Roman Fever" we are no closer to knowing anything substantive about Delphin's personality or character, and we know nothing at all of Horace.

For "Roman Fever" is primarily and essentially a woman's story. These pages contain comment elsewhere that Wharton resented being compared to James (and being found wanting) and even at one point had good reason to take offense at what were James's patronizing remarks about her craft. Is it possible that "Roman Fever," this great story written close to the end of her career, was her final literary response to Henry James? For it both acknowledges his own greatness by paying homage to him in its title and subject matter, yet establishes Wharton's uniqueness and singular talent and genius. [89]

"Confession"

"Confession," Wharton's last story about the role class plays in the lives of people of status, appeared in the British periodical *Story-Teller* in March 1936 under the title "Unconfessed Crime" and was reprinted a few months later in the United States in the May issue of *Hearst's International-Cosmopolitan*. Although the tale was "suggested by the Lizzie Borden case," Wharton wrote Mary Cadwalader Jones, its source was not very significant to her, although a good deal has been made of this in the lore of the story. "I do not think the story will suffer much from the Borden origin," Wharton continued in her letter to Jones, "as you will have seen by this time that it is of no importance in my fable, and my young woman would quite as well have murdered an intolerable husband" (*LEW* 584).

At least two critics have commented on the redemptive quality of the narrator Severance's marriage to Kate Spain. Barbara White suggest that Kate's "experience has split her in two, one half [getting her] to be happily married to a man who 'forgives her past'" (104). Lev Raphael speaks of "Severance [as] quite aptly named, having attempted to sever the ties between Kate and her former servant, and having successfully, it seems, severed her from her shameful past" and of "their marriage acting to heal shame" (109). These initially appear to be plausible conclusions: they take Severance's story at face value, granting him the credibility that one conventionally grants an omniscient narrator. But placing their emphasis on the substance of Severance's tale, they do not take into account certain elements of the narration that may very well suggest a relationship characterized less by romance and beneficence than by opportunism.

In other Wharton tales told by a first-person involved male narrator—"The Pelican" and "Miss Mary Pask," to name two—the retrospective story told may be seen to unveil elements that are beyond his intent and to lead the wary reader to conclusions not immediately apparent. In "Confession," it is important to note, Severance is telling his story not only to an at-large audience but also to a specific addressee or addressees: formulaic interpolations such as "of course, I couldn't," "I need hardly say" (II, 805), "I don't mind telling you" (II, 807), indicate this. Such expressions suggest also that the speaker is at pains to convince his audience of the truth of what he is saying. It is worth noting as well that Severance's story is being told seven years after the death of his wife Kate and that the events he is recapitulating are colored by the experiences of his intervening years. These things in mind, a careful examination of "Confession's" text reveals that Severance has concocted the tale of a rather idyllic relationship but which is undercut by elements that belie its truth: possibly unaware that he is doing it, Severance, in trying to convince his listener(s) of his love for Kate, is inadvertantly "confessing" that his motives for engaging her were less than worthy. In this regard it bears noting that the title was changed from "Unconfessed Crime" to "Confession" for the story's republication in *Hearst's International-Cosmopolitan.*

To be very abrupt about what happens in "Confession," Severance marries Kate Spain for her money. When he first sees Kate at Mont Soleil he is less struck by her beauty than by other aspects. Her attire draws much of his attention: she "was well-dressed (though overexpensively, I thought)" and a few lines later, "Dress, sober, costly" (II, 802). The truth about her superior affluence is reinforced when Antoine, the headwaiter, tells him that "The ladies have our most expensive suite, and they're here for the season" (II, 805) and that he cannot be granted his wishes in the matter of seating in the dining room. The strongest evidence of Severance's realization of how an alliance with Kate can improve his material condition comes in the matter of the comparison between the *pensions* at Orta and Mont Soleil. Severance has recommended Orta to Kate—"my favorite *pension* (II, 819)—but as he waits for her to come down on the occasion he has arranged to meet her there, all of his longing for a better life surfaces in his description of the Orta *pension's* public sitting room:

> There were three windows in a row, with clean heavily starched Nottingham lace curtains carefully draped to exclude the best part of the matchless view over lake and mountains. To make up for this privation the opposite wall was adorned with a huge oil painting of a Swiss waterfall. In the middle of the room was a table of sham ebony, with ivory inlays, most of which had long since worked out of their grooves, and on the table the usual dusty collection of tourist magazines, fashion papers, and tattered copies of *Zion's Weekly* and the *Christian Science Monitor*. (II, 818)

There are simply too many references, both direct and oblique, in Severance's monologue to the fact that "Kate was wealthy" (II, 806) to be ignored. Of course this theme plays in subtle counterpoint to Severance's insistence to his addressee(s) of his loving attachment to Kate and of his expressed detached altruism in removing her from a guilt-ridden situation. It must be said at the same time that an examination of the complex of Severance's protestations of love for and assistance to Kate shows it to be shot through with insincerity, with indications that beget suspicion. His early references to her by the formulaic "the dark lady" (there are five such on page 803); his insistence on pressing her to a hasty marriage despite her repeated protests that this is impossible; and especially his demonizing of Miss Wilpert, the only person, after all, who stands between Kate and dire consequences, more subtly point up his ulterior motives.

Severance's anxiety about securing himself of the comforts of Kate's hand comes to a climax in the dramatic meeting between him and Cassie Wilpert, which ends in her being stricken and, short weeks afterwards, in her death. Severance, the aspiring man of class, who equates class almost exclusively with wealth and is no respecter of persons of lesser status and of servants, rightfully envisions Cassie as the sole obstacle to his quest for Kate. While it would be an exaggeration to claim that he is Cassie's murderer, his conduct during their meeting shows him to be utterly insensitive to her agitated state and the immediate cause of her stroke, although he attempts to rationalize away his guilt by citing doctors' opinions "that in her deteriorated condition any medical shock might have brought about the same result" (II, 827). In fact, he has clearly brought on her cerebral accident: he saw "her discolored face [crimsoning] furiously," "her thick lower lip gaping queerly," "her jaw falling slightly," "her trembling" (II, 826, 827), but persisted with his provocations, claiming afterwards to be suffering from "distress and bewilderment" (II, 827).

It is instructive to examine Cassie's role as a defender of Kate Spain against Severance's onslaught. Of course, she has the strongest motivation for keeping Severance away from her friend. The bond that ties her and Kate is reciprocal: she is dependent for her considerable material comfort and security on Kate; the latter is indebted to her for her acquittal and for the safeguarding of her reputation and possibly her safety from the law. At the same time Cassie sees Severance for what he is, and some of her outbursts during their crucial meeting are on the mark. When she calls him a "dandified gentleman," (II, 824) she hits upon the fraudulance of his character; when she tells him, "If you think such a lot of her, I'd have thought you'd rather have gone away quietly, instead of tormenting her even more" (II, 825), she accurately diagnoses his hardness of heart. Both of Cassie's statements, and others like them during this meeting, point to the essential insensitivity of Severance, and Kate would have done well to heed her companion's advice to avoid him.

One senses that Severance has recognized the fact that Cassie has seen through him, and that is why his story stacks the deck so harshly against her. From the outset his tale is laden with reference to her servant-woman status, her common manners. He makes allusion to the fatness and redness of her fingers, her penchant for Pilsener, her "local vernacular" (II, 808). In fact Cassie is not the villain Severance makes her out to be, and one may surely make the point that she genuinely has the good and safety of Kate at heart. It is most likely that she, the trusted servant, has been convinced to turn false witness in favor of her mistress by her mistress, and it is not an exaggeration to say that her fidelity to Kate continues to motivate her. Severance's demonizing of Cassie is a rhetorical device (like his celebration of Kate as "the dark lady") whereby he seeks to gain the good favor of his audience in his campaign to establish the purity of his motivation in marrying Kate.

It says much of Severance that when he demeans Cassie he does so by castigating her class: this is, in fact, the ultimate kind of put-down for him. Even her abuse of alcohol (if indeed she is an abuser) is seen as a mark of her low status. And she is not the only victim of his disdain for servants: he has "long since classed the [Orta's] floor waiter as an idiot" (II, 816). In fact he is no respecter of persons generally, referring casually to his fellow hotel guests as "dull commonplace people" (II, 802) and as a "pack of hotel idlers" (II, 801). His habit of categorizing people in negative terms says much about his attitude about himself of course, but it reveals his disregard of people as individuals, a disregard that extends even to Kate, whom he characterizes at one point as belonging "to the class of intelligent but untaught travelers who can learn more by verbal explanations than by books" (II, 806). Kate was by Severance's estimation "not over thirty-two or three" (II, 806) when he first met her, a young woman. Their marriage lasted but five years. Although Severance says little about these five years, everything he reveals of himself in his monologue would suggest that his wife was also the victim of an uncaring disregard.

The closing paragraph of "Confession"—Severance's final words to his audience—reads:

> At the end of five years my wife died; and since then I have lived alone among memories so made of light and darkness that sometimes I am blind with remembered joy, and sometimes numb under present sorrow. I don't know yet which will end by winning the day with me; but in my uncertaintly I am putting old things in order—and there on my desk lies the paper I have never read, and beside it the candle with which I shall presently burn it. (II, 832)

The sealed letter, so frequently the subject of Severance's reference, has lain conspicuously on his desk during his entire narration.   But the letter, both actually and referentially, is a smokescreen with which he attempts to block out from his listener(s) the truth of his motivation in marrying Kate: in focussing on it he hopes to convey a sense of the extent of his devotion to his wife. In reality, the fact that he has not opened the letter will allow him to say, should he ever be obliged to, that he did not know his wife was a murderer, that he could not have been accused of any kind of complicity in hiding her crime from the law.

"Confession" is a story about social class that is different from most of the others discussed in this chapter.   Its protagonist fancies himself an American aristocrat who is lacking the only element that will make his status complete.   His story reveals his essential meanness.   His failings are not the so-called human ones: his conscious calculation and manipulation of persons show him to be inhumane; his attempts to obscure the truth and maintain the facade of goodness betray him as a hypocrite.   Wharton's first-person unwary narrators are invariably male, and the stories she tells through them are among her most gripping—if not always the most noted of her successes.

*   *   *   *   *

Being There and Getting There in New York and on the Continent

There is evidently considerable affinity between Wharton's stories of contact and conflict among persons of different upper social classes and those stories in which she limits herself to life within a given upper social class. The tales we have just examined continue to a degree to underline the vacuousness of upper-class life, although it is easier to find characters here who affirm meaningful values and show the potential and resolve to lead lives of personal and familial integrity.

Among the three stories that have the married relationship as their central interest, "The Line of Least Resistance," "The Other Two," and "Confession," it is the first that most glaringly sustains Wharton's critique of husbands and potential husbands in whom fear is a dominant quality. Mindon, the spouse of the socially-driven and philandering Millicent, is an extreme version—to the point of being a parody—of those inept husbands and lovers from "The Twilight of the God," "The Dilettante," "In Trust," "The Choice," "Atrophy," even "The Long Run," whose cowardice is betrayed by their fear of making a scene. Mindon is ineffectual in his efforts at communication with his wife, his servants, even his young daughters, and in the face of the three figures of authority who force him back to his family without giving him any assurance that the adulterous relationship that has brought on his attempt to escape will even be addressed, he capitulates in true form. In her other stories of boyish men Wharton is content to provide the symptoms of malaise and does not much seek to address the question of root cause. It is interesting that in "The Line of Least Resistance," a 1900 story that pre-dates many of her other tales of weak males, Wharton has offered a clue to the cause of the ineptitude she so often portrays. As Mindon examines the note incriminating Millicent in an illicit liaison with Frank Antrim, he experiences his vision of "the quivering imperceptible ego"; he sees elements of his psyche as if detached from himself. Might not such a vision be applied as well to other of Wharton's immature males?

Of the other two marriage stories "Confession" is of a similar slant as "The Line of Least Resistance." Its narrator/protagonist, Severance, is evidently a man who has an upper-class background, and he has married Kate Spain to improve his material condition. His lack of confidence shows through in his dissatisfaction with his lot in life and in his putting down of people of lower status, indeed of persons generally. "The Other Two" is of an entirely different cast. This oft-anthologized and attractive story, serious and whimsical at the same time, features two men who are without the often-seen limitations of Wharton's males. Both Waythorn, Alice's third and current husband, and Haskett, her first, impress us as confident and considerate. The latter especially transcends his poverty and sense of humiliation and insists on being a conscientious custodian of his daughter Lily's well-being.

It says much about the shift of focus in this present block of stories though that only three center on the married relationship. In fact Wharton is more interested here in impending marriages—which may or may not come about—than in the married state. Even "Confession," narrated by Severance after he has married and hence technically a marriage story, focusses for most of its length on the pre-marital lives of its husband and wife. "Souls Belated," "The Quicksand," "The Last Asset," "The Introducers," "Les Metteurs en scène," "His Father's Son," and "Autres Temps...," and to a lesser extent "Her Son" and "Roman Fever," have potential marriages as an important feature. It seems clear that for Wharton the subject of the interrelationships among upper-caste people of different levels in America and Europe could be best broached if marriage were in the offing, rather than actual.

Virtually all the stories under consideration here—the exception is "Autres Temps..."—contain examples of social climbing, and the majority have this phenomenon as their chief interest. In the tales centered on prospective marriage the principals or their patrons, usually their mothers, seek to make marriages that will better their social or financial standing, or in a few cases reject opportunities to join up with partners who will bring them advantages that the society at large

214

considers opportune. In the stories directed on married persons, social advantage has been the motivation for union in the first place, and this group contains one of the quintessential pieces in the entire literature on the subject of social climbing, "The Other Two." Invariably the spouse-seekers portrayed by Wharton are Americans—there are a few Europeans as well—and in most cases their search is fixed on other Americans in their own milieu. Sometimes Wharton presents her Americans as they visit or expatriate themselves to Europe and places their narratives of advancement in a continental setting. Thus she draws attention to the fact that they possess both the money and the leisure to take advantage of what they have been told is, or what they themselves appreciate to be, a more cosmopolitan atmosphere and lifestyle than they can experience at home. In a few of the stories Americans engage directly with Europeans and seek to better their standing by association with or marriage to French aristocrats.

Six tales place their scenes of marital life or of its social preambles in either New York or Newport. The two Newport stories, although published only a few years apart, are radically different in mood and tone. "The Line of Least Resistance" is striking for the unrelieved negative picture of its society: neither Mindon; nor his wife Millicent and her lover, who are both astonishingly insensitive and betray their aspiring-class status in the most blatant ways; nor the establishment trio who confront Mindon at the Newport hotel with the liabilities of the one genuine gesture he has made offer any hope of redressing the family's sorry situation. The story is surely one of Wharton's darkest portrayals of the higher society. "The Introducers" offers a far more cheerful portrait. Here, Wharton, as she does in a number of other stories, presents the latest generation of an old New York aristocracy come on hard times, their place at the top superseded by wealthy parvenus who hire the older class's young people as matchmakers, as "introducers," to assist their entry into the upper set. Wharton sustains the "upside-down" features of these social arrangements by having her two principals, Frederick Tilney and Belle Grantham, dally over the possibility of *nouveau riche* partners. In the end both abide by their better instincts and their love for each other and plan their own marriage. Tilney and Belle reflect something of the quality one would expect from an aristocracy, and in fact Tilney's expressed opinion about property, and his friend's echoing of his sentiments, may very well transcend the prevailing class attitude about ownership. Here is Tilney addressing himself as he looks at the morning seascape from his employer's shore: "Well—there's one comfort: none of the other fools really *see* it—it's here only for those who seek it out at such an hour—and as I'm the only human being who does, it's here only for me, and belongs only to me, and not to the impenetrable asses who think they own it because they've paid for it at so many thousand dollars a foot!" (I, 531)

The three out-and-out New York stories, "The Quicksand," "The Other Two," and "His Father's Son," demonstrate Wharton's on-going interest in the social climbing phenomenon. "The Quicksand" presents the plight of Alan Quentin, who runs, as his father did, a very lucrative enterprise, the scandal sheet *The Radiator*. Quentin's suit for the hand of Hope Fenno, whose family is from the old-money class whose assets have to a degree dried up and whose stock would benefit from a union with one of Quentin's ilk, will likely prove unsuccessful, for his mother's conscience awakens and she discourages the marriage. One finds in the story frequently used Wharton themes and ploys. Quentin's weakness of character, apparent in his willingness to make a living from yellow journalism, surfaces again in his getting his mother to plead his cause for marriage to Hope: this *nouveau riche* mother, from a tribe that characteristically take up their daughters' marital quests, is manoeuvered into acting on behalf of her son. "The Quicksand" also deploys Wharton's familiar device of defining the relative social status of the Quentin and Fenno families by detailed descriptions of their respective house decoration and furniture. In "The Other Two" the climber is the thrice-wedded Alice Waythorn, who has initially married out of her class and away from New York, then into a New York higher class, then to her present husband, who is a wealthier, more successful member of that class. In "His Father's Son" it is the ascent of both father and son that is accented. Ronald's widowed father, Mason, enjoys vicariously his son's ascent to wealth and standing. Indeed the story makes the point that Mason's delight in his own reflected status transcends his feeling for Ronald: after his wife's death he has moved to Brooklyn, where he keeps his contacts with Ronald to a minimum while enjoying via the social pages the news of his son's growing reputation.

As an example of a New York story and a tale of social climbing, "Autres Temps..." presents a special case. It is a story in which New York has major significance, although much of the action is set away from the city in Lenox, Massachusetts. The persons who come and go to and from Mrs Lidcote's daughter's home at Lenox and the relatives who close her off in her upstairs suite are the representatives of the New York she has feared since her arrival in her native land. "The huge menacing mass of New York" (II, 257) she has dreaded on her approach to the harbor is the New York that stalks her hours at Lenox. As for social climbing the "Autres Temps..." crowd have risen about as high as they are likely to rise on the social ladder: their fear is that their association with Mrs Lidcote will propel them to a descent, which they take radical measures to prevent.

In "Her Son," "Confession," and "Roman Fever," set in Europe, the principals are Americans who find themselves on the continent for a variety of reasons. "Her Son" sets its tale of social climbing in the context of the widowed and wealthy Catherine Glen's search for a son abandoned in infancy to adoptive parents. Catherine herself has been orphaned and taken in hand by a southern uncle, Colonel Reamer, who raises her despite the fact that he is "poor" and "impecunious" (II, 621): Colonel Reamer is one of Wharton's poor who are not so poor and may remind readers in this regard of Mrs Fenno from "The Quicksand" or Frederick Tilney and Belle Grantham from "The Introducers," later generations of a high society who have come on hard but scarcely impossible times. Boyden (Boy) and Chrissy Brown, the predators who use Catherine's vulnerability and ample means on which to make their social ascent, are surely among the most repulsive of Wharton's fictional characters. Severance, the narrator/protagonist of

"Confession" makes his climb on the resources of Mrs Ingram/Kate Spain, whom he marries. Cassie Wilpert catches some of his snobbery when she calls him a "dandified gentleman" (II, 825) and he completes the image when he informs his listeners of how he has sold himself to Kate: "She knew who I was, where I came from, who were my friends, my family, my antecedents; she was fully informed as to my plans, my hopes, my preferences, my tastes, my hobbies. I had even confided to her my passion for Brahms and for book collecting" (II, 815). Given his patronizing attitude to persons generally, his dissatisfaction with his allegedly meager material assets, his attempts to rush Kate into marriage, and his passing off of his interest in her as motivated by altruism and love, we may conclude that his social quality is merely nominal and that he is only somewhat less despicable than Chrissy Brown, for all his claims to class. In "Roman Fever" the social climbing has occurred years ago. Alida Slade's recognition that for all the success she and her husband have had—"his big *coup* on Wall Street, and when they bought in upper Park Avenue" (II, 835)—her daughter is still not as attractive as Grace Ansley's and she herself still feels outclassed by Grace is what propels her into the aggressive comments that bring on her ultimate shame at the story's end.

The three stories in which Wharton adds European characters to action that centers on transplanted Americans are somewhat more complex than her other tales of social striving, at least in the area of class distinctions. "Souls Belated," "The Last Asset," and "Les Metteurs en scène" all complicate these matters by inserting aristocrats or aristocratic pretenders and having them interact with the American personages. In "Souls Belated" the principal tale of Lydia Tillotson's tortured accomodation to life in the higher echelons of American society, into which she has been introduced by her marriage to Ralph Tillotson, is seen against the background of British snobbery in an Italian mountain resort. Another dimension is added in the persons of the British commoner Mrs Cope and Lord Trevanna, who are hiding at Bellosguardo as the married couple Linton. The Lintons effectively become objects against which Lydia's principles of integrity and independence are put to the test. Measured against "The Last Asset," a story published five years later, "Souls Belated" is somewhat loose in construction, but it is a highly interesting study of class ethics and politics.

In "The Last Asset" Wharton has created a small masterpiece hilariously comic and genuinely moving. Here Mrs Sam Newell of Elmira, New York marshalls a bewildering assortment of people representing the best and worst that America and Europe can offer of all classes and degrees of affluence, for the purpose of securing a successful marriage for her daughter Hermione and thereby assuring her own security and social standing. There is her impoverished, estranged husband, who had "lost heavily on Wall Street" (II, 604); Paul Garnett, the *New York Searchlight* reporter; the Woolsey Hubbards of Detroit (the millionaire Mr Hubbard's "standard of gentility was the extent of a man's capacity to 'foot the bill'") (II, 602); Lord and Lady Morningfield, "rich and immaculate" (II, 596); Lord and Lady Edmund Fitzarthur, "bankrupt and disreputable" (II, 596); Baron Schenkelderff, of dubious bloodlines; and the genuine article, Comte Louis du Trayas, son of the Marquis du Trayas de la Baume, who will marry Hermione. Wharton manages this *tour de force* without a hitch, at the same time chronicling the coming to moral and psychological maturity of the reporter Garnett.

Also set in Paris, "Les Metteurs en scène" looks again at social climbing in one of its most popular manifestations, the arrangement of marriages between socially aspiring partners and an established elite. The story will remind readers of "The Introducers," the tale of *ad hoc* marriage brokers plying their trade in America. "The Introducers" predates "Les Metteurs en scène" by less than three years, and one is tempted to ascribe to the two stories the kind of complementary relationship found in other pairs of tales in the Wharton canon. In "Les Metteurs en scène" Wharton sought to render the convention of match-making in a sophisticated Parisian milieu where matters were complicated by an established aristocracy as well as a nobility *du Faubourg*. (In "The Last Asset" Mrs Newell is ecstatic about Hermione's engagement to du Trayas: she had thought that "with her little dowdy air [her daughter] might very well 'go off' in the Faubourg") (I, 597). In "Les Metteurs en scène" Jean Le Fanois, apparently of the Faubourg himself, is assisted by Blanche Lambart in marrying off American *nouveau riche* women to nobles of his own kind. Le Fanois and Blanche fall in love, as do the American matchmakers in the earlier story, but the union is thwarted by circumstances that underline Le Fanois' worldliness and ennui: he is without the innocence and integrity of Tilney and Belle. Of note is the proliferation of blushing in both stories. This staple device of the fiction of manners—one sees it as well in "Roman Fever" and "Autres Temps..."—is an indicator of the embarrassment the couples feel about the demeaning activity in which they are engaged.

While the numerous references to blushing by characters with similar functions and under similar circumstances help to signal the similarities between "The Introducers" and "Les Metteurs en scène," and the common animus that lay behind their composition, the latter is an inferior story and off the standard of the tales of social climbing. By her own admission Wharton was hamstrung by her inability to express herself with required sophistication in French, her adopted language. A "Les Metteurs en scène" written in her own tongue, with its presentation of the underside of Parisian aristocratic life, its mix of American and European elements, its engaging characters, might well have added another story to the list of Wharton's "greatest hits."

The popularity and critical success of Wharton's short stories of life within the higher levels of the culture is self-evident. Her best and most frequently anthologized tales depict this life: "Roman Fever," "The Other Two," "Autres Temps..." "The Last Asset," "Souls Belated." Clearly she delighted in telling the stories of her own kind, her own observation, her own experience. Not surprisingly Wharton was not as successful when she ventured off her own social ground. None of the few tales she wrote about middle-class people shows the free-handedness and immersion in the subject of her upper-class narratives.

220

Notes

[86] The story is recorded in a Wharton notebook, dated 1924-1928, in the Edith Wharton Collection, Beinecke Library, Yale University.

[87] Writes Barbara Comins: "Alida mentally tallies the ways in which she feels superior to Grace. She, after all, has been part of the 'exceptional couple' as 'wife of the famous corporation lawyer', Delphin Slade. She believes that Grace Ansley and her husband made a 'good-looking, irreproachable, exemplary' pair, in short dismissing them as 'museum specimens of old New York'" (10). But Alida Slade's "dismissal" of the Ansley couple flies in the face of her grudging acknowledgement of their social superiority to her, of their old New York background. Alida does not feel superior to Grace, and Comins seems to have missed the point that social distinctions are at the root of the jealousy / envy that pervades "Roman Fever."

[88] The subject is broached in Alice Hall Petry, "A Twist of Crimson Silk: Edith Wharton's 'Roman Fever.'" *Studies in Short Fiction* 24 (Spring 1987): 163-166.

[89] The high reputation of "Roman Fever" remains undiminished. Hermione Lee, writing in her 2007 biography *Edith Wharton*, speaks of the story as being "most perfectly controlled and profound," whose "familiarity does not lessen its effect." It is "an impeccable, ruthless masterpiece...one of the best examples of the indirect, rich and surprising ways in which [Wharton] makes use of her own experiences" (718).

Chapter Five

The Middle Classes

Of the five stories considered in the present chapter, four had been published by the turn of the century. The exception, "Joy in the House," was the product of Wharton's late career. Only one of the earlier tales has much distinction about it, and one must conclude that the human struggle against economic deprivation, a major consideration in "Mrs. Manstey's View," "A Cup of Cold Water," and "Friends," had only a limited appeal for Wharton the fiction writer. By far the most interesting and successful pieces here are "A Journey" and "Joy in the House," each of whose female protagonists finds herself in a predicament that is other than financial.

"Mrs. Manstey's View"

Because "Mrs. Manstey's View" was her first published piece of fiction—it was accepted by *Scribner's* and appeared in its July 1891 issue—it has been a favorite subject of Wharton biographers and critics alike. Its author's refusal to include it in her earliest collection is most telling, for it constitutes her admission that it is a patently autobiographical story, in spite of the fact that it deals with a world and a character that do not directly reflect her own experience.

Cynthia Griffin Wolff's critique of "Mrs. Manstey's View" concerns the latent autobiographical nature of the story:

> It is a "given" of this little tale that Mrs. Manstey has relinquished all desires but one : the daily habit of peering out at the world from the unpromising, narrow vantage of the single small room to which she has retired. The view has little or nothing to recommend it: a disorderly back alley, yards strewn with the debris of life, slatternly windows, and yet Mrs. Manstey contrives to make a world out of it. She measures time by the slow passage of the seasons, waits patiently from one long year to the next for the blooming magnolia of the neighboring yard, and reaps the slender benefits of asking so

little. "Perhaps at heart Mrs. Manstey was an artist; at all events she was sensible of many changes of color unnoticed by the average eye and, dear to her as the green of early spring was, the black lattice of branches against a cold sulphur sky at the close of a snowy day." "It is a reduced diet, but it may be true" (as Wharton declared elsewhere) that "the creative mind thrives best on a reduced diet." Almost of necessity Wharton reveals her own situation, using this early story as a primitive representation of self (never mind that the "circumstances" are so different from her own—who in Wharton's position would not engage in clever disguise?) (65)

While it has become *de rigeur* to think of "Mrs. Manstey's View" as autobiographical, it is interesting that Alice Herritage Kinman's research has revealed that Wharton may have had other objectives than self-revelation in mind in telling her widow's story and that she may have told it more skillfully than is generally thought. Kinman's carefully researched and astutely written article "Edith Wharton and the Future of Fiction" opens up the tale to a less confessional and broader view than has hitherto been considered. She writes: "In ["Mrs. Manstey's View"] Wharton demonstrates her familiarity with the terms of discussion surrounding the state of American fiction as well as her desire to place her own work within the context of this discussion. At the same time, Wharton's story, through its language and structure, calls into question the very terms of the realism / idealism debate, making a case for both 'views' while suggesting that neither offers a satisfactory narrative perspective" (4). Kinman goes on to say that Wharton has injected into the story "a third discourse, the political discourse surrounding the spread of tenements in New York City" (7). In doing so, Wharton's story points to the necessity of nuancing the old realism / idealism debate and setting fiction's sights in a new direction.

Cynthia Wolff's references to "Mrs. Manstey's View" as "almost fiction" (96) and as "a tantalizing failure" (65) may very well be put in question by Kinman's reading of the story. The latter insists, for example, that the tale is "carefully structured to incorporate both a realistic and an idealistic account of [its] subject" (6) and that "the narrator's language, with its detached tone and classical references, evokes the scientific observer so typical of realistic fiction" (6). Of course, Kinman's fitting of the story into a context of American literary history in no way invalidates its autobiographical component: the association of "Mrs. Manstey's View" with the difficulty Wharton had in her own life of expressing her artistic talent in a hostile familial and social environment remains a salient element.

"A Journey"

Wharton returned to a middle-class milieu some eight years after "Mrs. Manstey's View" with the publication of "A Journey" in her 1899 collection, *The Greater Inclination.* (The story made no magazine appearance.) "A Journey" has a number of resemblances to its predecessor: its primary focus on one female character, its culmination in a death, its use of a privileged narrator. As well, like "Mrs. Manstey's View" it may be read (and has been read) as an autobiographical story, as in R. W. B. Lewis's remark, for example, that it is "an imaginative device, perhaps, for dispatching poor Teddy" (*EW,* 85). However, it may be preferable to assume that Wharton had other intentions with "A Journey." When one considers that a short time before she had proscribed the collection of a number of stories on the grounds that "they were the excesses of youth...were all written at the top of my voice" (*LEW,* 36), it is difficult to believe that she would have been so insensitive as to publish a tale that would be read as a veiled wish for her husband's death. But whatever Wharton's conscious or unconscious intentions, it is still instructive to look at the story within the fictional confines it sets.

"A Journey" limits its interest almost exclusively to its central character and reflector, the unnamed young woman who is accompanying her husband back to New York City after a period spent in the west in an attempt to bring the latter back to health. The critical commentary on the story tends to take a particularly sympathetic attitude towards the protagonist. Elizabeth Ammons includes her in a group of Wharton short-story women protagonists

> who come face to face with some bitter disillusionment, which often turns on discovering that the man she loves, or thought she loved, is a fraud. The hero of a woman's dreams turns out to be a coward in "The Lamp of Psyche" and "The Twilight of the God." The passionate sharer of her revolutionary notions about free love turns out to be convention-bound in "Souls Belated." The intellectual heroine of "The Muse's Tragedy" discovers that men cannot love her body and her mind; it must be one or the other.... The heroine [of "A Journey"] is a frontier schoolteacher who gets married to broaden and deepen

224

her lonely life, but the first thing her husband does is fall mortally ill. (6)

Barbara White sees the story as "quite literally [fitting] the incest paradigm—a man's hidden corruption accompanied by a woman's complicity" (49). But both Ammons' and White's opinions seem to fly in the face of the given facts of the story, and while possessing a certain marginal validity ignore more salient aspects of the young woman's character and temperament.

While the central character in "A Journey" surely elicits our sympathy, she is not one who would normally be called by critics "a sympathetic character." As a young wife rendered bereft of a husband soon after marriage and as a partner in a union in which "both had the same prodigal confidence in an exhaustless future" (I, 79) who now questions whether she is ever "to be allowed to spread her wings" (I, 80), she engages our solicitude. But her inner response to her husband's illness, immanent death, and actual passing do not strike this reader as particularly sensitive. It is a very telling point about her that at the time she is speculating about the possibility her family will tell her husband tactlessly, upon their disembarking the train, that "he was looking splendidly and would be all right in no time," her reference to "a certain coarseness of texture in the family sensibilities" (I, 81) excludes herself. In fact, she exhibits just such a coarseness of sensibility in her attitude and conduct towards persons. She has been unable to warm to her Colorado neighbors, she shows little attachment to the children she teaches, and when she leaves for New York she waves "unregretful farewells to the acquaintances she has never really liked till then" (I, 81). Her unease with people shows on the train: she somehow alienates the other passengers when in the process of trying to protect her husband from a curious child's attention. Most of all, her lack of warmth surfaces in her thoughts about her dying, then dead, husband. Although she observes the amenities related to conduct towards a sick and dying husband and insists on her love for him, her mind, as the train is eastward-bound, is more on her future and her "robust and buoyant family" and less on her husband. "How she had rejoiced when the doctors at last gave their consent to his going home! She knew, of course, what the decision meant; they both knew. It meant that he was going to die; but they dressed the truth in hopeful euphemisms, and at times, in the joy of preparation, she really forgot the purpose of their journey, and slipped into an eager allusion to next year's plans" (I,.80).

If the wife's response and on-going attitude to her husband's imminent death seem to be without the softer emotions that would normally attend such a prospect, her reaction when she discovers that he has passed away in his sleep during the night is singularly bereft of a sense of personal loss. "Suddenly, she shrank back: the longing to scream, to call out, to fly from him had almost overpowered her. But a strong hand arrested her. Good God! If it were known that he was dead they would be put off the train at the next station—" (I, 82). The strong hand that inhibits a normal display of emotion alerts her to the immediate unpleasant problem the corpse will cause aboard the train. Her fear of confronting a perplexing and macabre situation is stronger than any sense of loss. The immediacy with which her fear of unpleasantness dominates startles us, although we understand the fear itself to be perfectly real. During the day that ensues, the woman's total effort is turned towards assuring that the body will not be discovered so as to offset the predicament she so vividly fears.

The protagonist's fears reveal her weaknesses as a person: her lack of self-assurance and her distrust of others—the two obviously related. She is one "whom the routine of the sickroom bewildered: ...this punctual administering of medicine seemed idle as some uncomprehended religious mummery"(I, 80)—without the consolations of philosophy or religion that are often so helpful in times of distress such as hers. In this regard, although she has ample warning she is entirely unprepared, through no fault of her own perhaps, to cope with the death of a loved one. The story, so seen, appears to be more than simply about a woman of the middle class: it seems to suggest that her unpreparedness and inability to deal with a difficult but human problem is related to her social position and upbringing. We sense that Wharton is implicitly saying that a woman of her own social class would not be left to cope, without ritual, without assistance, without inner resources, in such a predicament as the one portrayed here.

"A Journey" realistically evokes the middle-class world of its protagonist, as does "Mrs. Manstey's View," but it is without the sentimentality of the latter. Indeed, it takes a situation that has been traditionally treated in sentimental fashion, one that virtually cries out for such treatment, and adopts a patently unconventional view of it. Critics are consistent in addressing the story's starkness: "It is one of Wharton's most hopeless tales" (Ammons, 6); "it is unlike any in the canon—a horror story inspired by de Maupassant" (Brown, 5-6); it is "unexpectedly realistic" (Nevius, 16). At the same time it is a remarkably strong story for a relatively inexperienced writer and a fairly young woman, rendering with impressive credulity the ordeal of its protagonist, a woman who engages both our sympathy and our dislike.

"A Cup of Cold Water"

Like "A Journey," "A Cup of Cold Water" appeared in Wharton's 1899 collection *The Greater Inclination* and had no periodical publication. The present decision to include it among stories of middle-class subjects will be considered questionable by some readers no doubt, for its central and point-of-view character, Woburn, has, from a perspective of social class, little in common with either Mrs Manstey or the young widow of "A Journey." He appears to have been born into a family with the financial means and social standing that would make him a legitimate contender for the hand of Miss Talcott, with whom he is in love. From what can be determined from the evidence of the story, the social set to which Miss Talcott belongs is the *nouveau riche* rather than the legitimate New York upper class. Details furnished about the background of guests at the Gildermere ball, the setting for Part I, establish that fact.[90] However, because of his father's financial failure and the inadequacy of the family's resources after the latter's death, Woburn has been forced to take a job as a bank cashier, and his investment failures have pushed him into embezzling a substantial sum of money so that he can keep up with the Gildermeres and hold his own in the competition for the hand of his beloved.

If Woburn is technically not a man of the middle class by birth, he has been rendered so by virtue of his misdemeanours and his lost means. There is no question but that he occupies, if artificially because of his unethical acquisition of money, a precarious middle ground between status and wealth and social and financial disgrace. As he rides away from the Gildermere home he is made aware of the delicate position he holds.

> At one corner he saw a shabby man lurking in the shadow of the side street; as the hansom passed, a policeman ordered him to move on. Further on, Woburn noticed a woman crouching on the doorstep of a handsome house. She had drawn a shawl over her head and was sunk in the apathy of despair or drink. A well-dressed couple paused to look at her. The electric globe at the corner lit up their faces, and Woburn saw the lady, who was young and pretty, turn away with a little grimace drawing her companion after her. (I, 156)

By the end of the story we are aware that his aspirations to move upwards again have been thwarted, that he is more likely to walk the shabby man's streets, to crouch on the destitute woman's doorstep—"To these he was linked by the freemasonry of failure"(I, 157)—than to frequent the Gildermere, let alone the Talcott, drawing room.

Wharton's evocation of Woburn's tenuous relationship to the Gildermere set and to his beloved Miss Talcott is astute. During his visit to the ball the night before his projected escape to Halifax, he is described three times as standing in the doorway of the ballroom and of not having any contact with the other guests. Miss Talcott — it is significant that Woburn never refers to her by her given name—has turned down his dining invitation of the previous evening, and although now at the ball she offers him the favor of a red enamel Legion of Honor, their dance together is silent and brief and her attention to him remote. Woburn's herculean efforts to secure the permanent favor of Miss Talcott show little sign of success, and readers will recognize in the latter a forerunner of those Fitzgerald women of two decades later whose beaux are chosen on the bases of the latters' real means rather than true measure.[90]

Part II of "A Cup of Cold Water" moves Woburn and the remaining action to a cheap New York hotel, "one which was known to offer a dispassionate hospitality to luggageless travelers in dress clothes" (I, 159). Here, the protagonist is on his own new-found ground, in a setting that more accurately equates to his present image of

228

himself. The introduction of Ruby Glenn to the action adds an unequivocally middle-class dimension to the story, and her own tale of misconduct and betrayal resembles Woburn's own to the point where "he was touched by the chance propinquity of two alien sorrows in a great city throbbing with multifarious passions" (I, 160-161). Woburn's intervention in Ruby's suicide attempt and especially his selfless act of generosity and assistance towards her demonstrate his innate goodness and make ironic comments on his rejection by Miss Talcott and on the disparity between the superficality and materialism that drive her other suitors and the natural goodness that informs his gestures on behalf of the helpless Ruby.

E. K. Brown has remarked that "A Cup of Cold Water" lacks unity, but in fact the ironic play between the two sections as well as the ongoing development of the subject of Woburn's ordeal effectively bring coherence to the story. Part I is more sure-handed than what follows, and one senses that Wharton feels herself on safer ground in her description of the dynamics of the social group she is examining and in her investigation of the consciousness of Woburn. In turning over the recapitulation of Ruby's story to that character Wharton sacrifices the sophisticated prose and outlook that characterizes the telling of Woburn's past. Wharton's prose is heavy-handed at times, as when she describes Woburn's looking through the keyhole after he hears the click of Ruby's pistol in the adjoining room: "After a moment or two of adjustment, during which he seemed to himself to be breathing like a steam engine, he discerned a room like his own, with the same dressing table flanked by gas fixtures, and the same table in the window. This table was directly in his line of vision; and beside it stood a woman with a small revolver in her hands" (I, 161). And the dialogue between Woburn and Ruby fails by excess, as in the following exchange:

"You haven't even told me your name," she said.
"No," he answered; "but if you get safely back to Joe you can call me Providence." (I, 169)

Wharton's title carries a hint of both of the major preoccupations of the story: the cup of cold water is at once the sustenance offered the needy in Jesus' name[1] and the draft thrown on those who aspire to greater things. The conceptualization behind the wedding of the two themes of social failure and moral transcendence demonstrates Wharton's early distrust of the false standards of her own class (even though the class she delineates here was not her own class). But the fictive rendering of the case is at best a mixed success.

"Friends"

With "Friends" Wharton took advantage of her connection with the weekly *Youth's Companion* where she had placed "April Showers" six months earlier. The story appeared there in two installments in the issues of August 23 and 30, 1900. Its publication in *Youth's Companion* was the result of its having been rejected by Scribner's for the 1899 Wharton collection, *The Greater Inclination*; she had sent it to Burlingame under the title "Something Exquisite," thinking it to be in the spirit of the title of that volume. (*LEW* 32)   Its suitability for a place in *The Greater Inclination* was, in Wharton's view, its similarity to "A Cup of Cold Water": "Friends" featured a protagonist who at great sacrifice to herself offered another human being the opportunity of escaping a predicament of potentially painful and enduring consequences. Penelope Bent, a successful school teacher in the small town of Sailport in New England, gives up her position so that her friend Vexilla Thurber may be able to support her own "helpless grandmother, a crippled brother and an idle sister" (I, 200). (Like "A Cup of Cold Water," "Friends" uses one of the staples of sentimental fiction: a wife or prospective wife left abandoned by a faithless man.)   What disqualified the story from appearing in the collection was the judgement of Burlingame, Scribner's book editor, that the tale was marked by "maudlin over-sensibility" (Wharton's rendering of Burlingame's assessment) and demonstrated too sharp a contrast between the heroine's rapture and the squalor portrayed (*LEW* 32).

"Friends" repeats the theme, subject matter, and sentimental tone of scores of novels and stories written in the United States during the late nineteenth and early twentieth centuries. If there is anything to distinguish it from the genre, to mark it as the product of Wharton's pen, it is its closing sentences, in which Penelope Bent, leaving Vexilla Thurber's home after foreseeing the dreadful consequences that would attend the latter's losing her teaching position, assesses her own sentiments vis-à-vis past and present:

> The experiences of the last weeks had flung her out of her orbit, whirling her through dead spaces of moral darkness and bewilderment. She seemed to have lost her connection with the general scheme of things, to have no further part in the fulfilment of the laws that made life comprehensible and duty a joyful impulse. Now the old sense of security had returned. There still loomed before her, in tragic amplitude, the wreck of her individual hope; but she escaped from the falling ruins and stood safe, outside of herself, in touch once more with the common troubles of her kind, enfranchised forever from the bondage of a lonely grief. (I, 124)

It seems relevant to say that here Wharton has raised "Friends" above the clichés of the popular genre. By imposing her own voice she has secured it a measure of quality.

"Joy in the House"

This very late short story "Joy in the House" appeared for the first time in the British periodical *Nash's Pall Mall Magazine* in December 1932. It differs significantly from the other tales in this group of studies of middle-class people by virtue of its focus group. The family on which the story centers attention might be considered upper middle class: Devons Ansley is a small-town (Stokesburg, U.S.A) real-estate agent, successful enough to employ a cook, a housekeeper, and a nursemaid, and to provide a very comfortable life for his wife and young son. Hence its theme does not turn on a question of economic need, but on one of infidelity and marital integrity. And although it will remind some readers of Wharton's stories of failed upper-class marriages, certain details of life in the Ansley household, particularly Devons' choice of decoration to welcome his estranged wife home, betray the family's small-town *parvenu* status.

"Joy in the House" is narrated in the third person with Christine Ansley, Devons' wife, as the point-of-view character, and portions of the story take the form of third-person interior monologue. Christine's interior monologue, set on shipboard as she returns to her family after leaving her lover, the painter Jeff Lithgow, serves to familiarize us with the context of the events that have brought her to this point and in the process reveal something of her disposition and character. The remainder of the story follows Christine as she is welcomed back into her family and then as she receives the surprise news of her lover's suicide, the result of her leaving him.

The recollections and considerations that constitute Christine's shipboard address to self demonstrate her ambivalence about her recent decision to return to her family. At sea, suspended between the bohemian world of Paris and Lithgow and the staid familial life of Stokesburg and Ansley, she rejoices in her return to husband and son while bewailing the loss of the man who has brought excitement and color to her life. It says much about Christine that the proximate cause of her departure has been the humiliation she has experienced at recent signs that Lithgow's artistic stock is failing. This, more than the separation from her son, Christopher, seems to have prompted her decision to abandon life in Paris. But even as she recalls the sense of satisfaction and pride she had earlier experienced at Devons' public displays of generosity, his liberal tipping, for example, she doubts her husband's facile conclusion that "It takes so little to make [the beneficiaries of his generosity] happy." "[H]er steamer trunk half unpacked," the narrator remarks, seizing on an apt symbol of her ambivalence, "she could only throw herself down on her berth and weep" (II, 711).

As Christine nears the American shore, her renewed commitment to family and home assumes a more and more dominant position in her thoughts. "[T]he happy tears rushed to her eyes" as she reads a telegram from Devons and Christopher: "In two days more there will be joy in the house" (II, 712). And in a brief passage of third-person interior monologue, she evokes the joys and familiarities of their home on Crest Avenue, "these small sensual joys." But even here the anticipated happiness is threathened by "something dark and looming on the threshold of her thoughts, the confused sense that life is not a matter of watertight compartments, that no effort of the will can keep experiences from interpenetrating and coloring each other" (II, 713).

The "something dark and looming" that encroaches on Christine's consciousness represents in a general way the fear that the broadened sensibility to life that she has acquired in her relationship with Lithgow will now be stifled. More particularly it harks back to the bantering conversation between Christine and Lithgow in which the latter forecast that her "crumbling" on him, to use her choice of verb, would eventuate in his suicide and subsequently her death. In fact, "Joy in the House," in concentrating the greater part of its length on Christine's return to her husband's house, documents the "death" Lithgow has forecast for her.

That "death" is one of psychological suffocation at the hands of a husband who has controlled and will control her life as if she were an immature child rather than his adult spouse. Christine's return to Ansley is marked by a new consciousness on her part of the terms of their married relationship. Although she must have felt subdued indeed prior to her six-month hiatus with Lithgow to the point where she was willing to abandon her young son, she does not appear to have been entirely aware of the extent to which she was in Ansley's control. What she has perceived as his generosity of spirit in allowing her her fling abroad was in fact a sign of his desire to be in charge of her life. Not only has Ansley allowed her to go to Lithgow, but also he has directed her as to when she might go, how long she would stay, and when she would return. Now, awakened to the possibilities of a freer life, she is alert to Ansley's manipulativeness, and she recognizes that the elements that attend her arrival bear the marks of his desire for control: her son is not brought to meet her at the train station; she is abruptly told of the dismissal of the nursemaid Susan; she is told by Ansley, who shakes "a pink finger admonishingly, 'Too much emotion. I want you to have only calm happy thoughts. Go up to bed now and have a long quiet sleep'" (II, 716).

Ansley's "Good night" to Christine demonstrates the "reign of reason" that prevails in his house where "scenes were the only thing strictly forbidden," where suffering is not permitted, and where Christine's lapse is "wiped out, obliterated, forgotten" (II, 715). The house is more fortress than home, bulwarked against the unhappy intrusions of Christine's past, where "You have only to forbid sorrow to look in at the door, or drive it out" (II, 716). In this anesthetized place where Ansley "smelt of eau de Cologne and bath salts" (II, 713) and where his mother's welcoming embrace of her "breathed of hygiene and Christian charity"(II, 714), Christine is doubtless reminded of Lithgow's remark to her about his own wife, that "she smells of soap" (II, 709). And in so identifying Lithgow's marriage with Christine's renewed union with her husband, the story is pointing to the impossibility of success for the new Christine's liaison with the vapid Ansley.

The absurdity of Ansley's attempt to keep trouble at bay manifests itself in the arrival of Mrs Lithgow with her announcement to Christine of the suicide of her husband, news that Ansley has tried, foolishly, to keep from his wife. Whatever hopes Christine might have harbored of freeing herself from the life-inhibiting confines of her home and returning to Lithgow are of course dashed with the widow's appearance. As Christine reflects, "the hand which had opened the world to her was dead, was stiff in the coffin already" (II, 721-722). Her lover dead, her husband an inhibiting force, she is thrown back on her young son, Christopher, for comfort, the child she had abandoned, who had greeted her return with the words "I thought you were dead" (II, 714), the son she has referred to in the course of the story as simply "the boy."

References to the fading and then dead roses that spell out the words "Joy in the House" point to the irony of the title, some might suggest, in heavy-handed fashion. Indeed, there is little to be joyful about in any of the elements of this story. If Ansley is hardly an exemplar of wholesome and mature humanity, neither is Lithgow, who has abandoned wife and children and left them, seemingly, without support. And despite the positive influence he has on Christine, he is patronizing and careless with her. Like Ansley, he treats her like, in fact calls her, a child. Absorbed entirely in himself and in his art, he leaves her on one occasion during a trip "to stagger under the burden of their joint bags and wraps, dive after the umbrellas, capture a porter and hunt for the hotel bus" (II, 710). Nor is Christine herself immune from criticism, for she has abandoned her little boy and her lover. As Lev Raphael remarks, "she comes off as badly as her husband in this story, and as Lithgow" (199).

"Joy in the House" is not a story that has garnered a great deal of comment.

R. W. B. Lewis's observation about it is much to the point. "It was turned down by a series of editors, because, as some of them explained, readers would be offended by the ugliness of its theme. It is in fact one of Edith Wharton's better and more bitterly ironic tales" (*EW* 5-6). It is certainly the best of her stories about middle-class people, reaching a stature that one usually finds in her stories of her own social group.

* * * * *

Lesser Lives and Greater Inclinations

R.W.B. Lewis writes that the title of Wharton's first collection of short stories, *The Greater Inclination*, "referred to a loftier as against a meaner moral propensity" (*EW* 87). Two of the tales discussed in the present chapter, "A Cup of Cold Water" and "A Journey," were placed in that volume, but only the former appears to qualify as a legitimate entry, given Lewis's explanation, in fact given the title itself. "Friends," another of Wharton's tales about people of the middle classes would have been an ideal representative. "A Journey" and "Mrs. Manstey's View," both from the same period, and "Joy in the House," a much later piece published in 1932, all take a decidedly more pessimistic view of the inclinations of their main characters.

"A Cup of Cold Water," a story with a notable spiritual and religious dimension, shows Wharton contrasting nouveau riche and working-class life, to the considerable detriment of the former. Observing the guests at the Gildermere ball, Woburn reflects: "...the women knew all about the men, and flattered them and married them and tried to catch them for their daughters. It was a domino party, at which the guests were forbidden to unmask, though they all saw through each other's disguise" (I, 157). The next morning he sees

> The signs of [downtown New York] life multiplying around him; he watched the cars roll by with their increasing dingy freight of dingy toilers, the shopgirls hurrying to their work, the children trudging schoolward, their small vague noses red with cold, their satchels clasped in woolen-gloved hands. There is nothing very imposing in the first stirring of a great city's activities; it is a slow reluctant process, like the waking of a heavy sleeper; but to Woburn's mood the sight of that obscure renewal of humble duties was

more moving than the spectacle of an army with banners. (I, 170)

Woburn has modeled his decision to face up to his crime on the "good and noble and unselfish" (I, 613) Joe, Ruby's husband, who has risked being fired rather than have another's act of vigilance attributed to himself. Thus the small-town mid-western telegraph operator, Joe, and the down-and-out and soon-to-be-charged nouveau riche, Woburn, both pluck up their courage and proceed to "face a scene" and stand in contrast to those upper-class men who cower at the prospect of confrontation.

Woburn's acts of preventing Ruby's suicide and assuring that she returns to her husband—Ruby too demonstrates her courage in her willingness to "face a scene"—derive from his essential goodness of heart and are of a piece with his sense of the vacuity and hypocrisy of life in the class from which he has fallen. The protagonist in "Friends," Penelope Bent, demonstrates similar selflessness in her decision to allow her friend Vexilla Thurber to take over her teaching position, given that the latter's financial needs are greater. She too sees beyond the superficial ugliness of her surroundings to the deeper significance of what seems mundane and unpleasant. "Sailport is an ugly town" (I, 197), the story begins, but to Penelope "Sailport had never appeared ugly; or only with the homely, lovable ugliness of a face that has bent above one's first awakenings; a face that has always been there, that one would not exchange for any Venus of the museums" (I 198). In this she resembles Woburn who, steeled by rejection and failure, has come to put a true face on life. Penelope's optimism has been an accustomed thing, one steeped in the hospitable social environment of small-town life, where she has always been successful, where her quality has never been put to the test. Now, after the distressing break-up of her relationship with her fiancé, she shares with Woburn the experience of rejection and failure, and is equal to the disappointment of losing her teaching job and up to the challenge put to her pride by the less-talented, less-attractive Vexilla's disruption of the status quo.

No such affirmative characters as Penelope Bent and Woburn inhabit Wharton's other tales of middle-class persons, "Mrs. Manstey's View," "A Journey," and "Joy in the House." Mrs Manstey, the seventeen-year widow of "a clerk in a large wholesale house" (I, 3) and mother of a daughter living in California, reserves her warmest sentiments for the urban flora and fauna. "She has never been a very sociable woman" (I,3), she corresponds but rarely with her daughter, she refers to servants in nearby houses as "noisy slatterns" (I, 4), she receives "rare" callers only with difficulty. She is clearly of an artistic temperament but, as Donna Campbell remarks, "Qualifiers flank Wharton's descriptions of Mrs Manstey as an artist" (172). In fact she is of too passive a nature to be called a creative artist, her occasional letters to her daughter "written...with difficulty" (I, 3), her real appreciation of natural things, color, form, and beauty not actualized in any outward creative way. The very title of the story, "Mrs. Manstey's View," paraphrases as 'what Mrs Manstey sees'. The emphasis, via the substantive, is on the view, not on the viewer, and this is consistent with the general inactivity of the protagonist—her final destructive action notwithstanding. It is surely Wharton's intention to present a sympathetic view of a sensitive, timid, private woman whose possibly real artistic potential has been thwarted.

The unnamed young wife, then widow, of "A Journey" lacks the love of the natural world and the artistic bent of Mrs Manstey but shares with her a disaffection for the human element. A teacher, she appears to have little sympathy for children, and she has been unable to make friends while living in Colorado. The warmest emotion she seems capable of summoning up for her dying husband is pity. As the train on which she and her now-deceased spouse are passengers arrives in New York, she senses that "the worst terror was past" (I,97): she would no longer fear that her fellow travelers would discover that they were riding with a corpse. As with Mrs Manstey, who dies as her story ends, the protagonist of "The Journey" suffers, if not a real, then at least a symbolic death: "She looked at [her husband's] hat and tried to speak [to the porter]; but suddenly the car grew dark. She flung up her arms, struggling to catch at something, and fell face downward, striking her head against the dead man's berth"(I, 87). "A Journey's" ending is informed by the same kind of ambivalence as is the close of Wharton's tale "After Holbein": in both cases readers are invited to consider the possibility that the protagonists have succumbed to the ravages of emptiness and disillusion.

"Joy in the House" asks readers to consider, in contrast to the literal widowhood of Mrs Manstey and the young protagonist of "A Journey," the figurative widowhood of Christine Ansley, twice deprived of a consort's companionship: her lover has committed suicide and her husband has rendered her place in his home virtually unbearable: "She must get away, get away at once from this stifling atmosphere of tolerance and benevolence, of smoothing over and ignoring and dissembling. Anywhere out into the live world, where men and women struggled and loved and hated, and quarreled and came together again with redoubled passion...but the hand which had opened that door to her was dead, was stiff in the coffin already" (II, 721-722). In Devons Ansley's house the nanny Susan has been fired because, as Devons puts it, "She made a dreadful scene—though she knew that scenes were the one thing strictly forbidden" (II, 715). Readers will be reminded of the fact that in the artificial atmospheres of the families of Wharton's fictive upper classes as well, scenes are to be avoided.

The fact that Christine sees clearly the problem she must confront if she is to take up again her relationship with her son is the one glimmer of hope in a story that is unreservedly grim. Indeed all of the middle-class tales, including "A Cup of Cold Water" and "Friends" are heavy, and ironically the only one in which Wharton engages her penchant for satiric lightness or whimsicality is "Joy in the House." Much of the ponderousness in these narratives comes from the unmediated style, but much as well is related to landscape—especially cityscape—description. "Mrs. Manstey's View" opens with "The view from [her] window was not a striking one" (I, 3); "Friends" begins: "Sailport is an ugly town" (I, 197). Mrs Manstey's view is not inspiring: "Being for the most part attached to boarding houses, [the yards beyond] were in a state of chronic untidiness..." (I, 4). Sailport's streets "are filled with snow and mud in winter, of dust and garbage in summer" (I, 197). The sordid hotel to which Woburn retires; the "unventilated coffee room" where he brings Ruby, where "a waiter who had a melancholy air...reluctantly brought them some tea made with water which had not boiled, and a supply of stale rolls and staler butter" (I,

170); the train in "A Journey" "rushing through a region of bare hillocks huddled against a lifeless sky" (II, 82) and its "windows...blocked by an expanse of sooty wall" as it "passed into the Harlem tunnel" (I, 87); all exemplify the physical ugliness that backgrounds those stories. True, Mrs Manstey, Penelope Bent, and Woburn transcend the ambient drabness in their own ways; nevertheless the atmosphere projected casts a pall over these narratives.

Blake Nevius has written about James's view—and Wharton's—of the pictorial in fiction: "'It is a singular fact,' Henry James remarked of Newport, 'that a society that does nothing is decidedly more pictorial, more interesting to the eye of contemplation, than a society which is hard at work.' Edith Wharton would have agreed. It was precisely this pictorial quality that attracted her and enabled her to demonstrate once again that she had 'the visualizing power' beyond any other novelist of her time" (279-280). In her visualizations of New York's underside, the inside of and view from a train speeding across the country, Sailport in New England, Wharton is as adept as she is at describing Newport, but one senses that she would much prefer sketching the latter.

Notes

[90] The description of the guests at the Gildermere ball (I, 156-157) establishes this: "The bald man with the globular stomach, who stood at Mrs. Gildermere's elbow surveying the dancers, was old Boylston, who had made his pile in wrecking railroads; the smooth chap with glazed eyes, at whom a pretty girl smiled up so confidingly, was Collerton, the political lawyer, who had been mixed up to his own advantage in an ugly lobbying transaction; near him stood Brice Lyndham, whose recent failure had ruined his friends and associates, but had not visibly affected the welfare of his large and expensive family.... The little ferret-faced youth in the corner was Regie Colby, who wrote the "Entre-nous" paragraphs in the *Social Searchlight*...."

[91] In fact, the whole of Part I of "A Cup of Cold Water" is similar to portions of Fitzgerald's fiction: its listing of names, the description of the ball, the meretricious splendor of persons as reflected in dress, furnishings, etc.

[92] "A Cup of Cold Water" contains other pertinent Biblical and religious references, one pertaining obliquely to sin, others to forgiveness and its absence. Early in the story the brownstone housefronts Woburn passes are described as having "the glamor of sword-barred Edens" (I, 151). Ruby Glenn tells Woburn she tried and failed "seventy times seven times" (I, 162). There is also, from Ruby's tale, the Baptist minister and Joe's mother, who find Ruby's sin too severe for forgiveness and who try to dissuade Joe from returning to his marriage.

Chapter Six

The World of the Arts

Wharton published eighteen short stories that are centered on the arts. Her characters of focus in these stories are usually painters (and mainly portrait painters), sculptors, writers (fictionists, poets, a philosopher), and performing musicians, but there are also tales whose interest is on persons who are in one way or another devoted to the arts and particularly to the pictorial arts: connoisseurs, critics, collectors, and art owners. In the eighteen pieces discussed in this chapter, ten feature in a major way painters or persons who have more than a passing interest in painting.

As with her ghost stories, Wharton's stories about persons involved with the creative arts tend to use the subject as a way of exposing issues of human and moral interest. Aside from making occasional bows to the distinction between authentic painters and commercial artists, the stories seldom involve themselves with the nature of the creative arts with a few exceptions: one does not often find discussions of technique or descriptions of the content of canvases. One of Wharton's biographers, Shari Benstock, notes that "Art historians Bernard Berenson and Kenneth Clark ...[observed] that she had no expertise or much interest in painting" (164). It seems safe to say though that her ample contacts with people such as Berenson, Clark, and Morton Fullerton, her intimate friend, provided her with more than a nodding acquaintance with the arts and a fascination with the particular human problems artists and art *aficionados* faced.

Most of the stories discussed in this chapter were the product of the first half of Wharton's fiction-writing career: only three of them appeared after 1910, for example. Of these three, the first published was "Writing a War Story," in which she discussed, among other things, artistic and technical problems challenging fictionists. Otherwise, as with the stories about painters and art connoisseurs and the one story she wrote about performing musicians, the six or seven tales featuring writers, or in which writers play some part, centered on the human dilemmas they confront in the course of the practice of their chosen vocation.

"That Good May Come"

Wharton's first story about a creative artist, "That Good May Come," appeared in *Scribner's* in May 1894. Its central characters are a family far removed from her own in wealth and social standing, yet her tale remains very close to home. It is set in New York City, and the Birkton family are, like the Joneses, members of an Anglo-Catholic high church. More importantly, the transition Wharton makes from poetry to fiction-writing is reflected in Maurice Birkton's recognition that the poetry he writes is *passé* and that "Nobody wants poetry nowadays" (I, 21) as well as in his aspiration to write "the great novel" (I, 25).

That said, "That Good May Come" is not much concerned with the question of literary genres but with themes of artistic integrity and personal morality. When pressure is exerted on him to provide financial support in a minor family crisis, Maurice Birkton succumbs to the temptation of "selling out" as an artist by writing a bit of contemporary scandal in a gossip publication. Because the money he gets from this venture is put to a religious purpose and because the woman who is victimized by his newspaper piece becomes part of the religious aspect of his dilemma, Birkton pays dearly for his indiscretion: although the victims of his impropriety do not turn on him, he is sorely pained in his conscience and unable to reconcile himself to what he considers his unpardonable action.

What triggers the crisis in "That Good May Come" is the poverty of the Birkton family. Because of the family's remote circumstances—Mrs Birkton is husbandless, for reasons we are not told about—and more immediate ones—Mrs Birkton's means of earning money, scrivening invitations for social events, have taken a bad turn on account of the cancellation of a huge ball and because "Lent comes so early this year" (I, 26)—resources are strained to the utmost. Dining fare is frugal, heat must be used sparingly, and family members must work by natural light as long as possible in the evening. Because Maurice is serious about making a living from his talent in a market uninterested for the most part in his literary work, he is unable to be of much assistance. The circumstance that attenuates the Birktons' problems and precipitates Maurice's rash gesture is that his sister, Annette, a deeply religious child of fifteen, is about to be confirmed in the Episcopal Church and needs to be appropriately dressed for the occasion, but there is no money to buy her the clothing she requires.

The poem Maurice sells to the *Social Kite* is evidently a bit of trivia, and we learn little of its content. He himself describes it as "that idiotic squib that I wrote the other day about Mrs. Tolquitt's being seen alone with Dick Blason at Koster & Beal's" (I, 24). Although he realizes that he must conceal from his mother and sister that this "squib" is the source of the hundred and fifty dollars he provides for the confirmation, he cannot escape his own guilt. His conduct with them reveals his self-recrimination. His mother "thought that he looked pale and spiritless." He offers Annette the money with "an awkward gesture" and speaks to her "abruptly" and with "a tinge of impatience in his voice" (I, 30). Initially he avoids all remarks and questions pertaining to the money and later responds by "[turning] sharply away" and speaking to Annette "with a violence which makes the women's startled eyes meet." Finally, he leaves them, slamming the door with "a crash that was conclusive" (I, 31).

But if Arthur keeps the explicit expression of his guilt under wraps within his own family, the nature and extent of his self-dissatisfaction is revealed in his conversation with his friend Helfenridge. Helfenridge is an ardent admirer of Birkton's poetry and shares his friend's high moral principles. His immediate response to Birkton's revelation is ambivalent, a reaction Birkton has sought to guarantee by having Helfenridge see Annette dressed in her new finery. To Birkton's question, "What do you think of a man who's sold his soul?" his friend answers, "I'm not sure if you have. It seems to me I'm not sure of anything" (I, 34). And although he parts company with Birkton rather abruptly, Helfenridge promises to attend Annette's confirmation ceremony.

The Birkton/Helfenridge dialogue resumes after the ceremony. Now Helfenridge has resolved whatever ambivalence he had previously harboured about his friend's guilt. "Even in church that little white seraph didn't seem to justify [your action] for a moment," he tells Birkton, "but I have been thinking hard all day—and now I've come" (I, 39). What he has come for is not to diminish the seriousness of Birkton's lapse but to assure him of his continuing friendship in the face of his human failure. Helfenridge does not seek to lessen the fault itself but rather to persuade his friend that "this good can come out of evil; that having done evil once it may become impossible to do it again" (I, 40). For his own part, Birkton is inconsolable. The sight of the subject of his scandal piece sitting a few places away in church with her about-to-be-confirmed daughter is "an intolerable rebuke"(I, 36), and he interprets the woman's tears during the service to be the result of his grossly insensitive attack. Helfenridge's final attempt to console Birkton, the information that "Blason was waiting for Mrs. Tolquitt outside the church, and I saw them drive away together in a brougham with the little girl between them" (I, 41), comes as a complete surprise to the reader, and doubtless to Birkton. Although the information seems to suggest that the effects of Birkton's action are not as devastating as he might have thought, they do not likely attenuate his sense of the seriousness of his scandal-mongering nor diminish his feelings of self-defilement.

Wharton's airing of the question of artistic ethics seems to be the chief *raison d'être* of "That Good May Come." That being said, the story is marred somewhat by the excessive use of extraneous material. The major offender is the section describing the Sunday morning confirmation service at the Church of the Precious Blood. Here Wharton's narrator launches into long flowery passages about the ceremony and its setting to a point considerably beyond what is necessary to establish the attitude of devotion that permeates the church and to heighten Birkton's sensitivity to the evil be believes himself responsible for. The temptation to indulge herself in the beauty of liturgical ritual with which she was familiar and of which she was fond was evidently too strong for the young writer just learning her trade to pass up. The story was among the first three or four Wharton wrote, but despite its flaws her *Scribner's* editor evidently saw the real promise it showed: "That Good May

Come" bared Wharton's ability to dramatize a moral conflict of some import. This was to become one of her most formidable talents.

"The Portrait"

With "The Portrait," published for the first time in her 1899 collection, *The Greater Inclination*, Wharton published the first of a number of short stories about painting and painters, subjects that would interest her during most of her career. Understandably, as with "That Good May Come," her first story about a creative writer, "The Portrait" shows the signs of apprenticeship work, and one of its major themes, the tension within the creative artist between being true to his talent and satisfying his need to act morally, is rendered with far greater dramatic impact and verbal compression in a story Wharton wrote a few years later, "The Potboiler."

Interestingly enough, as if she did not wish to stray too far from her own *métier*, Wharton uses as her primary narrator in "The Portrait" a novelist. It is this unnamed male, speaking in the first person, who tells Part I of the story, and who introduces the portrait painter George Lillo as his narrator for most of Part II. In turning over to Lillo the telling of what is by far the more important half of "The Portrait," Wharton may be making the point that what she is attempting to express is not easily done. In fact, Lillo, in the midst of his tale of the politically corrupt Vard, his struggle as to how he can paint him, and his burgeoning appreciation of Vard's daughter, expresses precisely this difficulty. Speaking of Miss Vard he tells the narrator: "My besetting fear was that I couldn't count on her obtuseness. She wasn't what is called clever, she left that to [Vard]; but she was exquisitely good; and now and then she had intuitive felicities that frightened me. Do I make you see her? We fellows can explain better with a brush; I don't know how to mix my words or lay them on. She wasn't clever; but her heart thought—that's all I can say" (I, 181). Lillo's statement underlines the difficulty of translating the substance of one art form into that of another and may be at the root of Lewis's characterization of "The Portrait" as "a somewhat confused affair" (*EW* 84) and of its general neglect by critics.[93] But more importantly, there are a number of evidences of Wharton's unsure and heavy hand in this story, and these may help to explain its uncertain status in the

244
canon.

In Part I the narrator/novelist functions as an observer, steering clear of participation in the conversation but revealing his presence by the attitudes he projects: the setting is a "Sunday afternoon" New York salon where a group of people are "talking about George Lillo's portraits" (I, 73). The conversation has evolved into a discussion of two opposed schools of portrait painting, and the group includes a practising representative of each school as well as a spokesperson for each school. In a longish statement, that the narrator somewhat obliquely describes as "a flushed harangue...not unfitted to the trivialities of the tea hour"(I, 74), Mrs Mellish, the hostess of the gathering, identifies Lillo's talent for capturing the "real person" who is the subject: "If there's one positive trait in a negative whole he brings it out in spite of himself; if it isn't a nice trait so much the worse for the sitter; it isn't Lillo's fault; he's no more to blame than a mirror. Your other painters do the surface he does the depths; they paint the ripples on the pond, he drags the bottom" (I, 174). Mrs Mellish's "harrangue" has been prompted by the patronizing and critical remarks of "little Cumberton" (as the narrator calls him) "the fashionable purveyor of rose-water pastels." Cumberton has called Lillo "a genius"—but with "an unfortunate temperament.... He sees only the defects of his sitters.... His peculiar limitations prevent him seeing anything but the most prosaic side of human nature." Cumberton himself has responded to the flattery of one of the gathering, identified simply as "the pretty woman," who has categorically registered her preference for the more romantic of the two painters. "[Lillo] makes people look so horrid," she announces. "I'd so much rather be done by Mr. Cumberton!" (I, 173). In her polarization of approaches, that is, in both her couching of Mrs Melish's apologia for Lillo as a semi-oration, and in her dismissal of Cumberton as "little" and as the ideal of a woman who is no less than five times addressed as the "pretty woman" and who is intent only on her appearance and clothing, Wharton show a heavy-handedness. And considering that the story comes to deal finally with matters that are only tangentially related to the polarity initially established, one might consider much of Part I superfluous.

But Part I does take on relevance as it moves to a conclusion. When we learn that Lillo has painted a portrait of Alonzo Vard, a corrupt city politician, and that the portrait is a failure, as his champion Mrs Mellish has to acknowledge, we are prepared for the story's second section. Here we are made privy via Lillo's narration to the unnamed novelist of the story, to the dynamic behind the protagonist's failure. If the effectiveness of Part I may be questioned because it dramatizes a situation that is only of minor importance to the story as a whole, Part II may be criticized because it transforms a series of potentially dramatic episodes into a narration which the reader experiences two or three persons removed from the action described. The very intense scenes between Lillo and the youthful Miss Vard are less recreated than told, with a resulting loss of immediacy. And considering that these scenes contain the essence of the story and are the stuff of compelling drama, "The Portrait" loses impact by presenting them as it does.

But Wharton's tale has elements to recommend it as well both for what it effects of itself and for what it anticipates of later stories. "The Portrait" ultimately turns on the displacement in Lillo's preoccupations about capturing the essence of Alonzo Vard on canvas by his developing sympathy for Vard's daughter. As in many of the best Wharton stories, the title holds more than initially meets the eye and justifies our seeing the tale in a broader sense than we initially perceived. Certainly the story is about Lillo's "botched" portrait of Vard, the portrait that is a failure despite its creator's undoubted ability to render it successfully, the portrait that has its verbal equivalent in the nuanced assessment of Vard that comes from the various sittings. And it is about the crayon likeness of Miss Vard, "The few lines—faint, yet how decisive—flowered out of the rough paper with the lightness of opening petals...a mere hint of a picture, but vivid as some word that wakens long reverberations in the memory" (I, 177), the product of Lillo's gradual coming into knowledge of the essential Miss Vard. But the story is also, and perhaps most importantly, about the verbal self-portrait of Lillo, the only portrait the reader is able to assess with any objectivity.

That self-portrait reveals a painter insightful enough to perceive the real person he paints and skilled enough to actualize his insights on the canvas. It also reveals a man of high sensitivity, appreciative of Miss Vard's delicacy and potential for being hurt, to the point where, as Lev Raphael expresses it, "Though he ultimately discovers that Miss Vard understands after her father has been arrested, he still botches [Vard's] face to make her feel 'that her miserable secret *was* a secret' just a bit longer to save her from the shame of further disappointment and exposure" (207). Thus Lillo resolves the tension between being true to his artistic commitment and serving the demands of conscience in favor of the latter. In so doing he has at least run the risk of jeopardizing his artistic reputation and diminishing his market value, although in the context of the story at least, this does not appear to have happened.

Both "That Good May Come" and "The Portrait," early entries in Wharton's life-long examination of the question of artistic integrity, reveal her inexperience as a short-story writer. Like the former tale, "The Portrait" can be criticized for its lack of firm focus. But already, the latter story shows considerably more interest in examining the subtleties of her theme than does "That Good May Come" and begins to approach the maturity of later stories about the practice and appreciation of the creative arts.

"The Muse's Tragedy"

If "That Good May Come" and "The Portrait" hinted at the talent of Edith Wharton for dramatizing complex moral and psychological states, "The Muse's Tragedy," written so soon afterward, and published in *Scribner's* in June 1899, saw her promise actualized. For where the earlier stories were overburdened with superfluous detail, "The Muse's Tragedy" is a marvel of economy, never giving the appearance of being arbitrarily or artificially shortened, in a word a story that finds its own proper length. It also demonstrates Wharton's early effective use of sophisticated narrative structures and points of view.

The restricted narrator who has access to the mind of the protagonist Danyers in the story's first two sections (a little more than half its length) introduces him initially at the moment of his first meeting with Mrs Anerton at Villa D'Este, an Italian resort. Then almost immediately he launches back into Danyers' past to contextualize his interest in Mary Anerton and the brilliant writer Vincent Rendle, who is responsible for bringing Mrs Anerton into the public eye. It is only at his third attempt at reconstructing the scene of Danyers' first encounter with Mrs Anerton that the narrator feels confident about proceeding with the present-time segment of the story: the development of the relationship between the two. Betraying his eagerness to get on with the action that most interests him, he has attempted twice before, in the story's first and second paragraphs, to introduce it, only to realize that he must present the background—without which "The Muse's Tragedy" will not be complete. Of course the narrator's hesitancy serves the additional function of offering to, then withdrawing from the reader, matter which he assumes is captivating enough to warrant his patience.

The narrator's digression into past time is made to be appealing and thematically related to his present-time story by its introduction of a friend of Danyers, Mrs Memorall. When Danyers learns that Mrs Memorall has been a schoolmate of Margaret Anerton in France and is at the present time corresponding with her, he is delighted, for it gives him a first-hand source of information about his idol and a possible means of contact with her. More importantly, it is from Mrs Memorall's "ex-cathedra" statements about Mrs Anerton that Danyers calibrates the image he has himself built up of his heroine from his readings of and musings about Rendle's *Sonnets to Sylvia* and *Life and Letters*. When Danyers does meet Mrs Anerton he does so with certain preconceptions, some of his own devising, others attributable to Mrs Memorall's rather superficial conclusions about her some-time friend. (Her name *does* suggest "know-it-all", or something like that, with the ironic coloring the expression conventionally carries.)

It must be noted that Danyers' fascination with *Sonnets to Sylvia* and *Life and Letters* extends to their author, Rendle, as well as to the woman who is memorialized in the books. And if the latter has gradually overtaken the former in Danyers' consciousness and affections, it must be remembered that it was Rendle—the writer—who first cast his spell, appealing to the young essayist and poet Danyers was. "The first reading of certain poems [including *Sonnets to Sylvia*] —had been epochs in Danyers' growth.... Danyers had written at college the prize essay on

Rendle's poetry...he had fashioned the fugitive verse of his own Storm and Stress period on the forms which Rendle had first given to English meter...(I, 67-68). When Danyers is in conversation with Mrs Memorall, he shows his great curiosity about Rendle as well, and although she answers to that curiosity, the information she proffers is largely hearsay and confined to Rendle's alleged eccentricities. There is no question though that she confirms Danyers' assumption, an assumption that seems to be widespread among devotees of Mrs Anerton and Rendle, that the latter two were involved with each other in a profound love relationship. That Mrs Memorall's comment, "[Mrs. Anerton] didn't marry [Rendle] when she had the chance," causes Danyers to "[wince] slightly at this rude fingering of his idol" (I, 69), suggests the wide gap that exists in the significance the perception of the Anerton-Rendle association has for the two people.

Subsequently Danyers assesses Mrs Memorall as if she were "a volume of unindexed and discursive memoirs, through which he patiently plodded in the hope of finding embedded amid layers of dusty twaddle some precious allusion to the subject of his thought" (I, 70), thereby more or less confirming his earlier judgment that "contemptuously classified her as the kind of woman who runs cheap excursions to celebrities" (I, 68). Once Danyers meets Mrs Anerton, his informant disappears entirely from the story, but Wharton, while using Mrs Memorall to supply necessary elements of time and plot has at the same time presented the reader with an enlivening and entertaining character.

Mrs Memorall has been the proximate cause of the meeting of Danyers with Mrs Anerton. By sending the latter the book including one of the young writer's critical assessments of Rendle, she has effectively set up their coming together at Villa d'Este. That coming together moves on the part of the principals from a position of mutual respect for Rendle as a writer to one in which the latter is seen as an obstacle to their mutual contentment. At this point Rendle is deposed from his privileged status in Danyers' consciousness and temporarily, at least, in Mrs Anerton's as well. From the outset, the relationship between the young writer and the older widow is directed by the latter. By the end of their first meeting, Mrs Anerton has flattered her young admirer by telling him that of the essays in the collection Mrs Memorall has sent her, his is "the best in the book," and that "he had penetrated the poet's inner meaning more completely than any other critic." She has also moved to ensure that their association will continue by adding that "There were certain problems...that he had left untouched, certain aspects of that many-sided mind that he had perhaps failed to seize—." Mrs Anerton's concluding statement at their first encounter, "But then you are so young, and one could not wish you, as yet, the experience that a fuller understanding would imply" (I, 71), inadvertently no doubt, draws attention to Danyers' callowness in matters other than literary criticism and points at the nature of their ensuing relationship.

That relationship continues over a period of some three and a half months, from the beginning of May until mid-August, and constitutes the subject matter of Parts II and III of "The Muse's Tragedy." In Part II we are privy to it from Danyers' point of view, his perspective provided by the story's third-person narrator. This portion covers the month of May Danyers and Mrs Anerton spend at Villa d'Este, during which the former "was with her daily" (I, 71). There follows a six-week period of separation, about which we learn next to nothing, though we must assume, in the light of subsequent events, that the emotions kindled at Villa d'Este only stimulated the desire for a reunion. Part III details the idyllic four weeks the two spend in Venice. Although technically speaking Wharton can be said to maintain the narrative technique she uses from the outset—the letter Mrs Anerton sends Danyers on August 14, the day after they part company, fits into the context of the third-person narration with Danyers as the point-of-view character—nevertheless, the piece of correspondence, reproduced verbatim, gives us access for the first time to the consciousness of Mrs Anerton, who up to this point has only been thought and talked about. The injection of the letter also serves another purpose, used as it is within the framework of the narrative perspective: the reader pictures the stunned Danyers reading the letter, his inability to respond directly to his beloved's discontinuation of the relationship a mute testimony to his inexperience and helplessness.

Besides establishing the fact of and the reason for her summer idyll with

Danyers, Mrs Anerton's letter serves at least two other important functions. In the first place, it sets the record straight: Rendle has never loved her. *The Sonnets to Sylvia* have been "A cosmic philosophy, not a love poem; addressed to Woman, not a woman!" (I, 75). Mrs Anerton has been to Rendle "like some perfectly tuned instrument on which he was never tired of playing." "The pity of it was that I wanted to be something more. I was a young woman and I was in love with him—not because he was Vincent Rendle, but just because he was himself" (I, 74). Thus, the public perception of Mrs Anerton as Rendle's illicit lover, the product of assumption, hearsay, rumor, and wishful thinking, was false. Less overtly perhaps, the letter also sheds light on the destructive impact Rendle has had on Mrs Anerton's psyche, and on the role Danyers has been manipulated into playing in helping to reinstate in his paramour a measure of wholeness. One realizes how seriously the woman's self-image has suffered when one examines the lures she feels she must set if she is to pursue her relationship with Danyers. The closing conversation between them as they prepare to leave Villa d'Este is enlightening in this regard:

> It was his last day with her, and he was feeling very hopeless and happy.
> "You ought to write a book about him," she went on gently.
> Danyers started; he was beginning to dislike Rendle's way of walking in unannounced.
> "You ought to do it," she insisted. "A complete interpretation—a summing up of his style, his purpose, his theory of life and art. No one else could do it as well."
> He sat looking at her perplexedly. Suddenly—dared he guess?
> "I couldn't do it without you," he faltered.
> "I could help you. I could help you, of course."
> They sat silent, both looking at the lake.
> It was agreed, when they parted, that he should rejoin her six weeks later in Venice. There they were to talk about the book. (I, 73)

Only the fact that she had been associated with Rendle and that she can satisfy Danyers' enthusiasm for Rendle will suffice, in her own mind, to attach Danyers to her. The questions that have obsessed her during the years with Rendle, "Why had he never loved me? Why had I been so much to him, and no more? Was I so ugly, so essentially unlovable, that though a man might cherish me as his mind's comrade, he could not care for me as a woman?" (I, 77), lurk behind Mrs Anerton's words to Danyers, revealing her panic that the experiment she is fomenting will not have a chance to continue.

That "psychological experiment"—it is Mrs Anerton who so characterizes it—the effort to see if Danyers "would not care for me as a woman," she is correct in identifying as only partly so, for she has "liked [him] from the first," been "drawn to [him]" (I, 77). That the experiment has worked in her favor is evident from Danyers' explicit statements to that effect and from more subtle evidence as well. For example, whereas her relationship with Rendle has not permitted her to evoke occasions of common joy, small acts of endearment, or the cherished little eccentricities of the beloved ("his way of always calling me *you—dear you* every letter began", "his childish delight in acrobats and jugglers") (I, 74), Mrs Anerton's letter spontaneously recalls to Danyers their first evening in Venice: "do you remember the music on the lagoon...from my balcony?" (I,78).

In view of the very satisfying relationship with Danyers she has just experienced, some readers will not be entirely persuaded by Mrs Anerton's conviction of the rightness of her decision to forego her relationship with the younger man. There is much ambivalence in her letter. She insists she is leaving Danyers because of the considerable age difference between them, yet declares, "It is because Vincent Rendle *didn't love me* that there is no hope for you. I never had what I wanted, and never, never, never will I stoop to wanting anything else" (I, 73). (The lady doth protest too much, some will say.) Her apprehension that "Perhaps it was you who had been flattering my vanity in the hope...of turning me, after a decent interval, into a pretty little essay with a margin" (I, 78) repeats her fear that Danyers will objectify her, as Rendle did, yet she fully acknowledges the recognition of her person and femininity by Danyers. In a word Mrs Anerton seems far more assured of her evaluation of the Rendle years than she does about the Danyers summer.

Among critics who have written about "The Muse's Tragedy" there has been the recognition of Mrs Anerton's objectification at the hands of Rendle. Both Cynthia Griffin Wolff (103, 107, 109) and Elizabeth Ammons (6) are cases in point.

More recently, M. Denise Witzig, in an article entitled "'The Muse's Tragedy' and the Muse's Text: Language and Desire in Wharton," has extended recognition of Mary Anerton's objectification to include the notion that "Wharton has given us not so much a tragedy as a revolt.... Her muse has appropriated pen, paper, and her own literary identity in the act of writing herself. By the end of the narrative, Sylvia has not so much become the text for Danyers and the readers as she has deconstructed and appropriated her own story" (263).

What is important about Witzig's comment is the realization that Mrs Anerton, in writing her letter, has written herself, dispelled the inaccurate images of herself constructed by others. What is also important, along with the fact that she has inscribed herself, is what she has inscribed of herself. It is interesting to note that in a short story featuring two "professional" writers and a woman who is immortalized by one of them, the only writerly text we are given is the latter's. That text, as suggested above, carries with it the complexities, contradictions, paradoxes, and ambivalences of a human being in search of herself.[94] And while it would be unfair to pass judgment on the contents of the works of the story's two male writers, which we never see, it is tempting to wonder about the one's preoccupations "about his theory of vowel combinations—or was it his experiments in English hexameter?" (I, 76) and about the other's with "the fugitive verse of his own Storm and Stress period" (I, 68).

"April Showers"

A few months after "The Muse's Tragedy" appeared Wharton published a tale about a young woman Theodora Dace who aspires to become a writer but whose novel is rejected by a Boston magazine. "April Showers" was accepted by *Youth's Companion* and carried in its issue of January 18, 1900. By the 1890's the long established *Youth's Companion* had become one of the most widely read magazines in the United States, boasting a circulation of over half a million (Mott IV 16), its success based on its having a readership of both children and adults. For whatever reason, its simplicity perhaps, Wharton submitted "April Showers" to *Youth's Companion*. It had been turned down by *Scribner's*.

As weak as "April Showers" is, it does establish Theodora Dace's awareness of the difference between mere popular fiction and serious fiction and her commitment, in theory at least, to the latter. Comparing her novel to the works of Kathleen Kyd, a "society novelist" who is a staple of the magazines, Theodora insists that if she lacks Kyd's "lightness of touch," her own novel "had an emotional intensity never achieved by that brilliant writer.... Her aim was to stir the depths of human nature..." (I, 190). In this regard Amy Kaplan, in one of the few comments made about it, remarks that "'April Showers,'[which] starts with a quotation from [Wharton's] own novella ['Fast and Loose'] demonstrates by this self-reference her concern about being 'mistaken' for a 'society novelist'" (73).

One of the signs of the weakness of "April Showers" is that we never learn if the rejection of Theodora's novel is a result of its general ineptitude or of its genuine and competent seriousness, hence its unsuitability for the popular magazine market. Indeed, that question is not raised at the time of the novel's rejection. As well, "April Showers" trails off into a sentimental ending of a kind that a Kathleen Kyd might rely on. The occasional inclusion of a self-deprecating remark betraying Wharton's sense of humor offers some relief to the reader. At one point Theodora's uncle refers to Kathleen Kyd as "a very pleasant, sociable kind of woman; you'd never think she was a writer" (I, 190). But such treats are too rare in this tale whose rejection by *Scribner's* may have been a sign to Wharton of its failure.

"Copy"

In "Copy," published in *Scribner's* in June 1900, Wharton took up again a format she used in a story that appeared in the previous year, "The Twilight of the God." Sub-titled "A Dialogue," "Copy" is written as a drama script, with the speakers' names preceding their spoken words, a description of the setting introducing the entire playlet, and stage directions appearing in parentheses in the text. Why Wharton departed from a conventional short-story format in "Copy" and chose to construct it as a short one-act play must remain a matter of speculation in the absence of any authorial commentary on the matter, but her inclusion of the piece in her 1901 short-story collection, *Crucial Instances*, suggests that her bit of experimentation was conceived less as an attempt to write something for presentation

254

on a stage than as an exercise in broadening the possibilities of narrative expression. It is interesting though that in Wharton's other story written in the same format, "The Twilight of the God," the main characters are also two ex-lovers meeting up later on in life.

In "Copy," the two principals are referred to "fervently" by Hilda, Mrs Dale's secretary, as "the greatest novelist and the greatest poet of the age" (I, 277), and the latter, Paul Ventnor, has come to visit his former lover some twenty years after their relationship has ended. Although the reunion is not without its emotional moments and one senses a real warmth behind the banter the two engage in, it becomes clear that the reason for Ventnor's visit is to retrieve his love letters to Mrs Dale so that his memoirs, which he is presently writing or contemplating, may provide immediate access to the past. The element of the love letters to each other, that both have kept and cherished, brings to the fore the main issue in "Copy," the dissatisfaction felt by both about their current public lives and their yearning for the earlier times when, as Mrs Dale puts it, "we lived instead of writing about life!" (I, 285). Their decision to burn the entire correspondence will ensure that at least that early "world" of theirs will remain their own secret preserve.

As Barbara White has remarked: "The threat [to authors] of becoming public property and other issues in the relationship between the artists' personal and public lives are explored at greater length in Wharton's first novella, *The Touchstone*" (38). "Copy," already written, or a least alive in Wharton's mind during the time she was working on the 1900 novella, provides a more dramatic and immediate—if less profound—airing of these issues. In playlet format, devoid of descriptive and expository passages, and consisting of a series of very brief exchanges between the two principals, "Copy" presents its theme in the context of the lively exchange between the ex-lovers. This dialogue, always witty, at times warm, at times acerbic, carries its own charm and satisfies what seems to be Wharton's purpose: to expose a personal concern of that time in her life as succinctly as possible.

"The Rembrandt"

"The Rembrandt," published in the August 1900 issue of *Cosmopolitan*, was unique among the group of stories about people in the arts that drew Wharton's attention at the turn of the century: it did not have a creative artist as one of its main characters. Its narrator/protagonist is the curator in an American art museum, and where the story touches upon art, its interest is on the artifact and not the artist.

Barbara White writes in part about "The Rembrandt": "As with 'The Pelican,' the reader is given just enough information to distrust the narrator but not enough to understand him. Although in both cases there is more than one possible interpretation, the possibilities are mutually exclusive" (62). By drawing attention to the narrational likeness between "The Rembrandt" and "The Pelican"—and, she might have added, a number of other Wharton first-person stories—White reminds us to look closely at the attitude the narrator projects about himself while in the process of telling his story.

But beyond the fact that the narrations serve in both cases as indications of their respective tellers' personalities and attitudes, there are few similarities between "The Pelican" and "The Rembrandt." Whereas the time lapse covered in "The Pelican" is of several years duration, "The Rembrandt" extends only to a few weeks. Consequently the dilettantish narrator of "The Pelican," an older man, reveals himself as one set in his ways, repeatedly revealing his sense of social superiority, his pedantry (sometimes false), and his tendency to patronize. Because the curator/narrator in "The Rembrandt" is younger, and because we observe him over so much shorter a period, we cannot say that Wharton is assessing him in as complete a way as she is the narrator of "The Pelican." The art curator is forced into making a decision about one immediate situation, and as a result we are shown him in a very limited way, although what we do see demonstratres a considerable amount about the man.

It must be said in favor of the narrator of "The Rembrandt" that his decisions in regard to the fraudulant painting that is the story's centerpiece are rooted in human compassion. His inability to tell Mrs Fontage the truth about her treasured canvas even as he realizes he is reneging on his professional obligations establishes this clearly. It is important to note as well that he immediately seizes upon the significance the painting holds for the owner in terms of its importance in her life.

256

Mrs Fontage's story of her acquisition of the work evokes in him a touching vision
not of the painting itself but of the difference it has made in its owners' lives. What
he is attempting to ensure by his inflated evaluation of her "Rembrandt" is the
continuation of the remembrances it conjures up for her:

> The old Belgian Countess, the wealthy Duke with a feudal castle in Scotland,
> Mrs. Fontage's own maiden pilgrimage to Arthur's Seat and Holyrood, all
> the accessories of the naive transaction seemed a part of that vanished Europe
> to which our young race carried its indiscriminate ardors, its tender romantic
> credulity; the legendary castellated Europe of keepsakes, brigands and old
> masters, that compensated by one such "experience" as Mrs. Fontage's, for
> an after-life of aesthetic privation. (I, 290)

The narrator is also moved by his better instincts in his interpretation of Jefferson
Rose's intention of purchasing the painting at its exaggerated price so that he can
assuage Mrs Fontage's privation. It is the narrator's realization that Rose's proposed
purchase, in the light of his obligations as the support of "an invalid mother and two
sisters on the slender salary of a banker's clerk" (I, 294), would create much
privation for the latter that motivates his second compassionate gesture. For all of
his astute and detailed vivisections of the personality, temperament, and motivation
of both Mrs Fontage and Rose, and Eleanor Copt for that matter, the narrator is more
a man of the heart than of the head.

Much of the curator's narration of his experience is given over to assessment
of the characters with whom he comes in contact. In the case of people he already
knew, Eleanor, Rose, and the committee member Crozier, for example, these are
usually preambles to his discussion of meetings with them. His analysis of Mrs
Fontage amounts to a running commentary on her personage, that presents an
evolving and more complete picture of the woman as his three meetings with her
ensue. The narrator's commentary about the other characters is invariably wry and
benevolently critical, but rarely bitter, unkind, or patronizing. It is well worth noting
that when the curator's comments do fall into the latter negative categories, they
reveal a man under the immediate stress of conflicting impulses. When his first
meeting with Mrs Fontage eventually leads him into an unspoken observation about
her "life-long habit of acquiescence in untested formulas that makes the best part of

the average feminine strength," he has just finished articulating to himself the nature of the dilemma in which he has been placed: "Looking at that lamentable canvas seemed the surest way of gathering strength to renounce it; but behind me, all the while, I felt Mrs. Fontage's shuddering pride drawn up in a final effort of self-defense" (I, 291). On his second visit he is again put under the gun by Mrs Fontage's persistent questioning of his willingness to buy the painting for his museum. Again he is prompted into another uncharacteristically negative narrational observation: "Even if the committee had been blind—and they all *were* but Crozier—I simply shoudn't have dared to do it" (I, 294).

Aside from these rare exceptions, the narrator is a man in control of his thoughts and careful about his evaluations. He obviously prides himself on his intelligence, aesthetic judgement, precision with words, and astuteness about assessing his fellow humans. But he is a young man with much to learn, and often lacks perceptiveness. He easily dismisses his cousin Eleanor as not being particularly knowledgeable about painting—and is surprised when Crozier, the only committee member he respects, tells him that his cousin's "encyclopedic information has often before been of service to me" (I, 299). As well, for all his self-alleged astuteness, he does not realize that Rose, whom he has previously identified as a suitor of Eleanor, would have provided information to her about the conditions pertaining to the purchase of the "Rembrandt." Under the narrator's somewhat vain, self-sufficient, confident, and professional exterior, a façade that falls away entirely during his dinner with Crozier, his acknowledged superior, resides a vulnerable innocence that is totally consistent with the goodness of heart demonstrated in his decisions in favor of the story's potential victims of misfortune.

Alongside the narrator's acts of human considerateness stands juxtaposed Crozier's cruel gesture of rewarding the former's "admirable promptness and energy in capturing [for the museum's collection] the Bartley Reynolds" (I, 299) with the bogus Rembrandt that has also cost him so much in human embarrassment. Crozier has secured the consent of the committees members to offer the false masterpiece to the narrator: his act is deliberate and calculated, and stands out in contrast to the

258

other's instinctive sensitivity and generous-hearted actions. Perhaps intended as a joke, Crozier's action is a cruel joke.

Wharton's early fiction was often seen to be of a piece with the work of Henry James. The narrator of "The Rembrandt" has the reflectiveness, loquaciousness and articulateness of a James narrator. And the theme of the evil, or wastefulness or ennui that lies behind refined exteriors, a favorite James theme, is incarnated here in the person of Crozier. To be sure, that theme is not a rare one in Wharton's short fiction either, as stories such as "The Eyes," "The Pelican," and "Mary Pask" demonstrate. But the theme that might be considered its obverse, the inherent goodness that resides behind a façade of fastidiousness and disinterestedness, seems to emerge more naturally from Wharton than from her famous contemporary.

"The Recovery"

The publication of "The Recovery" in the February 1901 *Harper's* and of "The Moving Finger" a month later in *Harper's* again draw attention to Wharton's particular interest at this time in subjects pertaining to the creative arts. In a period of ten months, between June 1900 and March 1901, five such stories appeared in the magazines, four of them reappearing in Wharton's 1901 collection, *Crucial Instances*.

"The Recovery" repeats themes found in the earlier "April Showers," but it advances considerably the satirical edge found in the latter: it is a tale of considerably more sophistication and elan than the *Youth's Companion* piece. Like "April Showers'" aspiring novelist, Theodora Dace, the painter Keniston is conscious of his responsibility of coming to the support of needy members of his family: in his case, a mother and a widowed sister. Thus, the notion of Theodora Dace's insistence on not "selling out" to the demands of popular magazine fiction editors is revisited in "The Recovery." In the story's early portions the third-person narrator adopts a satiric perspective on his subject. The president of Hillbridge University, where "The Recovery" opens, is called "a prehistoric relic who had known Emerson, and who was still sent about the country in cotton wool to open educational institutions with a toothless oration on Brook Farm" (I, 259).[95] And the central character, Keniston, also falls within the scope of the narrator's ironic glance: "It is known to comparatively few that the production of successful potboilers is an art in itself, and that such heroic abstentions as Keniston's are not always purely voluntary" (I, 261-262).

However, "The Recovery" does not maintain its satiric tack beyond its early pages. Indeed, there is a sharp demarcation in a number of ways between Part I of the story and its ensuing four sections. Whereas Part I is essentially narrative, covering in a general way Keniston's beginnings as a painter, his gradual emergence into prominence, and the interest taken in him by his future wife, the remainder of the tale is dramatic, presenting in a very particularized manner, i.e., by specific incident and much dialogue, the arrival of Keniston at an awareness of his own provincialism and inadequacy as an artist. Section II picks up events some ten years after Claudia Day and Keniston have met: now they are married, and the occasion that will bring about Keniston's epiphany, his first visit to Europe for an exhibition of his paintings in Paris, constitutes the substance of the remainder of the story. The transformation in Keniston is seen through the eyes of his wife: from the time of her introduction into the story in Section I, the third-person narrator presents matters through her view. Prior to that, the narrator sees things from his own ironic perspective, and when Claudia becomes the point-of-view character, "The Recovery" loses its satiric edge, and its critical commentary tends more towards direct attack than ironic indirection.

It is clear that in the ten years since Claudia and Keniston have first met the former has matured and sharpened her critical view considerably and the latter has began to question his pat assumptions about his own work. Of the three characters who share the foreground in the last three sections of the story, the Kenistons and Mrs Davant, a "worshipper" of the painter and "reckless purchaser" of his work, it is the last who is the butt of the narrator's jokes (and of Claudia's dissatisfaction). Mrs Davant "[reminds] Claudia of her earlier self...young credulous and emotionally extravagant...the self that, ten years before, had first set an awe-struck foot on [Keniston's] threshold" (I, 262).

The "newer" Claudia, on the other hand, has a far more critical appreciation of her husband's talent than has his young patron. Measured against Claudia's sense that "the true artist must regard himself as the imperfect vehicle of the cosmic emotion—that beneath every difficulty overcome a new one lurked, the vision widening as the scope enlarged" (I, 263), Keniston is found wanting. Of Keniston's admirers, only Claudia is not unequivocal in her acclaim, and Mrs Davant merely echoes the adulation of the Hillbridge view and shows up Claudia's judgement in bold silhouette: "'but now that his talent is formed,' says Mrs Davant, 'that he has full command of his means of expression,'—Claudia recognized one of Professor Driffert's favorite formulas—'they all think he ought to see the work of the *other* great masters, that he ought to visit the home of his ancestors, as Professor Wildmarsh says!'" (I, 264).

The experience of the Kenistons in London and Paris tends to favor and ultimately confirms both Claudia's suspicion that her husband's work will not hold up when measured against European art and her intuition that he himself realizes this. For Claudia though, the question of Keniston's paintings is not merely a professional matter from which she can maintain the proper impersonal distance. She is married to him in what seems to be a satisfying relationship, and her sensitivity is demonstrated throughout the story's examination of their relationship by its recognition of the tension within her of her loyalty and her suspicion that he is a mediocre artist. Her earlier sense that Keniston is "beginning to be dissatisfied with his work" relieves this tension, "[filling] her with a renovating sense of his sufficiency" (I, 265). Now standing alone in the beautifully appointed but empty Paris gallery where the paintings hang, she is struck by "a single conviction—the conviction that the pictures were bad" (I, 270), and once again the feeling that she is being disloyal comes over her. Her guilt manifests itself in different ways. She immediately tries to rationalize away her "conviction" by questioning her right as a non-professional to evaluate his art. Then, when she discovers Keniston is in the room, she is embarrassed beyond words, blushing and stammering as if her presence there were a betrayal.

As earlier, when Claudia's fear of having betrayed her husband is assuaged by her suspicion that he is beginning to question his own, and Hillbridge's, complacency, so now she is again relieved by his conviction about his work: "When I went to look at those things of mine," he tells her, "it all came over me in a flash. By Jove! It was as if I'd made them all into a big bonfire to light me on my road!" (I, 273). And if her joy is somewhat allayed by the practical consideration that he still must discharge his debt to Mrs Davant, Claudia will no doubt be convinced of his ability to make the most of his plan to "stay out here till I learn to paint" (I, 274) the panels that have been paid for but not done.

"The Recovery" has "a happy ending," Barbara White remarks, "as Keniston's recognition inspires him to start over, thus setting him on the road to recovery" (37). The story also concerns the psychological dynamic that Keniston's recognition and recovery bring about within Claudia, and it is surprising, given the attention White bids us pay to the role of point-of-view characters in her book on the short stories, that she does not include Claudia as an important aspect of the happy ending. It is just as surprising that White concurs with Patricia R. Plante's assessment of the story. "Plante criticizes the story at length," writes White, "noting justly that it lacks depth...." Then she cites Plante: "it does not really deal with any of the perennially important matters concerning the nature of man or the nature of art" (14).

But "The Recovery" has much to say about art and the human and, most important, about the interrelationship between the two. What has been hidden from the Kenistons, especially from Claudia's husband, during their lives in provincial Hillbridge is the recognition of the interplay of painting and the culture from which it emanates, the realization that "the pictures [in London's National Gallery] were simply the summing up, the final interpretation, of the cumulative pressure of an unimagined world" (I, 266). Unlike Mrs Davant—her name, in this context, is patently ironic, for her perspective is not an advanced one— whose statements are still governed by the sureties of home, and who reports that there had been a great crowd at the Keniston exhibition on the first day, and that the critics had been "immensely struck" (I, 267), Keniston and Claudia are, by the time they reach Paris, plainly embarrassed by the canvases. European art serves to awaken Keniston to his former blindness and to the vast gap between his paintings and what he sees in the National Gallery and the Louvre. London and Paris transform a man who, his wife recalls, had had at one time a "rather expressionless" face and "the habit of self-engrossed silences" (I, 266) into an excited and voluble man who is awakened to the possibility of achieving something beyond the narrow complacencies of his former work. Art impacts on the artist Keniston, raising in him the hope of becoming a more significant painter and allowing Claudia to trust his promise that in time he will satisfy his commitment to Mrs Davant. More importantly for Claudia perhaps—and this explains her light-heartedness in the story's closing exchange between the two—art impacts on Keniston the man, assuring her that he sees himself as he is and not as the construct of a provincial elite unaware of the world beyond itself.

"The Moving Finger"

Wharton followed up "The Recovery" with another story about a painter. "The Moving Finger" made its appearance in *Harper's* in March 1901. But this time the central character, Claydon, is not a painter challenging his own expertise but one who directs his expertise to what is finally a non-artistic end. While "The Moving Finger" is about the portrait painter and about one of his portraits, its focus is essentially psychological, extending beyond the painter to the story's other major character, the husband of the portrait's subject, to the point where the story's situation can be identified as a traditional—if far from conventional—love triangle.

"The Moving Finger" has elicited favorable comment from Henry James (Bell, 247), and the early critic E. K. Brown had high praise for it as well (11). Among recent critics, Barbara White has noted the self-parodic appropriateness of the story's title and the general intrusiveness of its narrative voices. A helpful examination of the tale has been written by Theodore Ziolkowski, who finds it "the most brilliant conflation of art and ghosts" (140) in Wharton's repertoire. "Grancy and Clayton (*sic*)," he writes, "represent two entirely different attitudes toward [the latter's portrait of Mrs. Grancy], even though both of them stand in a mystical relationship to the 'haunted' portrait.... The husband loves the painting only for the sake of the woman; the painter loves the woman only for the sake of the painting"

(141).

Ziolkowski's critique of "The Moving Finger" (140-143) is astute and provocative, yet it may not account for all of the elements in the story. Its antithesis about the objects of the artist's and the husband's respective devotion is both absolute and reductive. If Ziolkowski is arguing that Claydon is not attracted to the "real" Mrs Grancy but only to his own rendering of her, he may be overlooking the fact that the story insists on a genuine affinity between Claydon and his beautiful subject. Grancy tells the general narrator: "When Claydon painted her he caught just the look she used to lift to mine when I came in. I've wondered, sometimes, at his knowing how she looked when she and I were alone" (I, 307-308). This presents the possibility that Claydon is graced with the same "look" his wife gives to her husband and invests the story with a Browningesque touch by reminding us of its affinities to "My Last Duchess." Interestingly, Wharton draws on Browning in at least one other story, "The Duchess at Prayer," published in *Scribner's* just seven months prior to the appearance of "The Moving Finger." It is interesting also that Grancy's "wonder" as to Claydon's capturing a look he supposed was reserved only for himself is followed by his potentially, at least, ironic recapitulation to the general narrator: "I used to say to [Mrs. Grancy]...'If you grew tired of me and left me you'd leave your real self there on the wall!' It was always one of our jokes that she was going to grow tired of me" (I, 308).

That Claydon loves Mrs Grancy for herself seems verified by the final section of the story. The general narrator, coming upon the portrait "throned alone on the paneled wall [of Claydon's studio], asserting a brilliant supremacy over its carefully chosen surroundings," is convinced that "Claydon had heaped his treasures at the feet of the woman he loved. Yes," he thinks, "it was the woman he had loved and not the picture" (I, 312). When Claydon and the narrator confront one another on this occasion, the latter accuses the painter of trying to do "a cruel thing" (I, 312). But in the story's closing lines, Claydon establishes both the links that connect him to Mrs Grancy and the selfless love he has exercised in the direction of the married couple whose union he honors:

Cruel! Yes, it seemed so to me at first; and this time, if I resisted, it was for *his* sake and not for mine. But all the while I felt her eyes drawing me, and gradually she made me understand. If she'd been there in the flesh (she seemed to say) wouldn't she have seen before any of us that he was dying? Wouldn't he have read the news first in her face? And wouldn't it be horrible if now he should discover it instead in strange eyes?—Well—that was what she wanted of me and I did it—I kept them together to the last!... But now she belongs to me. (I, 313)

There can be little doubt that the narrator is convinced by Claydon's story: it merely verifies what he has already sensed. Given his conviction, and Claydon's declaration, we note that Claydon has been from the outset much in the forefront of his narration. Among the circle of friends that share the Grancy hospitality and warmth, Claydon is the only one singled out by name. His complimentary comments about Mrs Grancy are cited frequently by the narrator, and even during those later periods when he has withdrawn from the Grancys' company he remains a large part of the story-telling, conspicuous by his absence. It is clear that the narrator views Claydon as more than merely the painter of Mrs Grancy's portrait: he perceives the artist as having some special relationship to her as well, and that perception climaxes at the time of the intuition that it is Mrs Grancy Claydon loves and not the painting. The resentment this intuition raises in the narrator is sensed by Claydon, of course, and provokes initially his rhetorical question, "You think I killed Grancy, I suppose?" and then his closing explanation (I, 312).

Along with carefully charting the evolution of the narrator's recognition of Claydon's affinity for Mrs Grancy, the story also astutely establishes the rightness of Claydon's actions throughout, as consistent with the sentiments he expresses in his concluding remarks. When he first meets Grancy's new wife he remarks, "He *has* done [something great] —in marrying her!" and at the time he paints her portrait his unabashed praise expresses itself in flattering "metaphor" (I, 302). When the Grancys move to their country home, where the portrait graces the library wall, the narrator devotes much attention to Claydon's conduct during the Sunday visits of the Grancys' circle of friends. He notes: "we used to accuse Claydon of visiting Mrs. Grancy in order to see her portrait," and "One of us... said that Claydon had been saved from falling in love with Mrs. Grancy only by falling in love with his picture of her," and "We smiled afterward to think how often, when Mrs. Grancy was in the room, Claydon, averted from the real woman, would sit as if he were listening to the picture" (I, 303). Here, of course, the narrator and his friends might be said to be misinterpreting Claydon's action: given the latter's sensitivity to and respect for the couple's union as revealed in his closing declaration that "I kept them together to the last!" (I, 313), his turnings away from Mrs Grancy and his concentrations on the portrait might just as easily be interpreted as his effort to disguise his attraction for his host's wife—about which he might be somewhat embarrassed.

When Grancy returns to the country after serving a diplomatic mission abroad, the narrator is anxious to renew acquaintances with his widowed friend and his circle, but when he broaches the subject to Claydon, the latter turns down his invitation. If after their meeting, "Claydon was incalculable enough for me [the narrator] to read a dozen different meanings into his words" (I, 305), so too can the reader find a number of reasons why Claydon would be reluctant to return to Grancy's. His association with Grancy, and the fact that the former had prevailed on him to modify the portrait he loved might readily explain his reservations. We can better appreciate the reluctance of Claydon to visit Grancy when we examine the narrator's response to the modified portrait: "I stood speechless...a veil of years seemed to have descended on it. The bright hair had lost its elasticity, the cheek its clearness, the brow its light: the whole woman had waned" (I, 307). And if the narrator is somewhat mollified by Grancy's explanation of why he had the portrait transformed, Claydon is not privy to Grancy's rationale.

Claydon's second modification of his portrait into "the face of a woman *who knows that her husband is dying*" (I, 310), is initiated at the request of Grancy but effected according to the painter's own initiative as he is inspired by the spectral directive of Mrs Grancy. The moving finger of the story's title may very well be meant as an allusion to the warning embodied in the message that prompts the second modification. "But when I turned to the picture," Claydon tells the narrator, "... I swear it was *her* face that told me he was dying, and that she wanted him to know it!

She had a message for him and she made me deliver it" (I, 313). If we accept the fictive reality of the portrait's ghostly intervention into Grancy's life, we must just as surely admit the possibility of its impact on Claydon, who has his own claim to closeness with Mrs Grancy.

Like a number of Wharton's short stories, "The Moving Finger" is difficult to categorize, and it might have been discussed in these pages in the chapter devoted to the ghost stories. As with most of Wharton's ghost stories, this one uses the spectral theme to profile aspects of the psychological lives of characters, the latter emerging as the more important. What differentiates "The Moving Finger" from the other ghost stories is its emphasis on positive elements of love and human consideration that characterize the principals: in the bulk of the other ghost stories the evil side of the human psyche takes up our attention. The decision to include "The Moving Finger" in the present discussion of stories about the arts is based on a sense that this latter topic engages Wharton more fully than does the subject of ghosts. If, as Ziolkowski writes, Wharton "was obsessed both with art and ghosts" (140), this story is weighted in the favor of the former obsession, and one can readily imagine the story's maintaining its impact and point even shorn of its ghostly elements. In fact a case might be made against calling it a ghost story at all. Explaining the nature of the portrait's impact on him, Grancy says, "I'm not talking any psychical jargon—I'm simply trying to express the sense I had that an influence so full, so abounding as hers couldn't pass like a spring shower" (I, 308). Claydon evidently comes under the same full and abounding influence.

"Expiation"

With "Expiation," published in *Cosmopolitan* in December 1903, Wharton turned her hand to the writing of a light satirical and comic story about a first-time novelist named Paula Fetherel. The fact that Mrs Fetherel is a member of wealthy New York society and that the title of her fiction is *Fast and Loose* signals a certain autobiographical element in the story (See: *EW* 30; White 88), but Wharton's reference to her own social background and to her adolescent literary work seems little more than a bow to the past, and "Expiation" goes in its own direction, independent, in all but a general way, of its author's life and early work.

"Expiation" reveals Wharton's eye and ear for the humor inherent in the lives of the people of her own social set, her knack for isolating a selection of incongruous relationships and circumstances from the social context, and her skill at exploiting their comic possibilities. The story rides on the tension generated between Paula and her uncle, the bishop of Ossining, on the question of the moral suitability of her novel, which purports to expose the "hollowness of [society's] social shams" (I, 441). In the process it strikes out goodhumorously at such foibles as critical shoddiness, readerly carelessness, clerical self-importance, and husbandly doting.

The satire in "Expiation" derives from both the commentary of its privileged narrator and the actions and conversations of its characters. Although the status of Paula Fetherel as the central personage in all five sections of the story suggests that she is the point-of-view character, the narrator also assumes entry into the consciousness of other characters, making use of this broad access to full effect, often attributing to characters the possession of high sentiment, then undercutting it, as in "The Bishop was very fond of...Mrs. Fetherel, and one of the traits he most valued in her was the possession of a butler who knew how to announce a bishop" (I, 442). This device of deflating characters proliferates in the story and is a frequent source of humor and satire.

But most of the humor and satire in "Expiation" derives from the verbal and situational interplay of the characters themselves. The story is constructed as a series of interfaces between Paula and each of a number of persons who stand in various degrees of familiarity with her. Paula has two conversations with her cousin Bella Clinch, a successful if impoverished writer of popular science books. During these exchanges we learn that Paula's novel belies its title, is not the critique of high society it is supposed to be. The exchanges tell us as well that Bella , herself a niece of the bishop, is far more forthright in confronting the officious cleric than is Paula, who backs down in the face of his disapproval of her novel's title and thus puts into question her seriousness about writing a social critique in the first place. Bella also uncovers her cousin's desire to have a best-seller at any cost—despite the latter's explicit denial of any such wish—and prompts her into realizing that "a rousing attack on its morals" by her cleric uncle, "could run your novel up into the hundred thousands in no time" (I, 450).

Bella Clinch, like Mrs Roby of Wharton's best short-story satire, "Xingu," is the image and voice of good sense in "Expiation," rising above the pretentiousness of the other characters, hence free of the narrator's barbs. The bishop; Paula's husband, John; the bishop's friend, Mrs Gollinger, come under direct attack in the narrator's commentary and give themselves away by word and/or deed. John is seen as an uncultivated parasite. The bishop's standing on his own dignity is played off against the overweening intensity with which he pursues the acquisition of a new chantry window for his cathedral. Mrs Gollinger is set up as a type: the clergy-admiring woman who can see only good in her deceased minister/husband's former associate.

There is no doubt that satire dominates plot in "Expiation." Even the story's title, related no doubt to the price Paula pays for her pandering to material success when she is forced to sit silently through her uncle's taking credit in his dedication address for the acquiring of the funds for the chancery window, evokes parodic images of the grandiose cleric and his seething niece. The fact that the plot lacks focus—the story line is far off the point and precision of "Xingu"—suggests that Wharton was more conscious of developing a humorously critical statement than she was of making a well-crafted short story. Probably because the objects of her satiric thrusts reside in such diverse spheres of human activity as clerical life, social intercourse, and literary criticism, and because of the blurriness that inevitably brings to the story's action, "Expiation" is off the standard of Wharton's best short fiction.

"The House of the Dead Hand"

Wharton turned again to the subject of art in a story called "The House of the Dead Hand," published in *Atlantic Monthly* in August 1904. The fact that she did not include the story in any of her collections was perhaps used as a rationale for its virtually being ignored in the earlier commentaries on the short fiction. Lewis called it "her only inept effort in this period" (*EW* 81), and few had anything more to say about it until recently. Lately though, Barbara White has referred at some length to the connections between the story and Wharton's pornographic fragment, "Beatrice Palmato," reproduced in R. W. B. Lewis's biography and in Cynthia Griffin Wolff's critical study of Wharton's work, *A Feast of Words*. White has also incorporated Wolff's observations concerning the autobiographical elements of "Beatrice Palmato" into her discussion of the incestuous world that is the story's house of the dead hand.[96]

White's reading of "The House of the Dead Hand" incorporates many of the story's details. She writes, in part:

> In "The House of the Dead Hand" Lombard might be assumed to have symbolically killed Sybilla, accounting, in the traditional gothic connection between house and female body, for the cold and decay of the house. The painting probably stands for the incest itself, bought with Sybilla's female legacy, kept secret with keys, locks, and hidden doors; Dr. Lombard, guardian of the secret, understandably refuses to let the picture be photographed and makes Sybilla guardian after his death. The dead hand over the door of the house...could be the hand of the mother (or grandmother), too weak to protect the daughter. Or it might be the "third hand" of the Beatrice Palmato fragment, wherin Mr. Palmato and his daughter call his penis his third hand. Cynthia Griffin Wolff makes a convincing association between the third hand and the hand of Wharton's father, which forms a major part of her earliest recollection as recounted in *A Backward Glance*. If the dead hand is the third hand, it practically announces, "This is the house of incest." (40-41)

White extends her commentary to integrate such other aspects of "The House of the Dead Hand" as Siena, the locale, details of the Leonardo canvas, and the aura of Renaissance corruption projected by Doctor Lombard, and her argument in favor of interpreting the story as a case of incest is quite compelling. In characterizing the tale as an "Italian melodrama filled with Gothic trappings" (39), however, she is signaling the fact that her focus rests on the action observed by the story's reflector character, the youngish art connoisseur, Wyant, and not on Wyant as a participant in the action. Attending to the active presence of Wyant in "The House of the Dead Hand" is revealing of elements that complement the story of Dr Lombard and his house—in the broadest sense of that term—and useful in appreciating the story as a comprehensive unit.

Wyant has much in common with Dr Lombard. He has been drawn to Siena by his love of art, and his passion for the paintings of the masters is apparent at many points in the story. It is not an exaggeration to say, as well, that Wyant, like Lombard, places art above humanity in his scale of importance. It can be said of both men, of one to a greater, of the other to a lesser degree, that they have redirected normal affections and considerations in favor of fellow human beings towards objects of outstanding artistic accomplishment. Lombard, whether or not we accept the interpretation that he has abused his daughter in an incestuous relationship, has stifled her individuality and aspirations in a vicious way, controlling her life for the sake of the Leonardo he has forced her to purchase with the proceeds from her inheritance. Wyant's allegiance to Lombard's commitment to and representativeness of a certain aspect of the Renaissance ethos is reflected in his first meeting with Lombard:

> ...the young man was conscious of staring with unseemly intentness at his small round-backed figure, dressed with shabby disorder and surmounted by a wonderful head, lean, vulpine, eagle-beaked as that of some art-loving despot of the Renaissance—a head combining the venerable hair and large prominent eyes of the humanist with the greedy profile of the adventurer. Wyant, in musing on the Italian portrait medals of the fifteenth century, had often fancied that only in that period of fierce individualism could types so paradoxical have been produced; yet the subtle craftsmen who committed them to the bronze had never drawn a face more strangely stamped with contradictory passions than that of Doctor Lombard. (I, 509-510)

Beyond his eulogizing of Lombard, Wyant expends his enthusiasm on the *objects d'art* which he has come to Siena to see. Sybilla's Leonardo "was so dazzling, so unexpected, so crossed with elusive and contradictory suggestions, that the most alert observer, when placed suddenly before it, must lose his coordinating faculty in a sense of confused wonder" (I, 515). In the church of San Domenico, Sodoma's "St. Catherine" "under the momentary evocation of the sunset...emerged pale and swooning from the dusk, and the warm light gave a sensual tinge to her ecstacy. The flesh seemed to glow and heave, the eyelids to tremble. Wyant stood fascinated by the accidental collaboration of light and color" (I, 517-518).

Wyant's responses to the personages he engages in the story are not always marked by the enthusiasm with which he responds to Lombard or by the sensitivity with which he responds to *pièces d'art*. He is short with the Lombards' servant woman and becomes angered by what he calls the Count Ottaviano Celsi's unwarrantable liberty in soliciting his assistance in the former's love affair with Sybilla. Most seriously, he refuses his assistance to Sybilla at a time when she might have saved herself from the destructive influence of her father, even when he has become suspicious of precisely that negative influence. It is not unreasonable to conclude that Wyant's frequent retreat into Anglo-Saxon reserve as a method of explaining his reluctance to become involved in the affairs of the young lovers is a rationalization. And just as surely his love of art has served as a means of escape, justification for his holding himself from human entanglement.

Wharton has on at least two occasions in the story adroitly placed examples of this latter pattern in Wyant's conduct. As he leaves Lombard's house after his first visit, Wyant speculates about the mystery of the house. "What were the relations between Miss Lombard and her father? Above all between Miss Lombard and her picture? She did not look like a person capable of disinterested passion for the arts, and there had been moments when it struck Wyant that she hated the picture." What is interesting here is not only the relative importance he places in his two questions but also the alacrity with which his speculation is swallowed up in the aesthetic possibilities that invite him. "The sky at the end of the street was flooded with turbulent yellow light," the story continues, "and the young man turned his steps towards the Church of San Domenico, in the hope of catching the lingering brightness on Sodoma's 'St Catherine'" (I, 517). During Wyant's second visit to the Lombards we see the pattern reenacted. Here he finds himself alone with Sybilla.

> "I arranged it. I must speak to you," she gasped. "He'll be back in five minutes."
> Her courage seemed to fail, and she looked at him helplessly.
> Wyant had a sense of stepping among explosives. He glanced about him at the dreary vaulted room, at the haunting smile of the strange picture overhead, and at the pink-and-white girl whispering of conspiracies in a voice meant to exchange platitudes with a curate. (I, 525)

To be noted here is Wyant's assessment of the relative importance of things: "the haunting smile" of the picture overhead and the "platitudes" of the living woman beside him. Given the attitude projected here, it is difficult to take seriously the interest Wyant expresses about Sybilla's predicament in their ensuing conversation, and we are not surprised at his callous "Rubbish! She isn't walled in; she can get out if she wants to" (I, 526) as he leaves the house.

In his preference for art over life, Wyant is a milder version of Lombard, whose life is a drastic example of that principle and who is seen to express it in paradigms similar to those used to describe his young admirer. In a statement that begins as a comment about trivialities, Lombard repeats the pattern of Wyant's outlook on life and art. Speaking of Mrs Lombard's aunts in England, Lombard asks, "[Did] you mention that they never sleep in anything but linen, and that Miss Sophia puts away the furs and blankets every spring with her own hands?" Then, looking at his watch he says to Wyant, "Both those facts are interesting to the student of human nature. But we are missing an incomparable moment [to view the Leonardo]; the light is perfect at this hour" (I, 523-524). It is of more than passing interest in terms of the story's commentary on life and art, that only minutes before, Mrs Lombard has spoken to Wyant, to no effect whatsoever, words that are in diametrical opposition to the dominent ethos of the two connoisseurs of art. "I liked a picnic, too, or a pretty walk through the woods with young people of my own age. I say it's more natural, Mr. Wyant: one may have a feeling for art, and do crayons that are worth framing, and yet not give up everything else. I was taught that there were other things" (I, 523). In a brief "trivial" affirmation, the one character in the story whom we tend to dismiss, the woman whom Ottaviano refers to as "an idiot," puts in proper perspective the general question of the relative importance of life and art and the particular problem of her daughter's immediate dilemma, and establishes herself as the model of the principles she espouses, as the living antithesis of the lack of humaneness her statement exposes. Of course her statement, not surprisingly, falls on deaf ears.

There is no doubt that Wharton has told "The House of the Dead Hand" in such a way as to include Wyant in the malfeasance done to Sybilla. Beyond the aforementioned implicit evidence from the earlier periods of the story covered in Parts I, II, and III, there is considerable explicit criticism made of the young man's conduct in the periods described in Part IV, the time of Wyant's learning of Lombard's death and of his later visit to Siena. The criticism is seen in the narrator's commentary and in the story's unequivocal ending. Of the former, one might cite an instance from the first three paragraphs of Part IV, such as: "Wyant's justification [for his ineptitude] was complete. Our blindest impulses become evidences of perspicacity when they fall in with the course of events" (I, 526). As to the ending, in which Sybilla culminates her explanation of her inability to free herself of her deceased father's clutches by telling Wyant: "It is too late, but you ought to have helped me that day" (I, 529), it leaves no doubt about the story's position. It also gives rise to the possibility of reading the title to apply to Wyant's refusal to offer Sybilla the helping hand she so desperately required, at a time when she still appeared capable of quitting her father's house.

That Sybilla no longer has the capability of leaving the house is a measure of the power Lombard continues to wield over her. It is tempting to see "The House of the Dead Hand" as a ghost story, to read Sybilla's declarations to Wyant during his last visit— "No—he prevented me; he will always prevent me"; "I tried again and again, but he was always in the room with me" ; "I can't lock him out. I can never lock him out now" (I, 529) —as signs of her father's supernatural return. But— to turn our attention back to earlier considerations about the story—it is entirely consistent with what is now known about the residual impact of incest practised upon a young person and with what Wharton may have experienced herself, to view Lombard's posthumous visitations to his daughter as psychological rather than spectral. Is is also helpful to remember that very early in her career as a short-fiction writer, Wharton refused to include certain of her stories in her collections because they were too closely identified with her own experience. It adds fuel to the argument that "The House of the Dead Hand" was an acute reminder of pain to remember that Wharton also withheld this story from collection.

"The Potboiler"

Only four months after "The House of the Dead Hand" appeared, Wharton's "The Potboiler" was published in the December 1904 *Scribner's*. Inasmuch as the latter concerned itself with questions of art and conscience, it may be said to have certain general affinities to its predecessor, but "The Potboiler" can be clearly differentiated from "The House of the Dead Hand" for its placing of the artistical/ethical question in the context of lives of persons who are practising artists rather than connoisseurs of art. It is more appropriate to compare this latter story to "The Portrait," which seems in a number of ways to have been its model. Although there is no evidence to suggest that Wharton was consciously revisiting old territory for the purpose of reclaiming it, it is tempting to say just that, for "The Potboiler" makes use of the same polarities as the earlier story, as well as of some of its very paraphernalia, and fashions them into a more focussed and dramatic examination of the moral problems raised in the mind of a practising portrait painter who is sensitive to the needs of his fellow artists and other acquaintances.

"The Potboiler" has its own version of "little Cumberton, the fashionable purveyor of rose-water pastels" from "The Portrait" (I, 173) in Mangold, "the fashionable portrait painter of the hour" (I, 663), who caters to the "present generation [that] wants to be carved in sugar candy, or painted in maple syrup," that "doesn't want to be told the truth about itself or about anything in the universe" (I, 670). It also has its equivalent of the earlier story's Lillo in Stanwell, the embodiment of the honest artist, whose habit has been not to give in to the attempts of the agent Shepson to convince him to take lucrative commissions from sitters who wish to be painted according to the vogue of the day. As with "The Portrait," it is the insightful and genuinely talented painter in whom the moral dilemma of the story is played out: Stanwell makes certain decisions which bring into question his artistic integrity and must silently bear the criticism of the sculptor Arran, who is the unknowing beneficiary of his alleged fall from artistic grace. "The Potboiler" also repeats "The Portrait's" use of a young woman who draws the attention and attraction of the central character, although the nature of the dynamic that ensues is considerably different in the two stories. What bears noting too is the close similarity between the descriptions of the likenesses of Miss Vard and Kate Arran that the respective artists Lillo and Stanwell have sketched out. "The Portrait's" narrator is struck by Lillo's skill in transforming the subject's commonplaceness:

"The few lines—faint, yet how decisive—flowered out of the rough paper with the lightness of opening petals." He has rendered her "a memorable creature" ("The Portrait" I, 177). The narrator of "The Potboiler" draws attention as well to the primitive state of the drawing, dwelling on its unembellished attractiveness: "a young woman's head had been blocked in. It was just in that state of semievocation when a picture seems to detach itself from the grossness of the medium and live a wondrous moment in the actual; and the quality of the head—a vigorous dusky youthfulness, a kind of virgin majesty—lent itself to this illusion of life" (I, 665).

Both sketches establish their respective creator's authenticity and talent, of course. Beyond that, the use each story makes of its sketch may serve to stand for the relative artistic merit of the two stories in question. In "The Portrait," Lillo's crayon of Vard's daughter seems imposed on the story. It validates the artist's unquestionable talent, but at a point well beyond that when the talent has been amply established. And its superfluousness is rendered more obvious by the fact that the story does not in the end turn on Lillo's authenticity as an artist as much as on a larger question of human integrity. Stanwell's blocked-out head of Kate Arran, on the other hand, seemed more organically integrated in "The Potboiler." It does set its maker's quality as a portraitist and is a pervasive presence in the story, an object of attention in his studio, especially for Shepson, for whom Stanwell's insistence on maintaining his standard in the face of the pressures of selling out to popular demand is something of a mystery. What is more, the sketch of Kate encapsulates the major tensions of the story, for it captures the likeness of the person who is the motivation for Stanwell's exercising his ability to paint in a way that satisfies popular demand.

To the two characters Stanwell and Mangold, who represent respectively the principled and talented portraitist and the commercially successful but limited one, "The Portrait" has added in the person of the sculptor Arran a third "type," the erstwhile artist who is without either talent or success. It is the inclusion of Arran and his sister Kate that allows the philosophical polarities of the story to be brought sharply into focus. That, along with narration by a privileged voice, gives it its dramatic caste and makes it a more successful achievement than its predecessor.

Arran supplies the need for a spokesman to articulate the position of the pure artist, unaware though he is of his own lack, and Kate is brought into the story as the object of both Stanwell's and Mangold's love and the repository of their brotherly concern for the failing sculptor.

Of Stanwell and Mangold, the latter is scarcely developed beyond the type he represents. The former is the story's centerpiece, the point-of-view character, into whose consciousness we have the most access. In order that we be able to see his generosity to Arran as motivated by more than simply a means of entry into Kate's favor—and so establish the strong human feeling that pulls at his desire to produce only the highest art—he is set up from the outset as a man of patience, consideration, and kindness. His first conversation in the story is with the art dealer Shepson, whose repeated remarks about Mangold's commercial success—as compared to his—Stanwell counters with good humor.[97] The most striking manifestation of Stanwell's patience and forbearance comes later in his contacts with the Arrans, who are the beneficiaries of his largesse. If, as the critic Lev Raphael believes, "Stanwell decides to do the society portrait and anonymously commissions work for Arran with the money" (208), the painter's restraint is nothing less than admirable, considering the sculptor's challenging of his benefactor's acceptance of the lucrative commission and his taunting him over his lack of principle.[98] But whether or not Stanwell has been Arran's patron in the matter of his sculpture, his kindness and consideration for brother and sister is established without doubt when he rents a cottage on the New Jersey shore and invites them to join him there. Here, although his patience is put to the test by Arran's "denunciations of his host's venality" (I, 680), Stanwell transcends his friend's blatant insensitivity.

The question on which "The Potboiler" turns is posed early on when Stanwell asks Arran, rhetorically, "Why can't a man do two kinds of work—one to please himself and the other to boil the pot?" (I, 671). In the end it is Kate who takes on the role of spokesperson for her brother's idealistic position. Thus she is at once the desired one for whom Stanwell would at least indirectly, "boil the pot," and the demanding one, whose challenge to his integrity places him in an untenable position regarding the accomplishment of his desire. But if she does verbally insist on her preferred suitor's adherence to her imposed standard, Kate, as Raphael argues, compromises her own integrity. After she turns down Stanwell's proposal, "Kate announces she is marrying Mangold 'because though his pictures are bad, he does not prostitute his art.' The implication is clear enough, however, in her blushing and her attempt not to drop her head in shame that Kate knows full well that *she* is prostituting herself to help her brother" (209).

When Raphael adds, "An interesting question left open at the end is the nature of Stanwell's talent—if he truly has a gift of imitation, then perhaps he hasn't abandoned his standards so shamefully" (209)—he is, of course, advancing the possibility that the story is shaded in favor of Stanwell's position. The ending of "The Potboiler" has Stanwell sitting before "his unfinished head of Kate Arran...with a grim smile." He has decided not to paint Mrs Van Otley and not to accept "any more orders for the present" (I, 684). It is not likely though that this signals a change in his practice of exploiting his ability to paint for the market. Rather, it reflects his crestfallen spirit in the face of Kate's refusal of his recent proposal of marriage.

"The Potboiler's" sympathetic view of artists and art lovers who retain an allegiance to their human sides places it among a group of similar short stories that includes "The Portrait" and "The Moving Finger," to mention two. Compared to "The Portrait," on which it seems to have been modelled, "The Potboiler" is a more mature expression of one of the more pervasive themes found in these stories about the arts. Of Wharton's stories, Barbara White has noted, "[She] usually avoids didacticism...but she often has a message when it comes to art" (37). It must be said that "The Potboiler," for all its structural excellence, loses artistic impact because of the explicitness of its message.

"The Verdict"

Wharton reintroduced the subject of painting and the theme of the artist's moral responsibility four years after the appearance of "The Potboiler," in another *Scribner's* story, called "The Verdict," published in June 1908. What little recent commentary the story has garnered has drawn attention to the earlier "The

Recovery." Both Barbara White and Lev Raphael note that the two tales deal essentially with their protagonist/painters' recognition of their own artistic inadequacy when they measure their talents against those of the best of their peers and forbears, but neither critic goes on to explore the impact of this recognition on the respective protagonists.

"The Verdict" also provides an interesting contrast to its predecessor "The Potboiler" from the point of view of narrative approach. Dealing also with art and artists and the question of their moral responsibility, "The Verdict" limits its focus to one painter, considering the reasons for his resigning from the profession and the ramifications of his decision. It is a briefer, more concentrated tale, observing the unities of time and place, and less open than "The Potboiler" to the charge of overt didacticism. Viewing "The Verdict" in the light of "The Recovery," the story to which it is most often seen to be related in theme, offers a way of perceiving more clearly its very effective inferential quality.

If both "The Recovery" and "The Verdict" concern painters who come to recognize their own mediocrity, they differ substantially in the perspective from which their protagonists view this recognition. "The Recovery" dramatizes the process of the New England artist Kenniston's disenchantment with his own work, his realization that he has much to learn, and his resolve to "learn to paint" the panels he has already been paid for. Whether or not he has it in him to become the painter he would like to be is left in abeyance: he has rid himself of his illusions, and this recognition is of much worth in itself. In this developing self-knowledge Kenniston is the beneficiary of the burgeoning awareness of his wife, Claudia Day, who has feared her husband's complacency and self-satisfaction and who is delighted at his awakening to the truth.

"The Verdict" on the other hand catches Jack Gisburn, a one-time Chicago portrait painter, newly married and now living on the French Riviera, after he has made the irrevocable decision to give up his art. The tale of his "recognition" is recounted by himself in fewer than two pages at the beginning of the story. "I can tell you in five minutes—and it didn't take much longer to happen," he informs the narrator, Rickham (I, 660). What is dramatized in "The Verdict" is a few hours in the day of the desultory life of an ex-painter who has given in to the temptations of ease and wealth. The provider of Gisburn's ease and wealth is his wife: unlike Claudia Day, who challenges her husband, Mrs Gisburn aids and abets her spouse's escape to his easeful Mediterranean retreat. There is a reason why the present time of "The Verdict" is set where and when it is: the story is about what has happened to Gisburn, not about what has prompted his decision.

Gisburn the portraitist is characterized as follows by his friend Rickham in the latter's comments about Gisburn's portrait of his wife:

> [A]ll the characteristic qualities came out—all the hesitations disguised as audacities, the tricks of prestidigitation by which, with such consumate skill, he managed to divert attention from the real business of the picture to some pretty irrelevance of detail....Mrs. Gisburn...had lent herself in an unusual degree to the display of this false virtuosity.... [The picture] represented, on his part, a swelling of muscles, a congesting of veins, a balancing, straddling and straining that reminded one of the circus clown's ironic efforts to lift a feather. It met, in short, at every point the demand of lovely woman to be painted "strongly" because she was tired of being painted "sweetly"—and yet, not to lose an atom of sweetness. (I, 658)

This quality of Gisburn, "the quality of looking cleverer than he was" (I, 658), as Rickham describes it, had been the subject of his epiphanic realization as he sat beside the corpse of Stroud, his ideal, unable to fulfill the wish of the latter's wife that he paint him on his death-bed. "I dashed at the canvas furiously," he tells Rickham, "and tried some of my bravura tricks. But they failed me, they crumbled. I saw he wasn't watching the showy bits—I couldn't distract his attention; he just kept his eyes on the hard passages between. Those were the ones I had always shirked or covered up with some lying paint. And how he saw through my lies! (I, 661).

One cannot but admire Gisburn's awakening to the truth about his artistic pretense. It is the subsequent rationalizations, accommodations, and withdrawals that show themselves so patently in the remainder of his recapitulation of his experience at Stroud's bedside and in the present time of the story, that are less commendable. For Gisburn has managed to convince himself that he is beyond recovery as a practising painter and has placed himself in a situation where recuperation is virtually impossible. One senses, along with the alert Rickham, that Gisburn is dissatisfied with his decision to withdraw from a profession that gave him considerable satisfaction and might provide even more artistically significant fulfillment. But he is without the moral courage necessary to transcend his comfortable life and apply himself to the painful project of "learning to paint," as "The Recovery's" Kenniston has resolved to do.

The question of "learning to paint" is one that has arisen for Gisburn during his time with the dying Stroud: he has built the experience into a small myth for himself, imagining occurences there to the advantage of his weaker self. Indeed one wonders just how much of his recounting of his story to Rickham has been conditioned by his life since his comfortable marriage. Recalling the failed attempt to paint Stroud, he says, "If I could have painted that face, with that question on it, [i.e., 'Are you sure you know where you're coming out?'] I should have done a great thing. The next greatest thing to see was that I couldn't—and that grace was given me. But, oh, at that minute, Rickham, was there anything on earth I wouldn't have given to have Stroud alive before me and to hear him say: 'It's not too late—I'll show you how'?" Yet the answer, "It *was* too late—it would have been even if he'd been alive" (I, 662), belies the very questions and underlines the tension residing in the consciousness of Gisburn.

Gisburn's rationalizing continues in the brief conversation with Rickham that brings "The Verdict" to an end. This time it is Rickham who poses the question—because it seems, in the light of his friend's evident self-dissatisfaction, the obvious one. The response, couched as two questions, "Begin again? When the one thing that brings me anywhere near him is that I knew enough to leave off?" (I, 662), reminds us of Rickham's earlier characterization of Gisburn, "...that he had the same quality as his pictures—the quality of looking cleverer than he was" (I, 658): it avoids the question, attempting to rationalize it away with a bit of rhetorical smoke-screening.

What Rickham hears about Gisburn's experience at Stroud's bedside confirms what his afternoon visit in his friend's home has make him suspect. The following exchange during that visit verifies this:

> "Don't you ever dabble with paint any more?" I asked, still looking out for a track of such activity.
>
> "Never," he said briefly
>
> "Or water color—or etching?"
>
> His confident eyes grew vague and his cheeks changed color a little under their handsome sunburn.
>
> "Never think of it my dear fellow—any more than if I'd never touched a brush."
>
> And his tone told me in a flash that he never thought of anything else. (I, 659)

It is significant that this conversation occurs in the part of Gisburn's palatial home that he refers to as "my own lair." This is "a dark plain room...square and brown and leathery; no 'effects', no bric-a-brac, none of the air of posing for reproduction in a picture weekly...," and its dominant object is "a small picture above the mantlepiece—the only object breaking the plain oak paneling of the room" (I, 659), Stroud's sketch of a donkey, that so impresses Gisburn and is the proximate cause of his withdrawal from the practice of his art. The room is a shrine to Stroud, and in its isolation and simplicity might also be seen as a place that Gisburn has set aside to acknowledge that unactualized part of himself that would like to paint again. Rickham's conclusion to his description of the room, that it gave "no least sign of ever having been used as a studio" (I, 659), seems implicitly to recognize just that element.

The cause of Gisburn's refusal to recommit himself to painting in the face of the evident unease he suffers over that decision is a subject the story handles with some suggestiveness. We are not told in so many words what stands in the way of Gisburn's actualizing his unacknowledged desire to learn to paint like Stroud, but the information is embedded in the event and description of the text itself. If Gisburn has isolated a room where he pays homage to what Stroud represents, his life exists in the remainder of the luxurious home his wife has provided for him. When he shows Rickham around the house, the latter longs "to cry out: 'Be dissatisfied with your leisure'" (I, 659), but realizes that his host has become unconditionally attached to the house and to the amenities, tone, and life style that come with it. "He showed it to me with a kind of naive suburban pride," Rickham observes, "the bathrooms, the speaking tubes, the dress closets, the trouser presses—all the complex simplifications of the millionaire's domestic economy. And whenever my wonder paid the expected tribute he said, throwing out his chest a little, 'Yes, I really don't see how people manage to live without that'" (I, 658-659).

Gisburn's entrapment in a life style that effectively precludes his return to the artistic life is perhaps most aptly captured in a wonderful juxtaposition of action and dialogue that occurs early in Rickham's visit when he speaks to Mrs Gisburn in the absence of her husband:

> I turned to Mrs. Gisburn, who had lingered to give a lump of sugar to her spaniel in the dining room.
> "Why *has* he chucked the painting?" I asked abruptly.
> She raised her eyebrows with a hint of good-humored surprise.
> "Oh, he doesn't *have* to now, you know; and I want him to enjoy himself," she said quite simply. (I, 657)

The near-simultaneous occurrence of Rickland's question and the woman's gesture effectively accents the cause and nature of Gisburn's lassitude, and the latter's answer tells us that she knows nothing of her husband's deeper yearnings.

Because it was drawn from the lives of an American couple well known in the society Wharton frequented,[99] the scant attention "The Verdict" has received has focussed on this real-life connection. For whatever reason, "The Verdict" has never been given its critical due. It is a brief and compact dramatization of a not-uncommon human predicament observed and reported unobtrusively by a disinterested but sympathetic narrator. It makes its point by word and action, distributing detail significantly for maximum effect. Its particular use of interior household design and furnishing suggests that it was close to Wharton's heart, and this may help to account for its high quality.

"The Daunt Diana"

Wharton's July 1909 *Scribner's* tale, "The Daunt Diana," about art connoisseurs and collectors, resembles the earlier "The Rembrandt" and "The House of the Dead Hand," both stories in which the protagonists/art lovers are placed in predicaments in which their human qualities are measured against the attachment they have for objects of aesthetic value and for art generally. Shari Benstock's remark about "The Daunt Diana," that it deals with "the egotism of connoisseurship and art collecting" (244), suggests that the story takes a line that is consistent with its two aforementioned predecessors. The story is also reminiscent of "The Pelican," one of Wharton's short fictions about academic life written a decade earlier: its way of accommodating narratorial method to the subject matter repeats a technique used in the earlier story. Barbara White writes of "The Daunt Diana": "[It] might have been an intriguing study of the acquisitive instinct were it not for the elaborate point of view. The collector's story comes to us through the reminiscences of a first-person narrator, who is introduced by still another first-person narrator. While the narrators are scarcely characterized and have no part in the story themselves, their intervening presence makes the protagonist seem so far away that we can scarcely get interested in him" (64). In fact, the narrators are characterized and have an integral part to play in "The Daunt Diana," and we do become interested in all three of the principals, collectors and connoisseurs, narrators all, each of whose presence and verbalizations contributes to making the elaborate narrative structure an organic element of the story.

As with the unnamed narrator of "The Pelican," who unwittingly reveals aspects of himself as he tells his story of the itinerent lecturer Mrs Amyot, the principal voice in "The Daunt Diana" says much that displays facets of his personality and attitude as he recounts to his friend the ex-collector the tale of Humphrey Neave's acquisition, sale, and reacquisition of the Daunt Diana. Himself a collector—of enamel snuffboxes—Finney speaks of a world shared by his listener, an insider's world, male, affluent, sophisticated, and esoteric. As he speaks he reflects the exclusiveness of this world and the corollary tendency to negate elements foreign to it. Thus his comment when he describes his final visit to Neave, that the latter lives in a "black palace turned tenement house and fluttering with pauper linen," his three cold rooms smelling "of the *cuisine* of all his neighbors" (II, 59), smacks of his sense of social superiority and condescension.

Certain other remarks betray Finney's supercilious attitude towards women. Referring to Neave's early guide work in Rome "expounding 'the antiquities' to cultured travelers," he imagines "how it must have seared his soul! Fancy unveiling the sacred scars of Time to ladies who murmur: 'Was this *actually* the spot—?' while they absently feel for their hatpins!" (II, 51). The same attitude is evident in his sympathizing with Neave's own words and gestures. Recalling the latter's being driven mad by the requests to show his Daunt collection, Finney cites him:

> "The women—oh, the women!" he wailed, and interrupted himself to describe a heavy-footed German princess who had marched past his treasures as if she were viewing a cavalry regiment, applying an unmodulated *Mugneeficent* to everything from the engraved gems to the Hercules torso.
>
> "Not that she was half as bad as the other kind," he added, as if with a last effort at optimism. "The kind who discriminate and say: "I'm not sure if it's Botticelli or Cellini I mean, but *one of that school*, at any rate." And the worst of all are the ones who know—up to a certain point: have the schools and the dates and the jargon pat, and yet wouldn't recognize a Phidias if it stood where they hadn't expected it." (I, 55)

One can appreciate the satiric quality of some of Finney's and Neave's remarks, but their sallies go beyond satire. Both the limiting of the objects of the two's ridicule to the female sex and Neave's latter comment that relegates all but the most discriminating of art viewers to a status of stupidity reveal more about their sayers than they do about their subjects and ultimately turn the satire back on its intended makers.

Finney's tale, effectively his answer to the first narrator's queary "What's become of the Daunt Diana?" encompasses a period of some fifteen years: the time between Neave's first sight of the Daunt Diana and his reacquisition of it. His narrative surely satisfies his listener's expectations, for the latter characterizes Finney as "a psychologist astray among *bibelots*...[who] really has an unusually sensitive touch for the human texture, and the specimens he gathers into his museum of memories have always some mark of the rare and chosen"(II, 50). It is questionable though that Finney's addressee grasps the deeper psychological nature of Neave's existence, and the true purport of the story may have very well transcended the teller's ability to grasp it. Finney's Neave is a heroic romantic who by "persistent self denial" (II, 51) had begun to build his collection. "Year by year, day by day, he had made himself into this delicate register of perceptions and sensations—as far above the ordinary human faculty of appreciation as some scientific registering instrument is beyond the rough human senses—only to find that the beauty which alone could satisfy him was unattainable, that he was never to know the last deep identification which only possession can give" (II, 53). When he obtains the means of gratifying his highly developed faculties, he experiences, after a process of trial and error, the ultimate appreciation of his artistic acquisitions. In Finney's final evocation of his hero, as he sees him in the presence of his bronze Diana, "His face shone with an extraordinary kind of light as he spoke; and I saw he'd got hold of the secret we're all after. No, the setting isn't worthy of her.... But she rules here at last, she shines and hovers there above him, and there at night, I doubt not, comes down from her cloud to give him the Latmian kiss..."(II, 60).

The occasion that has brought on Finney's eulogism and initially caused him to gasp and say, "In the name of magic, Neave, how did you do it?" is the sight of his friend's bedroom, "a mere monastic cell, scarcely large enough for his narrow bed and the chest which probably held his few clothes: but there, in a niche, at the foot of the bed—there stood the Daunt Diana" (II, 50). The scene that so impresses Finney has been effectively prepared for from the inception of Neave's infatuation with the statue, and it marks the culmination of a progressing relationship that is expressed by both story-teller and subject in the vocabulary of sexual attraction and courtship. When Neave sees the Diana for the first time, "it was the *coup de foudre*," says Finney, "that day...the Diana followed him everywhere.... And on the threshold he turned and gave her his first free look—the kind of look that says: 'You're mine!'" (II, 52). For Neave the accumulation of the Daunt collection *en masse* has proved unsatisfying: "The transaction was a *marriage de convenance*," he says. "Why, my other things, my own things had wooed me as passionately as I wooed them," and even the Diana was "a cold bought beauty...a professional beauty [who]...expected every head to be turned when she came into a room" (II, 57-58). But the Diana's absence has served its purpose: "I wanted her to want me, you see, and she didn't then! Whereas now she's crying to me to come to her" (II, 58). And now that she has returned to his possession, Neave explains his former apparent indifference: "I lied to you that day in London—the day I said I didn't care for her. I always cared—always worshipped her—always wanted her. But she wasn't mine then, and I knew it, and she knew it...and, now at last we understand each other" (II, 59-60).

Finney's telling of the story of Neave's attachment to art, in particular his Diana, including his recapitulation of the subject's own words on the matter, in terms of a personal attraction, attachment, and union with a human love object is undoubtedly intended as a metaphorization of a man's passionate love of his own art possessions. There is no evidence that he ascribes to it anything more than comparative status. Readers may very well perceive an additional dimension of substance to be derived from Finney's narrative. The story's closing image conjured up by the sight of Neave's monastic cell, of an aging bachelor whose nights are spent in the company of a cold, nude, bronze statue of a chaste Diana may not produce in some the positive reverberations Finney derives from it. In fact the image serves to isolate the essential insularity, selfishness, and self-centeredness that has dominated Neave's life. Neave has courted, and captured—if only to his own satisfaction—the mistress Art in a literal and not merely metaphorical way. His life has been lived for himself and seems totally devoid of any human commitment, either personal or communal.

It is telling that Finney, subsumed into the aura of Neave's final exaltation, misses, in both the seeing and the recapitulation, the poverty of his subject's human situation. Given his attitude towards persons generally and women in particular, it is not surprising that he would fail to grasp the significance of his older friend's state. Although we are not given much information about "The Daunt Diana's" addressee character, its first narrator, we are no doubt meant to assume that he shares Finney's attitude, and there is nothing to suggest that his appreciation of his friend's "unusually sensitive touch for the human texture" of Neave (II, 50) will impart to him any deeper significance than it had for the teller. The two narrators enhance not a whit the starkness of the landscape of "The Daunt Diana."

"Full Circle"

Another of the half dozen or so stories Wharton wrote on the subject of writers, "Full Circle," appeared in *Scribner's* in October 1909. One extended examination of this tale is by Lev Raphael, who calls it "one of the best" and an "ironic *tour de force*" (209), but it is questionable whether "Full Circle" deserves such high praise. In any case, Raphael's discussion consists mainly of a summary of its somewhat complicated plot and falls short of demonstrating the high quality he would claim for it.

"Full Circle" features a running dialogue between its two major characters, the published novelist Geoffrey Betton and the failed writer Duncan Vyse, that is held together and given focus by the on-going commentary of a third-person narrator who adopts the perspective of Betton.

For sections of its length, the story shifts into portions of interior monologue that observe the elementary requirements of a third-person narration but in fact enter into the consciousness of Betton in such a way as to suggest that he is engaging in an address to self. In the following paragraph, in which Betton bemoans the imminent appearance of his second novel, one can see the transition from narration to interior monologue.

> Diadems and Faggots was now two years old, and the moment was at hand when its author might have counted on regaining the blessed shelter of oblivion—if only he had not written another book! For it was the worst part of his plight that the result of his first folly had goaded him to the perpetration of the next—that one of the incentives (hideous thought!) to his new work had been the desire to extend and perpetuate his popularity. And this very week the book was to come out, and the letters, the cursed letters, would begin again! (II, 74-75)

In the use of the technique Wharton resembles her contemporary Theodore Dreiser, a number of whose best short stories, such as "Free," "The Old Neighborhood," and "Sanctuary," derive their quality from their particular deployment of interior monologue. Although Wharton's use of the device in "Full Circle" is not nearly as pervasive as it is in the Dreiser stories mentioned, it nevertheless serves to provide the reader with a view of the inner intensity with which Betton perceives his predicament.

This uncharacteristic device aside, "Full Circle" seems undistinguished. Betton's aforementioned problem is, after all, trivial, as is the ensuing one that preoccupies him—his lack of popularity. And in any case we are unable to muster up much sympathy for a figure so egocentric and careless in his treatment of others. That Betton's preoccupations are dwarfed by Vyse's draws attention to the possibility of the latter's development as a character. His commercial failure as a novelist, his creative talent—as witnessed by Betton's appreciation of the high quality of his manuscript—his dire poverty, all cry out for our sympathy. Because of the story's focus on Betton, Vyse occupies only the background, a situation that is punctuated by the very limp ending. The state of critical neglect in which "Full Circle" finds itself seems warranted, and one is inclined to agree with E. K. Brown's early judgement that the story is without much value (25).

"The Legend"

Another *Scribner's* story, "The Legend," published in March 1910, takes up again the subject of a writer, this time a philosopher named John Pellerin, who, sensing that his work has not been appreciated by the public, disappears from view. In the present time of the story he has made a surprise reappearance as John Winterman, only to vanish again when he sees the abominations his writings have been subjected to, in particular by their chief contemporary interpreter, Howland Wade. Wharton herself drew attention to the tale in a March 19, 1910 letter to Morton Fullerton, when she wrote that she "thought of" Henry James when she "described the man in 'The Legend' as so sensitive to human contacts and yet so *secure* from them" (*LEW* 202). Commentaries on the story tend towards interpretations that reflect the seriousness of Wharton's words. R. W. B. Lewis and Nancy Lewis, in a footnote to Wharton's statement, emphasize Pellerin's (like James's) discouragement at the cold reception to his work (*LEW* 204) and Lev Raphael sees in Pellerin's disappointment an echo of "the shaming impact that contempt and indifference" (193) had on Wharton herself.

The Lewises and Raphael would surely agree though that there is much to provoke laughter in "The Legend," that its seriousness is mitigated and undercut and that irony and satire inform its earnest intent. (In fact, Raphael does comment on the story's satire) (215). But if "The Legend" is, as the Lewises say, one of Wharton's "most remarkable tales" (*LEW* 204), it is not among her best, and perhaps its major failure lies in its diffusiveness, in the uncertainty it shows about committing firmly to either a serious or a humorous center.

The beginnings of "The Legend" show little sign of the story's essential satiric turn. We are informed immediately of the first conjectures of the drama critic Arthur Bernald, the point-of-view character, that the down-and-outer called Winterman, whom the Wade family have sheltered on their Portchester estate since his discharge from hospital, is the famous but long-absent philosopher, Pellerin. (Bernald has written a manuscript about Pellerin's work that has remained unpublished, its appearance in print pre-empted by Howland Wade's popular book on the same subject.) It soon becomes clear that the physician Bob Wade and his mother are drawn to Winterman by his charismatic presence. They have no inkling, as Bernald does, of his real identity, although they both have a nodding acquaintance with Pellerinism, especially since Bob's brother Howland is an eminent Pellerin scholar. It is his dislike of Howland, whose integrity and intelligence he denies, that causes Bernald to anticipate with such relish his own presence at a projected meeting between the philosopher and his interpreter: "He hardly knew whether he was prompted by the impulse to shield Winterman from Howland Wade's ineptitude, or by the desire to see the latter abandon himself to the full shamelessness of its display; but of one fact he was assured—and that was of the existence in Winterman of some quality which would provoke Howland to the amplest exercise of his fatuity. 'How he'll draw him—how he'll draw him!' Bernald chuckled...and he felt himself avenged in advance for the injury of Howland Wade's existence" (II, 97).

The hotly anticipated meeting does not occur, however, and Bernald, happily for him as it turns out, finds himself alone with Pellerin in the cabin on the Wade property. They talk through the night, and Bernald is left in a state of exaltation, enchanted with Winterman and utterly convinced that he is the long-disappeared philosopher. This scene, recapitulated in Section IV, is a watershed in the story, bringing matters to a level of high seriousness they never again reach.

The larger portion of Section IV is a verbatim report by Winterman of his twenty-five-years withdrawal from public life. Although the story at no point attempts to expose the nature of Pellerinism as such—and Winterman makes no effort to do that in his "confession" to Bernald—we are able to glean from his oral biography something of the philosophical principles that govern Winterman's life, and we might assume that what constitutes Pellerinism includes tenets elaborated here. Clearly Winterman has been influenced by New England Transcendentalism. His words addressing the way he has confronted life's vicissitudes, "It is not a bad thing for a man to have to live his life—and we nearly all manage to dodge it," echo both the substance and form of Thoreau's advice to his readers. And his "I tried my hand at a number of things...adventurous, menial, commercial" (II, 102) are reminiscent of Emerson's words about his young friend. As well, Winterman's consciousness of the necessity of drawing directly from nature for his inspiration, "Our first round with the Sphinx may strike something out of us—a book or a picture or a symphony; and we're amazed at our feat, and go on letting that first work breed others...without renewed fertilization" (II, 102-103), smack of Emerson's own advice to the American scholars of his day.

If the high-minded idealism of Winterman's account of his life impresses and moves Bernald, the philosopher's reading from his latest manuscript convinces him that he has been faithful to his Emersonian tenets and "touched the earth between times," for "the earlier books have [dwindled] and [fallen] into their place as mere precursors of this fuller revelation" (II, 103-104). The earnestness inherent in the person and declarations of Winterman and in Bernald's adulatory response conspire with other elements in the first four sections of "The Legend" to instill the tone of seriousness that characterizes this part of the story. Among these elements are Bernald's dislike of Howland Wade, Mrs Wade's and Bob Wade's instinctive "taking to" Winterman, the precarious plight of Winterman himself. There is little, if anything, to prepare us for the shift to satire that occurs in the story's later stages. In fact the last sentence of Section IV seems to suggest that the reader had better be prepared for dire occurrences as Bernald "with a leap of rage...[pictures] Howland

Wade's thick hands on the new treasure [i.e., Winterman's manuscript], and his prophetic feet upon the lecture platform" (II, 104)

Berland's "leap of rage" never materializes into more than a metaphorical one: his realization that "the Interpreter's" dismissal of the Winterman manuscript has again driven the philosopher "East of everything—beyond the day spring. In places not on the map" (II, 94) instills in him more of a sense of disappointment and loss than of anger. In fact, after the intensity of the night-long meeting, the story changes into a comic and satiric commentary on human pretentiousness and vacuousness.

The fact that Bernald is the only character aware of the identity of Winterman is at the root of the story's satire, for it furnishes the necessary ironic possibilities for the reader. In this context, Bob Wade and Howland Wade are, respectively, innocent and inexcusable objects of ridicule in their unawareness and obtuseness. In his statement "Bernald himself has written a deep and thoughtful book on Pellerin which he knows could never survive the howling publicity granted to Wade's shallow and meretricious study" (103), the critic Lev Raphael has astutely noted the pun on the Howland name that suggests the pedestrian quality of the Wade family and the irreverent and empty rantings of the so-called Interpreter. Both the kindly doctor Bob and the fraudulant scholar Howland establish themselves as un-Emersonian men. When Bob, suggesting to Bernald that Winterman should hear Howland's lecture, explains: "It will give Winterman a chance to get some notion of what Pellerin *was*: he'll get it much straighter from Howland than if he tried to plough through Pellerin's books" (II, 105), and when Howland repeats verbatim his Kenosha lecture at the Uplift Club, they violate prescriptions expressly laid down by Winterman and his Transcendentalist mentors. Thus the practical, proudly un-intellectual doctor and the un-alert scholar reveal themselves as antithetical to the quintessentially Emersonian Winterman, the Man Thinking.

The other major objects of Wharton's satiric thrusts in "The Legend" are the ladies of the Uplift Club. Readers of the short story oeuvre will be reminded of their counterparts from "Xingu," the members of the Lunch Club of Hillbridge. Like the humor that is occasioned by Bob Wade's ignorance of what Bernald and the reader know, the humor that derives from their innocent remarks often verges on the hilarious—as when Miss Alice Fosdick says to Winterman for example: "We need someone like you—to whom [Pellerin's] message comes as a wonderful new interpretation of life—to lead the revival, and rouse us out of our apathy" (II, 107).

The occasion of Winterman's appearance at the Uplift Club is treated by the narrator and his reflector, Bernald, with mock-heroic effect. For Bernald, "The vision of Pellerin and his Interpreter, face to face at last, had a Titanic grandeur that dwarfed all other comedy," and "Winterman's fame, trumpeted abroad by Miss Fosdick, had reached the four corners of the Uplift Club." But Bernald's "fabricating...a Winterman legend which should in some degree respond to the Club's demand for a human document" is short-lived. Nor does his assurance that "in an hour or two [Winterman will] be telling me about his [conversation with Howland Wade]" (II, 109) ever materialize. Bernald's hopes of learning of his enemy's come-uppance come to naught.

In the closing lines of the story we learn that Howland Wade, having now rejected Pellerinism, continues blissfully in his blindness and that his unwitting encounter with his subject has driven the latter back to the oblivion—and peace—from which he had endeavoured to extricate himself. In light of the unhappy turn of events for both Bernald and Winterman and of the ongoing success of the fatuous Wade, it is possible to make some sense of the story's unlikely shift in tone and mood: the ironies and inanities of the last two sections may be seen to reflect something of the story's coming to terms with the absurdity of the denouement it exposes. Thus "The Legend" may be said to have a somewhat melodramatic cast, not a usual condition for a Wharton short story.

"Writing a War Story"

When "Writing a War Story" appeared in the September 1919 number of *Woman's Home Companion*, it marked the return of Wharton's short fiction to the magazines after an absence of three and a half years. She had published another war story, "Coming Home," in December 1915 in *Scribner's*, the only short fiction she had written since the beginning of the war. Her tremendously impressive work in the housing and rehabilitation of victims of the Great War had caused her to put aside the writing of fiction entirely, and "Writing a War Story" can be seen as an attempt to regain her writing hand. Its very title suggested the self-consciousness with which she returned to an exercise she had been practising assiduously for three decades.[100]

Although Wharton expressed the desire to turn her own wartime experiences into the stuff of fiction, she was not always able to do so with much aplomb. "Writing a War Story" offers ample proof of the difficulty she experienced, for it is a war story only in a marginal way and not a particularly well written piece in any case—"a flimsy tale" (*EW* 422), R.W. B. Lewis called it. It may not be inaccurate to say that the almost uniformly, and for her uncharacteristically short paragraphs, betray Wharton's uncomfortableness about writing the tale. This of course reflects the major theme of the opening half, wherein the protagonist, Ivy Spang, a neophyte fictionist, ignorant of the very bases of the story-telling art, encounters much hesitation in accomplishing her task. She faces the most rudimentary questions: Why must stories have beginnings and endings? How does Inspiration work? How, if one begins at the middle of an event, can one expect readers to understand what one is talking about? Do modern stories need a plot? Is treatment more important than subject? When she reads at one point that Ivy "sat down again to battle with the art of fiction" (II, 364), the reader understands that Wharton's long war-time layoff has contributed to her battle with her *métier*.

"Writing a War Story's" second half moves to the period after the appearance of Ivy's story "His Letter Home" in *The Man-at-Arms*, "a monthly publication that was to bring joy to the wounded and disabled in British hospitals" (II, 360). Here, matters turn on the fact that the magazine has published Ivy's photo with the story. She appears in her likeness, "exceedingly long, narrow and sinuous, robed in white and monastically veiled, holding out a refreshing beverage to an invisible sufferer with a gesture halfway between Mélisande lowering her braid over the balcony and Florence Nightingale advancing with the lamp" (II, 364). The quality of Ivy's story is mediocre, according to the published novelist and hospital patient, Harold Harbard, who reads it, and it is never allowed to become the principal point of interest. In fact,

Ivy discovers that her photo has so taken the soldiers that they have ignored the story and that Harbard and the rest have requested copies of her picture.

"Writing a War Story" has obvious feminist overtones. Josephine Donovan writes: "[W]hile Wharton unleashes heavy and contemptuous satire against Ivy throughout the story, in the end her sympathies are with the woman because of the men's attempt to reduce her to an object (the photo), reinscribing her in the system that treats women as objects of exchange" (78). But the story, thin as it is artistically, is most interesting in its dramatization of Wharton's own apprehensions about picking up an interrupted career again.

"The Temperate Zone"

In the last two decades of her life the number of short stories Wharton wrote about people in the arts dropped off considerably: only two such stories were published during the 1920's and 1930's. The first of these appeared in *Pictorial Review* in February 1924 and featured a complex array of painters and writers, four of whom we observe in three sets of relationships, the whole seen from the perspective of a character who sees the relationships either through an intermediary or at first hand. From the past time of the story there is the poet Mrs Emily Morland, the divorced wife of an English vicar, who has taken up a relationship with Donald Paul, a London barrister who "occasionally [wrote] things for the reviews" (II, 456), including two articles on Mrs Morland's poetry. From the past as well there is Horace Fingall, a transplanted American painter of portraits and landscapes, who has married after a very brief courtship a poor American art student, Bessy Reck, and lived with her in his Paris studio. After Mrs Morland and Fingall die, around the same time, Paul and Bessy marry one another and settle in the Morland home in London, where they are living at the onset of the story. These three relationships are seen, the first two by hearsay, the last directly, by Willis French, a young New Yorker who has tried unsuccessfully to be both a poet and a painter, and has been steered away from pursuing these careers by Mrs Morland and Fingall respectively. He has subsequently practised periodical art criticism, but abandoned it for the writing of books, and as the story breaks has come to London to interview Fingall's widow in connection with his work in progress, *The Art of Horace Fingall*.

"The Temperate Zone" also features a minor character named André Jolyesse, a portraitist. The inclusion of Jolyesse in the story reminds us of Wharton's penchant for dwelling on the distinction between the commercially successful painter and the more purely artistic one, a distinction she exploited earlier in such stories as "The Potboiler" and "The Verdict." Here the distinction is made by French who perceives that the intrinsic creative superiority of Fingall over Jolyesse has been ignored during his lifetime, his originality, however, acquiring posthumous fame for him; Jolyesse is much in demand and commands a high price, but his pictures have been the subject of Fingall's, and are the subject of French's scorn. As in "The Potboiler" and "The Verdict" Wharton signals the superior painter's status with the introduction of a preliminary sketch he has drawn. Here the piece in question is found in a sketchbook: "The drawing, in three chalks on a gray ground, was rapidly but carefully executed: one of those light and perfect things which used to fall from Fingall like stray petals from a great tree in bloom. The woman's attitude was full of an ardent interest; from the forward thrust of her clumsily shod foot to the tilt of her head and the highlight of her eyeglasses, everything about her seemed electrified by some eager shock of ideas" (II, 467).

In "The Temperate Zone," Fingall's sketch, which can be said to repeat a kind of signature device used in Wharton's stories about painters, is integrated into the plot structure. By acquiring it, French is given to believe that it is payment for the assistance he will give Paul in the latter's writing of his biography of the poet Morland. The sketch performs double duty for the Paul couple, functioning as well as the wedge whereby Bessy Paul forces French's intervention on her behalf with Jolyesse: she wants Jolyesse to paint her, but at a rate lower than the going one. Indeed Bessy's unlikely and surprising—to both French and the reader—strong-arming of French at the time she solicits his assistance confirms absolutely the writer's sense of the young woman's self-centeredness. Bessy's gesture of force brings to its apex French's disillusion about her and hence to a climax the major concern of the story: that a quest initiated in a spirit of admiration for the two potential subjects of his biography should end in such disappointment at their respective choice of mate.

French undertakes his trip to London with great enthusiasm. His publisher had suggested his writing a book on Fingall, and he seems, at least in the corner of his mind, to be contemplating also a biography of Mrs Morland. The happy alliance in marriage of the spouse of the former and the lover of the latter affords him a rare opportunity: "here was an occasion to obtain the desired light, and to obtain it at one stroke, through the woman who had been the preponderating influence in Fingall's art, and the man for whom Emily Morland had written her greatest poems" (II, 451). French's work on Fingall and Mrs Morland would be a labor of love because he has the highest personal regard for his subjects as well as a fervent admiration for their art. Although the two had "professionally speaking, discouraged their young disciple; the one had said 'don't write' as decidedly as the other had said 'don't paint'... both had let him feel that interesting failures may be worth more in the end than dull successes, and that there is range enough for the artistic sensibilities outside the region of production" (II, 450). French's assumption is that the understanding and appreciation of and commitment to art, and the human qualities that have drawn Mrs Morland and Fingall to him have been imbibed by the Pauls. "The Temperate Zone" is essentially the story of the disappointment of French's assumption.

French's disillusion begins inauspiciously enough and before he has even seen the Pauls. During his visit to their home in London—they have gone to Paris and he is received by a maid—he experiences a series of surprises. He is told the Pauls are staying at the Hotel Nouveau Luxe in Paris, which, with its evocation of *nouveau riche* and glitziness, causes him to wonder at the Pauls' taste. Then he sees on a writing desk that had once been Emily Morland's "an immense expensively framed photograph of Fingall's picture of his wife"(II, 453) that for him smacks of impropriety. "There was something shockingly crude," he reflects afterwards, "in the way it made the woman in possession triumph over the woman who was gone" (II, 454). He is shocked also that a trusted servant doesn't respond to the name Morland. The crowning event, that causes "all his disenchantment [to rise] to his lips," is the maid's invitation to tour the house: he, "a pilgrim to the shrine of genius...had been taken for a possible purchaser" of his saint's home (II. 453, 452).

The suspicions aroused by French's experience visiting the Pauls' home are entirely vindicated by his subsequent meetings with Bessy and Donald Paul, first on the crossing to France, then in Paris. His shipboard sighting of the Pauls is a particularly telling one because he is not aware of who they are when he and Jolyesse see them. Thus his mental comment about Bessy, "She seemed, in truth, framed by nature to bloom for one of Monsieur Jolyesse's canvases, so completely did she embody the kind of beauty it was his mission to immortalize" (II, 458), is uncluttered by the preconceptions about her that he has brought from London.

When French arrives in Paris for his interview with Bessy, his enthusiasm about his mission has been renewed, rekindled, no doubt, by his encounter with the detested Jolyesse and the latter's demeaning remarks about Fingall, whose growing posthumous reputation he as a biographer could help to affirm. Again his expectations of the assistance Bessy can offer are high and assume much about her sensitivity and artistic interest. "Would she understand that any serious attempt to analyze so complex and individual an art must be preceded by a reverent scrutiny of the artist's personality?" he asks himself. "Would she, above all, understand how reverent [his] scrutiny would be, and consent for the sake of her husband's glory, to guide and enlighten it?" (II, 460) But his first two-hour meeting with the woman "hardly added a grain to his previous knowledge of Horace Fingall" (II, 461), and he comes away with a "vision of the too-smiling beauty, set in glasses and glitter, preoccupied with dressmakers and theater stalls, and affirming her husband's genius in terms of the auction room and the stock exchange!" (II, 462). French's final meeting with Bessy reaffirms his earlier suspicion about her venality. Certainly the high hopes he had about being enlightened by his idol's wife are entirely dashed.

French's meeting with Donald Paul garners a similar outcome. He perceives him as dull and uncultivated as when Paul is slow to pick up on his metaphor of Joseph wrestling with the angel and its implications. Most of all he is stunned at Paul's lack of response to the drawing French finds in Fingall's old sketchbook: "There she sat—" he reflects, "Emily Morland —aquiver in every line with life and sound and color. French could hear her very voice running up and down in happy scales! And beside him stood her lover, and did not recognize her" (II, 467).

But French's meeting with Paul has had its compensations. He is the richer now for having in his possession the sketch of Mrs Morland. He is also rendered virtually speechless at the prospect of having put in his grasp Mrs Morland's papers, "heaps and heaps of letters—her beautiful letters!" (II, 468). French's last meeting with Bessy leaves him utterly speechless as well; indeed, Bessy has the floor for the final minutes of the encounter, and he leaves without a word as she calls to him "joyfully across the threshold" (II, 472). He has been "bewildered" and "confusedly aware that his misery was feeding some obscure springs of amusement in her" (II, 471). As with Paul, however, there is a compensation, albeit a small one: French has the satisfaction of knowing that Bessy's request that he intercede with Jolyesse to have the portraitist paint her at a reduced price is redundent, given Jolyesse's expressed desire to have her sit for him gratis.

French's silent departure from Bessy's company brings "The Temperate Zone" to a somewhat unsatisfying close. The story seems to have been left uncomplete, for there are elements that beg for illumination. Do French's feelings of disenchantment extend to Emily Morland and Horace Fingall? Is his disillusion about the young couple the result of his own idyllic image of the persons who so influenced him? These questions seem to be at least faintly suggested in the text, but one is never certain if they are meant to be part of the planned structure of the story. In the better stories where such questions arise as a natural outcome of the given text, they are given a response or at least a hint of a response. Here they seem to be overlooked, and for all its excellences "The Temperate Zone" remains, disappointingly, unfinished.

"A Glimpse"

"A Glimpse," the last short story Wharton wrote about people in the arts, was published in the November 12, 1932 issue of the *Saturday Evening Post*. Although it is unique in the fact that it focusses on two performing musicians, and removed some eight years in time from "The Temperate Zone," it bears a complementary relationship to Wharton's earlier tale about the ex-spouses of a famous painter and a famous poet. This relationship is signalled by a comment John Kilvert, the reflector character in "A Glimpse," makes to himself a few pages into the tale: "But what a power emotion is! I could lift mountains still if I could feel as those two do about anything. I suppose all the people worth remembering—lovers or poets or inventors—have lived at white-heat level while we crawl along in the temperate zone" (II, 692). The "those two" of his reflection are the objects of his observation and fascination, the pianist Margaret Aslar and the cellist Julian Brand. Those two stand in startling contrast to the married couple Donald and Bessy Paul who are at the center of Willis French's attention in "The Temperate Zone," and who also might be seen to have their equivalents in "A Glimpse" in "the dolls about Mrs. Roseneath's bridge tables" (II, 698), fashionable parasites whose lives are superficial and passionless.

The contrast between "The Temperate Zone" and "A Glimpse" extends to the characterization of the reflector characters as well. If French is a man committed to life in mind and profession, Kilvert is something of a hanger-on, dilettantish and uninvolved, seemingly without important personal relationships or occupational duties to anchor him. The supposedly well-rounded French is not drawn as one in whom there is much improvement possible: he is doomed to be somewhat of a stagnant character. Kilvert, on the other hand, leads an unsatisfying life, and he is aware of and somewhat anxious about that. "A Glimpse" documents his self-awareness and charts at least the beginnings of a commitment to something beyond his own ease and complacency, beyond an "existence [that] seemed to him too cushioned, smooth and painless" (II, 687).

The story settles on Kilvert at a time when he is sharply aware of the aimlessness and mediocrity that marks his fifty-sixth year: he has been summoned to Venice by a long-time friend and one-time lover, Sara Roseneath, "to help her about her fancy dress for the great historical ball which was to be given at the Ducal Palace" (II, 688). He chides himself for jumping so readily at her call and for assorted other self-dissatisfactions: letting himself go physically soft, hiring a car instead of travelling by train to Venice. We see as well that he is impatient with and fastidious about the simple people who travel with him on the ferry. His attitudes about these latter bespeak a loss of affinity with life and nature: references to "dull and dingy holiday makers," "fretful babies," "withered flowers," "a slatternly woman...supporting her sleep-drunken baby"(II, 688,689) suggest that the springs of human sympathy have dried up within him.

But Kilvert is soon roused from his state of negativism by the sight of the couple he eventually learns to be the eminent musicians Aslar and Brand. As "blousy and shabby" as they are, they are, "evidently persons of education and refinement," but his interest is perked by their noticeable passion. Initially they exude a "strong emotional glow" (II, 689), and as he watches them engage in heated discussion, "their look deepened from a feverish fire to a kind of cloudy resignation" (II, 690). Although he misreads the cause of their passionate talk to be a personal affair of the heart between them, there is no doubting his own involvement in their passion. His "interest deepened to excitement as he watched [Margaret Aslar]." Then "his own eyes filled with tears" (II, 691) and "he [watched] them in an agony of participation" (II, 693) as they continue talking.

Kilvert's misinterpretation of the source of the passionate feeling between the musicians is at the center of his involvement in their predicament and a factor in the inner discomfort he has been experiencing prior to his engagement with Aslar and Brand. Attempting to explain the natural sympathy he feels with them, he asks himself: "What was he mourning—the inevitable break between these two anguished people, or some anguish that he himself had once caught a glimpse of, and missed?" (II, 691-692). The story's title substantive is repeated here and recurs as a verb as Kilvert watches Margaret leave the ferry alone: "As Kilvert's gaze followed her he felt as if he too [with Brand] were straining his eyes in the pursuit of some rapture just glimpsed and missed" (II, 695). Seeing the musicians allow themselves such passionate engagement has reminded Kilvert of a lost opportunity and of the possibility of a relationship retreated from for the wrong reasons. He singles out a magical afternoon years before with "the gray-eyed Russian girl, the governess of his sister's children, with [whom] he had very nearly sounded the depths" (II, 692), and from whose arms he had withdrawn out of fear of being rejected—or accepted.

With the departure of Aslar and Brand and his own arrival in Venice, Kilvert is thrown back into his own accustomed world in one of its most spectacular manifestations: Sara Roseneath's dinner party. "But the women's vivid painted heads, the men's polished shirt fronts, the gliding gondoliers in white duck and gold-fringed sashes, handing silver dishes down the table, all seemed...remote and unrelated to reality" (II, 695). When he is given the chance of leaving the party and making contact with the world with which he has recently become reacquainted in the persons of Aslar and Brand, he virtually leaps at it, taking up with pleasure Mrs Roseneath's demand that he ensure the players' presence at her evening entertainment. Now the old lassitude about life and people is replaced with a new enthusiasm, and his contact with the broader world is marked by openness: "Kilvert was in a mood to like the shabbiness, the dinginess almost, of the little hotel on an obscure canal to which the gondola carried him. He liked even the slit of untidy garden in which towels were drying on a sagging rope, the umbrella stand in imitation of rustic woodwork, the slatternly girl with a shawl over her head delivering sea-urchins to the black-wigged landlady. This was the way real people lived, he thought, glancing at a crumby dining room glimpsed through glass doors" (II, 699).

Kilvert's meetings with Aslar and Brand, the former in her hotel room, the latter on the street, reinforce what he has seen of the couple as he observed them on the boat and his own approval of their passionate attachment to one another. Again he mistakes the nature of the tie that binds them and has to be set straight by Margaret as to that: music is the root of the strong emotional life they share. When Kilvert leaves Margaret's hotel after listening to her impassioned apologia and critique of Brand, he closes "the door on the greatest emotional spectacle he had ever witnessed" (II, 703). When he meets Brand, who is on his way to see Margaret, he has forgotten about his errand on behalf of Mrs Roseneath. "He seemed, for the first time in his life, to have his hands on the wheels of destiny.... He was still in the presence of the woman upstairs in the shabby hotel, and his only thought was: 'He's come back to her!'" (II, 704)

It may be possible to interpret the passionately expressed tension in the

Aslar/Brand relationship, as Kilvert at least initially does, as stemming from heterosexual attachment and jealousy. There is a third party involved in the person of "that Polish girl" whom undoubtedly Brand has been seeing and about whom Aslar is displeased. But if the latter's insistence that her obvious jealousy of the twenty-year-old with the "long eyelashes" who "pretends to swoon whenever he plays his famous Beethoven adagio" (II, 702) is more professional than personal, then Brand's statement that "we're chained to each other by something that we love better than ourselves, and she knows it" (II, 705) seems to favor the notion that it is music that both ties and divides the two performing musicians

It is likely that the reason why "A Glimpse" has attracted so little critical attention is that the change that takes place in Kilvert is not entirely convincing. Nevertheless, it is fascinating that this story that sets such high stock in the emotional life should be placed in the framework of the performing art of music, a form that Wharton chose to avoid in her large short-story oeuvre, and about which, like her point of view character, Kilvert, who admits to not being "much in that line" (II, 695), she freely acknowledged herself to be not highly conversant.

*   *   *   *   *

Writers, Painters, Sculptors, Musicians—and Their Champions

In the eighteen stories in which Wharton centers attention on characters for whom in one way or another the creative arts assume a more than casual importance, the question of social class is seldom a relevant issue. One exception is "That Good May Come," in which the strained means of the middle-class Birkton family drive the story's central action and exposes the tension within the poet and would-be novelist between fidelity to pure art and the pressure to accommodate a very practical and worthy purpose. In general though, class is not a consideration in most of these stories. If the artist/protagonists lead comfortable and affluent lives it is often the result of the proceeds from their practice, and we do not necessarily know whether or not they were of upper-class stock in the first place. The witty banter between the famous novelist Mrs Dale and the successful poet Ventnor in the playlet "Copy"reminds us of the exchanges in the upper-class Newport story, "The Twilight of the God,"—with the exception that in the former the male speaker is up to the verbal challenges of the woman. Whether or not Mrs Dale and Ventnor are of the social elite is a less important consideration than that their sparkling wit is a factor of their literary gifts. When there is "society" in a story, as there is in "Expiation," it figures little in the consequence of the story.

Eight of these tales of the art world place their primary focus on writers: novelists, writers of short stories, poets, essayists, biographers, critics. Not surprisingly Wharton has given more attention to the writing arts than to any of the others, and it should be added that writers often play minor roles in tales that are about the other arts. What is a little surprising is that only rarely in this group does she turn her attention to writers in the performance of their writerly arts. The critic Wyatt Mason, commenting on the work of the American fictionist Guy Davenport, writes: "Davenport isn't interested in dramatizing how a person comes to create art; he investigates, instead, how the sensitive individual who creates art survives in a society that is frequently inhospitable to such sensitivity. In many of his stories Davenport makes the struggles of the artist when not engaged in the act of creation the stuff of fiction" (88). This statement applies equally to Wharton in her narratives about writers, indeed in her tales of creative artists generally.

There are to be sure a few Wharton dramatizations of "how a person comes to create art." "April Showers" treats specifically of a writer as writer: Theodora Dace the aspiring novelist sees her first work struck down by a publisher whose carelessness in handling her manuscript initiates her into the disappointments of the writing life. As its title implies, "Writing a War Story" involves itself with the process of story-making. Here, the wartime nursing assistant Ivy Spang, who prior to the tale's time frame has been a published poet, is cajoled into writing a short story for *The Man-at-Arms*, a war-morale magazine. The narrator takes up her dilemma thus: "The more she thought of the matter, the less she seemed to understand how a war story—or any story, for that matter—was written. Why did stories ever begin, and why did they ever leave off? Life didn't—it just went on and on" (II, 361). She is reluctant and resists pursuing the project and is bothered by questions about inspiration, structure, plot, and veracity. Ultimately the story turns to other things and the failure of Ivy's composition is subsumed into non-writerly matters such as the impact of Ivy's photo on the soldiers and her own response to that.

Neither "April Showers" nor "Writing a War Story" demonstrates Wharton at her best however, and it is in tales in which the profession of writing is subordinated to considerations that are the by-products of writers' lives that she excels. The strongest pieces about writers' lives are "The Muse's Tragedy" and "The Temperate Zone," both tales of considerable narrative complexity and sophistication, and in which what happens to writers supersedes their professional performance. "The Muse's Tragedy" is a tighter composition than "The Temperate Zone" but not as complex. Here, the character who emerges as salient, Mrs Anerton, is not a practising writer at all, but her letter, which constitutes the story's closing section, establishes her real identity and the effectual use she makes of the written word. In her letter she demolishes the myth the world has built up about her, the one Danyers her young lover has lived by, the one Rendle, her lifetime companion and supposed patron, has never sought to destroy. The story is one of hope and lost hope, of initiation, of egotism and selfishness, as these elements apply to Mrs Anerton, Danyers, and Rendle respectively. "The Temperate Zone" manages a complex arrangement of relating couples from two time frames via the narration of Willis French, a critic and biographer. French rights the erroneous attitudes he has about his subjects that arise from information he receives from Lady Brankhurst with knowledge he obtains by direct experience. Here again the story focuses on the superficiality and venality of the spouses he meets—who are the ex-spouses of artists he admires—and on his own disillusionment. The two stories have much in common—including the presence of a woman in each, Mrs Memoral in "The Muse's Tragedy" and Lady Brankhurst in "The Temperate Zone," who provides the questionable assessments that force the reflector characters to reevaluate their initial perceptions of their subjects.

Of the remainder of Wharton's writer stories, "The Legend," whose central interest is the American Transcendentalist-like philosopher/essayist John Pellerin, exploits, along with other minor tales about writers, "That Good May Come," "April Showers," "Expiation," "Full Circle," the theme of society's rejection of the artist.

"The Legend" features a virtually parodic rejection of Pellerin, wherein his very "Interpreter" does not understand his work. "That Good May Come" addresses the theme by presenting a situation in which a good poet's serious work is rejected while his scandalous intrusions into people's private lives in verse form are acclaimed by the public. "Expiation" pokes fun at the issue of rejection of worthy fiction by exposing a novelist who exploits clerical censure of her work for commercial gain. "Full Circle," an unremittingly dour tale altogether devoid of color or zest, contrasts a commercially successful but vain, careless, and arrogant novelist Geoffrey Betton with the talented but unsuccessful writer Betton hires as his secretary. Only "Copy" eschews this theme of the public rejection of the literary by presenting two writers who have had seemingly unqualified success.

The question of the popular reception of the arts is also a frequent theme in Wharton's stories about painters, "The Portrait," The Recovery," "The Potboiler," and "The Verdict." Although a few of the painters highlighted in these tales work in other genres as well, the major emphasis is placed on portraitists, and only "The Recovery" features a painter for whom portraiture is not a relevant activity. It is clear why Wharton seized upon the portrait-painting genre rather than the landscape or still-life to exploit her themes. In the society she knew best, people of eminence, status, and wealth had their pictures painted routinely, and the entire enterprise had become a competitive one for the artists. Some painted romantic renderings of their subjects; others sought to individualize them and developed reputations for presenting subjects realistically while remaining true to some artistic principles. Wharton's treatment of this essential polarity in the portrait-painting trade takes on variations and refinements from story to story, but the polarity is evident throughout.

One sees the polarity simply put and the animosity generated by it in one of Wharton's writer stories, "The Temperate Zone," where it is not an essential ingredient of the tale. "Jolyesse, the eminent international portrait painter," says to Willis French, the point-of-view character, whose judgement we come to trust, "[Fingall] was a savage—he had no sense of solidarity. And envious! Could one help it if one sold more pictures than he did? But it was gall and wormwood to him, poor devil. Of course he sells now—tremendously high, I believe. But that's what happens: when an unsuccessful man dies, the dealers seize on him and make him a factitious reputation" (II, 457). Fingall, whose artistic quality is unquestionable, to the point where French intends to write his biography, is played off against Jolyesse, the crass commercial success. The same polarities occur in both "The Portrait" and "The Potboiler" but the latter story is a considerable improvement on its predecessor; it is surer-handed in being more focussed and it considerably fleshes out the earlier tale, banishing simplistic extremes, incorporating nuances, and putting the artistic elements to the service of the narrator's broader human themes.

Two of Wharton's other artist stories, "The Recovery" and "The Verdict," bear a complementary relationship to one another: the first centers on a painter who seeks to improve on what he comes to realize is a mediocre artistic product; the second exposes a commercially successful portraitist who is also dissatisfied with his work but is unwilling to pay the price improvement demands. Keniston, the protagonist of "The Recovery" paints in Hillbridge, a small New England college town, and his artistic as opposed to commercial success has left him a weak provider for his mother and sister. He is reminiscent of the sculptor Arran of "The Potboiler": when the astute Claudia, his future wife, first meets him "the girl's fancy instantly hailed in him that favorite figure of imaginative youth, the artist who would rather starve than paint a potboiler" (I, 261). Keniston is lacking in technique and subject, and his trip to Europe convinces him of his deficiency and encourages him to attempt recovery. Jack Gisburn, the focus character in "The Verdict," has difficulties of another order. In calling him "a rather cheap genius" (I, 655), Rickham, the narrator, is consigning him to that band of facile craftsmen who have sacrificed essence to style, and we have Gisburn's own admission that he has made a career of "bravura tricks" and "showy bits" and neglected "the hard passages between. Those were the ones I had always shirked, or covered up with some lying paint" (I, 661). Whatever the challenges Gisburn's *lacunae* present—and they are probably more demanding than Keniston's—he has passed them up and enjoys, despite the superficial amenities his wife provides him, a rather unsatisfying life, if we are to believe his sympathetic friend Rickham.

"The Moving Finger" is unique among Wharton's painter tales in its absolute concentration on one portrait: the artist Claydon's picture of Mrs Grancy. The questions the story invites as to the relative attachment of Mrs Grancy's husband and Claydon to both the woman and her portrait are intriguing enough to cause us to overlook a strong undercurrent of significance in the tale. Ralph Grancy's house and library, where the portrait hangs, is the meeting place of a group of his male friends, Claydon, the narrator, and others, whose visits are graced by woman and painting alike. We are reminded here of similar Wharton fictive homes and rooms— Merrick's of "The Long Run," Culwin's of "The Eyes," to mention two—which are the womenless retreats of males free of or fleeing from uncomfortable relationships. Grancy's sanctum includes a woman—one woman—of grace, beauty, and warmth, whose purpose is to serve her husband as spouse, her portraitist as sitter, her husband's friends as hostess, and who appears to have little identity or *raison d'être* of her own. And in the portrait as well she is manipulated at the will of both husband and painter. One is struck by expressions in the story that denote ownership of Mrs Grancy. "Claydon...had not set out to paint *their* [Wharton's italics] Mrs Grancy—or ours even," says the narrator (I, 303). Claydon's and the story's closing statement is "But now she belongs to me" (I, 313). Left twice a widower, the second time after a marriage of only three years' duration, Grancy joins the dubious company of two other surviving husbands of dehumanized wives, Severance of "Confession," whose marriage lasts five years, and Devons Ansley, who renders his own house a virtual widow's place.[101]

Wharton's fictive interest in the creative arts extends beyond their practicioners. In three stories especially she makes persons whose lives are identified with art in a professional or quasi-professional but not creatively artistic way the center of attention. "The Rembrandt," "The House of the Dead Hand," and "The Daunt Diana" focus respectively on a curator in a museum of art, two connoisseurs of Renaissance painting, and two collectors of expensive *bibelots*. The three stories deliver essentially the same message, albeit with varying degrees of subtlety: that life is more important than art and human beings more important than works of art; that respect for human health, dignity, and integrity ought to transcend devotion to objects of artistic beauty. To be sure Wharton raises the same tensions in some of her stories of creative artists. However, the question of the relative importance of life and art seems more salient in these stories, perhaps because persons who are not creative artists are more apt to be manipulated by compulsions and influences extraneous to art itself in their pursuit of objects of created beauty.

"The Rembrandt" approaches the subject of relative value by presenting an example of a man who, like certain writers and painters encountered in other Wharton stories, is willing, reluctantly, to suspend his respect for the authenticity of art in favor of something he considers to be a higher good. His decision is a reasoned one, made with eyes wide open, and alert to its possible ramifications. The curator reflects, "Reason argued that it was more cruel to deceive Mrs. Fontage than to tell her the truth; but that merely proved the inferiority of reason to instinct in situations involving any concession to the emotions," and he is unwilling to destroy "[her] faith in the Rembrandt...and the whole fabric of Mrs. Fontage's past..." (I, 291). The curator is true to his instincts, and he pays a cruel price in embarrassment at the hands of his less sensitive superior.

"The House of the Dead Hand" and "The Daunt Diana" approach the question of a proper hierarchy of values from another angle: by depicting characters who err against the principle of the primacy of human life and wreak damage upon other persons or upon themselves in so erring. Dr Lombard and his disciple Wyant of the first story inflict seemingly irrevocable harm on the youthful Sybilla in the name of art, and the predatory nature of the young woman's father is emphasized by physical descriptions that are unmistakable in their intent. Lombard is "vulpine, eagle-beaked" (I, 509) with "hooked fingers" (I, 523) and his hands "hang on the arms of the settle like the claws of a dead bird" (I, 524). The damage wrought by the collectors in "The Daunt Diana" is less severe, but regrettable in its perversion of human potential, its loss of a sense of human purpose. Both Finney, the teller of Neave's story and a collector of enamel snuffboxes himself, and his subject, Humphrey Neave, a man who has traded in his life for a bronze Diana, betray a sad withdrawal from life—the first by his confirmation of the acceptability of his hero's priorities, the other in his absolute commitment to his collection. Not to be missed about the story is the burden of its title and the frequent identification within of the bronze figure as the *Daunt* Diana. Whereas artistic objects are frequently referred to by the name of their creator—Michelangelo's *David*, for example—Neave's statue goes by the name of its collector. The likelihood is that Neave's treasure is not an original or significant piece of art at all but a replica, or at best a work of negligible artistic worth, unidentified or unidentifiable as to its maker, not unlike his other acquisitions, "bronze or lace, enamel or glass" (II, 52). The final irony is that the passion of Neave, and by extension of Finney, is directed to objects that are ultimately of artificial and market-inflated value.

Wharton's last tale about the arts, and one of the last short stories she wrote, centers on two performing musicians and constitutes her only overt venture into the realm of music and the interpretive arts. Besides serving a contrasting function to "The Temperate Zone" in its celebration of lives lived with passionate commitment to art, it also stands in interesting opposition to "The Daunt Diana." Whereas Neave gratifies exclusively himself and appears to withdraw from the ebb and flow of life, the pianist Margaret Anslar and the cellist Julian Brand of "A Glimpse" are performers, and share their talents with the world. Like Neave, the musicians are passionate in their love of the products they have amassed, but by the nature of their art form they communicate to an entity beyond themselves. As well, because Anslar and Brand prepare and play their music in tandem, they become enmeshed in the problems that naturally erupt between two persons interested in maximum performance and fair play. The passion their impressed observer Kilvert witnesses assures him that they are deeply involved in the process of living, and in the end he is convinced that they are capable of subsuming their individuality to an essential higher good. "A Glimpse" is a story about the significance of life and art both, and unlike a number of Wharton's other tales about the arts it does not as overtly engage a situation in which art must be subordinated to life.

"A Glimpse" brought to an end Wharton's life-long engagement in the fiction of art, and she seemed to have been conscious at such a juncture of making a summary statement about the larger place of the creative and interpretive arts. When Margaret Anslar says to Kilvert on the occasion of their one meeting, "We're the pipes the god plays on—not mere servile eyes or ears, like all the rest of you! And whatever branch of art we're privileged to represent, that we must uphold, we must defend—even against the promptings of our hearts" (II, 702), she is surely talking at a primary level about her own medium. Yet Wharton's choice of words for the start of Margaret's second sentence enlarges the scope to include all the "branches of art" and seems to be applying the statement to the non-musical arts as well. By insisting that "we must uphold...defend [whatever branch of art we're privileged to represent]—even against the promptings of our own hearts," Margaret is denying the validity of the actions of artists and art lovers (one thinks of Maurice Birkton of "That Good May Come," of George Lillo of "The Portrait," of Ned Stanwell of "The Potboiler," of Mrs Lombard of "The House of the Dead Hand," of the curator of "The Rembrandt") who are able to put aside their affinity to their given art form to effect a larger good, who insist on following the promptings of the heart. Margaret Anslar's declaration about putting aside "the promptings of our heart" seems remarkably short-sighted. It is after all because of the ability and willingness of Julian Brand to go beyond his partner's saying that her instrument is more important than his that their partnership and her career are able to go on.

Notes

[93] Barry Maine, who takes George Lillo to be a version of the American portrait painter John Singer Sargent, helps to dispel some of the confusion about the story in his carefully detailed examination of the progression in Lillo's attitude about his subject Vard during the latter's various sittings. Maine also makes an interesting parallel between Wharton and Sargent as social critics, but some readers will find it difficult to accept that "Wharton, in writing about her monde from the greater distance from her subjects that fiction allows, would pursue a greater inclination neither flattering nor excoriating the New York social register but urging upon it a higher standard of social conduct" (12-13). "Excoriating" does not seem to be too strong a term for the criticism applied to upper-crust New Yorkers in such stories as "Autres Temps...," "The Long Run," or "After Holbein."

[94] Laura Saltz writes that Mrs Anerton's letter "attempts to correct Danyers's misperceptions about her relationships both with him and Rendle" (16), but is not entirely certain that she is successful in her attempt to correct Danyers of his misperceptions about her relationship to him, or if, in fact, he *has* misperceived her feelings for him. It is entirely consistent with Mrs Anerton's "writing herself" (Witzig's contextual term) that her letter betrays a mixture of regret and longing, of protectiveness and desire, of nobility and practicality, of love and fearfulness. To deny the ambivalence in Mrs Anerton is to return her to the earlier iconic position to which Danyers and her

reading public had assigned her.

[95] The choice of discussing "The Recovery" in the present chapter rather than in Chapter Seven, "Town and Gown," is somewhat arbitrary. It might have taken its place with those stories set in Hillbridge and other fictional New England university towns. But because a large part of the story takes place in Europe, and because it takes more interest in the artistic than in the academic or intellectual life, it was thought best to include it here.

[96] Gloria C. Erlich's treatment of the story is similar to White's though not as detailed, and it includes a dimension of sexual conduct not mentioned by White. Erlich writes, in part, "The dead hand over the threshold may have a dual significance, abuse of Sybilla by her father as well as self-abuse" (42).

[97] Barbara White remarks: "The depiction of Jews makes some stories almost unreadable; in the early 'The Potboiler,' for instance, the Jewish Mr. Shepson has 'The squat figure of a middle-aged man in an expensive fur coat, who looked as if his face secreted the oil which he used on his hair'" (90).

[98] Raphael may be correct in surmising that Stanwell has secretly commissioned Arran's work and paid him in advance with the proceeds of his portrait of Mrs Millington. The story does not explicitly say as much, although the narrator has ample opportunity to do so. At one point the text does note of Stanwell's hosting the Arrans at a summer cottage for three weeks: "...Stanwell himself was consoled by the reflection that but for Mrs Millington's portrait he could not have performed even this trifling service for his friends" (I, 680).

[99] All of Wharton's principal biographers, R. W. B. Lewis, Shari Benstock and Hermione Lee, have noted that the Gisburns of "The Verdict" were modelled on a couple Wharton knew, Ralph Curtis and Lise Colt Curtis. Lewis writes of Curtis, a "second-rate" painter who has "given it up: He had married the former Lise Colt of Providence, Rhode Island, the decidedly wealthy widow (after a short marriage) of Arthur Rotch, and now lived in mild splendor at the Villa Beaulieu, near Monte Carlo. Lise, who could hardly have been pleased by the portrait of her as a woman of beaming stupidity, took enduring offense" (193).

[100] Julie Olin-Ammentorp expresses a mild reservation about the position that Ivy Sprang's anxiety reflects mainly Wharton's discomfort about returning to writing, a position taken by Barbara White. White writes: "Wharton must have been anxious about returning to her career after the war" (88). Olin-Ammentorp suggests that "Writing a War Story" "reflects perhaps not so much Wharton's anxiety about 'resuming her career' as the anxiety she underwent writing about war. One point is made utterly clear in this story: pitfalls await those who, not having been on the front lines, attempt to portray the experience of those who had" (104). Although Wharton had not been to the front, she had been close to it and knew first hand the immediate devastation and havoc wreaked by war. On March 11, 1915 she wrote Henry James about a trip to Verdun, when she saw "...soldiers coming and going, cavalrymen riding up with messages, poor bandaged creatures in rag-bag clothes leaning in doorways and always over and above us the boom, boom, boom of the guns on the grey heights to the east" (Letters, 351). War stories are not limited to tales of combat, and Wharton knew very well of what she spoke in her only short story of the war, "Coming Home."

[101] Of course it may be coincidental that two wives of Grancy, and Kate Spain, Severance's wife, die after relatively brief marriages to their respective husbands. It does not seem exaggerated to suspect, however, that Wharton, who knew what a stifling marriage was but who had a meaningful outlet in her writing and ultimately fled the marriage, might use the hyperbolic device of early death to suggest the ravages brought on women in dehumanizing unions. I am not suggesting that Grancy or

Severance mistreated or abused their spouses in an active way. But neglect, indifference, interference can also bring on death. The ease with which Grancy interfered with Claydon's portrait might very well be used by Wharton as a symbol of his treatments of the living Mrs Grancy. And Claydon *does* age the Mrs Grancy of his portrait before her time.

Chapter Seven

Town and Gown

Wharton published seven short stories that are placed in college and university settings. The first five, all appearing in *Scribner's* magazine, were the products of the early decades of her short-story-writing career; the last two, placed with the large-circulation slicks *Woman's Home Companion* and *Red Book* were from the 1930's. Only one of the tales makes use of a real-life institution; "The Debt" is set at Columbia University in New York. For the other six Wharton used the names of fictional college towns: in "The Pelican," "The Descent of Man," and "Xingu," she places the action in Hillbridge, a place she also uses in her 1900 novella, *The Touchstone*, where she calls it "the old university town"; in the other stories the events are played out in other fictional sites: "The Pretext" in Wentworth, "The Day of the Funeral" in Kingsborough, "Permanent Wave" in Kingsbridge. The strongest evidence for the location of these fictional places is to be found in "The Pretext," which cites New England as its location, and one somehow assumes that New England is understood to be the larger area in which these towns exist. The story that makes the most use of a college setting—of both interiors and exteriors—is "The Pretext," and it has been suggested that the story's Wentworth appears to resemble Harvard or an Ivy-League institution like it. Here it can be said also that there is an implicit conflation of town names and college names.

Of more importance, of course, is the particular nature of Wharton's use of academic life in these stories. Except for "The Descent of Man" and "The Debt," which center on professors as they are relating to their professional disciplines, the stories are concerned either with academics acting outside the borders of their professional lives, or with non-academic characters who are on the fringes of academic life—some at the distant fringes indeed!. A number of the major characters in these stories are professors and their wives and lovers, who are engaged in either intellectual or more amorous pursuits. There is often in these tales, as well, a tendency to satirize those who are at the center or on the borders of university life. It is because of Wharton's interest in the non-academic pursuits of people in and around the university that the chapter bears the title it does.

"The Pelican"

Wharton published "The Pelican," the first of a number of stories about the academic life, in the *Scribner's* issue of November 1898, and it immediately drew a very favorable response. Her editor called it "one of her most pleasing tales" (*EW* 81), her friend Walter Berry found it "first rate...very clever and very amusing and [a] heap original" (*EW* 85), and the *Literature* critic wrote: "Only a woman to the manner born in society, a woman, too, whose literary favorites or literary masters may have been Thackeray or James, since she partakes of the spirit of the one, and has followed the exquisite craftsmanship of the other, could have written [it]" (*EW* 88).

Until fairly recently criticism of "The Pelican" has been focussed on Wharton's portrayal of the central character Mrs Amyot, who prolongs her career as an itinerant lecturer on cultural topics beyond the time where its proceeds provide for her son's education, its intended purpose in the first place. Here, the comments of Cynthia Griffin Wolff are particularly pertinent: "And so the poor lady has prolonged the fiction of that child who needed support, prolonged it because without the excuse it offered, she would have had nothing. At the end of the story, the excuse has been torn from her, and she does have nothing" (101).

However, there has been a tendency of late to question both the flattering early assessment of "The Pelican" as well as the habit of placing the critical focus entirely on Mrs Amyot. Barbara White, taking issue with a 1903 evaluation proclaiming the story "one of the best short stories ever written," has pointed out that it "violates many of the principles of short story writing [Wharton] came to consider essential, such as the need for compactness and vividness and the preservation of unity of time"; she has also made much of the idea that there are "flaws in the point of view" (35). More importantly, both White and Amy Kaplan have in one way or another placed emphasis on the fact that the story is narrated by a male speaking in the first person and that attention to this fact gives rise to the possibility of an extended interpretation that includes the narrator within its purview. Thus White notes that "The critics who promote 'The Pelican' take [the narrator's disparaging comments about female intellectual endeavour]...as Wharton's opinion. However, it should be noted that his statement 'I don't think that nature had meant her to be intellectual,' along with others in the story, is clearly misogynistic; it is not only Mrs. Amyot who is being patronized but any woman aspiring to intellectual achievement" (61). And Kaplan reiterates and adds to White's contention when she points out that "the genteel dilettante [i.e., the narrator] maintains his own self-image by patronizing Mrs. Amyot" (73).

The reflections of White and Kaplan open up "The Pelican" to a closer examination than has been previously given it of the person of the narrator himself and of the particular artistic and psychological appropriateness of the fact that the narrator exercises his blatantly condescending attention on his subject over so long a period. White, however, though she evidently finds the story an important one and devotes considerable attention to it, does not go far enough in the assessment of these matters, perhaps thwarted by her sense that "we are not given enough information about the narrator to sustain our interest in him as more than a mere observer of events" (62). It is true that we are never told the narrator's profession, although we might safely speculate that as culturally aware and knowledgeable as he is, he is connected somehow, perhaps loosely, to the university in Hillbridge. More importantly though, there is much information to be gleaned about him from the story itself and indeed he does sustain our interest in the attitudes he projects and the responses he has towards people especially.

There is no need to dwell excessively on the narrator's patronizing attitude to Mrs Amyot and her female audiences: that has been sufficiently documented and is obvious in the story. It might be noted in this regard that his remarks about Mrs Amyot's intellectual capacity are almost invariably juxtaposed with references to her physical attractiveness, just as his comments about her women listeners are habitually joined to remarks about their rather unintellectual pursuits. Such allusions to Mrs Amyot as the following, "so ravishing a mixture of ... sham erudition and real teeth and hair" (I, 89), abound in the story; so do such descriptions as "the throng of well-dressed and absent-minded ladies who rustled in late, dropped their muffs, and pocket-books, and undisguisedly lost themselves in the study of each other's apparel" (I, 93). What are not as frequent in the story, but significant because they reveal a pervasive attitude, are comments that include males in their scope and suggest the narrator's attitude of social superiority that derives from his belonging to the intellectual elite. At one point he alludes to the usher at a public lecture as having "an educated mispronunciation" (I, 91); elsewhere he calls passengers in a Boston tram: "the line of prehensile bipeds blocking the aisle of the car" (I, 94). The attitudes these comments betray are of a piece with the narrator's image of women in the story, and one must at least consider the possibility that beyond the verbal prowess with which these remarks are delivered there lies a sense of inferiority and deep dissatisfaction with the self.

In this context it is interesting to look at the company the narrator keeps. For all his implied gestures in favour of male intellectual superiority, we never see him in the company of those men he assumes to be his social peers. Conversely, he describes his associations to be almost exclusively with women and in social settings. We see him frequently with the very women he patronizes: with Mrs Amyot, whose company he seeks out and whom he assists, and often with the attendees at Mrs Amyot's lectures. At the same time he assiduously avoids contact with women of intellectual accomplishment. Invited to meet Mrs Amyot's mother, a well-known writer, he is thwarted, as he puts it, by "the fear of encountering the author of 'The Fall of Man'"—in the context, can the implications of the title of her book be missed?—and passes it up in favour of another of his "dinner engagements" (I, 90). He also declines an invitation to the home of one of Mrs Amyot's aunts, "the aunt who had translated Euripides," rationalizing his refusal to go with the excuse that his "mood remained distinctly resentful of any connection between Mrs. Amyot and intellectuality" (I, 92). He is evidently more comfortable with Mrs Amyot and her patrons than he would be with her mother and aunt. The former buttresses his perceived sense of his status, her flattering statements that she considers him "dreadfully learned" and knowing he was in the hall "she had felt ready to sink through the floor" (I, 89) buoying up his weak ego.

It is a point worth making that for all his self-satisfied back-patting about his own success, the narrator at times betrays a striking deficiency in those two areas in which lie his claims to superiority: the social and the intellectual. His reneging on his promise to meet Mrs Amyot the day after he had refused to meet her mother is maladroit. (There is something suspicious as well about the circumstances of his refusal to meet Mrs Pratt; the excuse given, "the opportune recollection of a dinner engagement" (I, 90), somehow does not ring true.) As for his intellectualism it is self-conscious and often pretentious. His labelling of Mrs Amyot's memory as "capacious but inaccurate" (I, 89) raises the question as to whether an inaccurate memory is any memory at all. His over-zealous concentration on the fact that Mrs Amyot has misquoted a line from Emerson's lyric "The Rhodora" suggests a literal-mindedness that blinds him to the real issue. It is true that Mrs Amyot's citation is incorrect: she has substituted the word "seeing" for the last word of the verse "That beauty is its own excuse for being." Nevertheless the narrator's quibbling over the woman's error ignores her appreciation and understanding of the sentiment expressed by Emerson. This is yet another example of the narrator's underestimation of Mrs Amyot's qualities of mind, and the "overkill" he expresses is symptomatic of his sense of inadequacy. During the course of the story the narrator spends considerable time cataloguing his travels and social engagements. One wonders if the enforced holiday his doctors order him to take is less the result of work than of boredom and ennui. There may well be a point to Wharton's not mentioning his profession: he may not have one, and for all his verbal cleverness and knowledge about cultural matters, there is no mention of his having accomplished anything of any note.

One can surely make a case for seeing the narrator as Mrs Amyot's double. His continuing interest in her is based on the notion that she is masquerading as an intellectual, and even after he comes to understand the legitimate reason for her pursuing her means of livelihood he maintains his opinion as to her fraudulence. At some level of awareness the narrator is drawn to Mrs Amyot because he sees his own dishonesties reflected in her. Wharton's habit of bringing him so frequently together with her despite their independent itineraries suggests the author's desire that we understand that the former sees his semblance in the latter. This becomes explicit towards the end of the story when, watching the "poor lady" give a lecture, the narrator comments: "It was like looking at one's self early in the morning in a cracked mirror. I had no idea I had grown so old" (I, 99).

Amy Kaplan has drawn attention to the significance of the aforementioned passage: "Through this cracked mirror, we see that the genteel dilettante maintains his own self-image by patronizing Mrs Amyot, and that his style is as outdated as hers. Wharton here points to the collusion between the genteel man of letters and the sentimental and domestic woman artist" (73). Kaplan's statement is important because it alerts us to the cultural implications of the story, to the fact that it reflects a nineteenth-century phenomenon. But it is well to note that Wharton might have effected this without using a first-person male narrator. The psychological dimension of "The Pelican" is at least as important as the cultural, and that former dimension is a measure of what one can bring to bear on a study of the narrator's personality. To call the narrator of "The Pelican" "genteel"is to indicate that he represents a class; to examine him closely is to realize that he misrepresents that class, and that his departures from the conventions of that class distinguish him at least as much as do his adherence to the conventions.

Living in a pre-Boothian time less attuned to the relevance of narrative voice, early critics were not as apt to examine the role of the dilettantish narrator of "The Pelican." More recent readers, alive to the attitudinal self-betrayals of this narrator, find themselves face-to-face with a considerably denser and a considerably enriched short story.

"The Descent of Man"

In her second story of academia, "The Descent of Man," published six years after "The Pelican" in both the March 1904 *Scribner's* and the volume in which it was the lead piece, *The Descent of Man and Other Stories*, Wharton again chose the fictional college town of Hillbridge. Now she sets the action more pervasively in the town and focusses more squarely on its professional activity than she had in its predecessor. "The Descent of Man" is more notable for the commentary of its third-person narrator, who remains outside the action and uncharacterized, than for the action itself. As such, the story can be called a satire and in this regard can be said to differ essentially from "The Pelican," in which the satirical commentary of the personalized narrator is undercut when one realizes that that commentary is as effectual at betraying the foibles of the speaker as it is at denouncing the situation he portrays.

The immediate targets of Wharton's satire in "The Descent of Man" are two Hillbridge University graduates, both figures of heterodoxy during their student days and now both arrived at positions of prominence in their respective professional lives. Of the two, it is Professor Samuel Linyard, an entymologist at Hillbridge, who is the center of interest; his former college friend Ned Harviss, a publisher of popular books, serves as a kind of foil against whom the professor's fall from grace is measured, as well as the immediate trigger that sends him on his descent. That descent is from a life of intellectual and professional principle on which considerable pressure is applied by a wife's and children's legitimate and sometimes frivolous demands on his meagre material means, to a more easeful condition, one in which he can satisfy the family's financial requirements, but at the price of neglect and perhaps total forfeiture of his professional obligations and intellectual fulfilment. Harviss, whose own descent has occurred long before Linyard's, both oversees and engineers the latter's fall without qualm, indeed with scarcely any intimation that he seizes its significance.

Such a literal summing up of the major occurrences of "The Descent of Man" of course belies the essence of the story, hence the importance of the narrator's voice that imposes on these occurrences, that sees them, at least immediately, with a far less serious eye. "The Descent of Man" opens with a preamble, a passage of pure narrative, that brings us up to date on Linyard's recent activities, setting the stage for the events that constitute the story's present time. Here Wharton establishes the

320

tale's tone, casting her narrator's words as a kind of mock heroic. Unknown to Mrs Linyard, who is assured that he has gone off to the Maine woods on a solitary holiday, the Professor has in fact "eloped with an idea" so exhilirating that "he would not have changed places with any hero of romance pledged to a flesh and blood abduction" (I, 347).

> His real life had always lain in the universe of thought, in that enchanted region which, to those who have lingered there, comes to have so much more color and substance than the painted curtain hanging before it. The Professor's particular veil of Maia was a narrow strip of homespun woven into a monotonous pattern, but he had only to lift it to step into an empire.
> This unseen universe was thronged with the most seductive shapes; the Professor moved Sultan-like through a seraglio of ideas. But of all the lowly apparitions that wove their spells about him, none had ever worn quite so pervasive an aspect as this latest favorite. (I, 348)

In light of the current popularity and popularizing of science and the abuses thus engendered, the Professor will put his latest "apparition" to good use.

> The inaccessible goddess whom the Professor had served in his youth now offered her charms in the market place. And yet it was not the same goddess, after all, but a pseudo science masquerading in the garb of the real divinity. The false goddess had her ritual and her literature. She had her sacred books, written by false priests and sold by millions to the faithful.... And [his] idea—the divine incomparable idea—was that he should avenge his goddess by satirizing her false interpreters. He would write a skit on the "popular" scientific book; he would so heap platitude on platitude, fallacy on fallacy, false analogy on false analogy, so use his superior knowledge to abound in the sense of the ignorant, that even the gross crowd would join in the laugh against its augurs. (I, 349-350)

From this exalted pose of idealism, pride, self-assurance, and certitude Professor Linyard's descent takes place. When Harviss reads *The Vital Thing*, his friend's manuscript, the actualization of his "idea," he misses the author's satirical intention entirely, seeing in it rather the potential for a runaway success, a book whose popular appeal will derive from its defense of traditional values. Leaving aside the fact the Linyard has failed to satisfy the satiric muse and overestimated his imagined literary superiority, it is in the context of the exalted kingdom to which Linyard has claimed to belong and in which his grand idea has been spawned that his response to Harviss's trained intuition about *The Vital Thing* is viewed. Using as a point of departure Linyard's idyll in the Maine woods, where he seems to seal his commitment to the scholarly life, Wharton chronicles the series of decisions and rationalizations that bring him down, that determine what happens during Linyard's next eighteen months and probably the rest of his professional life. The Professor puts aside a life of scholarly integrity for peace in his family, where now even the most questionable of financial demands can be satisfied; an expanded social engagement with women, from which he was previously isolated by a secure, if unchallenging marriage; and a dusty, if inviting, laboratory and more equipment and specimens with which to pursue, at some receding point in the future, his research activities.

In his descent, Linyard is aided and abetted by Harviss, his iconoclastic undergraduate friend, whose own fall has been effected years before. In Harviss's hands, Linyard is as sodden clay. The publisher manipulates him, lures him, and lies to him, enriching his own coffers in the process. It is worth noting that Wharton has called her story "The Descent of Man," that is, the failure of the collective entity and not merely the individual person. One recalls, too, that one of Wharton' s early contemporaries, Edwin Arlington Robinson, had suggested more than once that the appeal of wealth might be too powerful to keep in check the two giants science and business that threatened to overwhelm twentieth-century American life.

"The Pretext"

Wharton published "The Pretext," her academic story most deserving of that designation, in August 1908 in *Scribner's*, changing the locale from the Hillbridge of "The Pelican" and "The Fall of Man" to the, again, fictional Wentworth. For the first time in these stories of academe, Wharton puts the college proper much to the fore, using the campus, buildings and grounds both, as the setting for much of the action, and more importantly perhaps, giving the college and the tradition behind it the role of an important force in the lives of the story's characters. Early commentary on "The Pretext" tends to be biographical: the fact that the story's *donné* was provided by Henry James, and the alleged similarity of the story's subject to Wharton's own relationship to Morton Fullerton have until recently been foregrounded at the expense of close attention to the text itself. Barbara White has given the story a thorough critical airing, commenting on its imagery and drawing the reader's attention to the necessity of looking closely at the reflector and central character, Margaret Ransom, in her own right. (18-24) It is difficult to take issue with White's reading as far as it goes. However, there are a number of additional facets to "The Pretext" that beg attention and whose pursuit add interesting dimensions to the story and may suggest a rather different emphasis from White's.

Wharton's artistic working out of the constrictions which regulate Margaret Ransom's life at Wentworth and which force her to seek a compensating interior existence is highly effective. The immediate and generic patriarchy to which it is seen to be her duty to submit and in the reflected importance of which she is expected to bask is the subject of two especially well-wrought scenes. In the first of these, Robert Ransom, finding out that his spouse, Margaret, is hesitant about attending "a banquet offered by the faculty of Wentworth to visitors of academic eminence" at which he will be a speaker, expresses his wishes without equivocation:

> Ransom laid a friendly hand on her arm: "Come along, Margaret. You know I speak for the bar." She was aware, in his voice, of a little note of surprise at his having to remind her of this.
> "Oh, yes. I mean to go, of course —"
> "Well, then—" He opened his dressing-room door, and caught a glimpse of the retreating housemaid's skirt. "Here's Maria now. Maria! Call up Mr. Dawnish—at Mrs. Creswell's, you know. Tell him Mrs. Ransom wants him to go with her to hear the speeches this evening—the *speeches*, you understand? —and he's to call for her at a quarter before nine." (I, 635)

Here Margaret's hesitancy breaks down completely in the face of Ransom's insistence, which is physical, and comprehensive to the point of his selecting and making arrangements for her to meet her escort. In the second scene, Margaret sits in the ladies' gallery, observing and listening to, but removed from the male celebration below. (Here we do not miss the ironic implications of the relative positioning of the sexes: Margaret and the other woman are above the men, looking down at them.)

A salient part of the patriarchal power that both restricts and eases Margaret's life is the university itself. The link between patriarchy and university is apparent to Margaret when after her descent from the gallery she sits in a committee room "confronted ... by a frowning college President in an emblazoned frame. The academic frown descended on her like an anathema" (I, 641). In a more pervasive way, she has been conscious until the present point in her life of the impact Wentworth has wielded.

> Wentworth, in fact, had always been the bond between [her husband and her]; they were united in their veneration for that estimable seat of learning, and in their modest yet vivid consciousness of possessing its tone. The Wentworth "tone" is unmistakeable: it permeates every part of the social economy, from the coiffure of the ladies to the preparation of the food. It has its sumptuary laws as well as its curriculum of learning. It sits in judgement not only on its own townsmen but on the rest of the world—enlightening, criticizing, ostracizing a heedless universe—and nonconformity to Wentworth standards involves obliteration from Wentworth consciousness. (I, 636)

The other major element that influences Margaret's life, also closely allied to the impact of patriarchy and the university, is, as she herself perceives, "her rigid New England ancestry" (I, 633). It is this that looms over her from the portrait of the college President in Hamblin Hall, and she perceives much the same kind of image peering back at her from her own mirror. When her husband accuses her of looking like the Brant girl, he is expressing the necessity of maintaining the ascetic New England tradition; her "plain prim dressing table, ... her stiff mahogany rocking chair, ... the scentless drawer" (I, 632, 633) in which she rummages for some articles that will enhance her appearance, are evidence of her own allegiance to it.

When Margaret decides to cultivate her attraction to Guy Dawnish, to "improve" her life, it must be kept in mind that she does so from a very ambivalent perspective. If her associations with a patriarchal town and institution have seemed in the past and now seem to thwart her from a more fulfilling life away from the shadow of husband and college, they have also provided her an easeful existence, the support of servants, and the interesting, if not particularly passionate pastimes of "her innocent and voluminous correspondence" (I, 639) and her work with the Higher Thought Club. The nature of her dalliance with Dawnish reflects the poles of Margaret's ambivalence: she is at once repelled by her married life to the point of making a move to alter it, and immersed so deeply in the Wentworth mode that her "new" life exists only as an extension of the patriarchal and ascetic milieu. In this regard it is interesting to see how her interior idyll of Dawnish is so fragile and quickly destroyed by Lady Caroline's unproven contention that he is using her as "a pretext". One realizes just how tentative and safe Margaret's move to a better life must of necessity be when one considers her attitude to the Wentworth world: "In a world without traditions, without reverence, without stability, such little expiring centers of prejudice and precedent [as Wentworth] make an irresistible appeal to those instincts for which a democracy had neglected to provide. Wentworth, with its 'tone,' its backward references, its inflexible aversions and condemnations, its hard moral outline preserved intact against a whirling background of experiment, had been all the poetry and history of Margaret Ransom's life" (I, 636). It is not altogether surprising then that Margaret's "new life" is squarely grounded in those very essences that made up her rejected world, "a world destitute of personal experience" (I, 637): in place of her husband she chooses another dominant man, in place of Wentworth she opts for a grander version of what Wentworth's stands for, to replace the New England ascetic tradition she removes herself to an interior place that repudiates the former yet allows her the comfort of living outwardly by its prescriptions.

Margaret cultivates the friendship, and what she assumes to be the requited love, of Dawnish because she is unfulfilled in her marriage. She has scarcely a kind thought for her husband, a sort of gray eminence in her life, "a solid bulk ... heavy, round-shouldered, a little pompous" (I, 644). As the two men appear to Margaret at the time of Dawnish's departure from Wentworth, Ransom is resolved to a "grayish stubble of beard, ... sallow forehead and spectacled eyes" while "Dawnish towering higher than usual against the shadows of the room, and refined by his unusual pallor ... [is] somehow more mature, more obscurely in command of himself" (I, 645). However, while Dawnish is much advantaged in the context, it is clear to see that the society from which he comes is thoroughly patriarchal, and that women's status is, as in Margaret's own culture, a reflected one. As she looks at photos Dawnish shows her, she sees "Guise Abbey, his uncle's place in Wiltshire, where, under his grandfather's rule, Guy's own childhood had been spent ... the walled garden ... [where] his uncle, Lord Askern, a hale gouty-looking figure is planted robustly on the terrace, a gun on his shoulder and a couple of setters at his feet" (I, 637). And if Dawnish's ancestral past is seen in male terms, his being at Wentworth is a factor of the same situation, for "he had been sent, through his uncle's influence, for two years' training in the neighboring electrical works at Smedden" (I, 638) to prepare for a career as an engineer and executive for the Smedden works in London.

In a word, there is an element of safeness for Margaret in the fact that the man to whom she is so strongly attracted exists in the same sort of social context and tradition as her husband, and in the unlikely eventuality that her relationship with Dawnish progressed beyond the limits of a secret platonic idyll, no large adjustment in attitude and life style would be demanded of her. That potential safeness is balanced as well by the actual security of knowing, as to her relationship with Dawnish, that Wentworth "has given her the domestic sanction without which ... any social relation between the sexes remained unhallowed and to be viewed askance" (I, 634). What is more, the relationship in question has the safeness of an age discrepancy that works to Margaret's disadvantage, and the photos of Dawnish's boating, and sporting tennis regalia in the company of attractive women closer to his own age remind her of the practical unlikelihood of her reaching any kind of mutually and permanently satisfying active involvement with the young man.

Dawnish's photographs demonstrate to Margaret as well "a life so rich, so romantic, so packed ... with historic reference and poetic allusion that she felt almost oppressed by this distant whiff of its air" (I, 638), and one is immediately reminded that what sustained Margaret in her life at Wentworth was "all the poetry and history" (I, 636) the community stood for. Again, the allure of Dawnish and his English aristocratic associations is less that it is a radical departure from what she has experienced in New England and more that it is an extension of it. "What subjugated her," she reflects—and it is instructive in the context of the present discussion to note Wharton's choice of verb—"was the unexampled prodigality with which [Dawnish] poured for her the same draught of tradition of which Wentworth held out its little teacupful. He besieged her with a million Wentworths in one" (I, 639). Just as in her attachment to Dawnish, Margaret's yearning for association with what his lineage represents is a factor of her own past and places no radical demands on her powers of adaptation.

One sees in Margaret a reluctance and ultimately an inability to press through to any essential change in her life style and status during her magic hour by the river with Dawnish on the evening of her escape from her husband's address at the university function. Here, just as in the story's opening scene when she is so self-conscious and guilty about making herself look attractive, she is thwarted by the ancestral Puritan morality that, at least for her, equates physical attractiveness with sexual evil and allure with prostitution. In this later scene, as elsewhere in the story, the opposed new permissive morality is embodied in the person of the Brant girl, the "laced, whale-boned, frizzle-headed, high-heeled daughter of iniquity ... from New York" (I, 636). In the following passage we perceive the presence of a third person, emblematic of the influence that continues to shape Margaret's words and actions and her very life.

> The young man leaned back luxuriously, reassured by her silence.
> "You see it's my last chance—and I want to make the most of it."
> "Your last chance?" How stupid of her to repeat his words on that cooing note of interrogation! It was just such a lead as the Brant girl might have given him. (I, 642)

Given her scruples about showing herself to be too forward here, is it any surprise that Margaret cannot imagine herself experiencing the unconventional predicaments an open assertion of love to Dawnish might bring about? Indeed, as she tells Dawnish, "[H]ow much safer to leave everything undisturbed" (I, 643).

Margaret's new life for the brief time it lasts is "a secret life of incommunicable joys" (I, 645), touching no one beyond herself, marked by self-gratification, and virtually devoid of sensitivity towards the beloved. The news that

Dawnish's marriage to Gwendolen Matcher has been called off triggers this response in her: "A gust of tears shook her, loosening the dry surface of conventional feeling, welling up from unsuspected depths. She was sorry—very sorry, yet so glad—so ineffably, impenitently glad" (I, 648). And for all its secret intensity, Margaret's interiorized life lacks any real substance, the fact of its being undermined by a statement of no provable truth, the suggestion that she was but a pretext for Dawnish's real involvement, the certain sign of its fragility.

Given the aforestated considerations, it is not unreasonable to examine the question of pretext in the story. In her review of the criticism of "The Pretext," Barbara White notes that "'the pretext' has been given two interpretations, one by several critics that Guy wooed Margaret to protect his real lover, and another by Millicent Bell that there is no other woman and Guy just needed an excuse to break an unwanted engagement" (21). White goes on to suggest that "it may have been Wharton's intention to indicate that Lady Caroline erred in concluding that Margaret could not have attracted her nephew" (23), and that in fact Dawnish was not using a pretext when he let it be known that he was in love with Margaret. Given the real possibility that there is no pretext here, perhaps one might consider that Lady Caroline's pretext is a smokescreen of sorts and look elsewhere in the story for further significance to be attached to its title substantive.

It may be reasonable to conclude that the pretext laying the greatest claim to being central to the significance of the story is the one lived by Margaret Ransom. For is her "secret life of uncommunicable joys" anything more than an excuse for not being able to live a fulfilling exterior life, either in the time-worn Wentworth ways, or in the potentially brave new world she envisages with Dawnish or with another unnamed companion with whom there would be a real deliverance? And in the final analysis, is not Margaret Ransom close to being a female version of those Wharton male characters such as the unnamed narrators of "The Pelican" and "Miss Mary Pask"—to mention two—dilettantes both, and unwilling hence unable both, to look at themselves clearly or to form permanently viable intimate human associations?

"The Debt"

Wharton once again turned her attention to academic life in "The Debt," published a year after "The Pretext" in the August 1909 number of *Scribner's*. Here, the only time she did so in these stories, she set her tale at a non-fictional university, Columbia, moving away from the make-believe Hillbridge and Wentworth of her earlier pieces. Although certain of the fictive details—book titles such as *The Arrival of the Fittest* and *Utility and Variation*, and the Columbia Chair of Experimental Evolution—suggest that Wharton was flirting with the idea of taking a satirical approach to her subject, "The Debt" in fact adopts the serious tack of its predecessor "The Pretext" and eschews the quasi-satiric and satiric slants of the earlier "The Pelican" and "The Descent of Man." But if "The Debt" resembles "The Pretext" in approach, it is a far cry from the latter's complex psychological inventiveness and wealth of color and allusion. In short, "The Debt" might be called a plain story, brief, direct, and effective enough, but without the richness one has come to expect of Wharton's fiction. It is not surprising that there is scarcely a comment to be found on the story in the growing body of critical writing about Wharton's work.

"The Debt" is told in the first person by a narrator who is a friend of the principal character and attempts to view personages and events objectively. His narrative tone is that of the raconteur: he will remind readers of the garrulous narrators in James's *The Turn of the Screw* and Wharton's own ghost story "The Lady's Maid's Bell," who adopt a familiar tone with their readers/listeners, luring them into the tale by assuming their prior knowledge of the context that gives rise to it. "You remember—it's not so long ago—the talk there was about Dredge's *The Arrival of the Fittest?*" (II, 61) "The Debt" opens, and we are launched into this tale of intellectual integrity. The fact of the narrator's self-consciousness as a story-teller is an important point to make, for here, as opposed to elsewhere in her short stories, Wharton plays down her first-person narrator as a character. This narrator is not one of those narrators who in the process of telling his story inadvertently gives away his hand and reveals himself to be an integral part of the psychological and moral action. By revealing next to nothing about his life, Wharton dismisses the possibility of seeing him as more than mere narrator.

The narrator's purpose in telling the story of Galen Dredge, the eminent Columbia biologist, is to take his listeners inside the man: if the world has perceived Dredge "simply as a thinking machine, a highly specialized instrument of precision," he would acquaint it with "the other, the personal side of Dredge's case [which is] even more interesting and arresting" (II, 61). Because he is a friend of the Lanfear family, probably a contemporary of the son Archie, the narrator is privy to the details of Galen Dredge's development. He has seen him grow from a bumbling student who has sufficiently impressed the great biologist Lanfear that he takes him under his wing, to a poised scholar who is confident enough to fend off the attacks of the Lanfear family but sensitive enough to understand its concerns.

It is the conflict between Dredge and the Lanfears, with the narrator serving as a moderator, that is the nub of "The Debt" and takes up nearly half its length. Summoned to a showdown by his former mentor's family, Dredge emerges vindicated. He has established to the satisfaction of all that his "personal," his human character transcends his scientific and intellectual personality. Not only does he convince his opponents that what they have interpreted to be a lack of respect for the deceased Lanfear is in point of fact the only way that he can satisfactorily repay his debt to his patron and mentor, but also he asserts his willingness to give up the tangible sign of his success, the Chair of Experimental Evolution, if his friends' sensibilities are to be hurt by his retaining the position.

In one of the very few critical comments made about "The Debt," R. W. B. Lewis writes: "when dealing with integrity, Edith Wharton was not much more than competent" (*ICSS* XXII). The following is a brief passage from the earlier part of the confrontation between Dredge and young Lanfear; the former has just become aware of the tension that lies behind the calling of the meeting:

> Dredge bent his slow calm scrutiny on his friend's agitated face; then he turned to me.
> "What's the matter," he said simply
> "The matter?" shrieked Archie, his fist hovering excitedly above the desk by which he stood; but Dredge, with unwonted quickness, caught the fist as it descended.

"Careful—I've got a *Kallima* in that jar there." He pushed a chair forward, and added quietly: "Sit down." (II, 68)

The incident brings color to the story, enhancing the tension-filled dialogue with gesture and action. Lanfear's anger and Dredge's command of himself and the situation are given substance. But there is too little of this kind of embellishment in "The Debt," a fact that lends credence to the corollary of Lewis's statement concerning Wharton's stories about integrity being merely competent: that the theme of intellectual integrity did not interest her enough to apply her best efforts to its depiction.

"Xingu"

If "The Debt" betrays in its artistic plainness the fact the Wharton was not greatly enthused with the theme of intellectual integrity, her next story of academe, "Xingu," illustrated, as R. W. B. Lewis has observed, that "it was the opposite— ... the pretence of intellectual seriousness—that engaged Mrs. Wharton's larger talent: that summoned into play [her] virile wit, trenchant, but just falling short of the merciless" (*ICSS* XXII). This story, also published in *Scribner's*, in December 1910, is much anthologized, probably because it is seen to represent the best of its author's satiric work. The product of the period immediately following the writing of *The House of Mirth*, "Xingu" echoes the manner in which the satire— to mention one of the categories under which that novel is justly praised—makes use of language. To cite Lewis again: "The language [of 'Xingu'] has the air of taking a rational delight in itself, as it cuts sharply into folly and hypocrisy" (*ICSS* XXII).

In "Xingu" the satire is pointed at the half-dozen members of Hillbridge's Lunch Club, singly and as a group, and to a lesser extent at Osric Dane, the Club's guest at the meeting on and around which the story is structured. One of the Club members, Mrs Roby, escapes the narrational barbs and indeed functions in concert with the narrator, effectively becoming the agent whereby her fellow clubwomen's fakery and pretentiousness are at once brought to life and uncovered.

That Wharton voice that "cuts sharply into folly and hypocrisy" is discernible in the tone of the narrator, who opens the story with a sardonic comment about the founder of the Lunch Club: "Mrs. Ballinger is one of the ladies who pursue Culture in bands, as though it were dangerous to meet alone" (II, 209) —and seldom relents in her onslaught as the story moves ahead. When the narrative voice gives way to the ladies' conversation, one still senses the former's hand as she superintends and manipulates the talk in a way that repeatedly holds the speakers up to ridicule. Often narrative commentary and conversation are brought together so as to produce optimum satirical impact, as in the following passage:

> "Well, my dear," the newcomer [Mrs. Van Vluyck] briskly asked her hostess, "What subjects are we to discuss today?"
> Mrs. Ballinger was furtively replacing a volume of Wordsworth by a copy of Verlaine. "I hardly know," she said, somewhat nervously. "Perhaps we had better leave that to circumstances."
> "Circumstances?" said Mrs. Van Vluyck drily. "That means, I suppose, that Laura Glyde will take the floor as usual, and we shall be deluged with literature."
> Philantrophy and statistics were Miss Van Vluyck's province, and she resented any tendency to divert their guest's attention from these topics.
> Mrs. Plinth at this moment appeared.
> "Literature?" she protested in a tone of remonstrance. "But this is perfectly unexpected. I understood we were to talk of Osric Dane's novel."
> (II, 214)

If it is the members of the Lunch Club who are the main targets of "Xingu's" satire—Mrs Bollinger for her protectiveness of her superficial enterprise; Mrs Plinth for her blind conviction that her material means ensure her a superior status in the Club; Mrs Leveret for her dullness; Laura Glyde for her pedantry; and the group as a whole for its artificiality and pretentiousness—the novelist Osric Dane absorbs a substantial share of barbs as well. Immediately she arrives at the meeting, her hauteur and self-absorption are held up to display and ultimately she falls prey, as the other women do, to Mrs Roby's ruse: her vanity deflated by her ignorance about Xingu and her unwillingness to acknowledge that ignorance, she settles at the level of the pack, or perhaps lower if one considers the exalted height from which she has fallen.

In "Xingu's" structure as the confrontation of opposed responses to high culture and to literature in particular, Mrs Roby stands at the opposite end of the pole represented by the Club ladies. She is discredited by the other women, who regard her as a failure in their organization and finally eject her. And understandably so, for she represents a natural forthrightness and an appreciation of literature that are foreign to them. She honestly admits to not having read *The Wings of Death*, the proposed subject of discussion for the day of Dane's visit. She is amused by Trollope. She dares to ask her fellow club members their opinions about *The Wings of Death*. Above all, she possesses a sense of humor almost totally absent in the other women, from whom scarcely the hint of a titter is heard on the two extended occasions during which we observe them. But Mrs Roby's humor is not appreciated in the club, a fact that is clear from the time of her introduction to it. When Miss Van Vluyck, in an effort to impress the new "biological" member with her own knowledge by her "offhand mention of the pterodactyl" elicits Mrs Roby's reply "I know so little about meters," it does not matter whether or not the latter knows that a pterodactyl is a prehistoric animal. She has effectively defeated Miss Van Vluyck's pedantry, a fact that is entirely lost on the latter and on the rest of the women.

Mrs Roby's pun on the word "pterodactyl" anticipates her play with "Xingu," and the Lunch Club's response to the former probably motivates Mrs Roby's injection of the latter term into deliberations during Osric Dane's visit. Although some of the members realize that this word-play has saved them from more embarrassment at the hands of the eminent writer, they choose to ignore this and focus rather on their own discomfiture, agreeing to dismiss her as a member and assigning that task to Mrs Ballinger, their leader and founder, who is sitting down to fulfill her task as the story ends. Meanwhile, after leaving everyone in a state of consternation over the significance of Xingu, Mrs Roby has walked blissfully off to her bridge game in mid-meeting, effectively pre-empting her dismissal and rendering it a gesture as empty as the minds of its perpetrators.

Whether Mrs Roby's up-ending of the Lunch Club is motivated by revenge or merely the love of fun—most probably it is the latter—her scheme works to perfection. In "Xingu," Wharton is as sure-handed as her central character, producing not only her most successful short satire but one of her most entertaining and best-wrought short stories as well.

"The Day of the Funeral"

After the publication of "Xingu" in December 1910, Wharton abandoned the college and the college town as a subject and locale until the 1930's when she took it up again in two short stories set, respectively, in the fictional American college towns of Kingsborough and Kingsbridge. The first of these, "The Day of the Funeral," published in the *Woman's Home Companion* in January and February 1933, is the better of the two, eclipsing its sucessor "Permanent Wave" in artistic tightness and psychological depth.

"The Day of the Funeral" captures the waking hours of Professor Ambrose Trenham on the day of his wife's funeral, her death by suicide a direct response to his refusal to give up his intimate relationship with the youthful Barbara Wake, herself the daughter of a Kingsborough professor. Focussing first on the interior consciousness of Trenham during the first part of the day, then on the verbal confrontation between him and Barbara in the evening, the story ends with a kind of coda which unequivocally establishes Trenham's despicableness and justifies the critic Barbara White's comment that he "[outdoes] Andrew Culwin of 'The Eyes' in selfishness and cruelty" (85).

The present-time action of "The Day of the Funeral" is picked up by the third-person narrator some time after the church service has been held, when Trenham is reflecting on the events of the immediate past: his wife's threat to end her life, her ensuing suicide, the inquest, the wake, and the funeral itself. The particular recollection that sets off and propels his thoughts and then the subsequent action of the story is his sight of Barbara at the end of the funeral service, and "In the reaction produced by the shock of seeing her, his remorse for what had happened hardened into icy hate of the woman who had been the cause to the tragedy" (II, 670). "The sole cause—" the narrator interposes," for in a flash Trenham had thrown off his own share in the disaster." Thus, triggered by his rationalizing away of his own responsibility and shifting it to his lover, "his indignation grew; it filled the remaining hours of the endless day, the empty hours after the funeral was over, it occupied and sustained him" (II, 670).

The "indignation," the false grief that sustains and nourishes Trenham is ritualized in his gathering together all the letters Barbara has sent during their relationship and presenting them to her as a sign of his disapproval. He imagines her receiving the letters: "It was so fortifying to visualize that scene—the scene of her opening the packet alone in her room—that Trenham's sense of weariness disappeared, his pulses began to drum excitedly, and he was torn by a pang of hunger, the first he had felt in days" (II, 671). Having satisfied himself that the responsibility for the suicide is Barbara's and not his own, he is relieved of the only grief that concerns any selfish person, grief for himself caused by personal psychological discomfort. The "pang of hunger" he feels, and his immediate satisfaction of it after this catharsis, functions as a sign of his insensitivity to the pain his wife has suffered. His almost voracious eating both at lunch and at the evening meal also effectively symbolizes the way—and here Wharton's choice of verbs highlights the connection—he is "sustained" and "nourished" by the guilty and soon-to-be-punished figure of Barbara.

The fraudulent nature of Trenham's grief as it is suggested and exposed in his many passages of interior consciousness in the first half of the story is anticipated in his recall of an early incident of the funeral day:

> It was when Mrs. Cossett, the wife of the professor of English Literature, came to him and said: "Do you want to see her?"
> "See her—?" Trenham gasped, not understanding.
> Mrs. Cossett looked surprised, and a little shocked. "The time has come—they must close the coffin ...."
> "Oh, let them close it," was on the tip of the widower's tongue; but he saw from Mrs. Cossett's expression that something very different was expected of him. He got up and followed her out of the room and up the stairs.... He looked at his wife. Her face had been spared.... (II, 669-670)

Trenham's answer to Mrs Cossett's first question might suggest that he is not of one mind with his questioner as to the antecedent of the pronoun "her." His response to Mrs Cossett's second remark betrays his insensitivity. The sentence that introduces the cited passage above ("Before the funeral one horrible moment stood out from all the others, though all were horrible.") might suggest to the wary reader, particularly in view of Trenham's conduct during the remainder of the story, that his moment of horror is a result of his being discovered in his own callousness.

In the incident alluded to above, Trenham finds to his own horror that he is without the real grief of the new widower, and one may interpret his seizing upon the person of Barbara Wake as proximate cause of Mrs Trenham's suicide as his method of inciting the required grief in himself. But the grief so incited is merely a *pro forma* grief, a fact evident in the exaggerated expression of many of the passages in which the narrator summons up the content of his central character's interior consciousness. In such passages Wharton uses a technique much in evidence in certain short stories of her contemporary Theodore Dreiser. In such stories as "Free" and "The Old Neighborhood"[102] Dreiser, while retaining the removed third-person narrator, seeks to capture the intimate thoughts and feelings of a character in what has the appearance and tone of first-person interior monologue. But while such interior monologues in Dreiser are normally sincere and genuine addresses to the self in which the latter is confronting a particular personal problem, in Wharton's "The Day of the Funeral" they function in a rather different fashion.

Here is Wharton's narrator recording Trenham's reaction to the sight of Barbara's letters to him:

> God! What dozens and dozens of letters there were! And all written within eighteen months. No wonder poor Milly ... but what a blind reckless fool he had been! The reason of their abundance was, of course, the difficulty of meeting.... So often he and Barbara had had to write because they couldn't contrive to see each other... but still, this bombardment of letters was monstrous, inexcusable.... (II, 673)

To be noted in the above passage is the vehemence of Trenham's protestations against Barbara, which betray—and belie—his attempt to put aside his own responsibility in the matter of "poor Milly's" suicide. For one thing, one assumes that the correspondence was a reciprocal one, that he had written as much as Barbara had. This interiorization of Trenham's blindness is the ultimate measure of his utter lack of human decency, a lack rendered more pathetic by the exclamations and the extreme nature of the diction, by the passion and intensity of his complaint.

That Trenham does protest too much is made amply manifest at the time he proceeds to Barbara's home to return her letters and deliver his own cryptic note that will end their association. As he nears her family's house, he sees her proceeding to the garage, the frequent site of their past trysts. Within seconds of "[wanting] to avoid going in to the garage. To do so at that moment would have been a profanation of Milly's memory" (II, 675), he is envisioning "the girl's slim figure"and contemplating the notion that "Real passion ought to be free, reckless, audacious, unhampered by the fear of a wife's feelings, of the university's regulations, the president's friendship, the deadly risk of losing one's job and wrecking one's career" (II, 675). As he watches Barbara move towards the garage, his attention settles on her hand. He is reminded "of the first time he had dared to hold it in his and press a kiss on the palm.... He could see now every line, every curve of her hand, with long fingers, slightly blunted at the tips, and a sensuous elastic palm. It would be queer to have to carry on life without ever again knowing the feel of that hand..."(II, 676). Virtually instantaneously Trenham's sympathy for Milly and his disaffection with Barbara have disappeared: rekindled by Barbara's person and the warmth evoked by the sight of her hand, his desire for her resurfaces.

The second half of "The Day of the Funeral" dramatizes Trenham's unsuccessful attempt to sustain his relationship with Barbara, and then her ultimate unimportance to him whose focus is inner-directed and self-centered. There is in this part of the story a shift of attention to Barbara. She is on her own ground, not only territorially but psychologically as well. Both before and after her discovery of the initial purpose of Trenham's visit, she maintains the initiative in the dialogue between the two, first expressing her attachment to him and insisting that her decision to go to California for a period of time is not a sign of a diminution of her attachment, then stating more and more intensely her shock at Trenham's disclosures about the period leading up to Milly's suicide. Barbara's accusation to Trenham of his, and her absolute acknowledgement of her own guilt in the matter of the wife's tragedy contrast her attitude and conduct sharply with Trenham's, and mitigate somewhat the absolute castigation by Barbara White that "all the characters [in the story] are repellent" (85).

In the end, Trenham's rekindled passion for Barbara is snuffed out as abruptly as it has arisen, and the pattern demonstrated in his easy dismissal of Milly's memory recurs as he contemplates a life with Barbara. Perceiving the potential parallel between the sentiments of the two women, he reflects and speculates: "Yes, that must have been the way Milly felt—he knew it now—and the way poor Barbara herself would feel if he ever betrayed her. Ah, but he was never going to betray her—the thought was monstrous! Never for a moment would he cease to love her. This catastrophe had bound them together as a happy wooing could never have done" (II, 683). But within seconds he is aware that because Barbara's guilt and pain will not soon disappear "his future would be burdened with long arrears of remembrance"; and in the face of this burden his inner protestations of unflinching fidelity have dissolved into the spoken words "I'd better go" (II, 684). As the story closes, Trenham has returned home, thoughts of either Milly or Barbara seemingly absent from his mind, and he is soothed by the "familiar slipping of the bolts and click of the chain" as the housemaid Jane lets him in: "It was his own house, after all—and this friendly hand was shutting him safely into it. The dreadful sense of loneliness melted a little at the old reassuring touch of habit" (II, 686). "The middle-aged disapproving maid" (II, 671) of a few hours earlier has suddenly become, in the absence of Milly and Barbara, the convenient and familiar source of comfort and domesticity.

Barbara White points out that "the preoccupation with vengeance...applies in all Wharton's late stories.... If the dead wife in 'Pomegranate Seed' reclaims her husband, the suicide in 'The Day of the Funeral' posthumously breaks up her husband's affair—and through letters too, as the husband's return of letters to his mistress initiates the split..." (100). This is an interesting speculation, giving something of a supernatural overtone to the story, but one may note at the same time that it is perfectly in keeping with Trenham's carelessness and casualness about his associations with women that the letters make the unfortunate appearance they do in the Wake garage. "The Day of the Funeral" is primarily a realistic story about human weakness and evil, particularly Trenham's, and less a tale about the play of fate.

As Trenham approaches the garage to meet Barbara, he thinks about the possibility of leaving Kingsborough by himself, of getting "as far away from that girl as possible." Then he continues his reflection:

> ...[W]hat he wanted was to get away to some hot climate, steamy, tropical, where one could lie out all night on a white beach and hear the palms chatter on the waves, and the trade winds blow from God knows where...one of those fiery flowery lands where marriage and love were not regarded so solemnly and a man could follow his instinct without calling down a catastrophe, or feeling himself morally degraded.... Above all he never wanted to see again a woman who argued and worried and reproached, and dramatized things that ought to be as simple as eating or drinking.... (II, 676)

Here is the real Trenham, for once true to himself, and the man here represented is the major point of interest in "The Day of the Funeral."

"Permanent Wave"

Wharton's last story of academic life, "Permanent Wave," was published in *Red Book* in April 1935 under the title "Poor Old Vincent." One of the weakest short stories she ever wrote, it has little, if anything, to recommend it, and Barbara White's suggestion that it reflects Wharton's tendency to go "commercial" in her late fiction is probably as valid a comment as any. It says something of the lesser quality of "Permanent Wave" that it was rejected by several of the slick American picture magazines before *Red Book* took it, and the opinions about the story have not apparently changed since, for one is hard-pressed to find any critical comment on it anywhere.

"Permanent Wave" repeats the narrative method of "The Day of the Funeral," taking the view of the central character, Nalda Craig, and expressing it from the perspective of a third-person narrator. For large portions of the story we are given access to Nalda's inner consciousness, and often that consciousness expresses itself in the diction and tone of a first-person interior monologue. That access reveals a person who is superficial, flighty, self-centered, and dim-witted, and corroborates the plight in which she finds herself: uncertain as to the day she is scheduled to run away from her professor husband and travel with her lover, a researcher of questionable talent, on an archeological venture to Central America. The fact that an adult woman who has made the decision to undertake such a major change in her life could be so careless about knowing the day of her elopement is simply not credible, and the evocation of the ambivalence she feels about leaving her husband is superficial and effected with an unsure pen. Wharton, who prided herself in not being utterly explicit about all the elements of her stories and who berated editors and readers who thought there were too many incertitudes in her work, would likely have been happy with the close of "Permanent Wave," which leaves in abeyance the final option Nalda takes. However, the story itself is not strong: and the ending has long ceased to be an issue.

*　*　*　*　*

On and off the Campus: Professors, Wives, and Other Lovers

Like Wharton's stories about persons occupied in or preoccupied with the creative arts, her tales of campus and off-campus life are generally marked less by an interest in academic professionals in the practice of their work and more by an absorption with the human occurrences that impinge on the daily lives of academics and academics' near ones and associates. To be sure there are narratives of academic life proper among the seven tales discussed here—two in particular that target college professors at work—but there are more whose central characters, if professors at all, engage in non-professorial activities or are caught up in non-professional predicaments. What all the stories have in common is their settings: each is placed on a college campus or in a town where the college is a significant place for its characters.

The setting for three of these academic short stories is the fictive Hillbridge, a college that is described most fully in Wharton's tale of a young painter's coming into self-awareness, "The Recovery." From its depiction in "The Recovery" readers can determine something of Hillbridge's status as an institution in Wharton's fictive world as well as the tone of those tales that use it as their setting. Hillbridge is introduced via the perspective of Claudia Day, the young woman who eventually marries the painter/protagonist of the story:

> In East Onondaigua where she lived, Hillbridge was looked on as an Oxford. Magazine writers, with the easy American use of the superlative, designated it as "the venerable Alma Mater," and "the antique seat of learning," and Claudia Day had been brought up to regard it as the fountainhead of knowledge, and of that mental distinction which is so much rarer than knowledge. An innate passion for all that was thus distinguished and exceptional made her revere Hillbridge as the native soil of those intellectual amenities that were of such difficult growth in the thin air of East Onondaigua.... The vision of herself walking under the "historic elms" toward the Memorial Library, standing rapt before the Stuart Washington, or drinking in, from some obscure corner of an academic drawing room, the President's reminiscences of the Concord group—this vividness of self-projection into the emotions awaiting her made her glad of any delay that prolonged so exquisite a moment. (I, 260-261)

Claudia's and her husband's maturing are closely tied to their realization that Hillbridge's artistic standards are limited and provincial, and in the three academic stories set at the college the reputation of Hillbridge as a bastion of intellectual life is undercut satirically. In "The Pelican," "The Descent of Man," and "Xingu" various aspects of intellectual, literary, and scholarly life, snobbery, elitism, fakery, for example, are held up to more or less humorous ridicule.

Perhaps because its publication predated "The Recovery's" appearance, i.e., before Wharton had so clearly pinned down Hillbridge's identity, "The Pelican" is not so obviously a Hillbridge story as its three successors. It is only later in the tale that the locale of the narrator's first meetings with his subject Mrs Amyot, "the New England University town where the celebrated Irene Astarte Pratt [Mrs Amyot's mother] lived on the summit of a local Parnassus, with lesser muses and college professors grouped on the lower ledges of the sacred declivity"(I, 89), is identified as Hillbridge. Because both narrator and subject lead peripatetic lives and seldom find themselves in Hillbridge, the story cannot truly be said to be "set" there, but both the narrator and Mrs Amyot are products of the place. The latter, no doubt inspired by the example of her grandfather, a student and perhaps professor of English literature; her mother, the "celebrated" poet of *The Fall of Man*; one of her aunts, "the dean of a girl's college" (I, 88); another aunt, a translator of Euripedes, has launched out on a career as a lecturer on literary subjects. The narrator himself is a walking exhibition of academic pretentiousness—although it does not appear that he is a professor at Hillbridge at all.

"Xingu" sustains Wharton's interest in satirizing aspects of life at the fringes of Hillbridge's academic endeavour. Although we are not told as much, the ladies of the Lunch Club may very well be professorial spouses. Certainly the presence of the college in town is what drives their need to form a literary discussion group: "We have a standard," insists Mrs Plinth, and the President, Mrs Ballinger, expands, "The object of our little club is to concentrate the highest tendencies of Hillbridge—to centralize and focus its intellectual effort. We aspire to be in touch with what is highest in art, literature, and ethics"(II, 216). No matter that virtually everything in their conversations betrays their lack of interest in and effort at giving substance to their lofty principles.

Among the Hillbridge stories, only "The Descent of Man" centers on a professor in the performance of his functions. Samuel Linyard is a Hillbridge entomologist of some renown, the writer of a "remarkable monograph on the Ethical Reactions of the Infusoria" and an investigator "into the Unconscious Cerebration of the Amoeba" (I, 349). Wharton's satire on Linyard and his professional interests, as the references to his research suggest, are in a mock-serious vein, and the professor's descent from academic gravity and marital probity to financial and material excess, professional mediocrity, and philandering are tracked via the same mock-serious techniques. Along the way Wharton levels her aim as well at Hillbridge's Ladies Debating Club and, ranging abroad beyond the college, at the corruption in the publishing industry as demonstrated by the connivance between publishers and critics to ensure healthy book sales—to which latter abuse Linyard gives at least tacit consent.

With the exception of the late and almost negligible story "Permanent Wave," which may be said to indulge in some satiric humor, Wharton abandoned the practice of satire in her remaining stories of academe, "The Pretext," "The Debt," and "The Day of the Funeral." Of these, "The Debt" comes closest to "The Descent

342

of Man" in its focus on a professor performing duties proper to his state. Galen Dredge is a zoologist at Columbia University, and his story is a highly serious study of moral integrity in the academy. But what obstructs its effectiveness somewhat are certain early references, a book title, the name of an academic chair, that seem to be taking the narrative in a satiric direction. However, the satire never materializes, and one suspects that Wharton did not give herself wholeheartedly to her tale.

Of the locales of Wharton's remaining academic narratives—Wentworth of "The Pretext," Kingsborough of "The Day of the Funeral," and Kingsbridge of "Permanent Wave"—it is the first that is by far the most amply identified and described. Although the tale's central character, Margaret Ransom, has no official status in the life of the university—she is the wife of a local lawyer who is "the legal representative of the University" (I, 636)—she identifies closely with Wentworth, and a number of the important scenes in the story are played out at the campus's exterior and interior places. These places serve to accent both the more romantic and the more inhibiting experiences Margaret faces in the course of the tale. On the sites of the most pastoral of Wharton's fictive campuses Margaret enjoys her idyll with Guy Dawnish; in the college halls where she hears her husband's address she is cowed by the portrait of the college President: husband and President come together to emblemize the prohibiting forces of patriarchy in her life.

No detail is provided about the campuses at either Kingsborough or Kingsbridge, and the action in both "The Day of the Funeral" and "Permanent Wave" is more of the town than of the gown, although there is an academic element to the tales. In "The Day of the Funeral," written for much of its length as the interior monologue of Professor Ambrose Trenham, we are not even informed of his academic discipline, and the action takes place away from the campus at his home and in and around his lover's parents' garage. Seeking to rationalize his extra-marital affair with Barbara Wake, the daughter of a professorial colleague, and the suicide of his wife, he seizes upon the forces of respectability that rule in university life as a way of unburdening himself of guilt. Thinking about the attendance of Barbara at his wife's funeral he imagines that she came "for the sake of appearances. 'Appearances' still ruled at Kingsborough—where didn't they in the university world, and more especially in New England?" (II, 670) Wondering how he will be able to return Barbara's love letters by mail without their being recognized at the post office, he exclaims interiorly, "How it complicated everything to live in a small prying community" (II, 672).

For all its triviality and inconsequence, "Permanent Wave" has a good deal to say about the impact of Kingsbridge life on Nalda, the wife of Vincent Craig, a renowned professor of economics. The thoughtless Nalda's life as a faculty spouse has been further dulled, redundent to say, by her husband's scholarly habits: "he would sit there all evening with his nose in a book" (II, 790); "when a man's life is wrapped up in economics, so little is left over for his wife" (II, 792); "Vincent measured his [hours] by college tasks, professional appointments, literary obligations, or interviewing people about gas and electricity and taxes" (II, 792). Nalda's disenchantment is buttressed by the attitude of Phil Ingerson, the young anthropologist with whom she has planned to flee to Central America. For Ingerson, "the grave was a circus compared with a university town. West of the Rockies academic life might have a little more ginger in it; but in the very capital of the Cut-and-Dried there was nothing doing for a young fellow of such varied ambitious and subversive views..." (II, 792-793).

In the end it does not appear that Nalda Craig satisfies her ambition to escape husband and Kingsbridge with Ingerson. Her affair is ended by her own stupidity and she seems doomed to a long life of four-hour "torture" sessions at Gaston's hair salon. In Wharton's academy the affairs don't work out: not Nalda's, nor Margaret Ransom's, nor Ambrose Trenham's. The known or nebulous forces that set the standards at Kingsbridge, Wentworth, and Kingsborough frown on such dalliance, and we remember with what fewer scruples the denizens of Wharton's higher social sets tolerated—and enjoyed—their illicit alliances.

Wharton's Hillbridge engages no such moral turpitude. Its flaws are mainly intellectual. Only "The Debt's" Columbia University escapes censure, but the tale of the probity of its academicians is not one to stir readers. One has the feeling that Wharton was not particularly at home rendering the American academy, but within that limitation was most comfortable when she took on the chore of holding up to ridicule its stolid insistence on its own importance.

Note

[102] See *Free and Other Stories*, New York: Boni and Liveright, 1918; for "The Old Neighborhood" see *Chains*, Boni and Liveright, 1927. Both stories reappeared in *The Best Short Stories of Theodore Dreiser*, Cleveland: World, 1947, 1956.

Chapter Eight

The Past

Between 1900 and 1928 Wharton published six tales set in the historical past. Of these, five are the products of her first decade of short-story writing and the by-products in one way or another of the writing of her "Italian" novel, *The Valley of Decision* (1902). The sixth story, "Dieu d'Amour," is set on the island of Cyprus, which Wharton visited while on a Mediterranean cruise in 1926. Five of the stories satisfy the periodical requirements of historical fiction. The sixth, "The Confessional," has a present-time setting, but because so much of its content is retrospective and because that retrospective period covers the same period as "The Letter," it qualifies as an historical piece.

Although the history tales do not represent Wharton's best work in the short-story genre, three of them "The Duchess at Prayer," "The Confessional," and "The Hermit and the Wild Woman," cannot be peremptorily dismissed as mediocre works, and they deserve considerably more attention than they have received. There is often a tendency among writers of historical fiction to focus on setting and atmosphere and to neglect probing into characters' psychology. The three aforementioned tales satisfy the latter requirement amply. Of the others, "A Venetian Night's Entertainment" is without much redeeming value, but "The Letter," with its political theme, and "Dieu d'Amour," with its hagiographical, religious, and moral dimensions, are quite readable entertainments.

"The Duchess at Prayer"

The first of Wharton's historical stories, "The Duchess at Prayer," published in *Scribner's* in August 1900, is one of several literary results of her interest in the Italian past, an interest that translated into four other tales and a long novel, *The*

Valley of Decision, in a period of six years at the beginning of the twentieth century. Like the rest of Wharton's historical stories, "The Duchess at Prayer" has not attracted a great deal of critical attention, commentary about it restricted mainly to the literary influences on its composition. Thus Blake Nevius, recalling that Balzac is mentioned oftener than any other fictionist in Wharton's own critical writings, sees the story as "unmistakably a reworking of [the] plot [of] *La Grande Breteche*," (154) and Patricia LaRose Pallis, expanding on Wharton's mention of Browning's impact on her work in *A Backward Glance* and on E. K. Brown's observation that the story is modelled on "My Last Duchess," speaks convincingly of the many analogies between that dramatic monologue and Wharton's tale.[103]

Readers of *The Valley of Decision* will recognize in "The Duchess at Prayer" a number of superficial likenesses to Wharton's 1902 novel. The Duchess's paramour, Ascanio, like Odo Valsecca, had as a boy "been meant for the Church" (I, 234), but had subsequently decided upon another career. There is also the detail of the rumor that Ascanio has tried to carry a nun away from a convent, which has its parallel in Odo's abduction of his future mistress, Fulvia Vivaldi, from the convent of Santa Chiara in Milan. Certain passages in the short story resemble, albeit faintly, the lush descriptions that chacterize Wharton's Italian novel. The detailing of the pleasures available to the Duchess at Benta is repeated in Wharton's evocations of life in the eighteenth-century Italy of *The Valley of Decision*: "Her father, it appears, had a grand palace there with such gardens, bowling alleys, grottoes and casinos as never were; gondolas bobbing at the watergates, a stable full of gilt coaches, a theater full of players, and kitchens and offices full of cooks and lackeys to serve up chocolate all day long to the fine ladies in masks and furbelows with their pet dogs and their blackamoors and their *abates*" (I, 233).

Readers familiar with Wharton's stories will also detect in "The Duchess at Prayer" the presence of a similar set of main characters and a situation that informs three of her ghost tales, "The Lady's Maid's Bell," "Kerfol," and "Mr. Jones": a wife of some social stature and wealth, neglected and/or abused by her husband, suffers the cruel results of his rancor, especially when he discovers that his continual absence has caused her to seek out, and usually to find, another companion. It is evident that a number of Wharton's ghost stories are historical tales in the same sense as are the stories discussed in this chapter.

Most of the historical stories use the same narrative approach: they begin in the fictive present—or at a time not far removed from it—each narrator proceeding to introduce a story-teller who recounts the tale which is the central focus of the short story in question. One critical element pertinent to the evaluation of these stories is, therefore, the extent and effectiveness of the organic relationship set up between the short story itself and its internal tale. In "The Duchess at Prayer" the narrator provides some four pages of description, commentary, and dialogue between himself and his aged story-teller before allowing the latter to begin his narrative and then removes himself entirely until the old man has almost concluded. The narrator's descriptions center on the appearance of the long-uninhabited villa he is visiting and accentuate the coldness he experiences there. As he emerges momentarily from the inside and feels the "lifeless" August air, even the latter "seemed light and vivifying after the atmosphere of the shrouded rooms.... Their chill was on me as I hugged the sunshine" (I, 229). The villa's outside space is suffused with an aura of ugliness, destruction, and death. The narrator looks upon "the mutilated vases of the gate" (I, 229), and "Everywhere were vanishing traces of that fantastic horticulture" of the place; "maimed statues stretched their arms like rows of whining beggars" (I, 230); "Lizards shot out of the cracked soil like flames and the bench in the laurustinus niche was strewn with the blue varnished bodies of dead flies" (I, 232).

In this mindset of coldness and disarray, of deterioration and death, the narrator is shown by the old story-teller the three pieces of art which become at once the *raison d'être* and point of departure for the latter's narrative journey back in time: the portrait of Ercole II, "the lips weak and vain" (I, 230) and that of his first Duchess, the face pliant and laughing; the sculpture of the same Duchess at prayer in the villa's chapel, the face now filled with "hate, revolt and agony" (I, 231). Though life and vitality have not been entirely absent from Ercole's villa during the two hundred years since the tale's events occurred—the Duke "brought home a new Duchess who gave him a son and five daughters" (I, 244); the old story-teller's grandmother, by whom he claims to have been told the tale of the villa, was able to smile, despite the tragedy she was privy to, when "they put her first child in her arms" (I, 233)—nevertheless it is the horrible deaths of Violante and her lover that have left their indelible mark on the place. By the time the tale proper begins, the narrator's opening philosophical reflections about the enigmatic façades of Italian dwellings have concretized into a view of the villa as a corpse "composed as a dead face, with the cypresses flanking it for candles" (I, 233).

The dialogue between the narrator and the story-teller also serves as an organic link between the short story *per se* and its internal tale. The narrator is astonished that the latter's grandmother could have been Violante's maid, for the story she has told her grandson when he was a child took place some two hundred years before. The story-teller does not deny the possibility that his claim as to the source of his tale has been exaggerated. "It's possible, you think," he says to the narrator, "she may have heard from others what she afterward fancied she may have seen herself? How that is it's not for an unlettered man to say, though I myself seem to have seen many of the things she told me" (I, 233). His statement, of course, acknowledges the possibility that his tale is partly an invention of his own—as many oral tales are in any case—and indeed the old man confounds his guest, and the reader, with the agility of his mind and the creativity and memory of his narration: he brings to a moribund setting and a devastating series of events a vitality that transforms and transcends the unpleasantness of the present and the horror of the past. Although the narrator initially responds negatively to the story-teller's agedness ("He was the oldest man I had ever seen; so sucked back into the past that he seemed more like a memory than a living being"), and although he suspects that his cooperativeness is motivated by pecuniary considerations ("The one trait linking him with the actual was the fixity with which his small saurian eye held the pocket that, as I entered, had yielded a *lira* to the gatekeeper's child") (I, 229), by the end of the story he has put aside his doubts about his vitality and good intentions and is left uncharacteristically speechless by his final disclosures.

The tale itself of Violante, Ascanio, and Ercole is marked by a subtlety and suggestiveness that is a trait of many of Wharton's stories. Indeed Wharton was the bane of popular magazine editors and readers, who expected her to be far more explicit than she was about explaining puzzling and mysterious happenings in her stories, and who sometimes rejected her material because they considered it too obscure. In "The Duchess at Prayer" the ending of the old man's story is shrouded in the kind of indefiniteness that teases the literal-minded to death. The reader is not told directly that Ascanio is sealed up in the chapel crypt, nor that Violante has been poisoned to death. Neither is he/she told who is responsible for Violante's death, nor of the exact nature and extent of the intimacy of the relations between Ascanio and Violante. But for all that, there is a marvellous revelation about the text, and most particularly about the dialogues between Ercole and Violante on the day of the latter's death. These dialogues are masterpieces of irony, innuendo, understatement, and euphemism: nothing is said but all is understood. In the first, which takes place in the chapel after the unexpected arrival of the Duke with the statue replicating his wife, the tone and nature of the conversation is set by Ercole's greeting: "Madam I could have had no greater happiness than thus to surprise you at your devotions" (I, 239). What ensues is a verbal sparring match between Ercole and Violante in which the former reveals to the latter his knowledge of Ascanio's presence in the crypt, and in which the latter at first parries with witty pleasantries and then, when she realizes fully the implications of her husband's intended placement of the statue, engages in a series of verbal attempts to forstall his plan.

Throughout the dialogue the Duke's irony and innuendo is directed to his wife's devotions, and here one sees the dual significance of Wharton's title. The Duchess in effigy is indeed at prayer, but the statue that memorializes her piety has snuffed out the real object of her devotions, Ascanio. Most of Ercole's words play off the *double entendre* of the story's title, from his aforementioned greeting to the Duchess to the statement of his purpose in placing the statue over the entrance to the crypt: "for not only would I thereby mark your special devotion to the blessed saint who rests there, but, by sealing up the opening in the pavement, would assure the perpetual preservation of that holy martyr's bones, which hitherto have been too thoughtlessly exposed to sacrilegous attempts" (I, 240-241). Ercole's *double entendre* is not lost on Violante and desperation replaces her early wit. As the two part, "the Duchess gave one look as the souls in hell may have looked when the gates closed on our Lord" (I, 242).

The last dialogue between Ercole and Violante takes place a short time later in the parlor to which the former has invited himself to dine with his wife. No doubt in an attempt to seduce her husband into reversing his drastic gesture, Violante has "dressed herself with extraordinary splendor, powdering her hair with gold, painting her face and bosom, and covering herself with jewels till she shone like our Lady of Loreto" (I, 242). The early part of the meeting has given the illusion to "the pantry lad who brought up the dishes and waited in the cabinet" that "the talk continued, with such gay sallies on the part of the Duchess, such tender advances on the Duke's, that the lad declared they were for all the world like a pair of lovers courting on a summer's night in the vineyard" (I, 243). But the Duke is unwilling to ignore the existence of his supposed rival, indeed may have deliberately built up Violante's hopes for a reprieve on Ascanio's life by appearing to succumb to his wife's allure. In any case the scene soon moves from softness to harshness, from innuendo to explicitness, and Violante's violent and fatal illness ensues.

A few final comments prompted by the closing Section V of "The Duchess at Prayer" are appropriate. Here we learn of the alleged origin of the change in the countenance of the statue of the Duchess from "the sweet and smiling look"of the day of its arrival to the "frozen horror" of "hate, revolt and agony"(I, 244) of the next day. The mysterious transformation of the statue's face is the stuff of myth and hearsay—and not very important in any final analysis of the story. What is important is that when the grandmother goes to the chapel to pray for her deceased mistress, she sees the transformed face and hears "a low moaning...that seemed to come from [the statue's] lips" (I, 244) but which in fact confirms—if any confirmation is needed—the presence of the buried Ascanio beneath. As for the other important revelation of this final section, that "the Duke had locked the chapel door and forbidden any to set foot there" (I, 244), one is surely put in mind again of that other Italian Duke who "gave commands/Then all smiles stopped together."

"The Confessional"

Wharton's second Italian story, "The Confessional," appeared in April 1901 in her collection *Crucial Instances*, only nine months after "The Duchess at Prayer," and it is a product of the same general interest that sparked the earlier story and *The Valley of Decision*. However, "The Confessional" and another story that appeared three years after it, "The Letter," are both inspired by a more recent series of events in Italian history, the *risorgimento*, the unification movement of the nineteenth century. Both *risorgimento* stories pay more than lip service to the movement, making use of the persons and actions associated with it and also placing their central characters in the very midst of its political events.

As with "The Duchess at Prayer," Wharton's narrative method in "The Confessional" is to tell her story using two narrators, each speaking in the first person. The primary narrator, a sophisticated New York accountant, Anglo-Saxon probably, makes the acquaintance of an older Italian priest, Don Egidio, who after some time takes his friend into his confidence and tells him the tale that accounts for his presence in America. "The Confessional" is a story of much broader scope than its predecessor: as a result, we learn considerably more about its primary narrator than we do about the primary narrator of "The Duchess at Prayer." Indeed the accountant/narrator's role is intimately connected by analogy with important elements in the saga of the priest, and a strong link is forged between the framing story and its inner tale that brings the two narratives close to having a seamless unity.

If at the outset the accountant's cultivation of a friendship with Don Egidio is motivated by his interest in what he refers to as the "local color" of the Italian community in which he lives, it is the common love of Italy, which the narrator has visited earlier in his life, that strengthens the friendship: that common attachment is strong enough to transcend the differences in age, vocation, language, nationality, and probably religious belief that might under other circumstances act as barriers between the two men. For the young man the friendship is manifested by his material assistance of the poor priest in the form of such luxuries as a gas stove and an easy chair, and by the psychological supports of conversation and companionship to one whose usual associations do not much furnish such support. For Don Egidio it is shown by his frequent appearances at the accountant's lodging and his willingness to confide in him.

Don Egidio's ultimate gesture of confiding to his friend the story of his past is a long time coming. It occurs after at least one abortive attempt on the narrator's part to draw it out, an attempt that is countered by Don Egidio's abruptly changing the subject of conversation. More importantly, it occurs after the narrator has established his concern for Don Egidio in a very substantial and active way in the matter that is closest to the priest's heart, the annual tribute he pays at the grave of his deceased friend and patron, Count Roberto Siviano. When Don Egidio realizes that his young friend is caring enough to follow the priest to the cemetary when the former fears for the old man's ability to survive the elements, he senses that he has found the potential perpetuator of his ritual of homage. But the narrator's spontaneous promise to maintain the tradition is not enough. "...[You] are young and at your age life is a mistress who kisses away sad memories," Don Egidio tells him. "But I will tell you [Roberto's] story—and then I think that neither joy nor grief will let you forget him" (I, 321).

This launches Don Egidio into his tale, Roberto's story, as he calls it. But it is his own life story as well, and this side of it is the more important one for the narrator. Don Egidio has underestimated his power to touch the narrator, and interestingly enough, the latter has already met the test the priest feared would be his undoing, for in order to seek out the priest on the day of his tribute at Roberto's grave he has passed up what his youth proffered: "a feminine alternative" to his cancelled business appointment, "a certain hospitable luncheon table" (I, 319). The tale Don Egidio tells the narrator serves the needs of both men, each in its own way: it satisfies the listener's curiosity about his friend, a curiosity that is motivated at this point by deep affection and not simply by his penchant for local color, and the speaker's need to confess his sacerdotal misdemeanour, his part in the violation of the seal of the confessional.

The critical portion of Don Egidio's tale is set against the background of the years immediately leading up to the abortive revolution of 1848, and culminates during the days of the bloody riots in Milan. Once we are provided early in the narration with the necessary family background of Don Egidio and Count Roberto Siviano, the major players in the drama that causes the forced emigration of both men to the United States, the story soon resolves itself into a political and nationalistic one. Don Egidio imparts a strong sense of his own and Roberto's fervor for the cause of Italian independence and unification and of their concomitant hatred of the Austrian oppressor. Within the extended Siviano family, sides form on the basis of members' allegiance to the Italian cause on the one hand or their mollifying or sycophantic attitude towards the Austrians on the other. Thus, Roberto and his sister, Marianna, distance themselves as much as is civilly possible from their younger brother, Andrea, and his wife, Gemma, because the latter's aunt has married an Austrian and has retained certain sympathies with the other side. As well, Roberto's father-in-law, "a beggarly Milanese of the noble family of Intelvi...had cut himself off from his class by accepting an appointment in one of the government offices" (I, 326). Don Egidio is also a staunch patriot, a liberal like most of the northern clergy, he explains, and his avowals of his political position are exceeded in intensity only by his declarations of Roberto's commitment to the Cause. Throughout, Don Egidio's tale is liberally sprinkled with the names of the familiar principals, places, and events that dominate the period: Cavour, Gioberti, Metternich and Raditsky, the Piedmont and Mantua, the election of Pius X and the revolt in Vienna.

Of course, it is the Italo-Austrian conflict that is at the heart of the personal elements of the priest's tale, and of the episode that seals the fate of both Don Egidio and Roberto. Here, the hitherto unproblematical Austrian connections in the Siviano family come together to disrupt Roberto's confidence in his young wife, Faustina, and his marriage: his brother and sister-in-law tell him that his wife has a lover, Frank Wilkenstern, the son of Gemma's Austrian aunt, whom she has met at the home of her brother-in-law, Andrea.

All things turn on the ensuing manipulation of the act of sacramental confession that Roberto engineers and acts out in order to satisfy himself about the truth or falsity of the accusation made about Faustina. In his desire to know the truth, Roberto is motivated not merely by the possibility that he has been cuckolded, and by a hated Austrian at that, but also by the recognition that if he is killed in the upcoming fighting in Naples, Faustina will be left alone to suffer the reputation of her infidelity, "the slow unsleeping hate...the lies [that] will fasten themselves to her and suck out her life" (I, 335). In his coercion of Don Egidio to cooperate in his sacrilegious plan, Roberto plays upon the question of Faustina's future, a legitimate concern in itself, if hardly a justification for breaking the seal of the confessional. But other aspects of Roberto's strong-arming of the priest are without any mitigating elements.

In the first place Roberto's attempts to break down Don Egidio's adament refusal to have Roberto replace him in the confessional make use of motives of patriotism. When he says to the priest, "We laymen are ready to give the last shred of flesh from our bones, but you priests intend to keep your cassocks whole" (I, 335), he is trying to shame him into believing that his abdication of his priestly function would be a patriotic act. In fact, Roberto's insistence that the defense of his wife's reputation is somehow related to the Cause is an exaggerated extension of his passionately militant pro-Italian and anti-Austrian sentiments and a reflection of what his life has been since the beginning of his patriotic involvement. His very marriage can be said to have been eagerly inspired by his desire to remove Faustina from the clutches of the Austrians, as from the eyes of the officers he sees ogling her on the morning of their first acquaintance. Once married, he has virtually abandoned her in favor of his devotion to his country. His exclamation of anguish when he considers the implications of Faustina's possible infidelity is most telling in this regard. Asked to "quiet" himself by Don Egidio, who fears his rising emotion, he replies: "Quiet myself? With this sting in my blood? A lover—and an Austrian lover! Oh, Italy, Italy my bride!" (I, 334).

But the most reprehensible aspect of Roberto's assault on Don Egidio's resistance is his summoning up of the priest's humble family roots and the role of the Siviano family in his taking holy orders. When Don Egidio invokes the fact that the dispensation from his priestly duty to protect the integrity of the sacrament is not his to grant—"[M]y cassock is not mine," he says—Roberto replies. "And, by God, you are right; for it's mine! Who put it on your back but my father? What kept it there but my charity? Peasant! Beggar! Hear his holiness pontificate!"(I, 335). Moments later upon Faustina's arrival to confess, Don Egidio capitulates, "no more than a straw on the torrent of [Roberto's] will" (I, 336). Don Egidio's sensitiveness about his family's poverty and his sense of indebtedness to the Sivianos is one of his first revelations to the narrator as he begins his tale. The Siviano villa was "the home of the kindest friends that ever took a poor lad by the hand" and the family offered an idyllic life to "an ignorant peasant lad." "Do you wonder," he asks the narrator, "I was ready to kiss the ground they trod, and would have given the last drop of my blood to serve them?" And of Roberto he recalls, "it seemed to me natural enough that such a godlike being should lord it over a poor clodhopper like myself" (I, 322). It may be said that Don Egidio's betrayal of his sacred trust derives from a flawed image of himself, just as Roberto's desecration of the sacrament derives from a flawed sense of patriotism.

Roberto's words to the intimate group gathered the following morning to see him off to Milan exonerate his wife: "I declare my wife innocent and my honor satisfied" (I, 338), he tells the family. Thus, backed by the alleged truth of Faustina's confession, Andrea's and Gemma's plan to disinherit Faustina's child is foiled. Of course, later events establish that Roberto has lied about his wife's confession and that, in fact, she has acknowledged her guilt. As she did in "The Duchess at Prayer" Wharton has veiled the closing event of "The Confessional" in inexplicitness. Much is left to the reader's surmise and conjecture. Given the later details of Roberto's secret expatriation to the United States and his decision to remain there *sub rosa* for the rest of his life, one has little choice but to assume that he is removing himself from what he considers an untenable future with an unfaithful wife and a rival's child. Other textual details as well conspire to suggest Faustina's guilt. At the moment of Roberto's revelation that he has taken Don Egidio's place in the confessional , "a strange look flitted over Faustina's face" (I, 337), and when he declares her innocent, "her face was a wonder to behold" (I, 338). Information

356

provided prior to Roberto's revelations also leads to the same conclusion. Faustina has for some time refused to go to confession; when she returns to the villa at Siviano after her time in Milan "one could not look at her without ransacking the spring for new smiles to paint her freshness" (I, 328); at the time she became pregnant Roberto was deeply involved with the Cause; there is a parallel situation to Faustina's in "the girl who met the Austrian soldier at the fair at Peshiera" (I, 331), for whom Faustina provides financial support.

Early in "The Confessional" when the narrator questions Don Egidio as to where he is bringing flowers on a snowy November morning and endangering his feeble health, the latter replies: "I go to place these on the grave of the noblest man that ever lived" (I, 318). And the closing words of his tale again attest to his friend's stature, to "his just life and holy death" (I, 343). Don Egidio is impressed by the immensity of Roberto's sacrifice, for although he is never told of the reasons for his friend's flight from Italy, he senses what they are. The closest he and the reader come to having an answer to that question lies in the brief exchange between Roberto and Don Egidio during their time of contact in New York. One day Roberto asks Don Egidio why he has been sent to New York. "The blood rushed to my face," the priest recalls, "and before I could answer he had raised a silencing hand. 'I see,' he said; 'it was your penance too'" (I, 342-343). If Don Egidio's bishop has exiled him to atone for his sin, Roberto's has been a self-imposed exile, away from his beloved Italy, his beloved Cause, and his beloved Faustina, and Don Egidio sees in him the nobility that would sacrifice his own passionate attachments rather than run the risk of prejudicing the future of his wife, and her child.

"The Confessional" ends with Don Edigio's eulogization of Roberto. Although the priest has opened his tale with the primary narrator squarely in mind— "You tell me that you know our little lake; and if you have seen it you will understand" (I, 321)—and although much of the earlier part of the story is given over to the relationship between Don Egidio and the narrator, the latter has disappeared as a focus of interest by the end, relegated solely to the role of listener. E. K. Brown praised Wharton's taking on such a complex narrative, adding that it did not entirely fail (11, 12), and Wharton herself acknowledged the trouble she was having with the story when she wrote Brownell at *Scribner's* that it required doing "on such a large scale with so much broader strokes than most of my stories" (*EW* 98). When Henry James suggested that the story's weakness lay in Wharton's difficulty handling the "completely foreign subject, the second-hand Italy of... 'The Confessional'," (Bell 247) he was probably acknowledging his own bias against historical fiction. The failure of "The Confessional" resides in its difficulty with the American subject, the New York portion. One senses that at a certain point, that is, immediately following the aforementioned exchange between Don Egidio and Roberto about their respective emigrations to America, Wharton has capitulated to the scope and complexity of her narrative and has seen that it required a longer form to be adequately realized. The sentence, "During the first few years [Roberto] had plenty of work to do, but he lived so frugally that I [Don Egidio] guessed he had some secret use for his earnings" (I, 343), passing up as it does the dramatic possibilities of the previous exchange, signals Wharton's waving the white flag. Nevertheless, one must applaud the skill with which she has merged widely different themes and especially the wit and originality with which she has managed the subject of the seal of the confessional.

"A Venetian Night's Entertainment"

For her third Italian story, "A Venetian Night's Entertainment," published in *Scribner's* in December 1903, Wharton drew upon the same general background of the eighteenth century as she had for *The Valley of Decision*, but her short story is in a much lighter vein. Barbara White's comment on it is to the point: "[It is] a colorful account of a con game in eighteenth-century Venice. Perhaps the story, absolutely all plot, succeeds in being entertaining because it attempts no more" (6). Possibly the lightest piece Wharton ever wrote, it has prompted scarcely a word from critics.

An interesting difference between "A Venetian Night's Entertainment" and the other Italian stories lies is in its narrative voice and perspective. Here there is but one narrator, an unnamed third-person voice, who introduces the tale of young Tony Bracknell's victimization by a gang of Venetian con artists. In a brief opening paragraph the narrator informs the reader of the habit of Tony, now a judge, of telling his tale to his grandchildren in his posh Boston home, one of the tangible fruits of the successful East India trading company in which his family has been a major partner. But for this opening paragraph, the entirety of the story is devoted to the Judge's tale: there is no attempt to tie the narrative context to the tale itself.

This tale sees Tony rescued from his predicament by his tutor, the Reverend Ozias Mounce, and by the Captain of the family trader the Hepzibah B, none the worse for wear. The most interesting facet of Tony's entrapment is the description of his predisposition for a fall. From the time of his childhood Venice had summoned up magical visions for Tony. The print entitled "St Mark's Square in Venice," which hung in the hall of the family home in Salem, had fed his fancy, had been "the first step of a cloud ladder leading to a land of dreams." Venice remained for him as he grew into young manhood a place "between reality and illusion," and Wharton catches Tony's state of suspension in her evocation of his first sight of the city as the Hepzibah B sails towards it: "And now here was his wish taking shape before him, as the distant haze of gold shaped itself into towers and domes across the morning sea!" (I, 476). When he steps off the boat some time later and walks on to St Mark's Square, he is in essence walking back into the picture of his childhood recollection.

Wharton insists on limiting her story to an entertainment in the face of ample potential within her text to make it considerably more than that. The fact that the beauteous Polixena Cador reciprocates Tony's attraction to and consideration for her is evident, but Wharton passes up the opportunity of entering into an examination of a love match that would be much complicated by the circumstances of the young persons' meeting. Nor does she follow up the other even more tantalizing prospect of the story: the tension between Tony's longing "to get away into such a world" as Venice promises and his awareness of the world of his Calvinist tutor and "the axioms in his hornbook [that] brought home to him his heavy responsibilities as a Christian and a sinner" (I, 476). The fact that Wharton weighted the story with such possibilities suggests something, perhaps, about her reluctance to indulge in writing a mere entertainment.

"The Letter"

With the publication of "The Letter" in *Harper's Monthly* in April 1904, Wharton returned to the familiar terrain of the *risorgimento*, the setting for her 1901 story, "The Confessional." Perhaps in an attempt to address the problems of length and control that had dogged her efforts with the earlier story, she seems to have deliberately limited her scope by using fewer characters and by restricting the byplay between the general narrator and the inside story-teller, Colonel Alingdon, to the story's two-page introduction: after the narrator has introduced Alingdon, an old freedom fighter turned art scholar, he removes himself entirely from "The Letter," presenting the Colonel's tale with the upper-case rubric "COLONEL ALINGDON'S STORY" and allowing the latter to spin his yarn in the first person. The result is that "The Letter" is a much tighter tale than "The Confessional," but lack's the latter's complexity and color. What little critical commentary "The Letter" has garnered is negative. It is a "superficial melodrama," (Brown 13) and "perhaps Wharton's worst effort [in the short story]" (White 78).

Besides its common historical background with "The Confessional," "The Letter" shares with that story the theme of admiration for a courage and nobility of a reticent passive kind. If Roberto Siviano of "The Confessional" is for Don Egidio "the noblest man that ever lived" (I, 318), Donna Candida's act of destroying the "deathbed" letter of her brother to their mother is, for Alingdon, "the bravest thing I ever saw done by a woman" (I, 494). Alingdon's early statement to the general narrator sets up the context of Candida's admirable act: "The Italian war of independence was really carried on underground; it was one of those awful silent struggles which are so much more terrible than the roar of a battle. It's a deuced sight easier to charge with your regiment than to lie rotting in an Austrian prison and know that if you give up the name of a friend or two you can go back scot-free to your wife and children. Thousands and thousands of Italians had the choice given them—and hardly one went back" (I, 494). Although Candida has not been jailed, her gesture resembles in spirit those of her fellow patriots.

That Candida's act transcends for Alingdon those other lives of passive valor is probably a measure of his romantic attachment to her and of the passage of the years, and readers may infer from his reference to the fact that "the Jack Alingdon she knew" (I, 498) died with her years ago that she has left him broken-hearted.

That interpretation would give rise to such a view as Brown's—that the story is a "superficial melodrama."

However, Alingdon's reference to his figurative passing, the death of "the Jack Alingdon she knew," may be merely to his change of occupation from revolutionary to art scholar, and it is the realization that the story is told by one who is passionately devoted to the study of Italian art that alerts the reader to the essential colorlessness of the tale. Compared to the evocative story of the old man of "The Duchess at Prayer" and to the sophisticated narrations of both Don Egidio and the young accountant of "The Confessional," Alingdon's recapitulation of events is prosaic and plain, devoid of the kind of references to art that his current avocation should enable him to bring to it. It is not, after all, the sentimental aspects of "The Letter" that render it unsuccessful but rather its plainness, its inability to exploit the possibilities of the rich background from which it is drawn, that is its final undoing.

"The Hermit and the Wild Woman"

When Wharton next returned to the historical short story with the publication of "The Hermit and the Wild Woman" in the February 1906 issue of *Scribner's*, she set her tale in a more remote period of the Italian past than she had previously exploited, late medieval times. As befits the story's distance in time, she chose to create a tale more fantastic than realistic and couched it in an idiom fitting for such a tale. For Lewis, Wharton's style here is "pretentious...founded on that of the lives of the saints" (*ICSS* XVIII), but all readers will not agree with that assessment. Some will see in the cadences of Wharton's sentences reflections of Biblical and mythical prose. Brown's comment that the story has exquisite charm and imparts a sense of late medieval history (19) seems closer to the mark than Lewis's blanket condemnation of it as "a tedious and contrived piece of work" (*ICSS* XVIII).

Criticism on the substance of "The Hermit and the Wild Woman" has centered on the autobiographical. For Lewis, "It becomes uncomfortably clear that the relation between the Wild Woman and the Hermit is an elementary version...of the relation between Edith Wharton and Walter Berry, during the period when she was escaping or trying to escape from her own convent, her marriage." The tale describes her "burning desire for total intimacy with Walter Berry, along with her tormented meditation on the sinfulness or lack of it of the extramarital physical relation" (*ICSS* XVIII-XIX). White extends Lewis's interpretation. "It seems more likely," she writes, "that the hermit and the wild woman represent two sides of Wharton herself, and the conflict should be construed more broadly." Like the hermit, Wharton is "a solitary person" whose "family [have] been dead to [her]"; she is a writer and gardener like the wild woman, she possesses intuitive powers, "openness to feeling" and "does not deny the erotic" (72). Without emphasizing exclusively the autobiographical aspects of "The Hermit and the Wild Woman," Josephine Donovan develops the notion of the wild woman as one who celebrates the erotic in the broadest sense of the term. "Bathing becomes a symbol of sensual participation in the green world, forbidden by patriarchy," she writes. "[The wild woman] lives her life out in the wilderness, tending her garden and eating as a vegetarian.... She is also adept at herbal medicine. She is, in short, a Diana figure..." (62).

Certainly there is much validity in the views of Lewis, White, and Donovan, and the elements they identify are important facets of the story. Yet it is possible to take a more comprehensive view of "The Hermit and the Wild Woman," Lewis's insistence that its "interest is almost entirely autobiographical" notwithstanding (*ICSS* XVIII). It is worth noting that the hermit's visit to the Saint of the Rock, described in Part III, is ignored in the aforementioned critics' comments, and that in a story where human contacts are at a premium it is perhaps important to attend to the few that do occur. An examination of the different approaches to holiness or closeness to God taken by the Saint of the Rock and the Wild Woman and of their impact on the Hermit suggests that Wharton's tale can be read as the dramatization of the preeminence of one form of spirituality over another.

Wharton immediately establishes the milieu and context in which her central character, the Hermit, will play out his days: his life is essentially one directed toward the salvation of his soul. Of a noble family, he has been orphaned after an attack on the family keep, and he flies from the horror to the wholeness of the "still woods" and "unmutilated earth" with "no wish to go back. His longing was to live hidden from life" (I, 571). He had been a religious child, delighting in listening to the histories of the Desert Fathers, "serving Mass for the chaplain in the early morning,...[feeling] his heart flutter up and up...till it was lost in infinite space and brightness," and watching the "foreign painter" draw forth his "celestial faces" on the chapel wall. (I, 511-512) Concomitantly he has possessed a strong sense and fear of evil as it is embodied in the "gnawing monsters about the church porch, evil-faced bats and dragons, giant worms and winged bristling hogs, the devil's flock...(I, 572). The massacre that sends him running to the woods incarnates the world of evil, and his aspirations to rise to God and to avoid sin meld into a single concern for eternal salvation. He settles in a cave on the side of a hill, within earshot of the church bells of his native town, separated from the body of the Church but living in its spirit. In this state he grows into manhood living the solitary life of a hermit through the cycle of the seasons," never restless or discontented" (I, 572), his simple needs provided for by his own resourcefulness and by the peasants who admire his godly life.

After many years the Hermit breaks his routine by undertaking a long journey to visit a man known in the land as the Saint of the Rock. The Hermit is drawn to this man, for he believes he recognizes in his holiness and austerity the ultimate model of godliness: the Saint has made his home in the hollow of a rock and lives seated there "[facing] the west, so that in winter he should have small warmth of the sun and in summer be consumed by it" (I, 574). But the Saint of the Rock receives his visitor indifferently and even angrily, and the latter is completely disillusioned with their meeting. He is "sorely abashed," and "his heart sank and for the first time he felt the weariness of the way he had traveled." Even the honeycomb offered by the Saint's attendant as the Hermit walks away is of no comfort to him, "for his heart hungered more than his body; and his tears made the honeycomb bitter" (I, 577). The Saint has considered the Hermit's visit an intrusion on his life of silence, has not communicated with him, has responded to him without warmth, ignoring the huge effort made by his visitor, and the human bond between them. Although the Saint shares with the Hermit the desire for holiness and salvation, he has chosen to lead a life devoid of human and natural relatedness. In aspiring to a higher life he has forsaken not merely the world of evil and material gain and comfort, but the world of humans and of the natural order. His rejection of the Hermit is of a piece with his avoidance of every "spreading tree" and "gushing fountain" (I, 574). Whereas the Hermit "felt such love for all created things that to him the bare rocks sang of their maker" (I, 575), the Saint views his barren rock as a fitting emblem and locale for his transcending of the dross of earthly existence. He is another version of the band of Flagellants the Hermit had once seen "showing their gaunt scourged bodies and exhorting the people to turn from soft raiment and delicate fare, from marriage and money-getting and dancing and games" (I, 572).

The Hermit returns from his visit to the Saint "heavy of heart, for his long pilgrimage had brought him only weariness and humiliation." What immediately lifts his spirits is the sight of his garden, about whose condition he had worried while he was away: "[its] soil shone with moisture, and his plants had shot up, fresh and glistening, to a height they had never attained" (I, 577). He soon realizes that the care of his garden has been effected by the woman he finds asleep in his cave, the Wild Woman of the story. In a word, the violence done to his soul by his repudiation at the hands of the Saint has been assuaged by the Woman. This moment, central to the meaning of the story because it juxtaposes the contrasting spiritualities represented by the Saint and the Woman, marks the beginning of an evolution in the awareness of the Hermit as to the nature of spirituality and ultimately forces him to bring about a change in his own notion of holiness.

The Hermit's observations of and conversation with the Woman when he finds her in his cave, and her ensuing recounting to him of her life story establish the important similarities and differences between her and the two male principals of Wharton's tale. Like the Hermit, she had taken up her abode in the woods, th' immediate reasons for her escape there reminiscent of his own: "the land...whe' she came was full of armed companies and bands of marauders, and...great li and bloodshed prevailed there" (I, 577). Her description of the armed m preyed on her reminds him of "his little sister lying with her throat slit a' altar, and of the scenes of blood and rapine from which he had fle' wilderness" (I, 578). Struck first by the "strange amulets about h' perceives "among the heathen charms, an Agnus Dei in her bosom" (I, 577), and she acknowledges that she is a Christian and recites piously the Angelus with him. She shares with the Hermit, and with the Saint as well, a commitment to formal Christianity and to a life of solitude, and a rejection of material attachments.

But at the same time the woman's spirituality has a unique flavor that distinguishes it markedly from that of the other two. Shocked that she is a renegade nun ("the thought of her wickedness weighed on him") the Hermit asks that the Woman explain "her abominable sin" (I, 578). Thus ensues the Woman's story, Part IV of Wharton's tale, told in the first person, as if Wharton did not wish the primary narrator, whose point of view is that of the Hermit, to intrude upon the Woman's thoughts. The Woman's story centers on the reason for her escape from the nunnery in which she has been "put" after her mother's death. Here her days and nights are dominated by oppressive heat and confinement and by the absence of even the sight of the beautiful natural things of creation. From her cell she sees all day long "the sun beat as with flails of fire...and the sweating peasants toil up and down behind their thirsty asses, and the beggars whining, and scraping their sores" (I, 579). When she convinces the Abbess to give her a cell overlooking the garden, she finds that at "the approach of midsummer the garden, being all enclosed with buildings, grew as stifling as my cell. All the green things in it withered and dried off, leaving trenches of bare red earth, across which the cypresses cast strips of shade too narrow to cool the aching heads of the nuns." In a word the Woman is virtually smothered physically and psychologically: she speaks of removing her "stifling gown" and "hanging it over her grated window, but the darkness choked me, and I struggled for breath as though I lay at the bottom of a pit" (I, 580).

Despite the Woman's praying for "the gift of holiness," her applying herself to "a devouter way of living" and her confiding her problems to the Abbess (I, 580), she is unable to transcend her plight, and she longs for the forbidden pleasure of bathing in the pool located in the convent. Discovered hovering close to the tank one day by the other nuns, she is reported to the abbess, who punishes her severely, ordering her "to sleep every night for a month in [her] heavy gown, with a veil upon [her] face." It is this penance that "drove [her] to sin," she tells the Hermit. (I, 581)

The Woman's description of her "sin," the violation of her vow of obedience, her immersion in the pool, is at the heart of her distinctiveness from the Saint of the Rock and to a lesser extent from the Hermit.

> To prolong the joy (of the ecstacy [of] that first touch of water on my limbs) I let myself slip in slowly, resting my hand on the edge of the tank, and smiling to see my body, as I lowered it, break up the shining black surface and shatter the star beams into splinters. And the water...seemed to crave me as I craved it. Its ripples rose about me, first in furtive touches, then in a long embrace that clung and drew me down, till at length they lay like kisses on my lips. It was no frank comrade like the mountain pools of my childhood, but a secret playmate compassionating my pains and soothing them with noiseless hands. From the first I thought of it as an accomplice, its whisper seemed to promise me mercy if I would promise it love. And I went back and back to it...; all day I lived in the thought of it; each night I stole to it with fresh thirst.... (I, 581-582)

For one thing, the Woman's action is a repudiation of the austerity of the penance imposed by the Abbess, an austerity that can be associated with that of the Saint of the Rock. In itself the action is one that acknowledges the integrity of the body and of bodily pleasure and sees no disparity between those and holiness. And when she is discovered in her forbidden bathings, the Woman escapes from the convent with a clear conscience, sure of her ground, "resigned to any hardship,...if only I may sleep under the free heaven and wash the dirt from my body in cool water" (I, 582).

The rest of "The Hermit and the Wild Woman" details, from the point of view of the Hermit, the remainder of the lives of the two title characters together, for they live virtually as one in spirit, though unjoined in the flesh, united in a common commitment to the salvation of their souls and the care of their fellow men and women. Although the Hermit is at first "dismayed that such sinfulness should cross his path" (I, 582), his negative feelings towards the Woman gradually fall away. Nevertheless he does not renege on his desire that she must be converted from her sins of fleshly indulgence until he realizes to his shame at the end of her life that he "had cursed a dying saint, and announced her aloud to all the people" (I, 588-589). It can be said that if he does not accept or understand during her life-time the intrinsic value of her respect for and celebration of her body, he acts in the spirit of the good

Christian who blesses the sinner though condemning the sin. Thus, remembering his own desire to exult in the lauds he has written, "he dared not judge his sister's fault too harshly" (I, 582); he promises not to betray her whereabouts to her Order and begins "to doubt whether she had any calling to the life enclosed" (I, 584); "his heart hung back" (I, 586) when he feels constrained to beg her to return to her convent.

As for the Woman, she remains true to herself. If at one point the Hermit becomes convinced that he has converted her from her attachment to the flesh, he has mistakenly interpreted her resolution "to embrace a life of holiness" (I, 585) as a renunciation of her desire to be cooled and refreshed by water. As well, she maintains her position about what the Hermit considers other departures from Christian orthodoxy, and in fact pierces beyond the restrictions imposed by contemporary thought and practice to a deeper Christianity. Thus, she would not have the Hermit think wholly ill "of the godless company she had been driven to keep...who are the masters of the pagan lore of the East, and still practice their rites among the simple folk of the hills" (I, 582-583). She honors the memory of "a faun and his female" with whom "she has found refuge"(I, 583); she wears pagan ornaments on her person presumably out of respect for her non-Christian connections; "she has learned from a wise woman how to stay [seizures] by a decoction of the *carduus benedictus*, made in the third night of the waxing moon, but without the aid of magic" (I, 584). But if she is "a Diana figure," as Bernadette Donovan rightly proposes (62), she does not stop at being that, for in the story that element is placed in a much broader context.

As time passes the reputation of the Wild Woman as a holy woman grows in the land: she is known to cast out devils and to cure the sick, and people who come to the Hermit's cliff are restored by her. During a plague that sweeps the country, the peasants who flee to the hills are tended by the Woman and the Hermit, and the former accepts the invitation of the burgesses of a nearby town to go to tend their sick, where she is "covered with the blessings of the townfolk, and thereafter her name for holiness spread as wide as the Hermit's" (I, 586). Throughout her life on the cliff, the Woman prays and observes the canonical hours with the Hermit. In a word her life is devoted to the Christian actions of prayer and good works. And her

Diana-like qualities complement her Christian life rather than conflict with it.

The Woman's death confirms her essential Christian spirit. She "has brought back from her labors among the sick a heaviness of body" (I, 586), the beginnings of her fatal illness: she has enacted the love than which there is none greater by laying down her life for her friends. Her death confirms in spectacular fashion the complementary nature of her Dianesque and Christian impulses, for she expires in the act of bathing and is blessed by both heaven and earth. The Hermit sees "above her head a brightness [floating]" (I, 588), and hears "a peal of voices that seemed to come down from the sky and mingle with the singing of the throng" (I, 589) of faithful and clerics who have come to honor the two anchorites. For the Hermit, the event serves to loosen the constraints that prevented him from seeing beyond his companion's sensuality and to create in him the sense of an alliance with her mode of spirituality and away from the absolute austerity toward which he tended.

"The Hermit and the Wild Woman" deserves more attention and credit than it gets. It is beautifully written, with the cadences, evocativeness, and universal quality of ancient myth. Beyond that, it has considerable relevance in the present day, and will come as a refreshing breeze to those whose interests are theological. Readers may be startled to find that one whose life and work was so taken up with the ways of the world could write with such articulateness and passion about the spiritual side of life. However, it should not surprise us that Wharton turned her hand to this theme, for there is not much of life that she did not touch in her impressive written output.

"Dieu D'Amour"

Wharton's last historical tale, "Dieu D'Amour," appeared twenty-two years after "The Hermit and the Wild Woman" in the October 1928 number of *Ladies' Home Journal*. The story originated during Wharton's ten-week Mediterranean cruise with friends aboard the 360-ton steam yacht the Osprey during the winter and spring of 1926. After visiting the twelfth-century castle called *Dieu D'Amour* on the island of Cyprus, Wharton began writing the story aboard the yacht the day after her visit to the castle. The beauty and romance evoked by the sight of *Dieu d'Amour* in its island setting, and her reading at the time of Mas-Latrie's *Histoire de l'Ile de Chypre sous les Princes de Lusignan,* as she told a correspondant, triggered her interest in the place and in its past importance (EW to Mr Conant, 30 April 1928, EW Collection), and the result was the short story "Dieu d'Amour." Among the stories of its genre it most closely resembles its immediate predecessor, "The Hermit and the Wild Woman," in its legendary quality and in its focus on characters preoccupied with their spiritual lives and their eternal salvation; however, the two stories are made distinct by their own emphases. Whereas "The Hermit and the Wild Woman" arbitrates among different approaches to the spiritual and moral life, "Dieu d'Amour," as Lewis notes, deals with "the conflict between sacred and profane love" (*EW* 470). As for the story's quality, E. K. Brown's assessment seems accurate enough: although "Dieu d'Amour" is a sumptuous evocation of Cyprus at the time of the crusades, it lacks psychological interest and compares unfavourably to "The Hermit and the Wild Woman" (32).

Initially the narrative's polarities reside in historical and legendary personages who have been identified with the castle, the former monastery. As the central and point-of-view character, the Norman page Godfrey, makes his way to the summit of *Dieu d'Amour* to visit his beloved, the Princess Medea of Lusignan, he is conscious of the myths and reputation of its historic inhabitants: "Saint Hilarion the Abbott, flying before the throngs of pilgrims who besieged his solitude in the Egyptian desert...[taking] up refuge in a cave of the inaccessible peak of *Dieu d'Amour*" (II, 551); and "centuries before Saint Hilarion's coming, Venus, Queen of Cyprus, [building] that towering pleasure house, and [reigning] there in mirth and revelry with her son Prince Cupid" (II, 552). Thus the story begins with a kind of time signature of its counter-thrusts.

As "Dieu d'Amour" moves from the past into the present and, via Godfrey, from reverie to action, the Princess Medea becomes the center in whom its conflict is worked out. Indeed Godfrey's first glimpse of her epitomizes the polarities between which she will ultimately choose: "The princess, lute in hand, stood penciled against this...light like a little dark saint on a gold ground. But in reality she was not dark: under her coif and veil her hair spiraled out like the gold wire of the old heathen ornaments which the laborers dug out of the vineyards in the valleys" (II, 553). The sacred/pagan duality represented in the imaged Medea appears to climax in her choice to elope with Godfrey rather than to become engaged in the planned marriage with her uncle. When she consents to escape secretly with Godfrey, she is opting for what her lover stands for: the life of innocence and goodness, and away from the disorder, license, and indulgence of the Lusignans, the life a marriage to her uncle would entail.

That latter life expands into clear and concrete focus when Godfrey accompanies his liege knight, John of Yvetot, to Famagusta where the latter is to make preparations for Medea's wedding to her uncle. At Famagusta, Godfrey comes in direct contact with, and is shocked by the moral corruption and unholy ease that have permeated the lives of the Christian elite and the holy places. He sees John of Yvetot "feasting with the archbishop in his lordship's golden-brown palace, facing the mighty spires and buttresses of his Cathedral Church of Saint Nicholas. Archbishop and knight were in their lordly cups, with many other knights and prelates, and the Moorish girls were dancing in clear veils, and plum-colored slaves fanning the Archbishop's concubine, and flies battening on the welter of meat-pasties, dismembered fowls, molten jellies, and disemboweled pomegranates that covered the tables" (II, 556). He hears, too, Famagusta's evils condemned by the ascetic and itinerant preacher Bridget of Sweden.

As the Venus of old is reincarnated in the spirit of excess and moral license that drives life in the Lusignan family and at Famagusta, so Bridget of Sweden reillumines the moral rigor of Saint Hilarion the Abbott, the founder of *Dieu d'Amour*'s ancient monastery. But Bridget's role is not limited to a merely representative one in the story, for she becomes an integral part of the action. Retreating to the Church of Saint George of the Latins to pray, Godfrey is drawn into conversation with Bridget, who asks him, "Is there anyone you wish me to pray for?" (II, 56).

When he answers Bridget's question with the name of his beloved, Godfrey inadvertently seals his own fate. On his return to *Dieu d'Amour* to carry off Medea, he finds that Bridget has preceded him and thwarted his plan to elope. Bridget has evidently convinced Medea of the higher good of escaping the House of Lusignan by committing herself to conventual life as opposed to seeking the embracing arms of Godfrey. We learn, as well, in the ultimate passages of the story, that Godfrey too has lived out his days as a friar in a Norman priory and that the thwarted lovers have never again communicated, hence Lewis's comment about the story that "sacred love won a somewhat melancholy triumph" (*EW* 470).

Thus "Dieu d'Amour" ends where it might have begun, and the story remains an allegorical and moral one, eschewing the psychological possibilities it invites. One suspects that Wharton's excitement was less with her "present-time" characters and more with the romance and history surrounding the striking edifice that was *Dieu d'Amour*. The story's strongest writing is found in those passages that evoke the aura of the place. The following half-paragraph describes the structure and surroundings as Wharton saw them from the Osprey's deck, and not as the youthful love-struck Godfrey imagines them as he mounts the long stairway to meet his love:

> It was different at noonday. Then, from the sheer pinnacle on which it was poised like a bird, rich slopes fell away from the castle in a dappling of spring colors, wheat and wine and mulberry, rosy orchard and dark carob grove; and the wild peaks, as though driven by a ceaseless gale, blew eastward to Buffavento the impregnable, to Kantara, and the holy convent of Antiphonissa. Far below, on the blue sea, lay Kyrenia, the guardian fortress, compact in her walls, and the sea was a tossing of laughter all the way to the Caramanian coast, where the snows of the Taurus floated in absolute light. At that hour, as befitted its name, *Dieu d'Amour*, turreted, balconied, galleried to catch the sun, seemed made for delicate enchantments.... (II, 552)

This passage and others like it betray Wharton's real enthusiasms about her subject.

* * * * *

Saints and Rebels, Heroes and Heroines: The Lore of Earlier Times

Nowhere in Wharton's short-story canon are the tales more overtly structured as told stories than in these narratives of times past. All but one are presented by a general narrator who turns over all or an essential portion of the short story proper to a clearly identified tale-teller who in turn proceeds with his or her narrative—which is often the bulk of the short story in question. "Dieu D'Amour" does not use such a device. In view of the footnote appended to the first page of the story (I, 551) in the Scribner's *Collected Short Stories*,[104] one might be justified in suspecting that Wharton felt herself so closely associated with her subject as to take on herself the narrator's role and forgo her usual habit in these history pieces.

Of the remaining five stories, two, "A Venetian Night's Entertainment" and "The Letter," begin with a more or less cursory introduction to the tale-teller by the primary narrator, then pass on to the former's verbatim rendering of his tale. It may say something about Wharton's lack of real interest in "A Venetian Night's Entertainment" that the narrative structure is carelessly set up. The six-line introduction reveals that "This is the story...Judge Anthony Bracknell...used to relate to his grandsons" (I, 475). But in the tale of adventure that follows, Tony Bracknell, the central character, is referred to in the third person. If we assume that Judge Anthony of the introduction is the original Tony "[relating his tale] to his grandsons," we would expect the telling to be done in the first person. In "The Letter," narrative matters proceed via the same sort of simple introduction, but without the inconsistency of person and with considerably more organic relatedness between introduction and tale proper. In the two-page introduction the unnamed first-person narrator, who has been hired as a kind of research assistant to the art scholar Colonel Jack Alingdon, establishes Alingdon's personal history, then engages him in conversation. During this conversation Alingdon is moved, as he rarely has been before, to speak of his life as a revolutionary in the nineteenth-century Italian struggles against Austrian domination, and it is this that prompts him to reminisce about the bravery of Italian women, and about one woman's bravery in particular during the insurgency. This latter matter becomes the subject of his tale, identified at the outset of "The Letter's" Section II as (COLONEL ALINGDON'S STORY). In neither "A Venetian Night's Entertainment" nor "The Letter" is there any reference after the introduction to the primary narrator: the tales told become the *raison d'être* of Wharton's respective stories.

In "The Duchess at Prayer" and "The Confessional" the tales told about the past are organically embedded within the larger compositions which are the short stories proper. Both stories return, towards their conclusion, to the primary narrator, to the context of the time at which the tale within is told. In "The Duchess at Prayer," the tale-teller is an old man—"the oldest man I had ever seen" (I, 229), says the unnamed primary narrator—and the tale he tells is not his own but that of his grandmother, who has known the tale's principal characters. Wharton's "The Duchess at Prayer" is a considerably more comprehensive statement than the old man's tale of the duchess. The age of the teller, the reliability of his memory and sources—his grandmother has not observed everything herself but relied on others for details—all raise questions about the nature of truth, for example. The moribund setting in which the raconteur speaks his narrative is in stark contrast to the vitality of the milieu recounted, and suggests that Wharton is interested in raising issues of contrast between past and present. "The Confessional" melds its inner tale of strife and sacrilege during the mid-nineteenth-century Italian troubles, told to the unnamed but involved primary narrator by Don Egidio, with the former's recounting of his association with the exiled priest in New York. If Egidio's tale is one of battle, bloodshed, treachery, and dishonor, his friend's is one of reconciliation, friendship, gentleness and honor. The two narratives are as one, complementing and balancing each other to compose a short story that is, despite its obvious flaws, emotionally satisfying.

"The Hermit and the Wild Woman" is closest to "The Confessional" in its narrative method. Its inner tale does not dominate the larger story. Told by the Wild Woman in the first person, it is the substance of Section IV and comprises only four of the total twenty-three pages of the story: coming about half way through Wharton's narrative, it can be said to be enveloped in the larger story, as the woman herself is subsumed within the consciousness of the Hermit, of whose point of view we are apprised throughout by the intermediary of a third-person narration. Of course the Wild Woman's significance is not to be reduced to the relatively small space given to her account of her life. She is the catalyst for the revolution in the Hermit's religious thought: it is because of what he learns from her that he is able to resolve finally the tension that has plagued his life, the tension that reaches back into his boyhood, when "There seemed to be so many pitfalls to avoid—so many things were harmless. How could a child of his age tell?" (I, 572) It can be said as a general observation about these short stories of the past that the quality of the story is in direct proportion to the successful integration of the framing story and its interior tale: "The Hermit and the Wild Woman," "The Confessional," and "The Duchess at Prayer" surpass "The Letter," "A Venetian Night's Entertainment," and "Dieu D'Amour" because they take their saints or rebels, their heroes and heroines out of the realm of pure legend and place them in a more realistically human context.

One does not find much that is new thematically in Wharton's history stories. They all include an actual or potential heterosexual relationship, and often a third party to complicate that relationship. The patriarchy and its exemplars are here, and their victims, the put-upon women. The protagonist of "The Duchess at Prayer" is a reincarnation of noble ladies from "Mrs. Jones" and "Kerfol," subjugated and isolated by absent husbands, or of contemporary women like Nora Frenway of "Atrophy" and Mrs Grancy of "The Moving Finger," abandoned or manipulated to serve the whims of indifferent or possessive mates. So is Faustina Intelvi of "The Confessional," although her victimization is more the result of her husband's patriotic obsession than of any intrinsic malice on his part. In the words of Don Egidio, "She was always the caged bird, the transplanted flower: for all Roberto's care she never bloomed or sang" (I, 327). Even the bogus Donna Polixena Cador of "A Venetian Night's Entertainment," the leading attraction in the gang of cons who try to trap Bracknell—"a pretty establishment, and a pretty lady at the head of it" (I, 489)—tells her potential victim, "They never give me anything but the clothes I wear" (I, 488).

But at the same time the history tales feature women of strength, initiative, and independence, and men who, taken with these women's striking courage, or motivated by genuine Christian love and concern, transcend conventional patriarchal roles and see their lovers or female friends proceed on their own way to establish lives outside the system to which they are expected to adhere. Such characters as Donna Candida Falco of "The Letter," Medea Lausignan of "Dieu D'Amour," and the Wild Woman are earlier versions of the Ruth Gaynors, Paulina Trants, and Mrs Lidcotes of Wharton's stories of contemporary life, just as the Hermit and the young page Godfrey of "Dieu D'Amour" have their later avatars in such understanding and supportive men as Ralph Gannett of "Souls Belated" and Julian Brand of "A Glimpse."

If these six Wharton stories set in earlier times repeat their author's themes and character types, there is a way in which they may be said to stake their claim to originality as well. In the canon generally there is not much interest in religion. Here there is: five of the stories engage the religious subject and most are pervasively religious, even if, as with "The Duchess at Prayer," the religion is mainly atmospheric. "A Venetian Night's Entertainment"—exceptionally, for the rest of the stories treat of Catholicism—features New England Calvinism, and a reason for the story's artistic failure is that the promise offered of a Puritan/Catholic tension is not delivered. "Dieu D'Amour" is patently religious in its many hagiographical references and in its resolution, but again the piece fails because it forsakes its religious/psychological possibilities in favor of a religious interest that is more allusive and atmospheric than penetrating. "The Confessional" and "The Hermit and the Wild Woman" are both fundamentally religious stories, the first implicitly, the second explicitly so. Sanctity, prayer, and the Christian sacramental life are salient factors in both, and the religious subject is addressed at once seriously and artistically.

Notes

[103] Patricia Pallis's commentary on the connections between Wharton's "The Duchess at Prayer" and Robert Browning's "My Last Duchess" was contained in a paper delivered in Boston in March 1994 at the annual conference of the North East Modern Language Association. The paper was titled "Robert Browning and Edith Wharton: Recreating the Dramatic Monologue."

[104] The footnote, written, one assumes, by the editor, R.W.B. Lewis, is as follows:
Dieu d'Amour was the name given by the Crusaders to the castle (formerly the monastery) of St. Hilarion in the mountains of Cyprus. In her second volume of memoirs, Autumn in the Valley (1936), Mrs. Winthrop Chanler tells of visiting the castle—built in the twelfth century by the ruler of Cyprus, Guy de Lusignan—during an Aegean cruise in May 1926, with Edith Wharton, on the chartered steam yacht Osprey. The Crusaders renamed the castle, Mrs. Chanler reports, "not for the Christian God of Love but after Eros, son of Aphrodite, "once liege lady of the island." She

continues: "It is the most fantastic fairy castle imaginable, built on a high rocky peak . . . two thousand feet above sea level and surrounded by sheer precipices." Edith Wharton did not herself, apparently, complete the arduous climb, and took her physical description of Dieu d'Amour from Mrs. Chanler, who did.

Chapter Nine

And the Rest...

Sixteen of the eighty-six stories collected by R.W.B. Lewis do not readily fall into the categories chosen as salient ones for purposes of this study. During the 1890's Wharton wrote two fantastical pieces: one, of a very experimental nature, both having a strong autobiographical leaning and about which she was later somewhat embarrassed. And in February 1934 *Hearst's International-Cosmopolitan* published her negligible pot-boiler "Bread upon the Waters." In the decades between, Wharton turned her hand to various out-of-the-mainstream (for her) subjects which attracted her interest: politics, business, murder, the war, religion, the gothic. She also attempted in two pieces to exploit genre stories by turning them around into mock, or counter tales: "A Coward" can be viewed as an anti-fiction of manners; "The Bolted Door" as a counter-murder mystery.

A number of these miscellaneous narratives are among Wharton's best, although they haven't all received their due, neglected, possibly, because they treat of matters with which critics, anthologists, and readers do not usually identify with Wharton short fiction. Among the finest, here and in the entire canon, are "Coming Home," Wharton's only story of active warfare; "A Bottle of Perrier," a murder mystery set in Morocco, a place she visited on occasion; "The Letters," a deft tale about a marriage relationship; and "The Young Gentlemen," a Gothic story covering for a penetrating socio-cultural study. Although in some of the stories discussed in this chapter Wharton may be said to be away from home ground, her insight into the psychology of characters transcends, in the better of the tales, the limited experience she may have had in the areas into which she ventures or with some of the new *genres* she essays.

"The Fullness of Life"

Of the first five stories Wharton published, two, "The Fullness of Life" and "The Valley of Childish Things, and Other Emblems," were fantasies, fables set in an imaginary place. The first of these "The Fullness of Life," appeared in *Scribner's* in December 1893 and was one of those tales Wharton considered unworthy of collection. "One long shriek," (*EW* 86) she called it, far too explicit about the unsatisfactory nature of life with her husband, Teddy. There are no fewer than seven direct references—including the story's closing words—to the creaking boots of the protagonist's husband: the tale is dominated by this audial manifestation of her husband's obstrusive presence in his wife's life, even in spite of the fact that the wife turns down her "kindred soul's" invitation to spend eternity with her, even in spite of her decision to await her husband's rejoining her after his death. The story is a reflection of both Wharton's unhappiness with her spouse and her resolution to maintain the marriage bond.

Like the rest of Wharton's initial stories, "The Fullness of Life" has been the subject of much commentary occasioned by the absence of novels during this earlier portion of her fiction-writing career. (The first short stories received an inordinate amount of attention by biographers and critics alike simply because there was little other fictional output to attend to. The corollary to this is evident as well: later stories ceased to garner such close scrutiny because they were displaced by the novels and novellas which began to appear in profusion after the turn of the century.) In the case of "The Fullness of Life," as with some of the other early stories, this commentary seizes upon the ways the tale reflects the author's personal life in a very particular sense.

One of the most enlightening of the discussions of "The Fullness of Life" ventures an opinion about the nature of the story's autobiographical disposition. Cynthia Griffin Wolff writes:

> But perhaps the most revealing thing in this piece, when we think of it in connection with the later work, is Wharton's almost complete inability to represent a convincingly adult relationship between the sexes. For example, the woman's "soul mate" is really nothing more than a replica of herself, and

their brief conversations sound distressingly like a parody of "Little Sir Echo." "'Did you never feel at sunset—' 'Ah, yes, but I never heard anyone else say so. Did you?' 'Do you remember that line in the third canto of the *Inferno*?' 'Ah, that line—my favorite always. Is it possible—' 'You know the stooping "Victory" in the frieze of the Nike Apteros?' 'You mean the one who is tying her sandal. Then you have noticed, too!'" This is not a relationship; it is an image of total oneness, fusion, a complete (an infantile) identification. It conjures no image of passion, only a chasm of uninterrupted boredom. The relationship with the husband gives no hint of passion either, and the wife chooses to wait for him solely because he needs her to take care of him. If we were to venture an assessment of the author's own emotional growth as revealed through this tale, we would have to conclude that she was still imprisoned in the modalities of childhood dependency and that she was not yet able to trace the map of mature experience and desire. (74-75)

One wonders if Wharton's embarrassment about "The Fullness of Life" stemmed at least in part from her own recognition of the kind of personal and artistic immaturity that Wolff identifies.

Examined without respect to its autobiographical side, "The Fullness of Life" can stand on its own as a respectable tale. Wharton's editor at *Scribner's* though it "a capital conception" (*EW* 65) and in accepting it for magazine publication acknowledged the considerable promise he saw in Wharton's early stories. For all its narcissism, the story is noteworthy for its lyric evocation of that world that was so important for Wharton, the world of the arts, of painting and sculpture and decoration and architecture and for its portrayal of the void created when recognition of and sensitivity to this world was lacking.

"The Valley of Childish Things, and Other Emblems"

Wharton's other fantasy, "The Valley of Childish Things, and Other Emblems," published in *Century* in July 1896, also bore witness to the personal problems she was experiencing. She wrote Burlingame on December 14, 1895:

Since I last wrote you over a year ago, I have been very ill, [and] I am not yet allowed to do any real work. But I have been scribbling a little [and] I have sent you a few paragraphs I hope you may like.
Please don't trouble yourself to answer this—I only write it because it is such a distress to me to send such a waif instead of the volume that Messrs. Scribner were once kind enough to ask for, that I cannot do so without a word

of explanation. And I still hope to get well [and] have the volume ready next year. (*LEW* 35)

Wharton's letter speaks of the difficulty she was having doing sustained work. The form of "The Valley of Childish Things, and Other Emblems," the "waif" mentioned in her note, suggests that she was having trouble generating longer and more complex pieces. The format she chose for this composition—it was the only time she used this format in her career—emphasized brevity, simplicity, and plainness: it was a group of ten narrative sketches, nine of them varying from five lines to a half page in length; one, the title sketch, only slightly longer. Cynthia Griffin Wolff called the story "the most bizarre piece that Wharton ever published" and "disjointed ramblings" (82).

Not much has been done to engage the bizarreness and disjointedness of "The Valley of Childish Things, and Other Emblems." Most of the commentary on the story is limited to the title parable and its autobiographical undertone. Wolff's own remarks about it suggest the elusiveness of the "other emblems" of the title:

> The tale is a collection of short parables, ...they swirl about the various problems that beset Wharton's adult life and haunted her from childhood, and several of them echo themes that we have encountered before in her fiction. The sixth parable, for instance, (in its entirety): "A soul once cowered in gray waste, and a mighty shape came by. Then the soul cried out for help, saying, 'Shall I be left to perish alone in this desert of Unsatisfied Desires?' 'But you are mistaken,' the shape replied; 'this is the land of Gratified Longings. And, moreover, you are not alone, for the country is full of people; but whoever tarries here grows blind.'" (82)

Wolff, like other critics, chooses to leave the other emblems unexplained and not to remark on common notes or connectedness among them.

Still there are a few observations to make about the strange tale, that may help to establish its significance in ways that need not be related directly to its author's life. There is a direct link to Wharton's earlier fantasy, "The Fullness of Life": the valleys in the two stories are places of peace, repose, and innocence, separated from a harsher everyday world of experience. Also, three of the "other emblems" can be tied together by their focus on marriage. However, they do not all take a negative approach to that institution. Although Section III does just that, presenting us with the prospect of a young married woman rendered foolish by her state, Sections V and VIII offer more hopeful views of wedded couples, ending in revised attitudes on the part of husbands about the positive value their life with their spouses has provided them. If there is a common trait in the emblems it is that some revelation of value is made by each central figure or by people who observe him or her. The brief vignettes all end in significant insights about the human condition.

That Wharton never repeated the form of "The Valley of Childish Things, and Other Emblems," even in an adapted way, speaks to her unhappiness about using it in the first place. That she did use it and manage to express notions that were not mere platitudes suggests her tenacity about developing her creative talent, her unwillingness to be put down by the circumstances of her life.

"A Coward"

"A Coward," one of the six previously unpublished tales Wharton collected in her eight-story 1899 volume, *The Greater Inclination*, bears a close resemblance to "The Lamp of Psyche," which had appeared in *Scribner's* in October 1895. The two pieces deal with the subject of cowardice, and we may safely conclude that the second was written with the first in mind: we have seen the phenomenon before in Wharton's short fiction that a second story in a similar vein seems to improve on the first, or to complement it, or to refine it.

In "The Lamp of Psyche" Corbett is revealed to have been unequivocally a coward in his declining to fight in the American Civil War: when his wife Delia confronts him with his pusillanimity, he neither denies it, nor explains it, nor regrets it, giving the impression that the whole question is beyond his consideration. The story's concluding paragraph suggests that the married couple is willing to put aside the principle that has been violated because confronting it cleanly would complicate considerably their currently comfortable life together:

> [Delia's] ideal of him was slivered like the crystal above the miniature of the warrior of Chancellorsville. She had the crystal replaced by a piece of clear glass which (as the jeweler pointed out to her) cost much less

and looked equally well; and for the passionate worship which she had paid her husband substituted a tolerant affection which possessed precisely the same advantages. (I, 57)

"The Lamp of Psyche" might well have been titled or sub-titled "The Coward," for Corbett has done nothing to lift the opprobrium from himself.

"A Coward" begins as a rather conventional story about the upper classes in America.[105] The point-of-view character, Vibart, is paying suit to the attractive Irene Carstyle in Millbrook, a summering place for the New York elite, where the Carstyle family has had to set up house year round, to the frequently proclaimed displeasure of Mrs Carstyle, because of the depleted condition of Andrew Carstyle's resources. But very early in the story Vibart's interest shifts away from Irene and towards her father. "I think [Irene] takes after her mother" (I, 131), Vibart tells his aunt, in so many words scuttling the love match the shallow, dissatisfied, grasping Mrs Carstyle so fervently desires.

Vibart's liking for Andrew Carstyle has been motivated by the latter's character. "Vibart's imagination had been touched by the discovery that this little huddled-up man, instead of traveling with the wind, was persistently facing a domestic gale of considerable velocity. That he should have paid off his brother's debt at one stroke was to the young man a conceivable feat, but that he should go on methodically and uninterruptedly accumulating the needed amount, under the perpetual accusation of Irene's inadequate frocks, and Mrs. Carstyle's apologies for the mutton, seemed to Vibart proof of unexampled heroism" (I, 131). Vibart's admiration for Carstyle only increases as he gets to know him better. The incident in which the latter attempts to prevent the potential disaster of a runaway horse and occupied carriage seals the younger man's conviction of Carstyle's courage, and it is after this incident that Carstyle tells Vibart of the act of cowardly withdrawal that years ago marked the latter indelibly and still plagues his memory.

The attachment Vibart feels for Carstyle is reciprocated by the older man, who initially seems to intuit the younger man's liking for him. At luncheon in his hosts' home where he has come to court Irene, Vibart finds himself "observed by Mr. Carstyle." The latter " sat contemplating his guest with a smile of unmistakeable approval." And if "[W]hen Vibart caught his eye, the smile vanished, ...Vibart was sure of the smile: it had established, between his host and himself, a complicity which Mr. Carstyle's attempted evasion served only to confirm" (I, 132). When on Vibart's first visit to Carstyle's simple office Carstyle learns of the other's genuine interest in Montaigne his sense of his visitor's intrinsic intellectual and moral worth is vindicated: Vibart has become a worthy and understanding repository for Carstyle's story of his one act of cowardice.

Whether or not Carstyle tells Vibart his story in order to explain his wife's and daughter's poverty of material and spiritual means and thus to rekindle in the young man his desire for Irene is not so much the point. Vibart has already realized that his suit to Irene has fallen on the rocks—evidenced by "an exchange, between mother and daughter, of increasingly frequent allusions to the delights of Narragansett, the popularity of Mrs. Highby, and the jolliness of her house; with an occasional reference on Mrs. Carstyle's part to the probability of Hewlett Bain's being there as usual" (I, 133). Nonetheless, the worthy father has the satisfaction of knowing that his new friend will not be drawn into the material and spiritual vacuum of life with his wife and daughter. The irony is, of course, that Mrs Carstyle squanders the opportunity of a better life for all—the possibilities of which she has been prevented from imagining by her unaltering and acute perception of her husband's ineffectiveness. To her Vibart is simply another Carstyle, and spells failure for her daughter.

The last several lines of "A Coward" are worth noting. Says Mrs Carstyle:

> "I was not obliged to do my visiting on foot when I was younger and my doctor tells me that to persons accustomed to a carriage no exercise is more injurious than walking."
> She glanced at her husband with a smile of unforgiving sweetness.
> "Fortunately," she concluded, "it agrees with Mr. Carstyle." (I, 139)

The events encompassed within the time frame of the story—indeed these few lines themselves—are a microcosm of the individual lives of the senior Carstyles. She is static, superficial, unforgiving, blind to possibilities; he is dynamic, curious, assured, aggressively seeking opportunities to rectify the grand failure of his life. In calling her story "A Coward," i.e., in using the indefinite article to modify the substantive, Wharton has taken the sting from the latter: here one sees highlighted the radical contrast between Carstyle and Corbett, *the* coward of "The Lamp of Psyche." Carstyle's very life is a running contradiction to the act that has marked him. In maintaining his dignity and authenticity in the face of his wife's perpetual "unforgiving smile," in sustaining the honor of his own family by recompensing those done injustice by his brother's misdemeanor, in risking to appear ridiculous in pursuit of chances to redeem his early cowardice, he is an example of courage.

"A Coward" is one of those stories that has not been given its due. It is at least as good as "The Lamp of Psyche," its progenitor that has drawn much more attention. Little has been written about it, and Lewis is not so much wrong as dismissive when he labels it merely "an anecdote with comic tonalities" (*EW* 81). Only E.K. Brown has seen its merit, calling it psychologically superior to "Souls Belated," its contemporary, and pointing out that it is not "geometrically simple" (7).

"The Angel at the Grave"

One of a number of stories in which Wharton engages New England Transcendentalist culture and thought—other salient examples are "The Long Run," "Atrophy," and "The Legend" —"The Angel at the Grave" makes the most overt use of it. Toby Widdicome writes of the story: "There is strong evidence that in creating Orestes Anson, Wharton deliberately created a Transcendentalist who would have to remain unidentified because unidentifiable; she created, that is, a sort of Transcendentalist Everyman" (50). Widdicome's analysis features a detailed account of Wharton's infusion of Transcendentalist elements to the detriment of the story's drama: it focuses more on the past-time Orestes Anson than on his grand-daughter Paulina, the story's present-time protagonist.

In "The Angel at the Grave," published in *Scribner's* in February 1901, Wharton centered her attention on Paulina, the grand-daughter of Orestes Anson and "solitary inmate of the Anson House" situated "a few yards back from the elm-shaded...street" (I, 245) in an unnamed New England village that is surely Concord, Massachusetts. Paulina's grand-father is a thinly disguised and loosely conceived

Orestes Brownson, the associate of the New England Transcendentalists, the one, according to the story, "who has been the mere mask through which [his better-known contemporaries] mouthed their lesson, the instrument on which their tune was played" (I, 253).

"The Angel at the Grave" initially presents Paulina as the custodian of the House and its collection of Anson materials: she has shown the intelligence to understand her grandfather's ideas and the enthusiasm to take on the responsibility of overseeing the premises and its contents, objects of curiosity to an international if limited public. But Paulina's life at the House is prey to a series of shifts in circumstance that tests her early enthusiasm before at least a certain measure of that first fervor is restored. Barbara White writes:

> [Paulina] loves her work and, like the New England nun, has no trouble giving up her suitor to preserve it. The event that changes the House into a tomb is not the loss of her beau but the *rejection of her manuscript*. Only when Paulina is denied communication with the world through showing the House to visitors, does she begin to feel walled in. Thus the restoration of communication at the end of the story immediately lifts the walls, and the promise that she can resume her work makes Paulina feel that she has not wasted her life. (55)

White goes on to praise Wharton for creating a tale that, with the help of a very distanced point of view, "coheres on several levels and can be read in terms of different themes, including art, fate, and the past" (56). It must be said that the narrator is a very overt presence in "The Angel at the Grave," distanced as she is. In fact, for the length of its first two numbered sections, the story proceeds as a straight narrative, amply editorialized upon, its incidents told with little or no dramatizing effects. Even the arrival on the scene of a suitor—described in the final segment of Part I—occasions no departure from this narrative procedure. We are given no account of the meetings between Paulina and Hewlett Winsloe, none of the dialogue that ensues between them, no imaging of their, doubtless, painful separation. Instead the narrator provides three paragraphs of distanced commentary about the response to the relationship by the townspeople and Paulina's aunts, the young man's unawareness of the importance of her grand-father in her life, and Paulina's own mixed reaction to Winsloe.

This method of describing Paulina's life's passage at a distance and in the past perfect tense changes abruptly with Section III, the transition signalled by its first brief sentence: "The bell rang—she remembered it afterward—with a loud thrilling note" (I, 253). What follows is a wholly unified scene, dramatized and highly dramatic, composed mostly of dialogue: first between Paulina and Katy, the servant woman who announces George Corby's arrival at the House, then between Paulina and Corby themselves. For the first time we see Paulina in the flesh, at first nervous, then excited and passionate, openly declaring her self-sacrifice and near death in a moribund cause, then finally her sense of revival. Wharton has rendered her protagonist's return to the living with the effective shift of the story from a descriptive to a dramatic stance.

This is not to say that the first two sections of "The Angel at the Grave" are unsatisfactory. Here one finds one of the first examples of the elegant Wharton style that is characteristic of so much of her narrative prose, of the voice that permeates *The House of Mirth*, for example. Barbara White remarks that "as is often the case in her best work, [Wharton] maintains a double perspective towards all [the] issues. The story may be read as a Hawthornesque satire of transcendentalism with its 'cloudy rhetoric' that doesn't deserve to survive, or of past doctrines in general.... On the other hand, only the angel's vigilance permits any continuity in individual consciousness or public tradition. The past must be come to terms with" (56). The third-person distanced narrator's voice, ironic and direct, satirical and straight, couches her description in a leisurely, articulate, and reflective manner that anticipates the best of Wharton's later longer and shorter fiction.

White's statement immediately above draws attention to the significance of the story's title: for her the angel at the grave is Paulina. The body of the story itself provides an extension to the meaning of the titular epithet: "There was a dreary parallel," says the narrator at the conclusion of Section II, "between her grandfather's fruitless toil and her own unprofitable sacrifice. Each in turn had kept vigil by a corpse" (I, 253). And the significance of the title can be extended farther still to include Paulina's two young men. Hewlett Winsloe, her unsuccessful suitor, attempts to rescue her from what she later recalls as a "ruined" life. "I gave up everything to keep [my grandfather] alive," she tells George Corby. "I sacrificed myself—others—I nursed his glory in my bosom and it died—and left me—left me here alone" (I, 257). George Corby restores life to Paulina by salvaging meaning out of her years of isolation. Winsloe and Corby, in their affirmative gestures, point to the double nature of Paulina's function, reminding us of Barbara White's identification of the story's dual thrust: the former draws attention to Paulina as satirical figure, the latter to her as idealistic one. The angels of the story serve to highlight its various dimensions. The truest angel would appear to be George Corby: the story's ending suggests that it is his person as well as his avocation that revitalizes Paulina:

> He went out with his bright nod. She walked to the window and watched his buoyant figure hastening down the elm-shaded street. When she turned back into the empty room she looked as though youth had touched her on the lips. (I, 258)

"The Reckoning"

"The Reckoning," published in the August 1902 issue of *Harper's*, may be said to imitate the design of its predecessor "The Angel at the Grave," whose magazine appearance in *Scribner's* was eighteen months earlier: both stories begin in a strong satirical vein but end in an aura of high seriousness. The key to the change of tone that occurs in "The Reckoning" is the point-of-view character, Julia Westall. In the early portions of the story, as she attends a Saturday afternoon event in the studio of the Herbert Van Siderens at which her husband is delivering a lecture on "The New Ethics," her preoccupations range outward to those around her. Here is the narrator's recapitulation of Julia's frame of mind concerning the Van Sideren circle: "It was vaguely felt...that all the audacities were artistic, and that a teacher who pronounced marriage immoral was somehow as distinguished as a painter who depicted green grass and a purple sky. The Van Sideren set were tired of the conventional color scheme in art and conduct" (I, 421). But as Julia begins to suspect that her husband is becoming attracted to Una, the Van Siderens' young daughter, her sardonic reflections cease, and she turns inward to thoughts of her past. Finally when her husband Clement confirms that he has decided to leave her—to call upon her to observe her side of the contract by which they may be untied from their marriage bond—she returns, not only in mind but also in body, to visit her first husband, against whom she has exercised the same option that is now being exercised against her.

During this brief visit, she enunciates to the surprised Arment the principle that is in direct contrast to the one by which her two marriages have been disolved. "If we don't recognize an inner law...the obligation that love creates...being loved as well as loving...there is nothing to prevent our spreading ruin unhindered...is there?" (I, 436). Formulations of the law that Clement Westall preaches and practises are liberally scattered throughout the story: "The marriage law of the new dispensation will be: *Thou shalt not be unfaithful—to thyself*" (I, 420) (from Westall's talk at the Van Siderens); "About the higher life—the full expansion of the individual—the law of fidelity to one's self" (I, 421) (Una Van Sideren, in conversation with Julia); "The new adultery was unfaithfulness to self" (I, 427) (from Julia's extended interior monologue in Section II); "I thought it was a fundamental article of our creed that the special circumstances produced by marriage were not to interfere with the full assertion of individual liberty" (I, 429) (Westall, in conversation with Julia).

Because it proclaims in word and deed ethical principles that are at polar opposites to each other, and draws two characters that espouse and put in practice these two standards, "The Reckoning" may be said to be a patently moralistic story and arguably the story the most overtly so that Wharton wrote. This does not dismiss it as a work of art, for the message it carries is enclosed in a context of dialogue, interior monologue, narratorial comment, and action that places drama at the forefront. Exemplifying the genuine dramatic impact of the story is the closing scene, Julia's brief meeting with Arment, and its aftermath. Here the description of Julia's apology to Arment and of his confused response might be used as a workshop example of how to avoid melodrama in a situation that is naturally conducive to it.

But there is another theme in "The Reckoning" that lies below the surface, that takes us somewhere beyond matters of marriage ethics as these are articulated in the polarities represented and personified by Julia and Clement Westall. This theme emanates especially from two of the story's descriptive paragraphs. The first of these paragraphs is placed in the middle of a mildly heated discussion between the Westalls on the subject of Clement's talk at the Van Siderens earlier in the day:

> Her eyes wandered about the familiar drawing room which had been the scene of so many of their evening conferences. The shaded lamps, the quiet-colored walls hung with mezzotints, the pale spring flowers scattered here and there in Venice glasses and bowls of old Sèvres, recalled she hardly knew why, the apartment in which the evenings of her first marriage had been passed—a wilderness of rosewood and upholstery, with a picture of a Roman peasant above the mantelpiece, and a Greek slave in statuary marble between the folding doors of the back drawing room. It was a room with which she had never been able to establish any closer relation than that between a traveler and a railway station; and now, as she looked about the surroundings which stood for her deepest affinities—the room for which she had left that other room—she was startled by the same sense of strangeness and unfamiliarity. The prints, the flowers, the subdued tones of the old porcelains, seemed to typify a superficial refinement which had no relation to the deeper significances of life. (I, 423)

Here one is struck by the sameness of her response to the drawing rooms in her two husbands' houses. Both rooms leave her with "a sense of strangeness and unfamiliarity." They are in no sense her rooms: she cannot see in their decoration any feature that is meaningful in her life. Indeed, they seem to have been devised according to an artificial standard that does not have any relevance even for their owners, "that seemed to typify an artificial refinement which had no relation to the deeper significances of life." The two pieces of art from Arment's drawing room whose subjects she singles out, "the picture of a Roman peasant above the mantelpiece" and "a Greek slave in statuary marble," are cases in point. They portray a humanity unrelated to the affluence in which they are expressed and by which they are surrounded.

The second description is set a week later after Westall has informed Julia of his intention to leave her for Una Van Sideren:

The clock struck another hour—eleven. She stood up again, and walked to the door: she thought she would go upstairs to her room. *Her room?* Again, the word derided her. She opened the door, crossed the narrow hall and walked up the stairs. As she passed, she noticed Westall's sticks and umbrellas: a pair of his gloves lay on the hall table. The same stair carpet mounted between the same walls; the same old French print, in its narrow black frame, faced her on the landing. The visual continuity was intolerable. Within, a grasping chasm; without, the same untroubled and familiar surface. She must get away from it before she could attempt to think. But, once in her room, she sat down on the lounge, a stupor creeping over her....(I, 431)

Now more than ever Julia feels herself an alien in the house; but her feeling has been merely accentuated, not brought on, by her rejection at the hands of her husband. The house is Westall's house and in no way hers, the decoration, and furnishings, and his personal belongings testifying to the fact. She has no place of her own, and in neither marriage has she *had* a place of her own.

Julia's conversation show her to be a woman of breeding, her interior monologue reveals a sensitive and sophisticated mind. It is surely Wharton's point that in the society in which she moves, neither outer nor inner resources of her own ensure Julia any personal individuality; women of the society Julia represents take their identity from their husbands. After Julia leaves the stifling confines of Westall's house she is acutely aware of her aloneness and of the conspicuousness a well-dressed and obviously affluent woman fosters. When she enters the Ladies' Restaurant she is aware that "two or three waitresses with their pert faces lounged in the background staring at her and whispering together" (I, 433). And as she innocently watches the Fifth Avenue traffic, "a policeman caught sight of her and signed to her that he would take her across. She had not meant to cross the street, but she obeyed automatically, and presently found herself on the farther corner" (I, 433). When she finds herself in Arment's drawing room again, it is the "Contradina still [lurching] from the chimney breast and the Greek slave [obstructing] the threshold of the inner room" (I, 434-435), details recalled from her earlier familiarity with the room, that initially dominate her consciousness. The "darkness" she enters at the last line of the story is her placelessness in a male-dominated world.

"The Reckoning" is about the ethics surrounding marriage, but it is also about broader matters of morality that are related to the dignity and significance of individual human beings. Julia Westall has been wronged by her second husband, and she had, as well, as she recognizes, wronged her first husband. Beyond that, Wharton is concerned with the plight of women in society, attention to which is drawn in this story by what happens to women in marriage and what happens when their marriages are dissolved. When we see Arment in his home during Julia's visit, we realize that he is surprised and moved by her gesture of apology. Of course, he has been easily able to make a new life for himself since Julia's departure, and his self-esteem shows no signs of having been impaired by it. Julia can hardly expect the same secure future for herself. The richness of "The Reckoning," a story that has been given little more than casual attention and whose subliminal theme seems to have been largely overlooked, lies in its broader moral implications.

"The Best Man"

The only short story Wharton wrote about politics, "The Best Man," was published in the September 2, 1905 issue of *Collier's*; it had been written after she and her husband were luncheon guests of President Theodore Roosevelt at the White House earlier in the year (Benstock 80). R.W.B. Lewis writes: "The presence of Roosevelt could be vaguely felt in the story Edith Wharton wrote in the wake of her visit to the White House, 'The Best Man,' which Senator [George Cabot] Lodge liked especially, but which in fact only showed the author's lack of sureness in dealing with political figures" (*EW* 146). The story's themes are the staples of politics fiction: scandal, corruption, nepotism, patronage, difficult terrain for one who has not observed first-hand and from the inside how the world of politics works. Wharton was attracted to the subject, no doubt, by its capacity to expose the pitfalls and victories of principle experienced by those in public life. As Wolff remarks, several of the stories from *The Hermit and the Wild Woman*, the 1908 volume in which the tale was collected, "'The Pretext,' 'The Verdict,' 'The Potboiler,' and 'The Best Man'...turn upon the problem of making moral choices" (151). In "The Best Man" Governor Mornway makes a political appointment based on principle, knowing full well that there may be negative repercussions for him resulting from his decision.

One can more readily see the "lack of sureness" of "The Best Man" if one examines the narrative approach. Not long before Wharton wrote this story she had produced two "tales" in a play-script format, "The Twilight of the God," published in 1899, and "Copy" in 1900. And only a few years later, in 1903, she had published "The Dilettante," in which she implemented the devices of the play-script format in a conventional short-story structure. "The Best Man" is just such a playlet transformed into a short story: its sections break down neatly into a series of dialogues between the point-of-view character, the protagonist Governor John Mornway, and a number of family and political figures with whom he converses on the subject of the reappointment of the controversial George Fleetwood as Attorney General of Midsylvania:

> I- Mornway and his sister Grace Nimick. Dusk on the day of his reelection as Governor.
> II- Mornway and his wife, Ella. Immediately following.
> III- Mornway and Rufus Gregg, a former employee. Thirty minutes later.
> IV- Mornway and Hadley Shackwell, a friend and political adviser. Same evening. Ten o'clock.
> Mornaway and George Fleetwood, his Attorney-general. (Shackwell remains on the scene but in the background as Mornway and Fleetwood converse.)
> V- Mornway and Mrs Mornway. Immediately following. (Fleetwood and Shackwell are on the scene when Mrs Mornway arrives but leave almost immediately.)
> VI- Mornway and Shackwell. Three days later, at the Capitol.

One notes that the unities of classical drama, of time, place, and action, are almost entirely adhered to. The exception is Section VI, which violates the unities of time and place. The story has relatively few passages of description, and where there is description it tends to function as stage setting or stage directions, as in a play script. It is the dialogue that carries this story, one of the other features that causes it to resemble a piece of drama writing.

It is a point worth raising as to whether the weakness of "The Best Man" is altogether related to Wharton's lack of direct exposure to political life (Lewis's contention). Certainly one has the sense that it was difficult for Wharton to maintain her interest in the subject she had chosen. There is a discernible sign of this in Section V when Mornway confronts his wife with what he has just heard about her earlier involvement with Fleetwood. The scene promises much in dramatic tension:

> ...finally [Mornway] said: "What did you do it for?"
> "Do what?"
> "Take money from Fleetwood."
> She paused a moment before replying: "If you will let me explain—"
> And then he saw that, all along, he had thought she would be able to disprove it! A smothering blackness closed in on him, and he had a physical struggle for breath. He forced himself to his feet and said: "He was your lover?"
> "Oh, no, no, no!" she cried with conviction. He hardly knew whether the shadow lifted or deepened; the fact that he had instantly believed her seemed only to increase his bewilderment. Presently he found that she was still speaking, and he began to listen to her, catching a phrase now and then through the deafening noise of his thoughts. (I, 700)

What Ella "was still speaking about" is the genesis and evolution of her association with Fleetwood, but Wharton has chosen to render Ella's story in a longish paragraph transmitted by the story's narrator: thus it is effectively removed from the dramatic texture of the scene as the latter has progressed up to that point. As a result Ella's story loses much of its urgency, and the method of its telling removes from Mornway the possibility of his having any dramatic involvement with it.

Also pertinent to "The Best Man's" use of a drama-like format and its consequences for the total impact of the story is the narrator's reference, in the last-cited passage from the tale, to "the deafening noise of [Mornway's] thoughts." This tells us that the Governor is thinking but not what he is thinking. It is true of the story in general that we are provided with few of Mornay's or anyone else's thoughts, not surprising, of course, because of the tale's emphasis on dramatic dialogue. It is unusual in Wharton fiction to find so little effort expended in exposing the reflections and feelings of characters, and the fact that Wharton avoids these elements here speaks certainly to the dramatic structure of the piece, and perhaps as well to the critique of those who see the story as an unsatisfactory one.

"The Bolted Door"

Written during Wharton's stay in England during the fall of 1908 (Benstock 244), "The Bolted Door" came out in March 1909 in *Scribner's*. When it appeared in Wharton's October 1910 collection of short stories, *Tales of Men and Ghosts*, some reviewers thought it "the best in the volume" (Benstock 244), a tall claim for a story that had as one of its companion pieces the superb ghost story "The Eyes" and a commentary on making snap judgements about works of fiction.

Most of the pertinent criticism on this rarely examined story points to its carrying the Poe-esque theme of "the prisoner of consciousness." Lewis comments on the relevance of this theme and cites one of the passages that illustrates its presence: "the feeling on the part of the main character that he has been 'visited by a sense of his fixed identity, of his irreducable, inexpugnable *selfness*, keener, more insidious, more inescapable than any sensation he had ever known'" (*EW* 253). The idea isolated by Lewis is implicit in the story's title, and the tale itself is shot through with statements pointing to Hubert Granice's psychological imprisonment. At the outset he is "tired, middle-aged;...baffled, beaten, worn out" (II, 3); the decade from forty to fifty has been "ten years of dogged work and unrelieved failure" (II, 5). His life is "a nightmare of living; he couldn't make himself a real life, and he couldn't get rid of the life he had" (II, 6). He refers to "the abyss within him" (II, 6), and "a sick despair possessed him" (II, 9). He thinks in terms of "meaningless days" and "his long agony" (II, 16). In short, this psychological study features a subject so disenchanted with life that, lacking the impulse to end it himself, he seeks by every means possible to have himself executed for his murder of a wealthy cousin, and is stalled at every turn, unable to convince anyone of his guilt.

In her discussion of "The Bolted Door," Barbara White writes: "One telling detail left unexplained is Granice's original motive for confessing [his murder]: he feels less guilty about the crime than depressed about his failure as a playwright" (74). It must be said that Granice's motivation for killing his cousin Joseph Lenman in the first place is not entirely unconnected to his ambition to be a successful playwright, and he speaks of this in his long narration to his lawyer Ascham:

"All the while, one phrase of the old man's buzzed in my brain....
'*I'll show him what money can do!*' Good heavens! If I could but show the
old man! If I could make him see his power of giving happiness as a new
outlet for his monstrous egotism! I tried to tell him something about my
situation and Kate's—spoke of my ill-health, my unsuccessful drudgery, my
longing to write, to make myself a name—I stammered out an entreaty for a
loan. 'I can guarantee to repay you sir—I've a half-written play as
security....'" (II, 12-13)

It is Lenman's immediate and absolute refusal to assist Granice that triggers the
latter's resolve to kill his cousin. The narrator resumes Granice's account: "He told
of his mounting obsession—how the murderous impulse had waked in him on the
instant of his cousin's refusal, and he had muttered to himself: 'By God, if you
won't, I'll make you.' He spoke more tranquilly as the narrative proceeded, as
though his rage had died down once the resolve to act on it was taken. He applied
his whole mind to the question of how the old man was to be 'disposed of'" (II, 13).
It is logical to conclude that Granice's motive for confessing is his failure as a
playwright, a condition that rightly or wrongly, he blames on his cousin's
unwillingness to back him financially.

The emphasis and detail deployed in telling Granice's life story is one of the
reasons why this very long tale loses its focus. So are other elements of the story.
White writes that it "bores instead of chilling, as Wharton concentrates on Granice's
efforts to make lawyers and reporters believe him" (74). Thus, in its counter-
detective story or anti-murder mystery aspect—the criminal is attempting to convince
his interrogators of his guilt rather than of his innocence—it is without the surprise
and anticipation of a conventional whodunit. "The Bolted Door" is not one of
Wharton's better stories, but it is hardly the "rotten little melodramatic anecdote"
Percy Lubbock called it—as Shari Benstock insists when she writes: "The story may
seem to create an atmosphere of excessive emotion in response to insufficient
motive, but it also shows that surface irrationalism and overstatement—the man's
claim to be a murderer—can hide a psychological truth that has its own logic" (244).

"The Letters"

Wharton's longish love story, long enough to be serialized in the August,

September, and October 1910 issues of *Century*, has not received many plaudits. Commentators such as Cynthia Griffin Wolff (202-204) and R.W.B. Lewis have focussed mainly on the autobiographical elements of the story, specifically its reverberations of aspects of the author's relationship with her husband and her intimate friend Morton Fullerton. Lewis remarks, for example, that "The Letters" "was written, as it were, from the top of Edith Wharton's imagination, possibly with the relevant documents spread out on her writing board." (The relevant documents were "the 1908 journal and the poems to her lover [Fullerton]" from which Wharton "borrowed richly" for the "description of [Lizzie West's] growing response to [Vincent Deering]") (*EW* 287).

Removed from the context of Wharton's life and relationships and examined as pure fiction, "The Letters" bears a close thematic resemblance to the earlier "The Lamp of Psyche." In both of these tales women who have loved their husbands deeply and without qualification discover that their husbands have been unworthy in one way or another of the high regard in which they have held them. In "The Lamp of Psyche," Delia Corbett learns that her husband Laurence has avoided fighting in the American Civil War when many of his peers have heeded the call to duty. In "The Letters," the wife, Lizzie Deering, suffers a revelation that touches the heart of her marriage: she discovers that most of the letters she had written Deering during his visit to the United States prior to their marriage have remained unopened, this lending considerable credence to her suspicion that he has married her mainly because she has been the beneficiary of an inheritance after all contact had broken off between them. Barbara White, in comparing "The Letters" with "The Lamp of Psyche," calls the former "vastly inferior.... The ending of the story is uncharacteristically didactic, as Lizzie powerfully argues her position [to stick with him] with the unmarried friend who serves as her double" (78-79).

For Allen F. Stein, Lizzie's decision signals a significant personal maturity. "Lizzie West...grows through her marriage to a less than perfect mate" (263). Stein reflects that "Such 'richer realities' as the quiet wisdom and intelligent love reflected here [i.e., when Lizzie sees that out of dross love may come]...are what marriage, as Wharton sees it, has to offer to those perceptive enough to take them" (265). It might be added that the maturing of Lizzie is a major feature of "The Letters" and figures prominently in the story prior to her marriage to Deering. One might consider that her decision to remain married is the natural outcome of a less naive and romantic view of life, a view that Lizzie has held for some time. We are confronted with two Lizzies in "The Letters": the earlier simpering, dependent, unconfident girl; and the later positive, independent, and self-assured woman. And the watershed in Lizzie's life is her acquisition of a small fortune.

The earlier Lizzie prevails to the point in the story when she writes Deering her final letter, knowing that the romantic marriage she so yearned for and worked towards will not materialize (the conclusion of Section IV). The letter is the very soul of romantic sentiment, expressing "the essence of Lizzie's devotion...the larger freedom of its object; she could not conceive of love under any form of exaction or compulsion" (II, 189). Earlier portions of the story speak too to Lizzie's inexperience, simplicity, and innocence—and to the narrator's very conscious expression of it. Here is the description of Lizzie's first romantic exchange with Deering:

> They kissed each other—there was the new fact. One does not, if one is a poor little teacher living in Mme. Clopin's Pension Suisse at Passy, and if one has pretty brown hair and eyes that reach out trustfully to other eyes— one does not, under these common but defenseless conditions, arrive at the age of twenty-five without being now and then kissed—waylaid once by a noisy student between two doors, surprised once by one's grey–bearded professor as one bent over the "theme" he was correcting—but these episodes, if they tarnish the surface, do not reach the heart: it is not the kiss endured, but the kiss returned, that lives. And Lizzie West's first kiss was for Vincent Deering. (II, 179)

The passage draws our attention to, among other things, the narrator's frequent use of the adjective "poor" in connection with Lizzie in the first four sections of "The Letters": "the poor little hat that *had* to 'carry her through' till next summer" (II, 177); "poor soul" (II, 178); "poor Lizzie" (II, 178); "her poor little protest" (II, 179; "her poor little swallow flight of devotion" (II, 186). In most of these places "poor" is being used in two senses: it has a tonal sense, expressing the narrator's sympathy for her subject, and a literal sense, commenting on the flimsiness of Lizzie's material resources and expectations. It may also be said by extension that it indicates something of the narrator's gentle criticism of Lizzie's romantic disposition. Nor does it seem an exaggeration to say that Wharton's frequent repitition of references to Lizzie's economic straits is unrelated to her propensity towards romantic dependence.

When we next see Lizzie, after an interval of two years (Section 5), she is an entirely different woman. Sitting in Laurent's restaurant on the Champs Elysées with her cousins from Providence and an American suitor, she is the picture of elegance, poise, and independence. The fortune she has come into has "destroyed her former world" (II, 191) and with it her former self. When Deering appears from the shadows, she maintains her calm; when he writes, asking for a meeting "she [grants] him a private hour" (II, 192). During most of that meeting, Lizzie is on the offensive, and the change her legacy has brought to her life is highlighted in the narrator's observation that "Gradually it came to [her] that her absence of resentment was due to her having so definitely settled her own fortune" (II, 193). And although Deering has resumed the ascendancy by the end of the meeting, having again won Lizzie's favor, we sense that her decision to return to him and reject "the spectral claim of Mr. Jackson Benn" (II, 197) is the decision of a clear mind. Even if there is considered to be some reversion to the former self in Lizzie, it is temporary and short-lived. When we see her after three years of "wedded bliss" with Deering, and in the face of the discovery that he has never even opened the letters she sent to him in America, she remains poised, controlled, and reasonable in her attempt to rationalize Deering's conduct and the validity of her position about maintaining the marriage bond.

Perhaps "The Letters" has been taken too lightly. As a pure love story, that is to say a love story in which the inter-personal relationship is not complicated by matters of class and status that would tend to make it into a fiction of manners, it deserves closer attention than it has been given. This dense psychological study of Lizzie West conducted by Wharton, complex and profound as it is, deserves better than a label of melodrama. More importantly perhaps, Wharton's explicit assertion of the empowering function of money in a young woman's life, which one would suspect might be of some importance to students of Wharton's interest in class, means, and the status of women, seems to have been almost entirely missed.

"The Blond Beast"

Very little has been written about this story of a business tycoon/philanthropist and his impact on two younger men, his son and his secretary. "The Blond Beast," published in *Scribner's* in September 1910, is to a large extent a mystery. Writing about the reception of the volume of Wharton stories in which it was collected, *Tales of Men and Ghosts* (also 1910), R.W.B. Lewis notes: "[Some reviewers] accused Mrs. Wharton of an excess of subtlety beyond anything the average magazine reader could enjoy," then concurs with these reviewers: "The latter charge, it might be said, could be justifiably leveled against 'The Blond Beast,' whose Nietzschean title is only skimpily fulfilled in the story, which has to do (apparently) with an unprincipled young man acquiring a moral sense. Edith argued with Hugh Smith that she had failed to pull it off—that 'it *was* a good subject,' but she had written it at a bad moment" (*EW* 296).[106]

The charge of "an excess of subtlety" seems entirely justified, and not only for the "average magazine reader," if we are to take seriously Lewis's parenthetical "apparently" from his declaration above. It is clear that the protagonist, Orlando G. Spence, as Barbara White puts it, "publicly denounces peonage abuses but privately transfers his stock to a dummy corporation instead of selling it" (76). It is also clear that when the press comes upon this knowledge, Spence engages his secretary, Millner, to prevail upon the junior Spence not to disengage from his good works, for this will be interpreted by the public as a sign of the truth of the allegations against the father. What is not clear is the nature of "the transaction" (II, 146) Orlando Spence and Millner conduct in order to ensure that Draper Spence is properly coerced. It is clear as well that Millner leaves the employ of Orlando Spence at the close of the story, thus denouncing his earlier opportunism and establishing his essential decency, but the conversation at the time of his resignation is veiled in mystery.[107]

In sum, "The Blond Beast" tells at bottom an uncomplicated story, and one wonders if Wharton did not try to impose on it more complexity than necessary so as to shield its intrinsic simplicity. In places the tale is shrouded in a layer of rhetoric, as in the two-page description of the newly-hired and ambitious Millner. Elsewhere the story suffers from an elliptical narration that draws attention to itself by not providing sufficient information to fill out the gaps. Of "The Blond Beast," Wharton's only "serious" story about big business, E.K. Brown has written that it fails because she didn't know the terrain (26). Perhaps his assessment is correct.

"Coming Home"

Of the three World War I stories Wharton published, "Writing a War Story," "The Refugees" and "Coming Home," only the last can be said to belong strictly to that genre. The first two are both set away from the battle zone; "Coming Home" pictures its characters acting out their adventures during the war, in battle areas, and in situations where they are directly privy to the horror, devastation, and inhumanity of war. Indeed the young French officer who is the story's central character has just been wounded in battle. "Coming Home," published in *Scribner's* in December 1915, has the distinction of being the only war story of this writer who had experienced war first-hand in her volunteer benevolent work and who had written copiously about the war in such non-fiction books as *Fighting France* and *French Ways and Their Meaning*. As Alan Price remarks: "For [Wharton's] contemporary readers in the United States it was a splendid war story with a wounded hero, an attractive heroine forced to sacrifice to save others, a vicious German officer, and an innocent American ambulance volunteer. For modern readers the story is less interesting for its structural than for its biographical and historical dimensions. Yet these biographical and historical facts argue strongly for our consideration of 'Coming Home' not only in Wharton's canon of literary achievements, but also in the larger canon of World War I literature" (99).

Comments made by Barbara White about "Coming Home" offer an opportunity of engaging some of the elements of a story that has been variously called "the best tale in [*Xingu and Other Stories*]" (*EW* 394), "the most interesting in *Xingu*" (Nevius 161), "propaganda" (Nevius 162), of a story in other words that has had a mixed reception. White writes: "'Coming Home' suffers from some typical Wharton failings. It has an unnecessary proliferation of narrators, an overcomplicated plot, and a confused ending (Jean may or may not deliberately kill a man who may or may not be Scharlach). But the story offers us an interesting heroine: a solitary, independent, and clever Parisian who has an incest secret in her past but during the war saves a part of France—in other words, Wharton herself" (86).

White's "unnecessary proliferation of narrators" and "overcomplicated plot" and "confused ending" seem overstated. "Coming Home" has two narrators who, effectively, blend into the one voice very early in the story. If at times backgrounds are provided by other characters, this information is integrated into the narration, and the method is not a source of confusion. One wonders, as well, what is overcomplicated about the plot. As for White's examples of the confused ending, the story seems to provide sufficient suggestion that de Réchamp has killed Scharlach. When de Réchamp informs Greer that there is a leak in the gastank, the latter recalls, "It struck me vaguely that he showed no particular surprise": evidently the former has recognized Scharlach at the onset of the trip and arranged matters so as to be alone with the German, who dies shortly after Greer leaves the scene, having just told his friend, "If we get him to the hospital before morning, I think he'll pull through" (II, 254). There is surely as much, and probably more, evidence for this as there is for Yvonne Malo having "an incest secret," something White insists on unequivocally and repeats later in her critique when she writes that "the French heroine has incest in her past" (101).

"Coming Home" is neither confusing nor overcomplicated. In some of Wharton's stories such failings are real, in the just-examined "The Blond Beast," for example, or in the 1901 historical tale of revolution in Italy, "The Confessional." In "Coming Home" the device of having a second narrator serves to verify the innuendo which is Whaton's way of presenting information: the first narrator, the unnamed American who listens to Macy Greer's story, understands the implications of what he is told—things do not have to be made explicit to him. It might be added as well that the implicitness the two narrators share draws the reader into the kind of "inness" the story invites. Indeed there are other elements of the story whose significance is not spelled out in specific terms which claim the narrator's and our understanding. The fact that the precaution is taken to remove the young de Réchamp boy from the premises when the German soldiers arrive surely speaks to the question of the atrocities of World War I.

Blake Nevius, who calls "Coming Home" the "most interesting" tale in *Xingu*, writes, "It proves that a novelist whose detachment was always precariously maintained could, when confronted by the reports of German atrocities, lose her head as easily as the average newspaper reader" (161). In calling the story "propagandistic" (162) he is, of course, correct in terms of its impact on its contemporary "Allied" readers. For to-day's readers it is less that than the story of an officer and a volunteer medic who respond to an enemy as men at war have universally responded to the enemy. In this sense it is a realistic war story told from the perspective of one side, but whose purely propagandistic "intention" is undercut by the fact that a French officer himself commits an atrocity of war when he kills a brutish enemy, and by the fact that an American medical volunteer is complicit in his friend's action, for he will surely not betray this confidence. Nevius's "average newspaper reader" might very well have cheered silently at the prospect of the two Allies walking off together arm in arm in search of an inn where they might innocently share a *café-complet* together, but both in terms of the killing itself, and in terms of what we have come to know about the virtually universal presence of brutality and atrocity in time of war, we can surely say that Wharton's position might not have been as unequivocally patriotic as it initially appears.

"Coming Home" is a successful war story because it transcends being merely propaganda. It is successful also because it dramatizes the impossible predicaments in which human beings find themselves in time of war, the ways in which war can complicate—even demolish—the moral standards of essentially worthy people. As Julie Olin-Ammentorp puts it, "The story suggests that, disturbing as it may be, war alters moral standards that, before the war, seemed unalterable" (54). Here a decent young woman allows herself to be used sexually by an enemy officer to offset the brutalization of her fiancé's family and the destruction of the family property; a mild-mannered young officer kills the man who has spared his family but victimized his fiancée; a member of the Medical Relief Corps, allegedly neutral, is put in a position where he must aid and abet a murderer. The ambiguity, the paradox, the irony of war is picked up in the story's title, "Coming Home."

It seems banal to say that Wharton came upon her adroitness as a war writer as a result of direct immersion. But such a sentence as "The sense of loneliness and remoteness that the absence of the civil population produces everywhere in eastern France is increased by the fact that all the names and distances on the milestones have been scratched out and the signposts at the crossroads thrown down" (II, 240) attests to the effectiveness of her observation while in the war zone. One had to be there to write that, and Wharton's experience at the front was surely a major factor in making "Coming Home" the credible and moving story it is.

"The Seed of the Faith"

Wharton's thoroughly religious story "The Seed of the Faith" was published in the January 1919 number of *Scribner's*. Cynthia Griffin Wolff notes that "the air of [her] Moroccan journey [1917] wafts through much of Wharton's fiction between 1919 and 1920.... ['The Seed of the Faith'] was clearly related to the blood ritual that she had witnessed at Moulay Idress" (411). In the story a minor character named Ayoub, an alleged convert of the American Evangelical Mission—Wharton's primary interest in the tale—has from time to time to be ministered to after he returns visibly scarred from "blood rituals" away from the mission. The story reflects Wharton's fascination with Moroccan life, in its descriptions of the beauty of the landscape and of the teeming life of Eloued, the city where it is set. Most importantly for the major thrust of "The Seed of the Faith," the Moroccan milieu provides the background for the Moslem faith, the force into which the Mission and its two representatives have been unsuccessfully trying to make inroads for several years.

"The Seed of the Faith" catches its two principal characters, the elderly Baptist missionary Mr Blandhorn and his young disciple Willard Bent, at the confluence of two events that force the dilemma of the two missionaries to a climax: Blandhorn and Bent receive a visit from a former member of the Mission, Harry Spink, who is now a rubber salesman; the ranks of the city are swelled by throngs of visiting faithful who have come to celebrate the feast of the "local saint," Sidi Oman, who "was held in great reverence by the country people" (II, 436).

From the moment of Harry Spink's arrival at Eloued—he comes across Bent in the bazaar—his presence is an explicit challenge to the missionaries: his constant questioning of the point of what they are doing and his noting of the obvious long-standing failure of their apostolate does not so much lead them to a new realization of their failure as bring to the surface of their consciousness the barely concealed sense of their lack of accomplishment. Spink peppers Bent with questions about the usefulness of the missionary project: "What's the good of it all, anyway?" (II, 422); "*What does it all amount to?*" (II, 424); and, in true salesman fashion, about the tangible success of their work: "I mean, what's the results?" and "What's your bag? How many?" (II, 424). Later we learn that he has asked Bent and Blandhorn, "*What is there in it for Jesus?*" a question the latter translates to "What have your long years here profited to Christ?" (II, 433).

Spink's pointed questions affect the older and the younger missionaries in different ways. Bent feels "unsettled," discouraged at the inefficiency of their work, at the fact that "Nobody's view of life was really affected by their presence in the great swarming mysterious city" (II, 431). But Blandhorn is rattled to the core of his being and impelled into taking the radical action of "[insulting the Moslems'] religion" (II, 434) as a way of inciting their fanaticism against himself and thus engineering his own martyrdom. His public acts of stealing the Koran from the mosque's school, spitting on the sacred book of Islam, and stamping on it on the ground—acts in which he is emulated by Bent—bring on his violent death at the hands of his enemies.

Blandhorn's initial actions of overt challenge to the Islamic community prefigure the twisted nature of his final sacrilegious gestures. His challenge is to the routine daily calling out of Allah's name by the muezzin. To "Only Allah is great," Blandhorn responds, "Only Christ is great, only Christ crucified!" When the muezzin answers with "Allah—Allah—only Allah!" Blandhorn "roared" in retaliation, "'Christ—Christ—only Christ crucified!'...exalted with wrath and shaking his fist at the aerial puppet" (II, 435). Blandhorn's words and gestures are more aptly seen as demonstrations of desecration of a religion and its symbols than as affirmations of his own Christian faith. His "martyrdom" is more an act of desperation and despair than one of commitment and hope. Beaten down by the death of his wife, by the lack of support from the Church at home, by years of frustrating work in an inhospitable culture and climate, he loses control, forsakes the principles that had always guided his zeal, "kindness...tolerance...the example of a blameless life" (II, 437), and rationalizes his disastrous last acts as the imitations of a wrathful God.

Although Bent sees the folly of his mentor's ways, he is ultimately moved by fidelity to follow him. "The sight of the weak unwieldy old man, so ignorant, so defenceless and so convinced, disappearing alone into that red furnace of fanaticism, swept from the disciple's mind every thought but the single passion of devotion" (II, 444). Bent's attempt to dissuade Blandhorn from his rash act, "But don't you see, sir, that that's the reason it's no use:[i.e., Blandhorn's statement "I'm too harmless...*they don't believe in me.*"] We don't understand them any more than they do us; they know it, and all our witnessing for Christ will make no difference" (II, 443), gets to the heart of the reasons for the missionaries' failure and frustration. Bent has noticed that his superior "had picked up a little Arabic (Willard always marveled that it remained so little)" (II, 437). He has also recognized Blandhorn's and his own "[ignorance] in everything that concerned the heathen."

> What did they know of these people, of their antecedents, the origins of their beliefs and superstitions, the meaning of their habits and passions and precautions? Mrs. Blandhorn seemed never to have been troubled by this question, but it had weighed on Willard ever since he had come across a quiet French ethnologist who was studying the tribes of the Middle Atlas. Two or three talks with this traveler—or listenings to him— had shown Willard the extent of his own ignorance. He would have liked to borrow books, to read, to study; but he knew little French and no German....
> As for Mr. Blandhorn, he never read anything but the Scriptures, a

> volume of his own sermons...and occasionally a back number of the
> missionary journal.... Consequently, no doubts disturbed him, and Willard
> felt the hopelessness of grappling with an ignorance so much deeper and
> denser than his own. (II, 441-442)

The religious conflict between the Christian missionaries and the Moslems that erupts at the end of the story and culminates in the death of Blandhorn is certainly a factor of the ignorance Bent expresses so articulately to himself in the last-cited passage. But for most of the story the concrete elements that weigh so heavily on the two missionaries, and which the reader is most conscious of their being burdened by, are less Islamic than non-sectarian: a pervasive evil that is more irreligious than religious. Blandhorn and Bent are overwhelmed by the profaneness of this "dark land": "the placid exchange of obscenities" (II, 421) in the bazaar; "fat merchants in white bunches on their cushions, Negresses coming and going with trays of sweets, champagne clandestinely poured, ugly singing girls yowling, slim boys in petticoats dancing"; "a sound of human wailing, cadenced, terrible, relentless, carried from a long way off on a lift of the air" (II, 432). It is this that accounts for the lack of focus in "The Seed of the Faith." There is a diffusion of elements that counters the story's overall effectiveness. In his comments on "The Seed of the Faith" E.K. Brown remarks, using the words of one of Wharton's earlier short-story collections, that the tale depicts a "crucial instance," dramatic and moving, but adds that the intrigue itself is developed in a mediocre and hesitant way (30). Here Brown may very well be alluding to the fact that the conflict which concludes the story does not follow naturally from what has gone on before.

If "The Seed of the Faith" concludes with the attack on the missionaries and the probable end of the missionary effort, and if the forces that prey on Blandhorn and Bent and the Society are seen in negative terms (as the missionaries' inadequacy is, in fact), there is nevertheless an affirmative strain in the story that brings to its anti-climatic close a positive note. Barbara White writes that "without his civilized half [i.e., Mrs Blandhorn] [Blandhorn] reveals 'the seeds of the faith' anger and hatred." White also comments on the story's conclusion: "Willard's survival..., as opposed to his supervisor's death from 'a weak heart,' implies that his experience may provide the seed of a new faith, one based more on Mrs. Blandhorn's healing than Mr. Blandhorn's racist egotism" (92).

It is well to note, however, that Mrs Blandhorn is not seen in an altogether approving light. She has been a somewhat overbearing presence in her marriage, a spouse to whom her husband was in the habit of yielding, a woman who was "the whole show"—as the reliable Spink might have put it. Although she has gained a reputation in Eloued for "miraculous healing powers," it is likely that she was merely a well-trained doctor and no miracle-worker, possessing little of the saintliness that would justify that elevated reputation. In one notable instance, against Mr Blandhorn's wishes she " in a white inarticulate fury...had banished her godson, little Ahmed, (whose life she had saved) and issued orders that he should never show himself again except at prayer meeting, and accompanied by his father" (II, 427). Like her husband and Bent, Mrs Blandhorn does not seem to have been up to the task of dealing with her charges with the warmth and acceptance one would expect of a Christian missionary. She too seems to have been worn down by the difficulties of life in Eloued.

One notes in all three of these erstwhile devotees a scarcity of the milk of human kindness. Spink senses this in Bent when the two meet in the bazaar and the latter makes a move to leave abruptly.

> Willard Bent rose and held out his hand.
> "Good-bye...I must go...If I can be of any use...You know where to find me..."
> "Any use...." Say old man, what's wrong? Are you trying to shake me?" Bent was silent, and Harry Spink continued insidiously: "Ain't you a mite hard on me? I thought the heathen was just what you was laying for." (II, 423)

Bent's coldness is demonstrated as well in his response to the boy Ahmed's invitation to Spink: "Show you Souss boys dance? Down to old Jewess's, Bab-el-Soukh." Bent takes the child's offer to Spink as a personal affront to himself, and "turning from red to a wrathful purple" says, "Get out, you young swine, you—do you hear me?"(II, 426) His reaction to the boy reminds us of Mrs Blandhorn's angry words and threats earlier on. On the other hand Spink's naturally amiable exchange with the child, whom he knew when he worked at the Mission, is in striking contrast to the words and attitudes of the others. When he sees Spink,

> Ahmed raised prodigious lashes from seraphic eyes and reverently surveyed the face of his old friend: "'Me' member."
> "Hullo, old chap....Why, of course...so do I," the drummer beamed.
> (II, 426)

It is difficult, since these variant responses to a child take place in a Christian mission and surround an attempt to get Ahmed to come to evening prayer, not to be reminded here of Jesus's admonition about suffering the little children to come unto him. One might make a case for "the seed of the faith" residing in Harry Spink, whose kindness, personal warmth, and respect for persons stand in striking contrast to the tendency of the Blandhorns and Bent not to acknowledge people primarily as people. Thus, little Ahmed is identified by the missionaries as the boy Mrs Blandhorn saved; Ayoub "was shown to visitors as 'our first convert'" (II, 429); we are never allowed to forget that Myriem is Jewish; the uncooperative masses are seen as heathens. And Spink is consistent with his better nature (and Wharton consistent in highlighting him to the end) when he saves Bent from death. One portion of the closing lines of the story shows Spink to be his brother's keeper. To Bent's question "You came back?" the salesman replies, "Of course. Lucky I did—! I saw this morning you were off your base" (II, 447). "The Seed of the Faith" is clearly a story of religion in its depiction of a sectarian conflict and religious in a more subtle way as well.

"The Refugees"

"The Refugees," from the January 18, 1919 *Saturday Evening Post*, was the second story based on Wharton's war-time experiences published in a little over three years: "Coming Home" had appeared in the *Scribner's* issue of December 1915. Its title clearly identifies its subject as do the settings of time and place that frame it: the story opens "On the 8th of September, 1914" on the railroad platform at Charing Cross (II, 570); at the start of the final section we find the central character standing "again on the pier at Boulogne" on a day in April 1918 (II, 590). Events in the interval take place in London and at an English country estate safely away from the war going on across the channel.

For "The Refugees" Wharton is clearly drawing upon the period of her benevolent work on behalf of widows and orphans during the Great War, a fact that R.W.B. Lewis recognizes in his biography. Wharton's war relief work was huge and drew her total commitment, so impressive that it elicited from Henry James, for example, some of the most enthusiastic praise to be found in the large correspondence the two writers engaged in. "Sometimes," James wrote Wharton on January 16, 1914, referring specifically to his friend's war work, "I let myself think that I form some sort of approximate image of your great life—and then again I fall back in conscious diminutive importance" (Powers 321). And again, on March 24 of the same year James wrote, "Your whole record is sublime" (Powers 331). Even if she seemed to Percy Lubbock to dislike what she was doing, it is difficult to conclude with Lewis that in "'The Refugees' she made a gentle mockery of it all" (*EW* 373). The story is satiric to be sure, but the object of the satire is not as much the benevolent work itself as the kinds of pretentiousness and self-serving that could sometimes surround it. In the story, the central and point-of-view character, Charlie Durand, lands by circumstance in an extended family of English upper-class do-gooders who are in competition over who will bring home the "best" refugees. The satire in the story is directed at such human foibles.

The most evident focus of satire in "The Refugees" is Aunt Audrey Rushworth. Cast aside in her own family, she sees taking in a refugee as the opportunity of asserting and establishing herself among her own. When she seizes on Professor Durand as her prize, she misses all the clues that he is an employed American professor and shows him off among the Rushworths and Beausedges as if he were a trophy, and is never rid of her illusion. When we see her at the close of the story—at the end of the war—she has lost all her timidity, is in officious command of some sort of hospice, and is shortly to marry the Bishop of the Macaroon Islands: presumably her taking on Durand, as illusory as it is, has given her the impetus to transcend her former "insignificance".

Durand is also, of course, a major object of the story's satire, for he too mistakes Aunt Audrey to be a refugee: both are the ironic refugees of the story's title. While his illusion lasts a shorter while than his imagined protégée's, he is slow to perceive the truth about the real nature of their association. When they board a hansom together in London, "Suddenly it struck him that it was *she* who had given the order to the driver. He was more and more bewildered, and ashamed of his visible incompetence" (II, 574). Then in a restaurant "He noticed a large sapphire on one of her [hands]" (II, 576). It is only later during this interlude in the restaurant, as Audrey embarks on a long, impassioned explanation of the difficulties the family has encountered in its attempts to obtain refugees, that Durand, beaten over the head with the obvious, understands.

Part of Durand's inability to recognize the real Audrey stems from his romantic disposition. Ignorant of her social status and predisposed to look on things in less than matter-of-fact fashion, he misinterprets Audrey's attitudes and statements. When she begins to announce her strong desire for a refugee of her own—"For weeks I've been simply suffocating with longing"—"[a]n uncomfortable redness rose on Charlie Durand's forehead. With these foreign women you could never tell: his brief continental experiences had taught him that" (II, 576). Indeed, a good deal of the satire in "The Refugees" is centered on this Professor of Romance Language's propensity to engage his penchant for fancy, a penchant one of his sisters acknowledges by referring to him simply as a Professor of Romance. Durand's motivation in allowing himself to be carried off to Lingerfield is to experience the aura of an English country estate. The description of his view from the cottage where he is quartered resembles a passage from some bucolic prose poem of earlier times: "When he pushed the window open a branch of yellow roses brushed his face, and a dewy clematis gazed in at him with purple eyes. Below him lay a garden, incredibly velvety, flower-filled, and enclosed in yew hedges so high that it seemed, under the low twilight sky, as intimate and shut in as Miss Rushworth's low-ceilinged drawing room, which, in its turn, was as open to the air, and as full of flowers, as the garden" (II, 583). The description of the scene Lingerfield offers Durand runs for an entire page and is shot through with his ecstatic notings of the trappings of Romance: "lattices," "stile," "forest of Arden," "ferny glades," "chapels," and "cloisters." When we see Durand four years later at Boulogne, "he was buttoned into a too-tight uniform, on which he secretly hoped the Y.M.C.A. initials were not always the first thing to strike the eye of the admiring spectator," and "he could never quite console himself for the accident of having been born a few years too soon to be wearing the real uniform of his country" (II, 590).

If Audrey Rushworth and Charlie Durand are individualized figures of gentle ridicule in "The Refugees," the English upper classes as an entity come in for a somewhat more severe castigation. Audrey's and the Professor's foibles are understandable, forgiveable, and in the end harmless, but the faults of the privileged English country set elicit less acceptance and understanding. Wharton exults in showing us a people of manners who are without manners. When Durand is ushered into the drawing room at Lingerfield, the room "seemed full of people and full of silence," and Lord Beausedge acknowledges his arrival by "[making] a step or two toward his guest, [taking] him for granted, and [returning] to the newspaper" (II, 584). Throughout the descriptions of Durand's stay at Lingerfield, Wharton's pen is sharp and telling, as in her portrait of the chatelaine of the manor: "Only Lady Beausedge, strongly corseted, many necklaced, her boa standing away from her bare shoulders like an Elizabethan ruff, seemed to Durand majestic enough for her background. She suggested a composite image of Bloody Mary and the late Queen" (II, 584). In one of the few extended discussions of "The Refugees," Lev Raphael writes that "the story has the sharpness and comedy of 'Xingu' (another extended play on embarrassment) and deserves to be better known" (168). One might add that although the product of a period several decades removed from *The House of Mirth*, "The Refugees" possesses some of the incisiveness of that novel, although, of course, here that quality is not put to such a lofty purpose.

"Velvet Ear Pads"

A little over five years after "The Refugees" appeared in the *Saturday Evening Post*, another of the relatively new mass-circulation slick magazines, *Red Book*, published "Velvet Ear Pads" in its issue of August 1925. The story was another light piece, centering its attention again on an American professor travelling in Europe, on the loose, as it were, away from his institution and the practice of his profession. As well, "Velvet Ear Pads," like its predecessor, has its professor's chance meeting with a woman trigger off the series of events that constitutes the story. The difference between the two tales is that the former is more satiric—more serious, if that can be said of "The Refugees"—whereas the latter is merely humorous and even trivial. E.K. Brown's comments on the story are appropriate: "une fantasie burlesque"; more caricature than real; an entertainment for a popular magazine (29).

This is not to say that "Velvet Ear Pads" is entirely devoid of satire: there is a bit of gentle fun made of both Professor Loring G. Hibbart of Purewater University in Clio, New York, and the Princess Balalatinsky. Each of the major characters is a parody of a type: Hibbart, of the learned academic whose *locus operandi* is the world of the abstract, who has written a book called *The Elimination of Phenomena* and is now in the process of refuting Einstein's theory of relativity, who regards pretty women and scenery as distractions to his retreats into Pure Reason and the Abstract, and who wears velvet ear pads to keep out the world of matter; Betsy Balalatinsky, of the dramatic, effusive, ostentatious parvenu Russian aristocrat. Beyond this there is little if anything that would qualify as satire. Rather the humor and good feeling in the story derive from such matters as names, mistaken identity, the fortunate confluence of circumstances, and mild sexual innuendo. As Barbara White remarks, "Wharton's post-war comedies rely heavily on plot and stories like 'Velvet Ear Pads'...are dominated by farcical action" (6). If nothing else, the story shows that Wharton was as capable as anyone of offering magazine editors and readers the light-hearted entertainment they wanted.

"The Young Gentlemen"

Pictorial Review published the Gothic tale "The Young Gentlemen," one of four Wharton stories that magazine carried during the mid-twenties.[108] Set in "Harpledon, on the New England coast somewhere between Salem and Newburyport" (II, 385), it exploits an isolated people's fear of intrusion from the outside, using its titular figures, the two dwarfs who emerge at the end of the story, as symbols of the village society's retardation. The criticism of the town is all the more pointed because it sees itself as a superior society of old property, of "artists and writers" (II, 385), whose spokesman, the story's narrator, is himself a writer of the most self-conscious pretensions.

The narrator's preamble to the story clearly establishes Harpledon's sense of exclusiveness and self-satisfaction: "How we resisted modern improvements, ridiculed fashionable 'summer resorts,' fought trolley lines, overhead wires and telephones...and bought up (those of us who could afford it) one little heavy-roofed house after another, as the land speculator threatened them.... Harpledon was, and is still, happily unmenaced by industry, and almost too remote for the weekend 'flivver'" (II, 385). The subsequent discussion of Waldo Cranch's family history suggests that the town had been characterized by the same insularity in its past: "...the Cranches had been prosperous merchants for three centuries, and had inter-married with other prosperous families," but "one of them, serving his business apprenticeship at Malaga in colonial days, had brought back a Spanish bride, to the bewilderment of Harpledon" (II, 386).

Of course it is this Spanish ancestry within the Cranch family that is seen to be responsible for the tragedy in which the story concludes. It is clear from the care-giver Catherine's recapitulation to the narrator of Waldo Cranch's last days that the latter holds his Spanish blood responsible in the birth of his dwarf sons. And it is also clear that the townspeople's attitude toward the Spanish presence in the Cranch family has been entirely negative. The sketchy Cranch family genealogy the narrator provides smacks of cultural and religious prejudice and of irrational judgements:

[Waldo Cranch's] Spanish great-grandmother's portrait still hung in the old house; and it was a long-standing joke at Harpledon that the young Cranch who went to Malaga, where he presumably had his pick of Spanish beauties, should have chosen so dour a specimen. The lady was a forbidding character on the canvas: very short and thickset, with a huge wig of black ringlets, a long harsh nose, and one shoulder perceptively above the other. It was characteristic of Aunt Lucilla Selwick that in mentioning this swart virago she always took the tone of elegy. "Ah, poor thing, they say she never forgot the sunshine and orange blossoms, and pined off early when her queer son

Calvert was hardly out of petticoats." A strange man Calvert Cranch was; but he married Euphemia Waldo of Wood's Hole, the beauty, and had two sons, one exactly like Euphemia, the other made in his own image. And they do say that one was so afraid of his own face that he went back to Spain and died a monk—if you'll believe it," she always concluded with a Puritan shudder. (II, 387)

This is a remarkable assessment of the Cranch family blood-lines, and the only basis we have in the story for the general conclusion that the trouble is all Hispanic and that "the young gentlemen's" condition is its result. One might as legitimately claim that the trouble was with the Cranch merchants whose time in Spain had exposed them too frequently to the intense rays of the Iberian sun. In fact, on the basis of what we are told, there is as much possibility of the faulty genes being from the Cranches or Waldos as from the undistinguished dowager of the portrait. It is testimony to Waldo Cranch's sense of racial superiority that he reflexively strikes out against his Spanish roots when what he considers his shame is about to be exposed to public view, and indeed when he has become vexed during his lifetime with the presence of the children in his house. It is from Catherine that we learn of Cranch's diatribe on the day he takes his final departure: "Not but what he would have hated me to say so, sir," she tells the narrator, "for the Spanish blood in him, and all that went with it, was what he most abominated;" and again, "Well, sir, he despised his great-grandfather more than he hated the Spanish woman. 'Marry that twisted stick for her money, and put her poison blood in us!' He used to put it that way, sir, in his bad moments" (II, 401).

Cranch's disappointment and pain over his fathering of dwarfs is certainly understandable. And it must be said that there is an element of consideration and love in his treatment of his offspring. He has seen to their welfare by putting them in the charge of a conscientious and sensitive care-giver and by assuring that every effort will be made to see to their care after his death. We must take Catherine's assurances about this aspect of Cranch's concern. When she tells the narrator after her employer's death that "He needed life and company himself; but he would never separate himself from the little boys. He was so proud—and yet so softhearted" (II, 402), Catherine is expressing the ambivalence in Cranch. But of course her bias in his favor prevents her from seeing the imbalance between his pride and his softheartedness. In fact, his pride has taken on the quality of a pathological obsession. In his need to shift off blame on his Spanish ancestor, in his extravagent efforts to keep hidden from the village the fact of his children, in his inability to face up to the secret being found out, and, possibly, in his treatment of the young servant woman who breaks the silence about his children, Cranch shows himself to be acting outside the bounds of control. (Does not the juxtaposition of Cranch's statement to Catherine as Hannah Oast leaves the house, "We'll have no trouble with her," and Catherine's declaration, "And this morning the police came," allow the possibility that the man has attempted or committed some harm on Hannah?)

Cranch's two-sided state of mind regarding his young gentlemen surfaces clearly, as well, in the note he leaves for the narrator just before he takes his own life: "I have appointed no one to care for my sons; I expected to outlive them. Their mother would have wished Catherine to stay with them. Will you try to settle all this mercifully? There is plenty of money, but my brain won't work. Good-bye" (II, 400). While his concern that the orphans be provided for is laudable, he totally misreads his fellow artist's potential to be a caring guardian for his sons. In choosing the writer/narrator he is assuming that one of his own kind—he is a painter, and the story suggests, a mediocre one—would be up to the task of helping fill a paternal role. In fact, the social and cultural superiority to which Harpledon and its inhabitants lay claim is based in part on the presence of creative artists in its midst; hence, Cranch, in reposing his faith in the narrator, acts through deluded motives. The narrator turns out in one sense to be a replica of Cranch, for his gestures *vis-à-vis* his new charges repeat the attitude of shame that characterizes their father's conduct. The final portions of the text are riddled with statements of his own distaste for his charges and his avoidance of them: "I hadn't the heart to go to that dreadful house again" (II, 400-401); "I never went back there"; "I am their other guardian; and I never yet had the courage to go down to Harpledon to see them" (II, 402).

The narrator of "The Young Gentlemen" takes his place among those several Wharton short-story male narrators who tend to withdraw from life, who avoid close relationships with women especially. Barbara White notes: "At the end of the story the narrator separates himself from Mrs. Durant, who is 'other' because of her female nature. He seems angry at her care for the dwarfs even addressing the putative male reader, 'Would you have believed it? She wanted it—the horror, responsibility and all,' and concludes with the sort of floating misogynist comment that brings so many Wharton stories to an abrupt end, 'Women are strange'." Whether the narrator is "a milder version of Waldo [Cranch]" (91), as White says, or whether the opposite is true, both of these males reflect the attitude that it is women in whom the responsibility for the dwarfs' plight resides: whether it be the Spanish ancestress of the portrait, or whether it be Catherine or Mrs Durant, women are seen by Cranch and the narrator as a means of deflecting responsibility away from themselves. "The Young Gentlemen" has, as seen earlier, a clear racist theme; it also has a sexist one: Harpledonians separate themselves from the outside on the basis of their New England, Anglo-Saxon, Puritan stock; the two male protagonists set themselves above women as well. The story of the discovery of a long-kept secret acts as a symbol of the letting of the racist and sexist cat out of the bag.

It is worth making the point that the narrator of "The Young Gentlemen" considers himself a writer and that when he speaks of Harpledon at the outset of the story as a place that has become "far more attractive, and far worthier of its romantic reputation, than when we artists and writers first knew it" (II, 385), he is including himself in that designated group. In many Wharton short stories, narrators tell their tales in informal ways and at least give the illusion that they are not structuring their narrative formally. In "The Young Gentlemen" the first-person involved narrator functions as a self-conscious, deliberate story-teller, giving his account of events that occurred twenty years earlier. And one might make a case that he is not a very good story-teller: like his friend Cranch, whose paintings none of the townspeople think to request when they organize their first "jumble sale," the narrator is a second-rate artist. For one thing, the ending of his account is "telegraphed": it is as if, like a student in a fiction-writing workshop, he has been told that a surprise ending must be properly set up in the body of the story if it is to be artistically effective, and has erred by overdoing his incidents of foreshadowing. Then too he can hardly be called astute in his conclusions about people, even about those to whom he is close. His inability to understand the urgency of Mrs Durant's need to go to Cranch's house after she has received the latter's message signifies his essential superficiality, as does his surprise at her devotedness on behalf of Cranch's dwarfs. His proposal to Mrs Durant on this occasion, "Hadn't we better stop and ask Aunt Lucilla what's wrong? She knows more about Cranch than any of us!" is particularly inappropriate.

Ultimately the narrator's artistic failings reflect his human failings. Wharton has written a good story about a poor story-teller and a less than admirable human being. In the portrayal of the narrator's weakness resides the author's skill. In "The Young Gentlemen," largely ignored in the commentary on Wharton's short fiction, what is being attempted is not necessarily immediately evident. The story deserves a much closer examination than it has received.

"A Bottle of Perrier"

Published in the *Saturday Evening Post* in its issue of March 27, 1926, a month after "The Young Gentlemen" had appeared in *Pictorial Review*, "A Bottle of Perrier" illustrates, when juxtaposed with its predecessor, just how wanting is the narrator's handling of the foreshadowing technique in the earlier story and lends credibility to the interpretation that Wharton was presenting the writer/story-teller of Harpledon as a flawed and pretentious artist. Because this first-person narrator is recounting his tale some twenty years after its salient events occurred and has direct knowledge of them—having been an actor himself in the events he is reconstructing—he is practising the narrative convention of suggesting or prefiguring a development in a literary work before it occurs (Frye, Baker, Perkins 199). His practice of the technique, though, is erratic because he is lured by his foreknowledge into overstating his case, with the result that much of the potential suspense in his story is diffused. We know for example after reading "The Young Gentleman's" brief first section that the romantic New England town has lost its charm for the narrator, that he has resolved never to return there. We are given clue after clue as his account progresses that the cause of his disaffection with Harpledon resides in a certain part of Waldo Cranch's house; in "The Young Gentlemen" the narrator's recounting directs readers to its bitter conclusion—long before that conclusion occurs.

In "A Bottle of Perrier" there is no such telegraphing of the story's ending. Rather, we are given evidence that does not register as evidence upon first reading but which later in the story or upon a second reading can be seen as foreshadowing subsequent discoveries. We wonder early on, after Medford's arrival at Almodham's desert home, why the servant Gosling insists that his guest drink wine when the latter wants only water without having any idea about the implications of Gosling's attempts at persuasion. Similarly, the false information Gosling gives Medford about one of Almodham's horses being lame initially has no impact on us, but later becomes part of Gosling's defensive posture.

All this to say that "A Bottle of Perrier" is one of Wharton's finest stories, and one whose excellence has elicited considerable critical comment. It would be more accurate to call it a "crime story," as Carol Singley does (271), than a "murder mystery" as R.W.B. Lewis does (*EW* 522), for the reader is virtually sure of the murderer's identity before the story's end. Its richness derives from the beauty of its prose descriptions as well as from the way it carries such a variety of substance. Wharton wrote it in less than a week; Bernard Berenson's understanding that she had done it in one day was incorrect (Benstock 423). Although it is the product of a period some thirteen years removed from Wharton's trip to the Moroccan desert, it powerfully evokes, like her other north African story, "The Seed of the Faith," the mixture of beauty, menace, and mystery that inhabits that terrain (Benstock 423).

In terms of characterization, the most interesting study in "A Bottle of Perrier" is that of the Maltese servant, Gosling. E.K. Brown doubtless had this in mind when he called the story a superior psychological study. One might make a case for Gosling's being the story's central character and that the change that occurs in him as the five days of Medford's visit ensue gathers to itself the other major dynamic, the burgeoning fear and suspicion of the young visitor. It is to these elements that the story's title is related. The "bottle" of Perrier that never arrives is the cause of Gosling's deterioration from a condition of assurance that he will be able to ride out the murder of his employer undetected by his guest. Had the Perrier water arrived on schedule, Medford might well have left Almodham's enclosure innocent of his host's state: it is the condition of the cistern water he drinks and in which he bathes, and Gosling's self-conscious defensiveness about it, that gradually arouses his suspicion and leads him to look into the well. The salience of Gosling in "A Bottle of Perrier" is emphasized by Barbara White when she notes, and with particular mention of this tale, that "the late short stories show...a greater lower-class presence with the perspectives of lower-class characters, especially servants, being presented more strongly and sympathetically." "Gosling," she writes "[is] in fact, presented sympathetically.... [His] murder of his master has been provoked; his tyrannical master is characterized as wholly evil, even in some respects resembling Culwin [of 'The Eyes']" (98).

But one would do great injustice to "A Bottle of Perrier" if one ignored the context, physical and psychological, in which the murder of Almodham and its discovery by Medford take place. Clearly, although Almodham is not literally a living presence in the story, he too is one of its major figures. It is clear that he is an older, experienced, predatory male who has taken into his sights the younger, callow, wholly innocent Medford. In its isolation, natural setting, and acquired conveniences Almodham's desert home suggests a place of potential entrapment for the recuperating Medford: "And what a place it was to rest in" is his first impression. "The silence, the remoteness, the illimitable air! And in the heart of the wilderness, green leafage, water, comfort—he had already caught a glimpse of wide wicker chairs under the palms—a humane and welcoming habitation" (II, 512). And until he is awakened by Gosling's growing anxiety, Medford finds himself easily taken by the ease and timelessness: "Life had the light monotonous smoothness of eternity" (II, 516). Then too there are the amenities of the place: Medford is plied with champagne and wine, he is treated to course after course of food prepared by a gifted cook, offered pipes of jade and amber for smoking opium.

Throughout, though, even from the outset of his stay at Almodham's, Medford is conscious of an offsetting aspect to much of what he observes and experiences both inside and outside the enclosure. In the courtyard "An ancient fig tree, enormous, exuberant, writhed over a whitewashed wellhead, sucking life from what appeared to be the only source of moisture within the walls." Beyond, "on every side, stretched away the mystery of the sands, all golden with promise, all livid with menace, as the sun alternately touched and abandoned them" (II, 511). For all its attractions the house is in poor shape: above "the habitable part...towered mighty dilapidated walls of yellow stone, and in their crevices clung plaster chambers, one above the other, cedar beamed, crimson shuttered but crumbling" (II, 513). "A Bottle of Perrier" is, like its sister Moroccan desert tale, "The Seed of the Faith," a case study in the effective wedding of theme and atmosphere. As White puts it: "Below the surface of the fortress's 'beauty' and 'peace' is Wharton's familiar underside—violence and corruption" (98).

Some idea of the richness of content "A Bottle of Perrier" carries can be gleaned from commentaries on the story by such critics as Candace Waid and Carol Singley which emphasize its psycho-sexual elements. Waid's critique puts these elements in the context of Wharton's effective blending of substance and setting. She notes: "'A Bottle of Perrier,' with its eroticized and cannibalistic landscape, is Wharton's vision of the monstrous and murderous feminine. Gosling is caught between 'masculine' assertion and 'feminine' service but he cannot escape from his feminine role. As a 'man-servant,' he is threatened with annihilation by the pastoral female timelessness of the desert's cycles. He in turn, assuming the woman's part, becomes deadly for his male master" (184). Singley frames her critique within a discussion of the story as an example of the "female gothic narrative," whose elements are "a young feminine innocent, a mysterious castle, and threatening or enigmatic male forces" (271). She goes on to note that here "a female writer engages issues of the male homoerotic gothic as well as the female gothic, giving us a rare vision of such a conflation from a woman's point of view" (272).

Such expositions of "A Bottle of Perrier's" effects only serve to emphasize the high quality of Wharton's observation of the human condition and her skill in elaborating her insights into coherent and eminently readable units of shorter fiction. It seems appropriate to say in this penultimate discussion of the author's eighty-six collected short stories, in which she uses a genre story, a crime story, as a vehicle for carrying profound observations about character, that in Wharton's short-story *oeuvre* we are dealing with a superb body of work. And to ask: Is there a more substantial and extensive collection of short fiction in our canon? Has any other American short-fiction writer as successfully taken into her/his sights such a variety of subjects and treated them with such a wealth of vision and such finesse of language?

"Charm Incorporated"

It does appear that in selling "Charm Incorporated" to *Hearst's International-Cosmopolitan*, where it appeared in the February 1934 number under the title "Bread upon the Waters," Wharton was being somewhat inconsistent with the principles she had expressed four months earlier in a letter to Rutger Jewett. "The fact is," she wrote at that time, "I am afraid that I cannot write down to the present standards of the American picture magazines. I am in as much need of money as anybody else at this moment, and if I could turn out a series of potboilers for magazine consumption I should be only too glad to do so; but I really have difficulty in imagining what they want" (*LEW* 572). Wharton seemed to have gauged correctly what *Cosmopolitan* wanted in the case of this story at least. Lewis reports that she received "the large sum of $ 5000" for what he characterizes as a "light-fingered tale" and "a trifle" (*EW* 507). One of the very few critical comments about "Charm Incorporated" comes from Barbara White, who uses it as an example of "the bad stories of the pre-war period." Calling it "a farce about a conservative American businessman who marries a Russian refugee and her family," she writes that "it is not funny enough to compensate for the shallowness in characterization and lack of import" (83).

It might be added that "Charm Incorporated" lacks unity, that it reads rather like two separate chapters of a frothy novel. In the first part, the point-of-view character, James Targatt, the businessman, finds out that he has not only married Nadeja Kouradjine but "taken on" all of her family as well, including some with questionable claims on the Kouradjine name. The application of the title to this part of the story is twofold: Nadeja and the Kouradjine clan parlay their good looks and personalities—their charm is emblemized by their long eyelashes, which seem to be a universal trait among them—into successful marital and financial arrangements;

Targatt puts their charm to work for him, using the alliances they make through his manipulations to his own business advantage. In the second part of the story, Targatt having been approached by a famous portraitist who wishes to paint Nadeja full-length, begins to wonder if she has lost interest in him and is falling in love with the painter. The story ends with Nadeja's reassurance of her love and fidelity; "Don't you think that now at last we could afford to have a baby?" she asks him (II, 762).

With its plethora of good-looking young people, its flimsy characters, its emphasis on money-making, "Charm Incorporated" was a natural for the movies, and Jewett sold it to the Eastern Film Company for $ 5000. It was subsequently sold to Universal Pictures who produced an adaptation of the story in 1934 under the title *Strange Wives* (Benstock 439). The generally affirmative assessment given *The World Over*, Wharton's last collection of new stories, and the one in which "Charm Incorporated" appeared, does not apply to this piece. Wolff writes of that collection that "it confirms the reclamation of [Wharton's] powers...the terrible shrillness of *Hudson River Bracketed* and *The Gods Arrive* had not prevailed after all" (396). "Charm Incorporated" could never be accused of being "shrill," but it is far off the standard of its collection companions "Pomegranate Seed," "Roman Fever," and "Confession."

* * * * *

The Immense Variety Show of Life

In the opening pages of Wharton's ghost story "The Eyes," the narrator refers to the central character, Andrew Culwin, as a "detached observer" of "the immense muddled variety show of life" (II, 115). If one excises the adjective "muddled" and substitutes the qualifier "passionate" for "detached," one has found an apt way of expressing the diversity and intensity of the Wharton short-story oeuvre. Adopting a genre approach to the stories as opposed to, say, a strictly chronological or largely biographical one, allows a reader to see not only the general scope of Wharton's interests but as well the broad range of situations, circumstances, and characters Wharton envisages and then fleshes out within a given genre of story, be the story a ghost story, a story of social striving or academic life, a story about the arts. But Wharton was not satisfied to limit herself to the well-trodden ways of her most preferred subjects. She assayed a number of tales that do not easily fit the niches that house most of her re-creations of life. The tales discussed in the present chapter represent her efforts when she strayed from home ground or when she sought to bring an original dimension to, or cast a familiar kind of story in a new light.

Wharton's forays into alien territory were in several cases written for the higher-paying, mass-circulation slick magazines, especially later in her life when she was feeling the need to reap higher financial gain for her writing. The majority of these were potboilers done to satisfy editors and readers eager for entertainment pieces. "The Refugees," in the *Saturday Evening Post* of January 18, 1919; "Velvet Ear Pads," in *Red Book* in August 1925; and "Bread upon the Waters," in *Hearst's International-Cosmopolitan"* in February 1934 (retitled for collection "Charm Incorporated") are all shallow and amusing performances. The first two present bumbling, endearing and morally upright professors, on the loose from their home universities in the United States, travelling in Europe, and taken in tow by convincing women: one is tempted to conclude that Wharton was attempting to soften the dour and sometimes dark view of the academic profession that emerges in her earlier tales of collegiate life. "Charm Incorporated," one of the two tales in which Wharton focusses on businessmen, is so light and frivolous as to invite a question about her possible motivation in writing it, even given the lucrative return it provided her.

The other story about entrepreneurs, "The Blond Beast," a more serious attempt to engage the world of big business, albeit in a limited way via the associations of three characters, is perhaps the most abject of Wharton's rare failures in the short story: its meaning is shrouded in narrative and verbal obscurity. Her only tale of political life, "The Best Man," is clearly written but has little distinction. It is one of those narratives that Wharton seems to lose interest in telling: confronted with a dramatic showdown between the protagonist/politician and his less-than-innocent wife, Wharton chooses to break off a promising dialogue and recount the confrontation via summary narrative. The other piece in this miscellany that hardly passes muster is the nondescript "The Valley of Childish Things, and Other

424

Emblems," one of her first fiction attempts, a collection of thematically but loosely related segments whose significance and interconnectedness beg for greater clarity.

The other fantasy Wharton wrote in the 1890s, "The Fullness of Life," a story that has been widely interpreted as an autobiographical statement on her unhappy marriage, is far more successful and holds up very well to critical scrutiny, even shorn of its engagement with the author's personal life. As a declaration about her own marital dissatisfaction however, it does stand in interesting contrast to another Wharton tale of love and marriage written a decade later. "The Letters" has been interpreted to reflect Wharton's growing attachment to her lover Morton Fullerton (*LEW* 287). It is also possible, based on details found in both stories, to read "The Letters" as Wharton's projection of a relatively happy union that might have been— with Teddy, or another husband of the same vintage, a marriage in which she has arrived at a satisfactory accommodation with her husband. Certain connections between items in the two stories are such as to suggest that Wharton may have had in mind "The Fullness of Life" when, a happier and more settled woman, she came to write "The Letters." The following passage from "The Letters" speaks of Lizzie West's state of mind on the day she discovers that her husband had not opened the letters he received from her while he was in America:

> The two friends were together in Lizzie's morning room—the room she has chosen, on acquiring the house, because when she sat there, she could hear Deering's step as he paced up and down before his easel in the studio she had built for him. His step had been less regularly audible than she had hoped, for, after three years of wedded bliss, he had somehow seemed to settle down to the great work which was to result from that state; but even when she did not hear him she knew that he was there, over her head, stretched out on the old divan from St. Cloud, and smoking countless cigarettes while he skimmed the morning papers; and the sense of his nearness had not yet lost its first keen edge of wonder. (II, 197-198)

Here we are reminded of the repeated sound of the husband's creaking boots which is recalled with such annoyance by the protagonist of "The Fullness of Life." We notice also that Deering has become lazy but that at least he is interested in painting and a far cry from the husband in "The Fullness of Life" who only read "railway novels" or novels "with a murder or a forgery and a successful detective" (I, 19, 20).

It is not a distant leap to imagine Deering as a more responsible and lovable Teddy Wharton, who if he "had sought [Lizzie] out when he learned that she was rich" (II, 203), "was not dazzled by money; his altered fortunes had tempted him to no excesses..." (II, 198). In the end Lizzie "understood...that she had gradually adjusted herself to the new image of her husband as he was, as he would always be. He was not the hero of her dreams, but he was the man she loved, and who had loved her" (II, 206). The fictive Deering stands somewhere between the real-life Teddy and the perhaps larger-than-life Fullerton in Wharton's affections.

The other marriage story in this grouping, "The Reckoning," is without the ultimate affirmation of "The Letters," and readers will notice that its ending closely resembles that of both "After Holbein" and "The Journey" in its evocation of bleakness. As Julia Westall leaves the home of her first husband, having gone there to seek his forgiveness for her insensitive departure from their marriage, "the footman threw open the door, and she found herself in the darkness" (I, 437). "The Reckoning" is a story of marriage *per se*, that is to say a story of marriage removed from considerations of status and wealth, the context in which Wharton's stories of marriage are usually seen. Julia has not brought money to her union with her second husband, and we are told that "Clement Westall was acknowledged to be a rising lawyer: it was generally felt that his fortunes would not rise as rapidly as his reputation. The Westalls would probably always have to live quietly and go out to dinner in cabs" (I, 426). She is alone now after two broken marriages, and the abjectness of her future, at least as she perceives it, is suggested by the apprehension she experiences as she walks in the New York evening: "she fancied the police was watching her, and this sent her hastening down the nearest side street" (I, 433).

Of Wharton's two pieces in which she plays variations on a genre story, "A Coward," an anti-fiction of manners, and "The Bolted Door," a counter-murder story, the first is the more successful. The latter fails in being too long: the substance of the story is not such as to sustain our interest, and the ending is telegraphed long before the end. Measured against another of Wharton's longer tales, "Her Son," where revelation after revelation carries us through to the final pages, where narrator and

426

characters have interesting interior lives or backgrounds, where Wharton's commentary about superficial characters amuses, "The Bolted Door" does not hold up. "A Coward," more compact, and fitted with characters and settings familiar to Wharton, carries off its counter-genre objective with aplomb. Beginning as a conventional fiction of manners ("My daughter Irene has had no social advantages but if Mr. Carstyle had chosen—"[I, 127], Mrs Carstyle exclaims as the story opens) "A Coward" soon turns Vibart's and the reader's attention away from Irene's predicament to her father's. The latter has forsaken status, style, and social advantage for the family in order to right a moral wrong, thus depriving Irene of the social advantages she and her mother both crave. Vibart's shift away from his campaign to woo Irene and towards an admiration for Mr Carstyle changes the axis of the story from manners to morality, an emphasis it retains until the end, despite Mrs Carstyle's regrets about the family's squandered opportunities.

The manipulation of literary genres Wharton undertakes in "The Bolted Door" and especially in "A Coward," where she turns one of her favorite and most successful genre of tale into something other than itself, may serve as an emblem for the general movement of departure from norms that characterizes many aspects of the stories under scrutiny here. For example, there is as much variety of geographical setting in these tales as there is breadth of subject matter and genre. Only three of these sixteen narratives have New York locales. The rest move about the imaginative and real world from Midsylvania to heaven, from Concord to Milbank and Harpledon in New England, from London to Paris to Monte Carlo, from the French wartime countryside to the Moroccan desert.

In her two Moroccan tales Wharton draws upon her memorable travels in North Africa and uses her texts to express her fascination with, as it is expressed in "A Bottle of Perrier," "the mystery of the sands, all golden with promise, all livid with menace, as the sun alternately touched or abandoned them" (II, 511). The stories themselves in their characters and situations reflect some of the ambivalence the setting represents. "The Seed of the Faith" suffers somewhat from a lack of focus, but its interest in religion, and particularly in Christianity, likens it to Wharton's other fundamentally Christian story, "The Hermit and the Wild Woman." Both of these latter tales favor the humanistic side of Christianity over the fanaticism and other-worldliness of the Baptist missionaries, and the stringent asceticism of the Saint of the Rock. "A Bottle of Perrier" is a superior story, more sharply centered, and assured of its direction. It is an interesting foil to "The Bolted Door" in its practice of a true crime story, and its tightness and concentration point up the short-comings of Wharton's counter-murder mystery.

Of the two New England stories in this group, "The Angel at the Grave" and "The Young Gentlemen," the former is the better known: it has been not infrequently anthologized, in part no doubt because of its appropriation of an important part of the American literary landscape. As are other elements of New England life, New England Transcendentalism is the object of considerable ambivalence in Wharton's short stories. In "The Angel at the Grave" the biographer of Orestes Anson, the story's central focus of interest, comes to see her subject as a virtual non-entity amidst of group of insignificant writers. At times Wharton plays upon this theme of the Transcendentalists' irrelevance and fustiness, but in other tales the movement is seen in a positive light. The hero of "The Legend," for example, is a philosopher who has drawn on Transcendentalist ideas, and in "The Long Run" it is the absence of Emersonian qualities that helps to identify the state of stasis into which the protagonist's life has sunk.

"The Young Gentlemen" stands at opposites to the New England-based academic stories in its portrayal of backwardness and provincialism—although it must be said that some of Wharton's colleges fall far off the ideal of openness and world-mindedness that ought to mark life in the academy. Set in Harpledon, "somewhere between Salem and Newberryport" (II, 385), and hence evocative of the Puritan foundation of the country, "The Young Gentlemen" is most fittingly compared to the ghost story "Bewitched," in which the rural community portrayed is still under the thrall of Calvinistic rigor and dourness, and the academic tale "The Pretext," where a kind of Puritan patriarchalism controls and inhibits the life of its female protagonist. "The Young Gentlemen" blends plot, character, and symbol into a masterful study of prejudice and warped human respect, and ranks with

428

"Coming Home" and "A Bottle of Perrier" at the summit of this anthology of miscellaneous Wharton short stories.

"Coming Home," the war story that has had to outlive its unjustified reputation as a piece of Great War propaganda; "A Bottle of Perrier," a murder story covering for a layering of psychological, social and regionalist themes; and "The Young Gentlemen," arguably Wharton's only piece of American Gothic, epitomize their author's aptitude with genres and subjects that were not her usual stock-in-trade and help to establish the immense variety of earthly life that she illuminated.

Notes

[105] Discussion of "A Coward" might have been included in Chapter Three, "The Upper Class": some of its characters are of the New York elite, others have been in another day. I have chosen to see "A Coward" as a kind of anti-fiction of manners, as a story that puts forth as exemplars persons for whom belonging to an elevated social group is less important than espousing and practising essential moral qualities.

[106] William Macnaughton's reading of "The Blond Beast" draws attention to the critical neglect that marks response to it, and focusses on its Nietzschean elements: "Almost all of the critical references ... have been either dismissive, perfunctory, or perplexed. Readers made aware, however, of how important Nietzsche is to the text should discover it to be an interesting complex one that is primarily about the education of a potential 'superman'" (13-14).

[107] Macnaughton argues that Millner's fundamental decency is not inconsistent with Nietzschean principles: "It could be argued ... that Millner's compassionate response to the suffering animal [the dog in Section I] and young man [Draper Spence] are intended by Wharton as implicit criticism of Nietzsche's sometimes ferocious doctrine because Millner, to live up to his conception of 'blond beast,'must become a less admirable human being. On the other hand, passages in the texts Wharton read suggest a more humane Nietzsche. ... In a section in *Beyond Good and Evil* entitled 'What is Noble,' for example, Nietzsche asserts that to be noble one 'must remain master of one's four virtues: of courage, insight, sympathy and solitude'" (16).

[108] The decision to discuss "The Young Gentlemen" in the present chapter was an arbitrary one, and the choice might have been made to include it with those stories of artists and writers treated in Chapter Six—The World of the Arts: its narrator is a writer who is telling his story as *raconteur* and not merely as one who has experienced its events. I have placed it here because of its subject matter. Its focus on the bizarre gives it a certain uniqueness in the Wharton short-story *oeuvre* and might be seen to justify its consideration in this Wharton miscellany.

Afterword

In 2001, The Library of America published its two-volume selection of Wharton's short fiction. The volumes, entitled *Collected Stories 1891-1910* and *Collected Stories 1911-1937*, each bore the introductory notice, "Maureen Howard selected the contents and wrote the notes for this volume." Howard's selection differs substantially from R.W.B. Lewis's *The Collected Short Stories of Edith Wharton*, itself a two-volume set. For one thing, Howard has included four longer pieces not in Lewis's collection: the novella *The Touchstone*, serialized in *Scribner's* in March and April 1900 and republished as a book by Scribner's a month later; her second novella, *Sanctuary*, run in *Scribner's* from August through November 1903 and reissued by Scribner's in book form immediately following; another novella, *Bunner Sisters*, written in 1893 but unpublished until 1916, when *Scribner's Magazine* carried it in its issues of October and November and Scribner's included it in its collection *Xingu and Other Stories*; and her brief war novel, *The Marne*, which appeared in the *Saturday Evening Post* in its issue of October 26, 1918 and again as an Appleton-published book on December 13 of the same year. Twenty-three of the eighty-six stories comprising the R.W.B. Lewis collection are not included in the Maureen Howard volumes, some of the excluded material of considerable literary quality. The exclusions are as follows: "That Good May Come," "April Showers," "Friends," and "The Line of Least Resistance," early stories that were not included in Wharton's own collections; "A Coward" and "The Portrait," from *The Greater Inclination* (1899); "Copy" and "The Confessional," from *Crucial Instances* (1901); "The Quicksand," "The Dilettante," and "A Venetian Night's Entertainment," from *The Descent of Man and Other Stories* (1904); "The Letter" and "Les Metteurs en Scène," two uncollected magazine stories from 1904 and 1908 respectively; "In

Trust" and "The Verdict," from *The Hermit and the Wild Woman* (1908); "The Bolted Door" and "The Blond Beast," from *Tales of Men and Ghosts* (1910); "The Choice," from *Xingu and Other Stories* (1916); "The Temperate Zone," from *Here and Beyond* (1926); "Dieu d'Amour" and "The Refugees" from *Certain People* (1930); "Diagnosis," from *Human Nature* (1933); and "Permanent Wave," from *The World Over* (1936).

There is no point in quibbling about Howard's decision to include *The Touchstone, Sanctuary, Bunner Sisters*, and *The Marne* in her collection. Clearly, their relative brevity qualifies them all as stories. (Lewis's omission of them was surely based on the fact that they were books that, short as they were, had nevertheless been issued as separate titles, and that he needed not add to an already bulging set.) Of more concern is that these four pieces have displaced twenty-three published stories, have in a word considerably diminished the Wharton short-story corpus.

In the first place, some of the short stories excluded from the Library of America volumes are of some merit. There is of course no accounting for varying responses to literary art by careful readers, but it is difficult to understand the elimination of some of Wharton's canon from the list. I would single out two: "The Confessional" and "The Dilettante," and there are more. "The Confessional," an artistic failure and admitted by Wharton to be so within the text itself, is a splendid and arresting failure nevertheless. The story, working within two time frames, takes on themes of family, politics, the seal of the confessional, friendship, and loyalty and finally collapses under its own weight, but what a stirring and intriguing tale it tells. "The Dilettante," the compact sketching out of a love triangle, has the subtlety, wit, and surreptitiousness of Henry James's fiction—without the garrulousness.

But beyond this elimination of stories of stature, there is also the question of the integrity of the Wharton short-story oeuvre. The 1968 Scribner's/R.W.B. Lewis *Collected* being out of print, the 1987 Scribner's/Macmillan reprint of the above having appeared in diminished form (Volume II never came out), the Library of America edition has become by default as it were the authoritative comprehensive collection, and readers are left with a much-depleted oeuvre. There are many reasons why the Library of America's incomplete collection provides an unsatisfactory picture of Wharton the short-story writer. Here are a few. Only two of the historical tales appear: readers are deprived of much of a sense of Wharton's interest in the historical past. Since "The Portrait" is left out of the collection, readers have no way of knowing that "The Potboiler" was a "rewrite" of the earlier story and that it improved considerably on it. If only as a curiosity—and there are other more substantial reasons—Wharton's only short story written in French might have been included. "A Coward" might have been included, for it serves as an interesting foil to "The Lamp of Psyche" in terms of the handling of the themes of courage and cowardice. Similarly, "The Verdict" might have been included, for it presents an interesting contrast to "The Recovery" on the question of the artist's response to wealth and comfort. In a word, if a collection implicitly purports to present if not the entirety then at least a representative gathering together of a writer's work in a genre, its choices may be questioned if they fail to allow readers to see for themselves the breadth, variety, and process of growth of the author's oeuvre.

It has been an advantage to have been able to work with the Scribner's/Lewis *Collected* volumes, which include the whole of the published short stories, warts and all. I have found it a distinct advantage as well to treat the stories not in the order of their over-all publication but chronologically within the categories I have chosen. This method, I came to realize only after I was well into the writing of my text, allowed me to see that among thematically homogeneous stories there were often connections that would likely not have been as perceptible had I chosen to write a completely chronological study. One assumes, for example, that Wharton herself, when thinking about and composing a story, say, about the arts, would have in mind the last time she had surveyed that territory, and indeed there are places in the oeuvre, as I have attempted to demonstrate, where this process seems to have been a very conscious and explicit one. It is surely no accident, for instance, that in "A Glimpse," a 1932 story about two impassioned performing musicians, the narrator notes that his musicians "have lived at white-heat level while we crawl along in the temperate zone" (II, 692), and that eight years earlier she had published a tale called

"The Temperate Zone," about two painters who led dispassionate and uncommitted lives.

* * * * *

In the early (1899) story "Souls Belated," the young unmarried lovers Ralph Gannett and Lydia Tillotson are travelling in Italy by train and stop at "the fashionable Anglo-American Hotel Bellosguardo."

> "Queer little microcosms, these hotels!" [Ralph says to Lydia on the first evening of their visit.] "Most of these people live here all summer, and then migrate to Italy or the Riviera. The English are the only kind of people who can lead that kind of life with dignity—those soft-voiced old ladies in Shetland shawls somehow carry the British Empire under their caps. *Civis Romanus sum.* It's a curious study—there might be some good things to work up here." (I, 112)

A few lines along we learn that "Gannett had made himself known as a successful writer of short stories and a novel which had achieved the distinction of being widely discussed" and that "The reviewers called him promising" (I, 113). What a temptation for us to think that it was she herself Wharton had in mind as she wrote about Gannett. That, of course, would have been premature on her part: her first novel had not yet appeared. But certainly her editors at Scribner's saw her promise. And certainly Gannett's "Queer little microcosms, these hotels!" and "there might be some good things to work up here" are highly evocative of Wharton's performance as a short-story writer. A yachting holiday on the Mediterranean, a trip to Morocco, her life with her husband, her remembrances of the days in old New York—the ordinary and the exceptional occurrences of her life, actual and recalled, were the materials from which were constructed the substantial houses of fiction we are privileged to read. And what a varied gathering of structures she made—what a breadth of good things she worked up here.

Bibliography

Works by Edith Wharton

Collected Stories 1891-1910. New York: Library of America, 2001.
Collected Stories 1911-1937. New York: Library of America, 2001.
"Preface." *Ghosts.* New York: Appleton-Century, 1937.
The Collected Short Stories of Edith Wharton. Edited by R.W.B. Lewis. 2 vols. New York: Charles Scribner's Sons, 1968.
The Valley of Decision. New York: Charles Scribner's Sons, 1902.
The Writing of Fiction. New York: Charles Scribner's Sons, 1925.

Works by Others

Ammons, Elizabeth. *Edith Wharton's Argument with America.* Athens: University of Georgia Press, 1980.
Anonymous. Review of *Certain People* by Edith Wharton. *New York Times*, November 1930, p. 9.
Anonymous. Review of *The Hermit and the Wild Woman and Other Stories* by Edith Wharton. *The Nation* 87 (26 November 1908): 525.
Anonymous. Review of *The World Over* by Edith Wharton. *Saturday Review of Literature* 14 (2 May 1936): 19.
Aronson, Marc. "Wharton and the House of Scribner: The Novelist as a Pain in the Neck." *New York Times Book Review*, 2 January 1994, p. 7.
Auchincloss, Louis. *Edith Wharton.* Minneapolis: University of Minnesota Press, 1961.
Bell, Millicent. *Edith Wharton and Henry James.* New York: George Braziller, 1965.
Bendixen, Alfred. "Wharton Studies, 1986-1987: A Bibliographic Essay." *Edith Wharton Newsletter* 5 (Spring 1988): 5-8, 10.
—. "New Directions in Wharton Criticism: A Bibliographic Essay." *Edith Wharton Review* 10 (Fall 1993): 20-24.
Benstock, Shari. *No Gifts from Chance.* New York: Charles Scribner's Sons, 1994.
Brown, E.K. *Edith Wharton: Etude Critique.* Paris: Librairie E. Droz, 1935.
Campbell, Donna M. "Edith Wharton and 'The Authoress': The Critique of Local Color in Wharton's Early Fiction." *Studies in America Fiction* 22 (1994): 169-184.
Comins, Barbara. "'Outrageous Trap': Envy and Jealousy in Wharton's 'Roman Fever' and Fitzgerald's 'Bernice Bobs Her Hair.'" *Edith Wharton Review* 17 (Spring 2001): 9-12.
Donovan, Josephine. *After the Fall: The Demeter-Persephone Myth in Wharton,*

434

Cather, and Glasgow. University Park: The Pennsylvania State University Press, 1989.

Drabble, Margaret. "Wharton's Sharp Eye." *Atlantic Monthly* 288 (July/August 2001): 166-170.

Dreiser, Theodore. *The Best Short Stories of Theodore Dreiser.* Cleveland: World, 1947, 1956.

—. *Chains.* New York: Boni and Liveright, 1927.

—. *Free and Other Stories.* New York: Boni and Liveright, 1918.

Erlich, Gloria C. *The Sexual Education of Edith Wharton.* Berkeley: University of California Press, 1992.

Esplund, Lance. "Resurrecting Matisse: A New Biography Revives the Life but Not the Art." *Harper's* 311 (December 2005): 90-96.

Frye, Northrop, Sheridan Baker and George Perkins. *The Harper Handbook to Literature.* New York: Harper and Row, 1985.

Garrison, Stephen. *Edith Wharton: A Descriptive Bibliography.* Pittsburgh: University of Pittsburgh Press, 1990.

Gilbert, Sandra M. From "Angel of Devastation: Edith Wharton on the Arts of the Enslaved." In *Edith Wharton: A Study of the Short Fiction* by Barbara A. White. New York: Twain, 1991, Pp. 164-170.

Going, William T. "Wharton's 'After Holbein.'" *Explicator* 10 (November 1951): 8.

Greene, Graham. Review of *The World Over* by Edith Wharton. *Spectator* 14 (2 May 1936): 19.

H., C. Review of *The Descent of Man and Other Stories* by Edith Wharton. *Reader's Magazine* 4 (July 1904): 226.

Hart, James D. *The Oxford Companion to American Literature.* Fourth ed. New York: Oxford University Press, 1965.

Heller, Janet Ruth. "Ghosts and Marital Entanglements: An Analysis of 'Afterward.'" *Edith Wharton Review* 10 (Spring 1993): 18-19.

Hemingway, Ernest. *The Sun Also Rises.* New York: Charles Scribner's Sons, 1926.

Howard, Maureen. "Note on the Texts." *Edith Wharton: Collected Short Stories 1911-1937.* New York: Library of America, 2001, p. 842.

James, Henry. *The Turn of the Screw.* New York: Scribner's, 1898.

Kaplan, Amy. *The Social Construction of American Realism.* Chicago: University of Chicago Press, 1988.

Kaye, Richard A. "'Unearthly Visitants': Wharton's Ghost Tales, Gothic Form and the Literature of Homosexual Panic." *Edith Wharton Review* 11 (Spring 1994): 10-18.

Killoran, Helen. "Pascal, Brontë, and 'Kerfol.'" *Edith Wharton Review* 10 (Spring 1993): 12-17.

Kimbel, Ellen. "The American Short Story: 1900-1920." *The American Short Story, 1900-1945.* Ed. by Philip Stevick. Boston: Twayne, 1984, Pp. 33-69.

Kinman, Alice Heritage. "Edith Wharton and the Future of Fiction." *Edith Wharton Review* 18 (Fall 2002): 3-12.

Lauer, Kristen O., and Margaret P. Murray, eds. *Edith Wharton: An Annotated Secondary Bibliography.* New York: Garland, 1990.

Lee, Hermione. *Edith Wharton.* London: Chatto & Windus, 2007.

Lewis, R.W.B., and Nancy Lewis, eds. *The Letters of Edith Wharton*. New York: Charles Scribner's Sons, 1988.

Lewis, R.W.B. *Edith Wharton: A Biography*. New York: Harper and Row, 1975.

—. Introduction. *The Collected Short Stories of Edith Wharton*. Ed. by R.W.B. Lewis. 2 vols. New York: Charles Scribner's Sons, 1968.

Macnaughton, William. "Edith Wharton's 'The Blond Beast' and Friedrich Nietzsche,' *Edith Wharton Review* 15 (Fall 1999): 13-19.

Maine, Barry. "'The Portrait': Edith Wharton and John Singer Sargent." *Edith Wharton Review* 18 (Spring 2002): 7-14.

Mason, Wyatt. "There Must I Begin to Be: Guy Davenport's Heretical Fictions." *Harper's* 308 (April 2004): 87-92.

McDowell, Margaret B. *Edith Wharton*. Boston: Twayne, 1976.

—. "Edith Wharton's 'After Holbein': A Paradigm of the Human Condition." *Journal of Narrative Technique* 1 (January 1971): 49-58.

—. "Edith Wharton's Ghost Stories." *Criticism* 12 (Spring 1970): 133-152.

Mott, Frank Luther. *A History of American Magazines*. 5 vols. Cambridge: Harvard University Press, 1966.

Nevius, Blake. *Edith Wharton: A Study of Her Fiction*. Berkeley: University of California Press, 1953.

Olin-Ammentorp, Julie. *Edith Wharton's Writings from the Great War*. Gainesville: University Press of Florida, 2004.

Petry, Alice Hall. "A Twist of Crimson Silk: Edith Wharton's 'Roman Fever.'" *Studies in Short Fiction* 24 (Spring 1987): 163-166

Pierpont, Claudia Roth. "Cries and Whispers." *The New Yorker* 77 (2 April 2001): 66-75.

Powers, Lyall H., ed. *Henry James and Edith Wharton: Letters, 1900-1915*. New York: Charles Scribner's Sons, 1990.

Price, Alan. "Edith Wharton's War Story." *Tulsa Studies on Women's Literature* 8 (Spring 1989): 95-100.

Purdy, Jr., Theodore. Review of *Human Nature* by Edith Wharton. *Saturday Review of Literature*, 22 April 1933, p. 549.

Raphael, Lev. *Edith Wharton's Prisoners of Shame*. London: MacMillan, 1991.

Repplier, Agnes. Review of *The Hermit and the Wild Woman and Other Stories* by Edith Wharton. *Outlook*, 28 November 1908, p. 693.

Rogers, J.T. Review of *Here and Beyond* by Edith Wharton. *North American Review* 223 (June 1926): 225.

Saltz, Laura. "From Image to Text: Modernist Transformations in Edith Wharton's 'The Muse's Tragedy.'" *Edith Wharton Review* 19 (Fall 2003): 15-19.

Singley, Carol J. "Gothic Borrowings and Innovations in Edith Wharton's 'A Bottle of Perrier.'" *Edith Wharton: New Critical Essays*. Ed. by Alfred Bendixen and Annette Zilversmit. Hamden, CT: Garland, 1992, pp. 271-290.

Smith, Allan Gardner. "Edith Wharton and the Ghost Story." *Women and Literature* 1 (1980): 149-159.

Stein, Allen F. *After the Vows Were Broken: Marriage in American Literary Realism*. Columbus: Ohio State University Press, 1988.

436

Stengel, Ellen Powers. "Edith Wharton Rings 'The Lady's Maid's Bell.'" *Edith Wharton Review* 7 (Spring 1990): 3-9.

Waid, Candace. *Edith Wharton's Letters from the Underworld*. Chapel Hill: University of North Carolina Press, 1991.

White, Barbara A. *Edith Wharton: A Study of the Short Fiction*. New York: Twayne, 1991.

Widdicome, Toby. "Wharton's 'The Angel at the Grave' and the Glories of Transcendentalism: Deciduous or Evegreen." *American Transcendental Quarterly* 6 (1992): 47-57.

Wilson-Jordan, Jacqueline S. "Telling the Story That Can't Be Told: Hartley's Role as Diseased Narrator in 'The Lady's Maid's Bell.'" *Edith Wharton Review* 14 (Spring 1997): 12-17, 21.

Witzig, Denise. "'The Muse's Tragedy' and the Muse's Text: Language and Desire in Wharton." *Edith Wharton: New Critical Essays*. Ed. by Alfred Bendixen and Annette Zilversmit. Hamden, CT: Garland, 1992, pp. 261-270.

Wolff, Cynthia Griffin. *A Feast of Words: The Triumph of Edith Wharton*. New York: Oxford University Press, 1977.

Zilversmit, Annette. "Edith Wharton's Last Ghosts." *College Literature* 14 (Fall 1987): 296-305.

Ziolkowski, Theodore. *Disenchanted Images: A Literary Iconology*. Princeton: Princeton University Press, 1977.

Index

Ainslee's, 16, 43n26
American Literary Realism, 1
American Magazine, 36, 38, 42
American Transcendentalist Review, 1
Ammons, Elizabeth, 223-224, 226, 251
Appleton and Company, 18, 24, 25, 27, 28, 29, 30, 31, 35, 40, 45n56, 45n62, 45n68, 429
Appleton's Booklover's Magazine, 18, 43n31, 118
Appleton-Century, 37, 39, 41, 45n74, 46n77
Astor, Caroline, 137
Atlantic Monthly, 2, 3, 16, 23, 24, 43n26, 44n47, 124, 268
Auchincloss, Louis, 15, 39, 138, 199-200

Baker, Sheridan, 417
Balzac, Honoré de, *La Grande Breteche*, 346
Bell, Millicent, 9, 10, 13, 14, 21, 262, 327, 357
Bendixen, Alfred, 1
Benjamin, Albert, 36
Benstock, Shari, 121, 135, 140, 239, 283, 311n99, 391, 394, 395, 418, 422
Berenson, Bernard, 239, 418
Berry, Walter, 314, 360
Best Short Stories of Theodore Dreiser, The, 344n102
Booth, Wayne C., 318

Borden, Lizzie, 39, 206
Bromfield, Louis, 36
Bronté, Emily, *Wuthering Heights*, 102n81
Brown, E.K., 13, 18, 23, 48, 56, 61, 118, 122, 124, 140, 153n85, 161, 170, 184, 226, 228, 262, 287, 346, 357, 359, 360, 368, 384, 400, 412, 418
Brownell, William Crary, 10-11, 12, 13, 14, 15, 16, 17, 18, 19, 21, 184, 357
Browning, Robert, "My Last Duchess," 263, 347, 350, 374n103
Brownson, Orestes, 385
Burlingame, Edward L., 7, 11, 12, 15, 17, 18, 20, 22, 26, 110, 229, 379
Burton, Harry Payne, 38

Campbell, Donna, 236
Cavour, Camillo Benso, 353
Century, 8, 20, 22, 44n41, 44n44, 44n45, 56, 121, 122, 187, 379, 396
Chambers, Charles E., 25
Chanler, Mrs Winthrop, *Autumn in the Valley*, 374-375n104
CLA Journal, 1
Clark, Kenneth, 239
Clark, Walter Appleton, 14
Codman, Ogden, *The Decoration of Houses* (with Edith Wharton), 152
Collier's, 14, 18, 38, 42, 43n23, 43n29, 170, 391

438

Comins, Barbara, 220n87
Cosmopolitan,12, 13, 14, 15, 43n15, 43n22
Curtis Brown Ltd, 37
Curtis, Lise Colt, 311n99
Curtis, Ralph, 311n99

Dashiell, Alfred Sheppard, 32
Davenport, Guy, 303
De Ivanowski, Sigismond, 20
De La Mare, Walter, 41
Delineator, 27-28, 30, 33, 38
De Maupassant, Guy, 226
Dickinson, Emily, 56
Donovan, Josephine, 294, 361, 366
Drabble, Margaret, 2, 3, 4, 5
Dreiser, Theodore, "Free," 287, 335, 344n102; "The Old Neighborhood," 287, 335, 344n102; Free and Other Stories, 344n102; Chains, 344n102

Edel, Leon, 92
Edith Wharton: Collected Stories (Library of America), 2
Edith Wharton Review, 1, 102n79, 102n81
Emerson, Ralph Waldo, 131, 258, 290, 291, 427; "The Rhodora," 317
Erlich, Glorira C., 185, 311n96
Esplund, Lance, 4
Everybody's Magazine, 25

Fedorko, Kathy, 1
Fitzgerald, F. Scott, 227, 238n91; The Great Gatsby, 137
Freud, Sigmund, 48
Frye, Northrop, 417
Fullerton, Morton, 20-21, 122, 239, 288, 322, 396, 424-425

Garrison, Stephen, 11
Gilbert, Sandra M., 2, 81-82
Gioberti, Vincenzo, 353
Going, William T., 136

Good Housekeeping, 38, 42
Greene, Graham, 39

Harper's, 13, 14, 15, 16, 24, 43n17, 43n19, 43n21, 43n22, 43n25, 110, 113, 166, 258, 262, 358, 387
Harper's Bazaar, 38
Harriman, Karl Edwin, 27
Hart, James D., 11
Hawthorne, Nathaniel, 23, 386
Hearst's International-Cosmopolitan, 36, 38, 39, 42, 45n70, 45n73, 206, 377, 421, 423
Hearst, William Randolph, 26, 33-34, 36, 37, 38
Heller, Janet Ruth, 102n79
Hemingway, Ernest, The Sun Also Rises, 151
Hoeller, Heldegarde, 1
Holbein, Hans (the younger), 136
Howard, Maureen, 5, 429, 430
Huxley, Aldous, 36

James, Henry, 9, 12, 13, 15, 16, 17, 19, 20, 21, 109, 118, 184, 206, 238, 258, 262, 288, 311n100, 314, 321, 357, 409, 430; The Turn of the Screw, 49, 63, 328; "Daisy Miller," 173, 205
Jewett, Rutger, 25, 26-27, 28, 29, 30, 31-32, 33, 34, 35, 36, 38, 40, 41, 421, 422
Jones, George Frederick, 102n82, 188
Jones, Mary Cadwalader, 29, 39, 206

Kaplan, Amy, 253, 315, 318
Kaye, Richard A., 48
Killoran, Helen, 102n81
Kimball, Alanzo, 19
Kinman, Alice Herritage, 6n2, 222-223

Lacan, Jacques-Marie Emile, 48

Ladies' Home Journal, 29, 30, 32, 33, 34, 35, 37, 38, 42, 45n59, 45n61, 45n63, 77, 132, 140, 367
Lane, Gertrude, 34
Lapsley, Gaillard, 23
Lee, Hermione, 220n89, 311n99
Lengel, William, 36-37
Letters of Edith Wharton, 199, 223
Lewis, Nancy, 288, 289
Lewis, R.W.B., 2, 6n1, 430; Edith Wharton, 9, 11, 16, 20, 21, 28, 31, 36, 56, 61, 121, 132, 161, 184, 185, 199, 223, 234, 243, 266, 268, 293, 311n99, 360-361, 361, 368, 378, 384, 391, 392, 394, 396, 399, 409, 418, 421; Introduction to The Collected Short Stories, 48, 49, 70, 124, 135, 170, 329, 330; Letters of Edith Wharton (with Nancy Lewis), 288, 289, 421, 424
Liberty, 36, 37, 38, 45n71, 199
Library of America, 2, 429, 430
Lippincott's, 12, 42n12, 161, 166
Literature, 314
Lodge, George Cabot, 391
Lubbock, Percy, 395, 409

Macmillan (publishing house), 16
Macnaughton, William, 428n106, 428n107
Maine, Barry, 310n93
Mansfield, Katherine, 170
Mas-Latrie, Louis de, Histoire de l'Ile de Chypre sous les Princes de Lusignan, 368
Mason, Wyatt, 303
Matisse, Henri, 4
McCalls', 33, 38, 42
McClure's, 25, 29
McDowell, Margaret B., 48, 51, 61, 63, 70, 72, 74, 77, 82, 84, 140, 159-160
Metropolitan, 25, 29
Metternich, Clement, 353
Mott, Frank Luther, 252

Mugnier, Abbé Arthur, 86
Murray, John, 10

Nash's Pall Mall Magazine, 34, 45n66, 230
Nation, The, 19
Nevius, Blake, 13, 22, 61, 109, 137, 138, 170, 187, 226, 238, 346, 400, 402
New Yorker, 2
New York Times, 31
Nietzsche, Friedrich, 399, 428n106; Beyond Good and Evil, 428n107
Nolan, Becky, 182
North American Review, 28
Norton, Sarah, 19

Olin-Ammentorp, Julie, 311n100, 402
Outlook, 19

Pallis, Patricia Larose, 346, 374n103
Parrish, Maxfield, 13, 15
Pascal, Blaise, 102n81
Perkins, George, 417
Petry, Alice M., 220n88
Pictorial Review, 26, 27, 28, 33, 34, 38, 44n52, 44n53, 44n55, 69, 294, 412, 417
Pierpont, Claudia Day, 3; Passionate Minds, 2
Pinker, Eric, 38, 39, 40, 42
Plante, Patricia R., 261
Poe, Edgar Allan, 20, 394; "William Wilson," 63
Price, Alan, 400
Purdy, Theodore, 35

Raditsky, Joseph Wenzel, 353
Raphael, Lev, 126-127, 132, 206-207, 233, 246, 276, 277, 278, 287, 288, 290, 291, 311n98, 411
Red Book, 27, 37, 38, 44n54, 45n72, 313, 338, 411, 423
Revue des Deux Mondes, 17, 43n27,

182

Repplier, Agnes, 19
Riis, Jacob, 6n2
Robinson, Edwin Arlington, 321
Rogers, J.T., 28
Roosevelt, Theodore, 391
Roach, Arthur, 311n99

Saltz, Laura, 310n94
Sargent, John Singer, 310n93
Saturday Evening Post, 25, 29, 30,
  33, 35, 36, 37, 38, 45n57, 45n58,
  45n60, 45n65, 45n 69, 80, 136,
  298, 408, 411, 417, 423, 429
Saturday Review of Literature, 35,
  39
Schuler, Loring A., 35-36
Scribner's (magazine), 6n2, 7, 8, 9,
  12, 13, 14, 15, 18, 19, 20, 21, 22,
  23, 24, 26, 31, 32, 40, 42n3, 42n4,
  42n5, 42n6, 42n8, 43n13, 43n14,
  43n16, 43n20, 43n22, 43n23,
  43n28, 43n30, 43n32, 44n34,
  44n35, 44n36, 44n37, 44n38,
  44n40, 44n42, 44n46, 44n48,
  44n51, 45n64, 47, 48, 61, 63, 68,
  104, 184, 193, 221, 229, 240, 246,
  252, 253, 263, 273, 277, 282, 287,
  288, 292, 313, 314, 318, 321, 328,
  330, 345, 357, 360, 378-379- 381,
  384, 387, 394, 399, 400, 403, 408,
  429
Scribner, Charles, 10, 18, 21, 22, 23,
  26
Scribner's (publishing house), 8, 10,
  11, 12, 14, 18, 19, 21, 24, 40,
  42n9, 43n18, 43n24, 43n33,
  44n43, 44n49, 184, 229, 379, 429
Sears, J.H., 25
Shakespeare, William, *Henry IV*
  (Part I), 91
Singley, Carol, 1, 48, 418, 420
Sitwell, Osbert, 95
Smith Allan Gardner, 48, 56-57, 59,
  61, 63-64, 70, 75, 92
Smith, Hugh, 399

Spreter, Roy F., 34
Spurling, Hilary, 4
Stein, Allen F., 170-171, 396
Stengel, Ellen Powers, 48
Story-Teller, 45n73
Strange Wives (film), 422
Studies in America Fiction, 1,
  220n88

Thackeray, William Makepeace, 314
This Week, 42
Thoreau, Henry David, 290
Twayne's Studies in Short-Fiction
  Series, 2

Vance, Arthur T., 27, 28

Waid, Candace, 81, 420
Weaver, Gordon, 2

Wharton, Edith: advances, royalties
  stipends, 14, 19, 24-25, 26-27, 28,
  29-30, 32, 34, 35, 36, 37, 38, 39;
  and Hearst publications, 34, 36,
  38; and Henry James, 12, 15-16,
  17, 19, 21, 184, 206, 311n100,
  409; autobiography, 11, 46n 77,
  108, 121, 221, 223, 377, 378,
  424-425; break-up with
  Scribner's organization, 24, 32;
  classical myth, 80-81, 84, 104,
  340, 367, 368, 369, 375n104;
  didacticism, 11, 277; ghost
  stories, 40-42, 47-48, 93, 95;
  incest as theme, 2, 92, 268, 269,
  273, 401; move to Appleton and
  Company, 24; play-script
  narration, 9, 109, 110, 113-114,
  166, 178-179, 253-254, 392;
  satire, 23, 112-113, 149, 258,
  259, 266, 267, 268, 284, 291,
  292, 314, 319, 328, 330, 331,
  332, 340-341, 386, 387, 409,
  410, 411, 412; war effort, 22, 29,
  409

NON-FICTION
Backward Glance, A., 46n77, 269, 346
Decoration of Houses, The (with Ogden Codman), 152
Fighting France, 400
French Ways and Their Meaning, 400
Writing of Fiction, The, 47

NOVELS AND NOVELLAS
Age of Innocence, The, 185
Bunner Sisters, 23, 429, 430
Fast and Loose, 11, 253, 266
Gods Arrive, The, 31, 422
House of Mirth, The, 113, 164, 330, 386, 411
Hudson River Bracketed, 422
Marne, The, 429, 430
Reef, The, 18
Sanctuary, 429, 430
Touchstone, The, 81, 254, 313, 429, 430
Valley of Decision, The, 14, 345, 345-346, 346, 351, 357

SHORT STORIES
"After Holbein," 29, 30, 31, 46n60, 103, *136-140,* 145, 147, 149, 150, 151, 236, 310n93, 425
"Afterward," 1, 20, 41, 44n39, *56-61,* 68, 69, 77, 78-79, 80, 82, 97, 98, 99, 102n79
"All Souls'," 3, 40, 41-42, 47, *92-95,* 96, 97-98, 102n83
"Angel at the Grave, The," 13, 43n16, *384-387,* 387, 427
"April Showers," 11, 42n10, 229, *252-253,* 258, 303, 304, 429
"Atrophy," 29, 30, 45n59, *132-136,* 136, 140, 141, 144, 147, 149-150, 152, 212, 373, 384
"Autres Temps...," 22, 24, 156, 165, *187-193,* 213, 216, 219, 310n93
"Best Man, The," 18, 43n29, *391-393,* 394, 423,
"Bewitched," 25, 26, 28, 41, 44n53, *69-73,* 73, 77, 97, 98, 101, 427
"Blond Beast, The," 21, 44n42, *399-400,* 401, 423, 428n106, 430
"Bolted Door, The," 20, 44n34, 377, *394-395,* 425, 426, 429-430
"Bottle of Evian, A," ("A Bottle of Perrier"), 29, 45n58
"Bottle of Perrier, A," 30, 39, 41, 46n77, 377, *417-421,* 426-427, 428
"Bread upon the Waters," ("Charm Incorporated"), 36, 38, 45n70, 377, 421, 423
"Call, The," ("Afterward"), 102n80
Certain People, 29, 30-31, 32, 35, 45n62, 430
"Charm Incorporated," 35, 36, *421-422,* 423
"Choice, The," 18, 22, 44n44, *121-124,* 124, 147, 151-152, 212, 430
Collected Short Stories 1891-1910, (Library of America), 2, 429
Collected Short Stories 1911-1937, (Library of America), 2, 429
Collected Short Stories of Edith Wharton, The (Scribner's), 4, 41, 46n75, 102n84, 104, 182, 199, 371, 374n104, 377, 429, 430, 431
Collected Short Stories of Edith Wharton, The, (Scribner's reprint), 430
"Coming Home," 22, 23, 24, 44n48, 292, 311n100, 311-312n101, 377, *400-403,* 408, 428
"Confession," 35, 38, 39, 45n73, *206-211,* 212, 213, 216, 216-217, 307, 422
"Confessional, The," 13, 16, 345, *351-357,* 359, 360, 371-372, 373,

374, 401, 429, 430

"Copy: A Dialogue," 12, 43n13, 113, 153n85, 166, *253-254*, 302, 305, 392, 429

"Coward, A," 9, 377, *381-384*, 425, 426, 428n105, 429, 431

Crucial Instances, 12, 13-14, 43n18, 253, 258, 351, 429

"Cup of Cold Water, A" 9, 221, *226-229*, 229, 234-235, 237, 238n90, 238n91

"Daunt Diana, The," 20, 44n36, 282-286, 307, 308, 309

"Day of the Funeral, The" 31, 34, 313, *333-338*, 338, 341, 342-343

"Debt, The," 20, 44n37, 313, *328-330*, 330, 341-342, 343-344

"Descent of Man, The," 15-16, 43n23, 313, *318-321*, 321, 328, 340, 341

Descent of Man and Other Stories, The, 14, 15, 17, 43n24, 318, 429

"Diagnosis," 31, 32, 45n63, 136, *140-144*, 147, 149, 152, 430,

"Dieu d'Amour," 29, 30, 45n61, 345, *367-370*, 371, 373, 374, 430

"Dilettante, The," 14, 15, 43n22, *113-118*, 118, 141, 147, 149, 150, 152, 153n85, 184, 212, 392, 429, 430

"Duchess at Prayer, The," 12-13, 43n14, 263, 345, *345-350*, 351, 360, 371-372, 373, 374

"Duration," 35, 39, 103, *145-147*, 147, 148, 150

"Expiation," 15, 43n22, *266-268*, 303, 304, 305

"Eyes, The," 20, 21, 41, 44n40, 48, *61-63*, 63, 97, 98, 152, 307, 333, 394, 419, 422

"Friends," 11-12, 42n11, 221, *229-230*, 234, 235, 237, 429

"Full Circle," 20, 44n38, *287-288*, 304, 305

"Fullness of Life, The," 7, 8, 42n4, *378-381*, 424-425

Ghosts, 41, 46n76, 46n77, 47, 74, 92, 96, 98; Preface, 95, 96, 102n84

Ghost Stories of Edith Wharton, The, 46n77

"Glimpse, A," 31, 34, 45n65, *298-302*, 309, 310, 374, 431

Greater Inclination, The, 9, 10, 11, 12, 13, 42n9, 109, 156, 223, 226, 229, 243, 381, 429

Here and Beyond, 25, 26, 28-29, 31, 44n52, 45n56, 430

"Hermit and the Wild Woman, The," 18, 19, 43n30, 345, *360-367*, 367, 368, 372, 373-374, 374, 426-427, 429

Hermit and the Wild Woman, The, 19, 43,n33, 391

"Her Son," 6n1, 31, 32, 35, 45n64, 156, *193-199*, 199, 213, 216, 220n86, 425

"His Father's Son," 20, 44n35, *184-187*, 213, 215-216

"House of the Dead Hand, The," 16, 43n26, *268-273*, 273, 274, 282-283, 307, 308, 310

Human Nature, 35, 45n68, 140, 430

"In a Day" ("The Day of the Funeral"), 45n67

"Introducers, The," 16, 17, 43n26, *178-182*, 182-183, 213, 214, 215

"In Trust," 18, 43n31, *118-121*, 147, 151, 212, 429

"Journey, A," 9, 221, *223-226*, 226, 234, 235, 236-237, 238, 425

"Joy in the House," 31, 33, 34, 45n66, 221, *230-234*, 236, 237

"Kerfol," 1, 22, 23, 24, 41, 44n48, *68-69*, 77, 78, 97, 100-101, 102n81, 346, 373

"Kouradjine Limited" ("Charm Incoporated"), 36

"Lady's Maid's Bell, The," 14, 16, 41, 43n20, 47, *48-56*, 57, 60, 80, 85-86, 97, 99, 101-102, 328, 346

"Lamp of Psyche, The," 8, 42n6, 103, *104-109*, 110, 111, 145, 147,

148, 149, 150-151, 223, 381-382, 384, 396, 431
"Last Asset, The," 17, 18, 43n28, 156, *173-178*, 178, 213, 218, 219
"Legend, The," 20, 44n40, *288-292*, 304, 305, 384, 427
"Letter, The," 16, 43n25, 345, 351, *358-360*, 371, 373, 429
"Letters, The," 20, 44n41, 377, *395-399*, 424-425
"Line of Least Resistance, The," 11, 12, 42n12, *161-165*, 166, 212, 214, 429
"Long Run, The," 22, 23, 44n47, *124-132*, 132-133, 135, 136, 140, 141, 144, 147, 149, 150, 152, 153, 212, 307, 310n93, 384, 427
"Looking Glass, The," 1, 35, 37-38, 39, 46n77, *85-92*, 96-97, 98, 101
"Metteurs en Scene, Les," 17, 43n27, *182-184*, 213, 218, 219, 429, 431
"Mirrors, The" ("The Looking Glass"), 45n73
"Mission of Jane, The," 14, 43n21, *110-113*, 147, 149, 150, 153
"Miss Mary Pask," 25, 26, 27, 29, 41, 44n53, 69, *73-77*, 77, 97, 99, 101, 207, 258, 327
"Moving Finger, The," 13, 43n17, 258, *262-266*, 277, 307, 311-312n101, 373
"Mr. Jones," 29, 30, 35, 41, 45n59, *77-80*, 100-101, 346, 373
"Mrs. Manstey's View," 6n2, 7, 42n3, 101, *221-223*, 223, 226, 234, 235-236, 237
"Muse's Tragedy, The," 9, 42n8, 223, *246-252*, 304
"Other Times, Other Manners" ("Autres Temps..."), 22, 24, 44n45, 187
"Other Two, The," 1, 15, 16, 43n23, 156, 165, *170-173*, 178, 212, 213, 214, 215, 219
"Pelican, The," 9, 42n8, 207, 255,

283, 313, *314-318*, 318, 319, 327, 328, 340
"Permanent Wave," 1, 35, 37, 313, 333, *338-339*, 341, 342-343
"Pomegranate Seed," 35-36, 41, 45n69, *80-85*, 97, 99, 337, 422
"Poor Old Vincent" ("Permanent Wave"), 37, 45n72, 338
"Portrait, The," 10, 118, *243-246*, 246, 274-275, 277, 305, 306, 310, 429, 431
"Potboiler, The," 17, 18, 43n28, 118, 243, *273-277*, 277, 278, 295, 305, 306, 310, 391, 431
"Pretext, The," 18, 19, 43n32, 313, *321-327*, 328, 341, 342, 391
"Quicksand, The," 14, 43n19, *166-170*, 213, 215, 429
"Reckoning, The," 14, 43n19, *387-391*, 425, 431
"Recovery, The," 13, 14, 43n17, *258-262*, 262, 277-278, 305, 306, 311n95, 339-340, 340
"Refugees, The," 29, 30, 45n57, 400, *408-411*, 411, 412, 423, 430
"Rembrandt, The," 13, 43n15, *254-258*, 282, 307, 308, 310
"Roman Fever," 3, 35, 36, 37, 39-40, 45n71, 156, 165, *199-206*, 213, 216, 217, 219, 220n87, 220n88, 202n89, 422
"Seed of the Faith, The," 25, 26, 28, 44n51, *403-408*, 418, 420, 426-427
"Something Exquisite" ("Friends"), 11, 229
"Souls Belated," 9, 156, *156-161*, 161, 165, 173, 213, 217-218, 219, 223, 374, 384, 432
"Stage Managers, The" ("Les Metteurs en Scène"), 182
Tales of Men and Ghosts, 20-21, 44n43, 394, 399, 430
"Temperate Zone, The," 22, 25, 26, 44n52, *294-298*, 298, 299, 304, 305, 309. 430, 431

"That Good May Come," 7-8, 42n5, *240-243*, 243, 246, 302, 304, 305, 310, 429

"Triumph of Night, The," 22, 23, 24, 41, 44n48, 48, *63-67*, 68, 69, 97, 99, 100

"Twilight of the God, The," 9, 12, *109-110*, 111, 113, 118, 147, 149, 151, 166, 178, 212, 223, 253, 254, 302, 392

"Unconfessed Crime" ("Confession"), 45n73, 206, 207

"Valley of Childish Things, and Other Emblems, The," 8, 42n7, 378, *379-381*, 423-424

"Veloet Ear Pads," 25, 27, 28, 44n54, *411-412*, 423

"Venitian Night's Entertainment, A," 14, 43n22, 345, *357-358*, 371, 373, 374, 429

"Verdict, The," 17, 18, 19, 43n32, 118, 119, 182, *277-282*, 295, 305, 306, 311n99, 391, 429, 431

World Over, The, 39-40, 45n74, 85, 145, 422

"Writing a War Story," 25, 44n50, 239-240, *292-294*, 303, 304, 311n100, 400

"Xingu," 22, 23, 44n46, 268, 291, 292, 313, *330-332*, 333, 340, 341, 411

Xingu and Other Stories, 23-24, 44n49, 400, 402, 429, 430

"Young Gentlemen, The" 25, 27, 44n55, 377, *412-417*, 417, 417-418, 427-428, 428n108

UNPUBLISHED FRAGMENT
"Beatrice Palmato," 2, 268, 269

Wharton, Edward ("Teddy"), 7, 9, 121, 223, 378, 424-425

White, Barbara A., 1, 2, 6n1, 48, 92, 114, 132, 135, 138, 139, 141-142, 147, 170-171, 188, 204-205, 206, 223-224, 254, 255, 261, 262, 266, 268, 269, 277, 278, 283, 311n96, 311n97, 314-315, 322, 327, 336-337, 337, 338, 357, 359, 361, 385, 386, 394, 395, 400, 400-401, 412, 416, 419, 420, 421

Widdicome, Toby, 384

Williams, John L.B., 35, 37, 38

Wilson-Jordan, Jacqueline S., 101-102n78

Witzig, M. Denise, 252, 310n94

Wolff, Cynthia Griffin, 16, 28, 31, 35, 61, 104, 108, 110, 121, 122, 161, 170-171, 193, 221-222, 223, 251, 268-269, 314, 378-379, 380, 391, 396, 403, 421

Woman's Home Companion, 25, 34, 38, 39, 42, 44n50, 45n67, 229, 292, 313, 333

Youth's Companion, 11, 42n10, 42n11, 252, 261

Zilversmit, Annette, 48, 49-50, 77

Ziolkowski, Theodore, 262-263, 266

Joseph Griffin

Dr. Joseph Griffin, now retired, was an Associate Professor in the English Department at the University of Ottawa, Canada. Dr. Griffin completed his Ph.D. at the University of Notre Dame.